Florida Media Law

Florida Media Law

Second edition

Donna Lee Dickerson

University of South Florida Press
Tampa

Printed in the U.S.A. on acid-free paper⊗

The University of South Florida Press is a member of University Presses of Florida, the scholarly publishing agency of the State University System of Florida. Books are selected for publication by faculty editorial committees at each of Florida's nine public universities: Florida A&M University (Tallahassee), Florida Atlantic University (Boca Raton), Florida International University (Miami), Florida State University (Tallahassee), University of Central Florida (Orlando), University of Florida (Gainesville), University of North Florida (Jacksonville), University of South Florida (Tampa), University of West Florida (Pensacola).

Orders for books published by all member presses should be addressed to University Presses of Florida, 15 NW 15th St., Gainesville, FL 32611.

The activities of the University of South Florida Press are supported in part by the USF Research Council.

Library of Congress Cataloging-in-Publication Data

Dickerson, Donna Lee, 1948–
Florida media law / Donna Lee Dickerson.—2nd ed.
p. cm.
Includes index.
ISBN 0–8130–1039–X.—ISBN 0–8130–1035–7
1. Press law—Florida. 2. Freedom of the press—Florida.
3. Mass media—Law and legislation—Florida. I. Title.
KFF316.D52 1991
342.759'0853—dc20 90–44163
[347.5902853] CIP

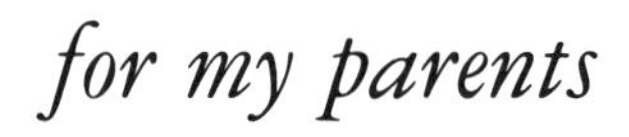
for my parents

Contents

Preface

In his book *Florida Law of the Press,* Kenneth Ballinger said there were no major trends in First Amendment interpretation in this state because no major Florida case involving freedom of the press had been heard by the U.S. Supreme Court. That was more than 30 years ago. By 1990, the Court had heard more than two dozen cases from Florida, representing almost every major news medium and every region of the state. These cases have been either landmarks such as *Adderley* v. *Florida* and *Miami Herald Publishing Co.* v. *Tornillo* or First Amendment stepping-stones such as *Pennekamp* v. *Florida, Time, Inc.* v. *Firestone,* and *Chandler* v. *Florida.* Florida cases have set national precedents in libel, privacy, cameras in the courtroom, and right of access to the media. At lower court levels, major precedents and important persuasive cases have dealt with privacy, libel, news gathering, and reporter's privilege. Additionally, the Florida Legislature has become a leader in opening up government meetings and records.

Florida Media Law provides the editor, news reporter, public official, attorney, or student of the media an exhaustive yet readable guide to the law of the press in this state. By analyzing statutes, the common law, provisions of the Florida and U.S. constitutions, and court decisions, this book helps the user understand and deal with current legal problems. Areas covered include prior restraint, libel, invasion of privacy, reporter's privilege, restrictive and exclusionary orders, news gathering, and the Florida open meetings and open records laws. These areas are explored first by examining federal precedents, then by juxtaposing state cases and laws against the national trend.

There are many questions in communications law that have yet to be answered by the U.S. Supreme Court. When dealing with these questions, each state must find answers that fall within the broad mandates of the First Amendment. Such areas include intrusive news gathering, the use of tape recorders, restrictive access to court records, retraction laws, and access to records, meetings, and prisons.

Legal advice is expensive. For those media without access to a staff counsel, this book will explain current law. It can be used as a tool for self-protection, providing the legal precedents necessary for an editor to decide whether or not to pursue a certain course of action. Editors may use it to thwart those who harass with empty threats. It should be used by every reporter preparing sensitive material. The problems of libel, privacy, news gathering, and covering the courts are the same whether a newspaper reporter or a broadcast journalist is covering the story. The additional obligations of license requirements that fall on broadcasters should not overshadow their need to know basic communications law.

With access to a law library, a lawyer can use this book as a base for advice, research, and argument. The book should be especially valuable to the lawyer who only occasionally represents the media and thus does not make communications law a specialty.

The Judicial System

Both the federal and state judicial systems are hierarchical with many courts at the bottom and one court of final resort at the top. The systems are parallel; they only overlap when a case involving a constitutional issue is appealed from a state supreme court to the U.S. Supreme Court or when the ruling of a state court is considered by a federal district court to result in irreparable harm to the public or the parties involved.

At the foot of the federal system are the district courts, which are the only trial courts in the system. District courts handle diversity cases, federal question cases, and certain other enumerated cases. These courts are distributed across the country within state boundaries. States may contain from one to four federal district courts; Florida has four. The majority of district court cases are appealable to a U.S. circuit court of appeals. The country is divided geographically into 12 circuits. Eleven of the circuits are numbered; the twelfth is the U.S. Court of Appeals for the District of Columbia. The courts of appeals review lower court decisions and decisions of certain federal administrative agencies. Effective November 1981, Florida, Alabama, and Georgia were removed from the Fifth Circuit to create the new Eleventh Circuit, which sits in Atlanta. Cases filed from these three states before November 1, 1981, were heard by the "old" Fifth Court of Appeals.

A court of appeals decision may be appealed to the U.S. Supreme Court, which is the court of last resort in this country.

Appeals will only be accepted when a federal question—one involving the U.S. Constitution or a federal law or treaty—is at issue and when the resolution is of importance to more than just the parties involved.

The Florida state court system has three parts with numerous inferior courts on the bottom and a court of final resort at the top. The circuit court is the trial court. Thee are 20 judicial circuits in Florida with any number from 3 to 51 judges in each. The circuit courts have exclusive and original jurisdiction in all actions not covered by county and municipal courts. They also may hear appeals from inferior courts (municipal and county). Circuit court decisions as well as administrative actions are appealable to a district court of appeal. There are five district courts in the state. Three judges hear each case. The Florida Supreme Court, composed of seven justices, is the state's court of last resort and may hear appeals from circuit courts or district courts of appeal. Circuit and district judges and supreme court justices are nominated to their posts and retain their position by running against their own record every four years. Inferior court judges are elected in the same manner as other public officials.

The U.S. Supreme Court may review a decision of the Florida Supreme Court if the Florida court has declared a federal treaty or statute invalid. Similarly, it may review final decisions where the state supreme court has ruled that a state law is valid in face of challenges that it is repugnant to the Constitution, treaties, or laws of the United States.

The American judicial system is responsible for interpreting constitutions, statutes, treaties, and the common law. When a higher court hands down an interpretation, that interpretation must be followed by all lower courts within its jurisdiction. A precedent gives lower courts direction on how to decide similar cases. Precedents set by the U.S. Supreme Court must be followed by all state and federal courts. Decisions of a U.S. court of appeals must be followed by all federal district courts within that circuit. Likewise, when the Florida Supreme Court hands down a decision, it must be followed by all state courts in Florida.

While one court's decision may not be a binding precedent on another court, it may be persuasive. In other words, a decision from one jurisdiction can be used to bolster or even form a legal argument in another jurisdiction. For example, while the Florida Supreme Court is not bound by decisions announced in Georgia, it may listen to arguments that incorporate Georgia precedents. The court may even adopt the Georgia precedent as its own if it is persuasive enough.

Media law is evolving so fast that it is no longer sufficient just to look at the precedents established in this state. Precedents are being set every day in courts all over this country dealing with problems Florida has not yet encountered but may in the near future. To help understand some of the changes that are occurring in other parts of the country, this volume uses numerous cases outside of Florida that may be perceived as persuasive precedents. What is the rule in a neighboring state this year may be the rule in Florida next year, because persuasive precedents were tactfully used by persuasive lawyers.

Chapter One

The First Amendment in Florida

The First Amendment to the U.S. Constitution reads, "Congress shall make no law . . . abridging the freedom of speech, or of the press." This prohibition against the U.S. Congress presumably left to the states the power to regulate expression. However, many states also included in their own constitutions statements guaranteeing press freedom. Section Four of the Declaration of Rights of the Florida Constitution reads, "Every person may fully speak and write his sentiments on all subjects being responsible for the abuse of that right . . . no laws shall be passed to restrain or abridge the liberty of speech or of the press."

As long as sanctions against the press occurred after publication and not before, it was considered within the state's power to define how it would punish the abuse of that right. The result was state laws dealing with such press misconduct as libel and invasion of privacy. In 1925, the U.S. Supreme Court in *Gitlow v. New York* held through the Fourteenth Amendment that the prohibition of the First Amendment's order against Congress applied also to the states.[1] The Fourteenth Amendment forbids states to deprive any citizen of "life, liberty, or property, without due process of law." Of those liberties protected against state infringement, the liberties of speech and press are considered the most vital. By making the First Amendment applicable to the

1. 268 U.S. 652 (1925).

states, the Court was clearly protecting the freedom of the press against state laws or actions.

The *Gitlow* case created no major changes in state law. In fact, many states had already conferred greater privilege upon the press than even the federal courts had acknowledged. Other states, such as Florida, had not encountered enough press freedom cases to have established any major precedents contrary to the First Amendment.

THE EXTENT OF PERMISSIBLE REGULATION

The First Amendment is not absolute nor has it ever been considered so by a majority of the U.S. Supreme Court. A civilized society requires the promulgation of rules to maintain an ordered system, and some of those rules may limit expression in order to promote certain desired ends. As Chief Justice Frederick Vinson said in *Dennis* v. *United States,* "[T]he societal value of speech must, on occasion, be subordinated to other values and considerations."[2]

In 1931, the U.S. Supreme Court suggested in *Near* v. *Minnesota* that the three types of expression that fell clearly outside the boundaries of the First Amendment were obscenity, expression that threatens national security, and expression that results in a breach of peace or property.[3] The Supreme Court repeatedly has upheld the right of government and states to censor and regulate material that has fallen into these categories.[4] However, because our form of government depends upon freedom of expression, any restraint carries with it "a heavy presumption against its constitutional validity."[5] To protect freedom of expression from unjustified restraint, important guidelines have been developed for each of the proscribed categories.

Traditionally in the United States, these guidelines have been

2. 341 U.S. 494, 508 (1951).
3. 283 U.S. 697 (1931).
4. *See* Roth v. United States, 354 U.S. 476 (1957).
5. Bantam Books, Inc. v. Sullivan, 372 U.S. 58 (1963).

set in cases involving persons or organizations that hold opinions that run against the current popular belief. The 1920s and 1930s saw cases involving socialists, Marxists, and Jehovah's Witnesses; the 1940s and 1950s, Communist sympathizers; the 1960s, atheists and antiwar and civil rights demonstrators; and the late 1970s and 1980s, Nazis and the Ku Klux Klan. All of these groups have sought public access to challenge ideas and change opinion. Because such groups and others have been outside the mainstream of contemporary society, they have been the targets of arbitrary state and local laws that have impinged on their expression of opinion.[6] Hence, in our constitutional development, atheists have strengthened religious freedoms, Nazis have reaffirmed freedom of speech, Communists have given greater meaning to freedom of association, and pornographers have buttressed a sometimes sagging freedom of the press.

National Security

In cases involving national security, the Court has held that expression cannot be censored unless it creates a clear and present danger to national security. This danger, said the Court in *Brandenburg* v. *Ohio,* must be imminent; mere advocacy of an idea is not sufficient justification for censorship.[7] Rather, the expression must be likely to incite or produce immediate lawless action.

The bulk of First Amendment cases touching upon national security were litigated during the cold war years of the 1950s and 1960s. Fear of communism was rampant, stirred first by Senator Joseph McCarthy and later by the Cuban missile crisis. Florida was the source of only two major cases involving expression and national security; even those cases sat on the periphery of the issue as national security became synonymous with internal security. Congress as well as state legislatures established numerous investigative committees to detect Communist infiltration

6. *E.g.,* Collin v. Smith, 578 F.2d 1197 (7th Cir. 1978).

7. 395 U.S. 444 (1969); *see also* Yates v. United States, 354 U.S. 298 (1957).

into such groups as the National Association for the Advancement of Colored People and the American Civil Liberties Union.

The Florida Legislative Investigation Committee was a typical investigative arm empowered "to act and protect the state's legitimate and vital interest." The committee ordered the president of the Miami branch of the NAACP to appear before it and produce records that identified members and contributors.[8] The stated purpose was to detect Communist infiltration into organizations involved in race relations. The defendant refused to produce the records or identify persons and was found in contempt of the legislature. On appeal, the U.S. Supreme Court held that a legislature's power to investigate is limited; certain tests must be met to balance the state's needs against the individual's rights. The Court stated that a clear "nexus" must exist between the information sought and the subject of the state's interest. No substantial connection between the NAACP and Communist activities was demonstrated and the contempt charges were dismissed.

Another Communist-era case in Florida involved the pervasive loyalty oaths. Florida's statute required public employees to swear that they had never "knowingly lent their aid, support, advice, counsel, or influence to the Communist Party." The U.S. Supreme Court in *Cramp* v. *Board of Public Instruction* held that the wording of the loyalty oath "completely lack[ed] terms susceptible of objective measurement."[9] *Cramp,* decided in 1961, was the first in a series of cases nationwide that resulted in the demise of public employee loyalty oaths in most parts of the country. The only loyalty oaths to survive are those that pledge loyalty to the constitutions of the United States and the state or those that specifically disavow the overthrow or the advocacy of overthrow of the government by violent and imminent lawless action.

Only twice have the news media been censored to prevent the

8. Gibson v. Florida Legislative Investigation Comm., 372 U.S. 539 (1963).

9. 368 U.S. 278 (1961).

publication of information that the government considered a clear and present danger to national security. The first case arose in 1971 when the *New York Times* began publishing its version of the Pentagon Papers, classified documents relating to the history of U.S. involvement in Vietnam.[10] An injunction was issued against the newspaper to stop publication. Seventeen days later, the U.S. Supreme Court held in a three-paragraph per curiam decision that the government had failed to carry the heavy burden necessary to justify prior censorship.

The second incident occurred in the spring of 1979, when the *Progressive,* a liberal public opinion magazine, was preparing to publish a story, "The H-Bomb Secret: How We Got It, Why We're Telling It." An injunction was issued to prevent publication.[11] The government feared that information contained in the freelance piece could be used to construct a hydrogen bomb. The government eventually dropped its suit and the injunction was lifted seven months after imposition when the information appeared in another publication. The government decided, as it did in the Pentagon Papers case, to investigate and bring criminal charges against persons who provided the information to the media.

Breach of Peace

Despite the broad rights of the First Amendment, government is not precluded from regulating expressive conduct that may clash with other private rights such as property, health, and safety. The U.S. Supreme Court has defined as constitutional those regulations that contain specific guidelines as to time, place, and manner of expression. The rules must be enforced uniformly against all persons and groups, must be reasonably aimed at protecting the state's interest, and must not turn on the question of content or subject matter.[12]

10. New York Times Co. v. United States, 403 U.S. 713 (1971).
11. United States v. Progressive, 467 F. Supp. 990 (D. Wis. 1979).
12. Kovacs v. Cooper, 336 U.S. 77 (1949).

In the 1930s and 1940s, the United States and Florida supreme courts handed down numerous decisions that dealt with prior restraint in public areas. For example, a Melbourne ordinance prohibited the distribution of literature at certain busy intersections in that town. The Florida Supreme Court said in 1941 that while the material being distributed was protected by the First Amendment, its manner of distribution was creating a safety hazard.[13] The city, said the court, must preserve human life and ensure safety of the streets. Reiterating the need to balance freedom of expression against public safety, the court held that the presence of persons in crossings or intersections was dangerous and that other areas were available for the distribution of literature.

Two years later, the Florida Supreme Court heard the case of a Jehovah's Witness who was arrested in Tampa for distributing religious tracts without a license.[14] A city ordinance required a $50 license fee from all peddlers, vendors, or canvassers. Although the U.S. Supreme Court never has held license fees unconstitutional, it has held that such fees must have an overriding public purpose and must not be based upon the content of the material being distributed. The Florida Supreme Court upheld Tampa's ordinance with one exception: The ordinance could not be enforced against the distribution of religious materials. "To confer a free exercise of religion then lay a tax on the performance of that right when no question of morals, ethics, safety, and convenience is involved is contrary to the constitution," said the court.

The U.S. Supreme Court has held that certain areas of a city such as streets and parks have been "immemorially" and in "time out of mind" used for discussing public questions.[15] However, during the civil rights and antiwar demonstrations of the 1960s and 1970s, protestors chose areas and buildings that were much

13. Stephens v. Stickel, 200 So. 396 (Fla. 1941).
14. State *ex rel.* Singleton v. Woodruff, 13 So. 2d 704 (Fla. 1943).
15. Hague v. CIO, 307 U.S. 496 (1939).

closer to public officials in an effort to convey their message more clearly. Jailhouses, courthouses, public libraries, state capitol grounds, draft board headquarters, and various municipal and state buildings were typical demonstration sites. In 1965, students at Florida A&M University in Tallahassee marched to the Leon County jail to protest the earlier arrest of fellow students.[16] The demonstrators, singing and clapping, marched directly to the jail, where a deputy sheriff ordered them to move away from the door. The students moved to the jail's driveway where they continued to block the passage of vehicles. Refusing to vacate jail property, the students were arrested.

Justice Hugo Black, writing for the U.S. Supreme Court in *Adderley* v. *Florida,* held that a state has the right to control the use of its property for its own lawful and nondiscriminatory purpose. He affirmed the strong notion that protestors or those wishing to express views have no constitutional right to do so whenever, however, and wherever they please. The sheriff, said Black, was the custodian of the jailhouse; he was authorized to order the students off the grounds in order to maintain the premises for jail use. The sheriff did not act out of his disagreement with the protestors' opinions but only out of his concern for the integrity of the jail grounds and the safety of the prisoners and personnel, said the Court.

Not all expression takes the form of printed or spoken words. Some individuals choose to express opinions through symbolic behavior such as burning draft cards, wearing black armbands, or defying patriotic symbols. This type of conduct often gains protection as speech because of its political context. Most of the cases involving symbolic speech arose out of the Vietnam conflict and civil rights protests. However, the U.S. Supreme Court has warned that not all conduct intended to express an idea can be labeled speech. A sufficiently important governmental interest (such as preserving the selective service system) in regulating the

16. Adderley v. Florida, 385 U.S. 39 (1966).

nonspeech element (burning draft cards) can justify incidental limitations on First Amendment freedoms.[17]

The issue of flag burning came to the U.S. Supreme Court in 1989 and 1990. In the first case, the Court held unconstitutional a Texas statute making the destruction of the American flag a criminal offense.[18] The decision set off a movement in Congress that resulted in a federal flag antidesecration statute. But, once again, the Court held the law to be in violation of the First Amendment guarantee of freedom of speech.[19]

Whenever pure speech is involved, the expression cannot be completely prohibited, only regulated with finely honed laws. However, there is one area of public expression that, because of its ability to provoke listener reaction, can be repressed. The U.S. Supreme Court in *Chaplinsky* v. *New Hampshire* termed this type of speech "fighting words" because the words by their very utterance are apt to provoke the average person to retaliation or are likely to incite an immediate breach of peace.[20] Justice Frank Murphy explained that "such utterances are no essential part of any expression of ideas, and are of such slight social value as a step to truth that any benefit . . . is outweighed by the social interest in order and morality."

Florida has several statutes that attempt to regulate speech that may create retaliation, but most have been disregarded or declared unconstitutional because of vagueness. Florida Statute 847.04 prohibited any profane, vulgar, or indecent speech in a public or private place so as to be heard by another. This statute was declared unconstitutional in *Brown* v. *State,* where the defendant used the term "mother fucker" toward his father.[21] The Florida Supreme Court said the statute failed to require that the offensive words tend to result in some breach of peace or to inflict

17. United States v. O'Brien, 391 U.S. 367, 376 (1968).
18. Texas v. Johnson, 109 S. Ct. 2533 (1989).
19. U.S. v. Eichman, 50 S. Ct. Bull. (CCH) B3341 (June 11, 1990).
20. 315 U.S. 568 (1942).
21. 358 So. 2d 16 (Fla. 1978).

injury. Prohibiting mere utterance without more stipulation resulted in an impermissible chilling effect, said the court. A similar law, Florida Statute 847.05, was aimed at repressing the public use of indecent and obscene language. This law was held unconstitutional in *Spears* v. *State,* where the high state court held that the term "indecent" made the law overbroad because it criminalized protected speech.[22] In several cases involving Florida statutes that proscribe certain types of speech or conduct, the state supreme court has said that when mere words are used as a tool of communication they are protected. However, that protection ends when the speech is accompanied by acts that invade the rights of others or create a willful disturbance.[23]

Obscenity

Those cases protecting vulgar, indecent, offensive, or profane speech attempt to meet the constitutional balance in that uncertain area between socially acceptable language (either because of its harmless nature or its political and social value) and language that has never been constitutionally protected—obscenity.

For more than 50 years, the courts of this country have been grappling to define material that falls under the rubric "obscenity." The foundation for the present definition of obscenity was set in 1957 in *Roth* v. *United States,* which declared obscenity to be beyond the protection of the First Amendment.[24] The *Roth* definition, added to by *Memoirs* v. *Massachusetts,*[25] held material obscene if, to the average person applying contemporary community standards, the dominant theme of the material taken as a whole appeals to prurient interest, is patently offensive, and is utterly without redeeming social value.

Following the *Roth* case, the Court became "an unreviewable

22. 337 So. 2d 977 (Fla. 1976).
23. White v. State, 330 So. 2d 3 (Fla. 1976).
24. 354 U.S. 476.
25. 383 U.S. 413 (1966).

board of censorship for the 50 states," subjectively judging each sexually explicit film, magazine, and book brought before it.[26] The problem was further complicated by the fact that no majority of the Court was able to agree on what was obscene. Justice Potter Stewart's concurring opinion in *Jacobellis* v. *Ohio* demonstrates the dilemma: "I shall not today attempt further to define the kinds of material I understand to be embraced within the shorthand description; and perhaps I could never succeed in intelligibly doing so. But I know it when I see it."[27] Until 1973, this type of indecision made the regulation of obscenity one of the most controversial areas in the First Amendment debate.

In 1973, a five-judge majority of the Court finally agreed on a definition in *Miller* v. *California*.[28] The Court, disturbed by the vagueness of obscenity laws, required the states to define specifically the types of depictions of sexual conduct that were illegal. For the first time, the Court suggested what types of sexual activities were patently offensive and hard-core. States were free to adopt either the *Miller* suggestions or to develop their own list of proscribed depictions.

A second change was that the "utterly without redeeming social value" test was replaced with the stricter "serious literary, artistic, political, or scientific value" test. The determination of whether a work meets the serious value test is to be made according to a local standard rather than a national one. "Our nation is simply too big and too diverse for this court to reasonably expect that such standards could be articulated for all 50 states in a single formulation."[29] Thus, in *Miller* the Court left it to the states to decide what community value test, short of a national one, would be used.

Florida's obscenity law, Florida Statute 847.011 et seq., was passed in 1971 and adhered to the *Roth-Memoirs* definition. Through judicial decision the statute has been augmented, mod-

26. Miller v. California, 413 U.S. 15, 22 n.3 (1973).
27. 378 U.S. 184, 197 (1964).
28. 413 U.S. 15.
29. *Id.* at 30.

ified, and reinterpreted so as to stand the test of the stricter *Miller* definition. The law defines obscene material as that which is "lewd, lascivious, filthy, indecent, sadistic, or masochistic"; only the last two terms are defined in the law.

In *State* v. *Papp,* the Florida Supreme Court held that, taken together, the law's catalog of terms, the definitions used, and applicable court decisions identifying certain sexual activities were sufficient to meet the *Miller* requirement of specificity.[30] An example of a judicial definition is found in *State* v. *Aiuppa.* In that case the Florida Supreme Court said that the law's definition of prurient interest—"shameful and morbid interest in nudity, sex, or excretion"—could include cunnilingus, sodomy, and fellatio.[31]

For community standards, Florida since the mid-1960s has adopted the view that a local standard was the only one that made constitutional sense. As early as 1967, a district court judge upheld the use of a citywide standard to apply a Pensacola ordinance governing pornographic material.[32] A year later, the same judge applied a county standard in determining the applicability of a county ordinance.[33] He said, "[T]he judge and other citizens of the community are better equipped to know [their community] standards than [are] appellate judges living far away." And in 1970, in *Meyer* v. *Austin,* a federal district court judge used a Florida-wide standard to determine the constitutionality of the state obscenity law.[34]

In 1987, the U.S. Supreme Court held that a community standard does not have to be used to determine whether material "lacks literary, artistic, political or scientific value."[35] The jury needs only to assess whether a reasonable person would find such

30. 298 So. 2d 374 (Fla. 1974).
31. 298 So. 2d 391 (Fla. 1974).
32. Felton v. City of Pensacola, 200 So. 2d 842 (Fla. Dist. Ct. App. 1967).
33. Nissinoff v. Harper, 212 So. 2d 666 (Fla. Dist. Ct. App. 1968).
34. 319 F. Supp. 457 (D. Fla. 1970), *cert. denied,* 413 U.S. 902 (1973).
35. Pope v. Illinois, 481 U.S. 497 (1987).

a value. The Court reasoned that the ideas a work represents do not need majority approval and the value of an idea does not vary from community to community. The case left community standard in place but said it only applied to determinations of prurient interest and patent offensiveness.

Whatever community is used to set the standard, the U.S. Supreme Court has determined that children may not be included as part of that community.[36] In *Pinkus* v. *United States,* the Court stated that only adults can be used to determine the hypothetical "average person" in the collective community. Adults can include "sensitive persons" as well as "deviant sexual groups." The decision in *Pinkus* does not deny a state the power to take extra measures to protect its youth from obscene material. In fact, in 1968 the Court held that a state does have the power to regulate minors' access to obscene material and to establish a stricter definition of obscenity for minors.[37]

Florida Statute 847.012 applies the *Miller* standard to juveniles by stating that the material is obscene if it appeals to the prurient, shameful, or morbid interest of juveniles. In addition, the law prohibits the display of pictures or written material that depicts or describes nudity, sexual conduct, or sadomasochistic abuse. The law specifically defines these last terms.

In an effort to protect children from displays of nudity as well as to protect the privacy of unwilling adults, Jacksonville passed an ordinance forbidding the showing of films that display buttocks or breasts in public drive-in theaters. The ordinance was challenged in *Erznoznik* v. *Jacksonville,* and the U.S. Supreme Court held the ordinance vague and overbroad for it did not consider the context of the nudity.[38] "Clearly, all nudity cannot be deemed obscene even as to minors." As for the privacy aspect, the Court said that an unwilling viewer could easily avoid exposure by averting his eyes from the screen.

Enforcement of city and state obscenity statutes must be

36. Pinkus v. United States, 436 U.S. 293 (1978).
37. Ginsberg v. New York, 390 U.S. 629 (1968).
38. 422 U.S. 205 (1975).

cloaked carefully in procedural safeguards that balance the individual's right to sell or display material not yet determined obscene against the state's interest in stopping distribution if there is reasonable cause to believe the material is unprotected. These safeguards revolve around the Fourteenth Amendment's due process clause and the Fourth Amendment's proscription against unreasonable search and seizure.

In *Marcus* v. *Search Warrants,* Justice William Brennan recognized that the use of the search and seizure power to suppress obscene publications could involve abuses because the procedures lacked the safeguards to assure nonobscene material the constitutional protection it deserves.[39] Some of these safeguards were established in *Marcus* and *A Quantity of Books* v. *Kansas.*[40] Materials deemed obscene by a policeman or state prosecutor cannot be seized for evidence unless there is a clear and unmistakable determination that the law is being violated. That determination must be made by a proper judicial authority at an adversary hearing. Additionally, according to *Freedman* v. *Maryland,* such a hearing must be prompt and the burden of proof rests with the state.[41]

In December 1969, Allen Ginsberg delivered a poetry reading at Miami Marine Stadium. In the middle of the performance, the manager of the stadium determined that the material was obscene and disconnected Ginsberg's microphone. The poet sued the city of Miami. A federal district court held that the manager's arbitrary judgment of propriety "fell short of required procedural safeguards"; the determination of obscenity must be made by a judge and only after a hearing on the evidence.[42] The court ordered the city to make the stadium available at no cost so Ginsberg could resume the reading.

It is not uncommon for police to harass owners of adult book-

39. 367 U.S. 717 (1961).

40. *Id.;* 378 U.S. 205 (1964); *see also* Fort Wayne Books, Inc. v. Indiana,—U.S.—; 109 S. Ct. 916 (1989).

41. 380 U.S. 51 (1965).

42. Ginsberg v. Miami, 307 F. Supp. 675 (D. Fla. 1969).

stores by parking near the store, entering several times a day, questioning customers, or threatening the owner. In *P.A.B., Inc.* v. *Stack,* the Florida Supreme Court held that such harassment was unconstitutional because it forced the bookstore owner to practice self-censorship and it resulted in economic loss to his business before any finding that the business was illegal.[43]

Impermissible Restraints

American courts have spent more than 60 years establishing and articulating the limits in which persons may express ideas. Along the way, they have encountered numerous prior restraints from states, which fell clearly outside of the *Near* limitations on obscenity, breach of peace, and danger to national security. These attempts at limiting expression are the result of well-meaning but often overzealous lawmakers attempting to protect other legitimate interests, such as the election process or taxation.

Taxes

The city of Tampa passed an ordinance requiring newspapers to pay a business license tax based on their circulation. Newspapers under 10,000 would pay $40 a year; those between 10,000 and 30,000 were taxed $500; and papers over 30,000 would pay $700. The *Tampa Times,* with a 1942 circulation of slightly over 10,000, argued that the classification of newspapers by circulation was arbitrary and discriminated unjustly against large newspapers. Following the U.S. Supreme Court's 1936 decision in *Grosjean* v. *American Press,*[44] which held a similar Louisiana statute invalid, the Florida Supreme Court held that any license tax that discriminated on the basis of circulation volume was unconstitutional.[45] The Florida court failed to say why such a tax was unconstitutional. In fact, a close reading of the opinion reveals

43. 440 F. Supp. 937 (D. Fla. 1978).
44. 297 U.S. 233 (1936).
45. City of Tampa v. Tampa Times, 15 So. 2d 612 (Fla. 1943).

that the justices had no real opposition to the law since it was not actuated by anything other than good motives.

In 1943, the *Tampa Times* challenged another city ordinance that taxed the volume of sales. Not only were retailers required to pay the tax, but so were wholesalers. Consequently, each issue was taxed twice. The *Times* itself was paying 30 cents for each $1,000 of gross sales with a minimum tax of $10 a year. The effect of this gross receipts tax, argued the *Times,* was the same as the gross volume tax—to force larger newspapers to pay more taxes than smaller newspapers. The Florida Supreme Court, not as solicitous this time, held that newspapers are not immune from ordinary forms of taxation as long as the tax is not aimed solely at the media and does not control content.[46] The court's holding followed an Arizona precedent where a standard city business tax was upheld against challenges from an Arizona newspaper.[47]

Today it is widely accepted that the media are businesses and may not use the shield of the First Amendment as immunity from nondiscriminatory and standard forms of taxation or business regulations.

The Election Process

In an attempt to regulate and protect the integrity of the election process, the Florida Legislature has passed several laws limiting political expression. Beginning in 1973, Florida's newspapers took on the burden of challenging these laws. The result was a landmark First Amendment case and the invalidation of several laws.

A right of reply law was passed in 1913 to ensure that persons in the political arena had access to the public through the printed media.[48] The law required newspapers to give free and equal reply space to any candidate whose record or personal character was

46. Tampa Times v. City of Tampa, 29 So. 2d 368 (Fla. 1947).
47. Giragi v. Moore, 64 P. 2d 819 (Ariz. 1937).
48. 1913 Fla. Laws ch. 6470, § 12.

attacked by the press. Failure to grant reply space was punishable as a misdemeanor. In 1974, the U.S. Supreme Court in the landmark decision *Miami Herald Publishing Co.* v. *Tornillo* declared the law unconstitutional and reaffirmed the notion that no state can tell a newspaper what not to print nor what to print.[49]

The case arose when Pat L. Tornillo, a candidate for a position on the Dade County Board of Education, was criticized by the *Miami Herald.* After asking for space to reply and being refused, Tornillo brought charges against the *Miami Herald* under the 1913 law. The Florida Supreme Court held the law constitutional, saying that such a law was not a deterrent to free press but an aid, for it furthered the broad societal interest in the free flow of information.

Chief Justice Warren Burger, however, overturned the Florida court and held the law in violation of the First Amendment. The chief justice reasoned that anytime a law, no matter how good its motives, promotes a governmental mechanism to enforce responsibility in the media, it must be held to be in direct confrontation with the First Amendment: "A responsible press is an undoubtedly desirable goal, but press responsibility is not mandated by the Constitution, and like many other virtues it cannot be legislated." Faced with a penalty as a consequence of not running a reply, "editors might well conclude that the safe course is to avoid controversy," thus dampening the vigor and variety of public debate.

This decision was widely condemned by those who contend that freedom of the press is a right belonging not only to the press but to the public as well. These "Right of Access" proponents, led by law professor Jerome Barron, argue that the public's right to know, which is implicit in the right of a free press, requires that the media cover all sides of an issue or provide access to spokespersons from all sides.[50] Because many newspapers have not taken it upon themselves to offer this type of free access,

49. 418 U.S. 241 (1974).
50. J. BARRON, FREEDOM OF THE PRESS FOR WHOM? (1973).

some proponents feel access is a ripe area for legislation. While the Supreme Court disagreed with these arguments, the press did begin taking a look at its responsibility to the community, and many newspapers adopted various methods, including op-ed pages, ombudsmen, expanded letters to the editor sections, and space for guest editorials, to encourage access and full exposure of public issues.

Another early law regulated preelection charges against candidates. Florida's eleventh hour law, passed in 1913, prohibited any charges against a candidate to be circulated within 18 days of a primary election unless that candidate was notified 18 days before the election.[51] The law was first challenged by N. Vernon Hawthorne, who made charges over radio against a candidate for the Florida House of Representatives. Newspaper articles reporting the charges were also printed. In 1934, the Florida Supreme Court held the law to be reasonable because it was interpreted to apply only to handbills and campaign literature and not to the news media.[52] The court stated that anyone being attacked needed time to answer charges by the same means in which they first were disseminated. If the charge is made by a handbill, then 18 days is a reasonable time in which to print up handbills rebutting the charges. The court surmised that the legislative intent was to promote fair play and fair competition in elections and to compel the making of late charges in an open forum such as a rally or campaign speech. Because Hawthorne's charges were made over radio and not written, his conviction was overturned. The court also held that the eleventh hour law did not apply to news stories reporting that such charges had been made. However, editorials, letters to the editor, and advertisements that originated the charge were illegal.

Florida's eleventh hour law eventually was extended to prohibit the publication or distribution of pictures, cards, literature, or other writings against a candidate on election day.[53] Gore News-

51. 1913 Fla. Laws ch. 6470, § 10.
52. *Ex parte* Hawthorne, 156 So. 619 (Fla. 1934).
53. 1951 Fla. Laws ch. 26870, § 8.

paper Company, publisher of the *Fort Lauderdale News* and the *Pompano Beach Sun Sentinel,* challenged the law in 1975. A U.S. district court held in *Gore Newspapers* v. *Shevin* that the law was unconstitutional; the Fifth Circuit affirmed.[54] Although the Florida law had been passed to prevent last-minute smear tactics against candidates, the district court stated that press responsibility cannot be legislated. The court cited *Mills* v. *Alabama,* which declared a similar Alabama law unconstitutional.[55] In *Mills,* the U.S. Supreme Court said that "no test of reasonableness can save a state law from invalidation . . . when that law makes it a crime for a newspaper editor to do no more than urge people to vote one way or another in a publicly held election."

Meanwhile, a city ordinance in Lantana that prohibited charges against a candidate seven days before an election was held unconstitutional. James Pelczynski had circulated a letter the day before a mayoral election charging the incumbent with failure to discharge his duties. The mayor lost the election, and Pelczynski was convicted of violating the ordinance. Following the holding in *Mills,* a Florida appellate court stated that prior restraint on the First Amendment cannot be justified on the basis that there might be some abuse.[56] The court asked rhetorically, "Is it constitutionally permissible to prevent dissemination of all true, newly learned charges which electors should know simply because they were learned after some arbitrary date?" The time just before an election, continued the court, is the time when the public's need to know is at its height. Although the *Mills* case specifically concerned the mass media, the Florida court expanded the case's application, saying that one does not have to be a "card-carrying member of the Associated Press or *New York Times*" to be entitled to the protection of the First Amendment.

In *Gore Newspapers* v. *Shevin,* the same case that held Florida's

54. 397 F. Supp. 1253 (D. Fla. 1975), *aff'd,* 550 F. 2d 1057 (5th Cir. 1977).

55. 384 U.S. 214 (1966).

56. Town of Lantana v. Pelczynski, 290 So. 2d 566 (Fla. Dist. Ct. App. 1974).

eleventh hour law unconstitutional, the newspapers also challenged a campaign financing law that, in part, had been on the Florida books since 1913.[57] The law originally forbade publishers and broadcasters to charge political candidates any more than the regular rates available to advertisers.[58] However, in 1973, the legislature passed a comprehensive campaign financing law and revised the advertising rate section to prohibit the media from charging any more than the lowest rate available. A violation of the law would subject the newspaper to a $10,000 fine and forfeiture of its right to do business in the state. Individual editors and advertising managers would be subject to imprisonment for one year or a fine of up to $1,000 or both.[59]

The newspapers argued in federal district court that the political advertising rate statute imposed an unconstitutional restraint upon the press by singling it out for discriminatory economic regulation. They contended such regulation made the press vulnerable to be "taxed" out of existence or into silence. The newspapers also noted that such a statute was an attempt by politicians in Tallahassee to give themselves a preferred status in the marketplace of ideas.

The district court upheld the newspapers' argument, stating that the fact that the statute was aimed at revenue rather than content did not insulate it from the constraints of the First Amendment.[60] The court ruled that the constitutional protection against prior restraint extended to the preferred status of candidates where advertising revenue was concerned. The state appealed the judgment, asserting that the statute was a valid exercise of police power to ensure candidates who lacked substantial financial backing access to the news media. The Fifth Circuit affirmed the judgment of the lower court.[61]

Another election law to be invalidated was one of the new

57. 397 F. Supp. 1253.
58. 1955 Fla. Laws ch. 29934, § 27.
59. 1973 Fla. Laws ch. 128, § 16.
60. Gore Newspapers v. Shevin, 397 F. Supp. 1253.
61. 550 F.2d 1057 (5th Cir. 1977).

sections of the Florida election code that prohibited any candidate from buying advertising or renting a hall before the official filing date.[62] The law was challenged by William Sadowski, a candidate for the Florida House of Representatives. The Florida Supreme Court declared the law "a restraint of free speech and a restriction on the quantity of a candidate's communication and diversity of political speech. . . . The public's 'need to know' is most critical during an election campaign."[63] This holding followed the U.S. Supreme Court's decision in *Buckley* v. *Valeo,* which invalidated restrictions placed on political campaign expenditures during federal elections.[64]

The most recent challenges to Florida's numerous election laws have involved access to and around polling places. In *CBS* v. *Smith,* the U.S. district court in Miami held that a statute prohibiting the solicitation of voters within 150 feet of a polling place could not constitutionally be applied to journalists.[65] The case arose out of exit polls conducted by CBS during the 1988 elections. Because "solicitation" was defined to include the soliciting of opinion, CBS would be forced to conduct its interviews too far from the polls. A polling expert testified during the course of the case that the farther away from the polls the interviewer was stationed, the less reliable were the results.

The court ruled that the law could not be enforced against exit polling or other reportorial activities. The court reasoned that the law was overbroad by restricting nondisruptive and protected speech in public areas and resulted in the loss of valuable information about voters and voting.

A year later, the Florida Supreme Court attacked another polling place law that prohibited nonvoters from within 50 feet of a polling room. In *Firestone* v. *News-Press Publishing Co.,* a photographer assigned to take pictures of a candidate voting was told to

62. 1973 Fla. Laws ch. 128, § 15.
63. Sadowski v. Shevin, 345 So. 2d 330 (Fla. 1977).
64. 424 U.S. 1 (1976); *but see* FLA. STAT. ANN. § 106.15(1) (1985).
65. 15 Media L. Rep. 1251 (S.D. Fla. 1988).

leave the polling place.[66] The court stated that the 50-foot boundary restricted access to areas outside of the actual polling room, thus prohibiting exercise of First Amendment rights and everyday activities, regardless of any effect on voting. The court ruled that the law was unconstitutional but noted that a state can legitimately prohibit nonvoters within a voting room itself.

Commercial Advertising

While political advertising gained constitutional protection rather quickly, commercial advertising's protection has been slow in coming. Until recently, commercial advertising was not regarded as a form of expression embraced in the First Amendment's definitions of "press" and "speech." Advertising was tainted by its commercial nature and hence possessed little public interest value. The U.S. Supreme Court said in 1942 that "the Constitution imposes no such restraint on government as respects purely commercial advertising"; therefore, government could regulate such activity as it saw fit.[67]

Florida enacted statutes prohibiting advertising by pharmacists, optometrists, dentists, chiropractors, lawyers, and osteopaths. Florida law also banned the advertising of abortion services, lotteries, "freak shows," and endurance contests such as marathons.

In 1964, as the U.S. Supreme Court was altering the law of libel, it also took the first steps toward modifying its philosophy of advertising regulation. *New York Times Co.* v. *Sullivan* involved a libel suit against an "advertorial" bought by the Southern Christian Leadership Conference.[68] The editorial advertisement included false charges against police who had used questionable methods to quell protesting students in Montgomery, Alabama.

66. 538 So. 2d 457 (Fla. 1989).
67. Valentine v. Chrestensen, 316 U.S. 52 (1942).
68. 376 U.S. 254 (1964).

The plaintiff, a Montgomery city commissioner in charge of the police, argued in part that the First Amendment had no bearing on this case, since the false and misleading information was contained in a paid commercial advertisement.

The Court disagreed; the advertisement "communicated information, expressed opinion, recited grievances, protested claimed abuses, and sought financial support on behalf of a movement whose existence and objectives are matters of the highest public concern. . . . That the Times was paid for publishing the advertisement is . . . immaterial." With that statement, the Court initiated new protections for advertising that communicated ideas rather than sold products.

In 1975, the Supreme Court took up the task of distinguishing between advertisements that were purely commercial and those that contained material of a "substantial individual and societal interest." In *Bigelow* v. *Virginia,* a commercial advertisement for an out-of-state abortion service was considered protected because it contained information of public value and interest to the citizens of Virginia.[69] What followed were numerous decisions at both federal and state levels protecting formerly prohibited forms of advertising. Florida repealed several advertising laws in 1977. Pharmacists now may advertise the price of prescription drugs, lawyers may advertise terms of routine services, dentists may advertise prices and services, nonprofit organizations may advertise legal services, and drug companies may advertise contraceptives.

Even if an advertisement is used only to sell a product and has no substantial public information, a state may not completely suppress it as long as it is truthful. In a footnote to *Virginia State Board of Pharmacy* v. *Virginia Citizens Consumer Council,* Justice Harry Blackmun stated that some First Amendment protection "is necessary to insure that the flow of truthful and legitimate commercial information is unimpaired."[70]

As more commercial speech cases came to the courts, a set of

69. 421 U.S. 809 (1975).

70. 425 U.S. 748, 771 n.24; *see also* Linmark Assocs., Inc. v. Township of Willinboro, 431 U.S. 85 (1977).

guidelines was adopted to balance the right of the public to receive vital economic information against the need of the state to protect the health, safety, and welfare of its citizens. The guidelines ask: Does the state have the power to regulate in the area (e.g., cigarettes, drugs, professional services)? Is the regulation unrelated to the content of the message? Is there a substantial government interest in the regulation (e.g., health, safety, and welfare)? Does the regulation bear a substantial relationship to the interest? Is the regulation narrowly tailored and no broader than reasonably necessary to meet the government's interest?[71]

States may also regulate the time, place, and manner of any advertising as long as such limitations are reasonable and applied uniformly. For example, Florida law specifies the content of advertisements a dentist may buy in a newspaper or magazine.[72]

States and the federal government also may prohibit advertisements that are false, misleading, and deceptive or advertisements for products, services, or activities that themselves are illegal. For example, one traditionally proscribed area of advertising was lottery information. Beginning in the mid-1800s, states passed laws prohibiting the publication of any lottery information or advertisement for lotteries because they had become recognized as a form of gambling.

In the 1960s and 1970s, as it became necessary for states to create new sources of revenue, the state lottery was instituted. As state lotteries gained popularity, it became impossible to enforce laws that banned lottery advertising. In January 1975, the federal lottery law was revised so as not to apply to the broadcasting or mailing of advertising, lists of prizes, or information about state-sanctioned lotteries.[73] The law also did not apply to

71. *See* Central Hudson Gas & Electric Corp. v. Public Serv. Comm'n, 447 U.S. 557 (1980); Posados de Puerto Rico Ass'ns v. Tourism Co. of Puerto Rico, 478 U.S. 328 (1986); Zauderer v. Office of Disciplinary Counsel of Supreme Court of Ohio, 471 U.S. 626 (1985); Shapero v. Kentucky Bar Ass'n, 486 U.S. 466 (1988).

72. FLA. STAT. ANN. § 466.019 (1987).

73. 18 U.S.C. §§ 1302, 1307 (1982).

broadcasters and newspapers in states bordering lottery states where the media have a reading or listening audience.

Florida's lottery was established in 1988, and advertising of lotteries in Florida newspapers is legal. Also, the state cannot prohibit the distribution in Florida of a newspaper published in another lottery state and carrying lottery advertising.[74]

The major burden of regulating advertising falls to the federal government and its many agencies involved with commercial transactions. These agencies include the Federal Trade Commission, U.S. Food and Drug Administration, Federal Communications Commission, U.S. Postal Service, and the Securities and Exchange Commission.

Summary

The freedoms guaranteed in the First Amendment are the fundamental rights guaranteed by the U.S. Constitution. But the U.S. Supreme Court has stated repeatedly that these rights are not absolute. It has been up to the Supreme Court since it heard its first freedom of expression case in 1919 to define the limits of these rights. In *Gitlow* v. *New York,* the Court held that the Fourteenth Amendment prohibits states from abridging these rights. Therefore, any decisions interpreting the meaning of the First Amendment are binding on the states.

Over the years the Court has declared that the only type of prior restraint allowed is that which prevents violence or a breach of peace, dangers to the national security, or obscenity. In each of these permissible restraint areas, the Court has established unique procedures and definitions for assessing whether the expression is protected.

Protected expression can be regulated as long as the regulation is not aimed at content. Statutes that specify time, place, and manner of expression are constitutional as long as they are reasonable, are administered impartially, and are specific. Symbolic

74. 18 U.S.C. §§ 1307 (1982).

speech—expression that involves action—can be regulated if the government can show an overriding governmental interest in controlling the action.

The Court has also overturned numerous state statutes that attempted to regulate content in the name of the public good. For example, the Court has held arbitrary taxation and mandatory right of reply unconstitutional.

One area of expression slowly being acknowledged as legitimate for First Amendment protection is commercial advertising.

Chapter Two

Libel

American libel laws have been developing for more than 200 years to protect the property value of reputation as well as to guarantee press freedom. This balancing of fundamental rights has resulted in a complex system for awarding damages, presenting evidence, and setting up defenses that is cluttered with mitigating factors. The antiquated and cumbersome common law tort of libel has been complicated further by a recent line of U.S. Supreme Court decisions. The burden placed on state courts in recent years has been to determine how the Court's translation of libel law fits into traditional legal structures. The most utilitarian approach to libel is to study the present trends, pulling from the past only what still serves the law.

Basic to an understanding of libel law is the concept that reputation is property due protection. If the Anglo-American legal tradition has one predominant characteristic, it is that of individualism. This intense individualism can be traced to the eighteenth- and nineteenth-century philosophies of natural law and natural rights as well as to the English common law attempts to define, protect, and limit these rights.[1] Our legal system, a product of this tradition, therefore is concerned with individual rights, liberties, and properties.

In the American legal tradition, fundamental rights are categorized as the right to life itself, the right to enjoy liberties basic

1. R. Pound, The Spirit of the Common Law 111 (1921).

to one's integrity, and the right to own property—both tangible and intangible. Property has come to encompass all the valuable interests persons hold outside their life and liberties. One of these intangible possessions is reputation. A property right in reputation means a person has a right to be secure in the knowledge that he is socially functional, accepted by others, and able to enjoy social interaction for his own mental well-being. This property right in reputation is secured by the due process guarantees of the federal and state constitutions.

Section 4 of the Declaration of Rights of the Constitution of Florida reads, "Every person for any injury done to him in his . . . reputation shall have remedy by due course of law." This section is construed as being of equal force with Section 13, which provides, "Every person may . . . publish his sentiments on all subjects but shall be responsible for the abuse of that right." Thus, the Florida Constitution sets the stage for balancing these two guaranteed rights. Some of this balancing is attempted in Florida's libel laws.[2] However, most of the balancing is carried out through courts, which have the responsibility to interpret the state constitution, the statutes, the common law of libel, and the First Amendment.

Definition and Elements of Libel

Libel is any false communication by print, signs, pictures, or broadcasting that holds a person up to ridicule, contempt, or hatred, lowers the person's reputation, causing him to be shunned by others, or causes mental distress. Several elements must be present in a story before it can be considered defamatory. The plaintiff must establish that (1) he or she has been identified, (2) the statement was published, and (3) the statement was indeed false and injurious. Establishing these three elements is tedious because they are fraught with numerous exceptions.

2. FLA. STAT. ANN. chs. 770, 836 (1984).

Identification

In the majority of cases, establishing identification creates no problem because the defamatory material directly identifies the individual by name, address, age, or occupation. Nevertheless, there are numerous instances where identification can be established without a name being used. One example is to show that identification is accomplished by "colloquium." Colloquium refers to some description of the plaintiff other than standard demographic information. It is not essential that the plaintiff be named if, by intrinsic reference or description, others may identify the plaintiff.

In *O'Neal* v. *Tribune Co.*, the *Tampa Tribune* and *Tampa Times* ran news stories that falsely stated that the owner of a children's nursery had beaten a child.[3] The owner was not named, nor was the nursery, nor was the address given. However, the story did give the name and address of the child's parents. The court concluded that persons who knew nothing of the incident prior to reading the stories could identify the owner of the nursery if they knew the parents and knew that the child went to that nursery. In fact, several persons including nursery patrons did identify the plaintiff in such a manner.

Reporters, knowing that to identify someone outright in a possibly libelous story is dangerous, may try to hedge on the identification. One columnist chose satire to conceal the identity of a person she was writing about. Betty Bush wrote an allegorical tale for the *Jupiter-Tequesta Beacon* in which the main character was "Harwood the rat."[4] Harwood, "a sleek, fat, gray rat," had followed the writer onto a yacht, peered through her window, scratched at her window "not unlike that [scratching] made by a 16 mm camera," and had pillaged a neighboring yacht, destroying its food supply. John Harwood, a well-known private investigator, claimed the tale referred to him, and he proved that

3. 176 So. 2d 535 (Fla. Dist. Ct. App. 1965).

4. Harwood v. Bush, 223 So. 2d 359 (Fla. Dist. Ct. App. 1969).

many persons identified him as "the rat." Apparently, Harwood had been the subject of recent articles that criticized his conduct as a private investigator. A district court of appeal held in 1969 that the allusion was apparent, particularly since the rat's name was Harwood and since the description and references to facts and events were the same as those surrounding the plaintiff. In addition, the court stated that identification is sufficient when those who know the plaintiff can identify him or her in the material.

Establishing identification is almost impossible when the plaintiff is a member of a large group. For example, if an article defamed the Florida Press Association, no individual has been identified; however, if the group were a small one, an individual might well be able to sue. The problem is that there is no court definition of what is a small group and what is a large group. For example, in a 1952 case, *Neiman-Marcus* v. *Lait,* a book about the Texas-based department store accused "some of the" store's models and "the" saleswomen of being high-priced prostitutes and "most of" the menswear sales staff of being homosexuals.[5] Neiman-Marcus employed 9 models, 382 saleswomen, and 25 salesmen. A federal district court held that the salesmen and models had a cause of action against the book's author. But because of the size of the female sales force, the court felt that no one would believe that all 382 were prostitutes, nor could any one saleswoman reasonably be identified.

Twenty-five appears to be the magic number in group libel cases. However, the *Restatement of Torts,* an explanation of current trends in tort law, says that liability exists when the group is so small that the matter can reasonably be understood to refer to an individual or the circumstances reasonably lead to the conclusion that there is a particular reference to one person.[6]

A Florida circuit court applied this rule to the 400-member

5. 13 F.R.D. 311 (D. N.Y. 1952).

6. *See* Tyler v. Garris, 292 So. 2d 427 (Fla. Dist. Ct. App. 1974); RESTATEMENT (SECOND) OF TORTS § 564A (1977).

Fraternal Order of Police in Fort Lauderdale.[7] The *News and Sun-Sentinel* published an editorial cartoon that was a takeoff of the well-known poster for the movie *The Sting* and depicted the characters in police uniforms. The Fraternal Order of Police sued the newspaper, claiming that the cartoon defamed local police. The court refused to find that the editorial identified any single policeman or that the cartoon could be reasonably understood to refer to any particular policeman.

Group libel cases can be further complicated by a publication's use of such qualifiers as "all," "some," "many," and "most" before the group's name. For example, to say that "all" members of a group are hooligans and thieves is going to create more problems than if the writer says that "some" or "many" members are hooligans and thieves. The problem of group libel is fuzzy, and there are no clear answers.

Publication and Liability

Technically, only a third party needs to see libelous material. But when the media are concerned, publication means that the libelous material has reached the intended general audience. Few cases have raised questions about the actual publication of material in the media. Questions of publication are raised primarily in nonmedia libel suits where the offending material is in a letter, a note, a credit report, or another document and the court must determine just how widely that document was distributed.

Media cases mostly involve questions of responsibility for the publication or the number of times the media can be sued for one publication.

Responsibility in a libel suit resides in the publisher. Yet, it is possible for any party to the preparation or publication of a de-

7. Fraternal Order of Police v. News and Sun-Sentinel, 12 Media L. Rep. 1619 (Fla. Cir. Ct. 1985); *but cf.* Fawcett Publishing Co. v. Morris, 377 P.2d 42 (Okla. 1962) (60-member football team won group libel suit after magazine charged team members used drugs).

famatory article to be named in the suit. That is as far as liability extends. It does not extend to the seller or distributor of the material. This was settled in a personal injury suit against a bookstore. Although it was not a defamation suit, the ruling is applicable. The suit involved a recipe in a cookbook.[8] Ellie's Book and Stationery in Sarasota sold a cookbook by Norma True, titled *Trade Winds Cookery.* The book described how to use various tropical plants in cooking. One recipe suggested using the poisonous roots of the elephant-ear plant. A buyer tried the recipe and became ill. The buyer sued the bookstore. A Florida district court of appeal held that a distributor is not responsible for the content of the publications it sells, nor is the distributor obligated to evaluate every book or magazine it sells. An earlier court stated the reasoning more eloquently: "Those who are in the business of distributing the ideas of other people, perform a unique and essential function. To hold those who perform this essential function liable, regardless of fault, when an injury results would severely restrict the flow of ideas they distribute."[9]

In an early precedent, the Florida Supreme Court limited the liability of a newspaper that publishes a defamatory wire service story. In a Prohibition-era case, *Layne* v. *Tribune Co.*, the *Tampa Tribune* carried wire stories from the Associated Press and the International News Service that falsely stated that the plaintiff had been indicted after trunks of liquor were delivered to the House Office Building in Washington, D.C.[10] The court held that no newspaper can take the time to authenticate every wire item, and unless the items are reproduced inaccurately, there can be no liability on the part of the media. In a more recent case, an AP wire story inaccurately reported that the officers of a firm were convicted on criminal charges and that the firm was bank-

8. Cardozo v. True, 342 So. 2d 1053 (Fla. Dist. Ct. App. 1977).

9. *Id.*, quoting Sexton v. American News Co., 133 F. Supp. 591 (D. Fla, 1955).

10. 146 So. 2d 234 (Fla. 1934); *see also* MacGregor v. Miami Herald Publishing Co., 119 So. 2d 85 (Fla. Dist. Ct. App. 1960).

rupt.[11] The court entered summary judgment for the newspaper based on *Layne.*

In yet another move to limit liability, the Florida Legislature in 1967 passed the single publication law. This law defines time of publication, states where a suit may be brought, and limits the number of causes of action based on one libel.[12] A single publication law has been passed in many states in response to the growing number of multiple suits being brought against publications. Before 1967, a suit technically could be brought every time a publication was sold at a newsstand. For example, a plaintiff could stretch the statute of limitations (which in Florida is four years for a libel suit), claiming another, separate occurrence when a magazine was purchased six months after its publication date.

Under the present law, only one cause of action exists for each publication—a single publication is presently seen in Florida as one issue of a newspaper or magazine that is circulated at one time. A plaintiff does have the choice of where to bring that one action. In *Perdue* v. *Miami Herald Publishing Co.,* the choices of venue were held to be the following: (1) the county where the publisher has its headquarters; (2) the county where the publication is published; (3) any county where the publisher has a bureau for editorial, advertising, or circulation purposes; and (4) any county where the publication is distributed or sold.[13] The choices of venue give the plaintiff a chance to shop around for the Florida court that will be the most conducive to the complaint. Also, the court held that the statute of limitations takes effect when the publication is first sold.

For a newspaper, any one daily or weekly issue is considered a publication. Thus far, the question of multiple daily editions has not come before Florida courts; however, a Georgia court set a

11. Merritt-Chapman & Scott v. Associated Press, 33 Fla. Supp. 102 (Fla. Cir. Ct. 1970); *see also* Nelson v. Associated Press, 667 F. Supp. 1468 (S.D. Fla. 1987).

12. FLA. STAT. ANN. § 770.05–.08 (1984).

13. 291 So. 2d 604 (Fla. 1974).

disturbing, persuasive precedent. Georgia has a single publication rule similar to Florida's. In *Cox Enterprises* v. *Gilreath,* the plaintiff was libeled in an article that appeared in all four editions of the November 13, 1974, issue of the *Atlanta Constitution.*[14] A Georgia appeals court held that separate causes of action existed for each of the four editions. The reasoning: News stories may be rewritten for each edition, and with rewrites it would be possible to libel a person in different ways and degrees in each edition.

Litigation is further complicated when defendant and plaintiff reside in different states. Normally, the case will be handled in a federal district court. But in order to determine in which state the case will be heard, courts generally look at factors such as the availability of witnesses, access to evidence, and convenience to the parties. Unless the balance strongly favors the defendant, the choice of venue will rest with the plaintiff.[15] The district court then uses that state's prevailing law of libel to render its decision.

Adding to the problems of jurisdiction, many states have long-arm statutes which provide that any person is subject to a state's jurisdiction if that person conducts business in the state or commits a tortious action (such as libel) in that state. Two cases involving long-arm statutes were decided by the U.S. Supreme Court in 1984. In *Calder* v. *Jones,* the Florida-based *National Enquirer,* its editor, and a reporter were sued by actress Shirley Jones for alleged libels committed in California.[16] In *Keeton* v. *Hustler Magazine,* a woman who lived in New York sued the Ohio-based *Hustler* in New Hampshire because the statutes of limitations had run out in the two states of residence.[17] In *Calder,* the Court held that although neither the editor nor the reporter ever entered California to gather the story, the fact that the story was drawn from California sources, the injury was suffered in California, and the editor intended to cause injury was sufficient for a finding of jurisdiction in California. In *Keeton,* the Court agreed that the

14. 235 S.E. 2d 633 (Ga. Ct. App. 1977).
15. Silvester v. ABC, 9 Media L. Rep. 1051 (S.D. Fla. 1983).
16. 465 U.S. 783 (1984).
17. 465 U.S. 770 (1984).

plaintiff could sue in New Hampshire although neither party was a resident of the state and only 1 percent of the magazine's circulation was in New Hampshire. The Court reasoned that the plaintiff was suing for injury that occurred in all states and that New Hampshire had a right to discourage the deception of its citizens.

In *Anselmi* v. *Denver Post,* the *Los Angeles Times* carried an article insinuating that three Wyoming politicians were involved in various "high crimes."[18] The Wyoming long-arm statute was found to apply in this case and jurisdiction was held to be in the Wyoming courts. The Tenth Circuit said that tortious conduct had occurred in Wyoming because the story was gathered in that state, carried a Wyoming dateline, was sent into Wyoming, and injured a Wyoming resident. In addition, the court noted the *Los Angeles Times* conducted business in Wyoming when it sold syndicated features to newspapers and solicited advertising.

Magazines are more likely to encounter long-arm jurisdiction problems than are newspapers. When *Ring* magazine, a New York publication, was sued by a Florida resident, a federal district court dismissed the suit for lack of jurisdiction.[19] According to the court, *Ring* had insufficient contacts with the state. Only 3.5 percent of *Ring*'s circulation was in Florida, and there was no office, no stringer, and no active solicitation of advertising or subscriptions in the state.

If a plaintiff chooses to use the long-arm statute of a state and if that state has a single publication law, the plaintiff is also bound by that latter law in deciding where in that state to bring a suit. Also, if a person brings a suit in one state, no other suits may be brought against that publication in any other state that has a single publication law.

The significance of the long-arm statutes for the media is that the plaintiff who is limited to one action by a single publication

18. 552 F.2d 316 (10th Cir. 1977).

19. Ziegler v. Ring Publications, 556 F. Supp. 329 (S.D. Fla. 1982); American Fed'n of Police v. Gordon, 8 Media L. Rep. 1392 (Fla. Cir. Ct. 1982).

law is able to bring his action in the state where the evidence is available, where the plaintiff's reputation resides, and where witnesses are familiar with the plaintiff.

Defamation

Before a judge determines whether a cause is proper for submission to a jury, he must evaluate the pleading and proof to determine whether the material is capable of a defamatory meaning. Defamation has been defined in this state as any unprivileged publication of false statements that naturally and proximately result in injury.

It is impossible to list all the statements that carry a defamatory meaning; however, a general classification is possible. A statement may be defamatory if it:

1. Charges a person with a felony. To say falsely that one accepted a bribe, was arrested for drunkenness, is a murderer, a bigamist, a tax dodger, or a thief are just some of the statements that have been held defamatory in the state.
2. Lowers a person in esteem or social standing by religious or racial slurs, by name calling, or by charging a woman with being immoral or unchaste. For example, falsely charging that someone is a Communist is libelous.
3. Makes a person appear to be foolish, stupid, or ridiculous. This has seldom been a cause of action in recent years.
4. Accuses someone of having a loathsome disease or mental illness. Time and social climate will dictate what falls under this category. Some of the standards include leprosy, venereal disease, alcoholism, retardation, or drug addiction.
5. Charges a person with misconduct, mismanagement, or other unethical conduct in his or her business, trade, or profession. Some examples: that a pollster was a phony, that a comptroller of a shipping company was incompe-

tent and dishonest, that a stockbroker was a poor businessman, that a private investigator was unethical.

6. Makes accusations of mismanagement or misconduct against a corporation. It was held defamatory to state falsely that a stock brokerage firm was bankrupt and its officers convicted on criminal charges.
7. Results in emotional distress, mental anguish, and personal humiliation.

There are some imputations that, though embarrassing or hurtful, have never been considered defamatory, such as falsely accusing someone of committing a misdemeanor. A libel suit cannot be brought for falsely stating that someone has died. Nor can a relative bring a libel suit against a relative or on behalf of a dead person.[20]

Whether material does carry a defamatory meaning is often the most difficult allegation for a plaintiff to establish. Important in determining defamatory content is how the ordinary and reasonable reader will interpret the story. A statement may be defamatory on its face, defamatory only when extrinsic facts are added by the reader, defamatory only if one of its reasonable meanings is used, or defamatory by insinuation or innuendo.

In common law, a defamation was classified either as libel per se (damaging on its face) or as libel per quod (damaging only when facts unknown to the publisher are added to the material by the reader). An example of libel per se would be to state falsely, "Bobenhausen is a thief and a crook and he stole me blind."[21] An example of libel per quod may be a vital statistic entry such as "divorce granted Hazel M. Pitts from Philip Pitts."[22] On its face, the wording is not defamatory, but the divorce had been granted over a year earlier and Pitts had since

20. Estill v. Hearst Publishing Co., 186 F.2d 1017 (7th Cir. 1954).

21. Bobenhausen v. Cassat Avenue Mobile Homes, 344 So. 2d 279 (Fla. Dist. Ct. App. 1977).

22. Pitts v. Spokane Chronicle, 388 P.2d 976 (Wash. 1964).

remarried. Some readers interpreted the statement to mean that Pitts had been married to two women at once and was thus a bigamist. The distinction between these two types of libel was important in common law because the existence of a charge that was libelous on its face meant that the plaintiff undoubtedly suffered whether or not any injury was ever proven or any fault was present. Thus, a plaintiff could recover damages even if a defamation was the result of an innocent mistake. In libel per quod, however, the injury was not as apparent and no injury was presumed; the plaintiff had to prove actual monetary loss as well as ill will or intent to injure on the part of the publisher.

This burdensome distinction has all but been eliminated by recent U.S. Supreme Court rulings that prohibit damages based on strict liability—the mere existence of a libel per se or an innocently published libel per quod. The Court, in *Gertz* v. *Robert Welch, Inc.*, held that a publisher may no longer be liable merely upon a presumed injury nor without some proof of fault or negligence.[23] Interestingly though, many courts still go through the rhetoric of establishing whether a defamation is per se or per quod although the distinction should make no difference in the outcome. The Florida Supreme Court has noted that the only reason the term "libel per se" is used is as a convenient shorthand for saying that the words being sued on are facially defamatory.[24]

Often, the language of an article can have more than one meaning, and the jury decides whether or not the communication is understood in its defamatory sense. When John Perry, former editor of the Clearwater *Sun*, was fired by that newspaper's publisher, several readers expressed their concern over the action. Publisher Richard Cosgrove wrote a letter to one reader saying he would not give any details about the firing because he did not want to "embarrass" Perry any further. The Second District Court of Appeal ruled that the term "embarrass" was defamatory be-

23. 418 U.S. 323 (1974).
24. Mid-Florida Television v. Boyles, 467 So. 2d 282 (Fla. 1985).

cause it could imply that Perry had conducted himself in a "shameful manner or manner inconsistent with the proper exercise of his profession."[25]

Of course, there is an exception to every rule. In *Adams* v. *News-Journal Corp.*, an editor criticized the actions of a local attorney as unethical.[26] The lawyer was representing a notorious client who had resisted arrest several years earlier. When the client was apprehended, his lawyer used a technicality to apply for and receive a writ prohibiting the municipal judge from exercising jurisdiction. Apparently the client had been abused during the original arrest and the lawyer convinced the judge that the police had acted unlawfully in the arrest. The editor criticized the attorney, saying it was unethical to accuse law officers of a crime in a technical move to save a client from a trial. The attorney sued the newspaper.

The Florida Supreme Court said in this 1955 case that there was no defamation since the attorney did what the law allowed him to do; following the law does not reflect on the integrity of the attorney. As to the accusation of unethical conduct, the court reasoned that the article was really not a personal attack but a criticism of the system that allowed the attorney to keep his client out of court. Yet, interpreting this editorial using the "common mind" or "reasonable reader" test, it would be difficult to imagine that a reader would interpret it as the court did since the editorial failed to say the lawyer's action was legal under Florida law. An ordinary reader would probably feel the lawyer was guilty of illegal and unethical conduct.

Generally, a story will be considered as a whole, but if the headline is defamatory and the story is not, courts will probably find defamation. Since the public frequently reads only the headline, the impression left is that imputed by the headline. It is also possible to have a situation where two elements, such as a picture and a story, standing apart are innocent but when com-

25. Perry v. Cosgrove, 464 So. 2d 666 (Fla. Dist. Ct. App. 1985); *see also* Wolfson v. Kirk, 273 So. 2d 774 (Fla. Dist. Ct. App. 1973).

26. 84 So. 2d 549 (Fla. 1955).

bined impair someone's reputation. Publishing the wrong picture with a story charging criminal conduct is a cause for a libel action. In *Miami Herald Publishing Co.* v. *Brown,* the newspaper ran an article about Lottery King Emmett Caraker, who had entered guilty pleas to charges of attempted bribery and operating a lottery.[27] The story was accompanied not by a photo of Caraker but by a photo of the plaintiff, Frank Brown. When Brown and Caraker had their picture taken together several months earlier, the *Miami Herald* had cut the photo in half and separately filed each half, transposing the names. The newspaper ran a retraction and an apology. Fortunately for the *Miami Herald,* there was no proof that the mix-up damaged Brown's reputation or feelings. Six witnesses testified that the plaintiff's reputation remained unimpaired. Also, only five copies of the paper were distributed in Brown's hometown of Bartow and none in his former home of Fort Meade. Only nominal damages were awarded in this 1953 case.

While material normally is read as a whole, rather than by taking statements out of context, some Florida courts have suggested that the best way of assessing whether defamation exists is to exercise parts that are alleged to be defamatory and then determine what overall impression is left. If the article without the false information still carries a defamatory meaning, then the article is not libelous. Such a "different effects" test allows the media to defend themselves on the general truth of an article rather than on specific portions.

For example, in *McCormick* v. *Miami Herald Publishing Co.,* the newspaper printed an article that said that the plaintiff, a city commissioner, owed over $40,000 in back taxes, that his $150 paycheck was being picked up by federal agents, and that there were four liens against his income and property.[28] In fact, he

27. 66 So. 2d 679 (Fla. 1953).

28. 139 So. 2d 197 (Fla. Dist. Ct. App. 1962); *see also* Gadd v. News-Press Publishing Co., 10 Media L. Rep. 2362 (Fla. Cir. Ct. 1984) (falsity is such a minor part of story that context would not change if false material were removed).

owed only $1,758.47, the balance having already been taken care of; the federal agents were not picking up his paycheck but did institute a levy action against it; and there were three liens rather than four. The court, in 1962, suggested and used the different effects test to determine whether the article was libelous. The conclusion was that the article was substantially true, and even with the false material removed the reasonable reader could still infer that the plaintiff had indeed willfully failed to pay his taxes, a criminal offense under federal law. The newspaper was found not liable since it could not be accountable for the truth, no matter how much it hurt the plaintiff's reputation. This test had provided the media a better chance in libel suits where information has been misinterpreted by a reporter.

In another case, the *Lakeland Ledger* ran a story stating falsely that the attorney general of Florida said a former Winter Haven mayor was in criminal violation of Florida's conflict of interest statute because his chemical firm sold supplies to the city while he was mayor.[29] In fact, the mayor was unaware of the purchases and, once informed, directed that the city be reimbursed. The attorney general did not tell the reporter that the mayor himself had specifically violated the statute. A district court of appeal, using the different effects test, said that if the incorrect information attributed to the attorney general were left out of the story the reasonable reader could still come to the conclusion that the mayor was in violation of the law.

Sometimes reporters will insinuate some wrongdoing rather than specifically state it, thinking they will be protected from a libel suit if they write "around" the problem. For example, the report that "the mayor, who was sober at last night's meeting, voted yes on all resolutions" does not directly state the mayor is usually drunk at meetings, yet insinuates that his soberness at this meeting is an unusual state. The innuendo must be in the statement and not brought to it by the reader. For example, in

29. Hill v. Lakeland Ledger Publishing Co., 231 So. 2d 254 (Fla. Dist. Ct. App. 1970).

the statement "Mary Jones, an 'acquaintance' of the young man, was called to the stand," the innuendo is carried in the quotes around "acquaintance," leaving the reader to believe the relationship was more than casual. The absence of the quotation marks would allow only the meaning that the woman was indeed just a friend.

Retraction

After proving identification, publication, and defamation, a plaintiff in Florida must cross one other hurdle. Florida law requires that five days before any action for libel can be brought, the plaintiff must serve written notice on the defendant specifying the statements that he alleges to be defamatory.[30] The defendant is not obligated to retract, although the law looks upon a retraction as a means of reducing, if not altogether eliminating, certain damages.

Florida's retraction law has been tested frequently; it was held constitutional for the first time in 1950. In that case, *Ross* v. *Gore,* the *Fort Lauderdale Daily News* ran a defamatory editorial.[31] The Florida Supreme Court explained that the purpose of the Florida law was to ensure that the media would be relieved of punitive damages and would have the opportunity in every case to make a full and fair retraction. The court explained that by retracting, a newspaper or broadcaster can mitigate or offset damages and be saved the annoyance and expense of answering unfounded complaints.

Twenty-three years later, in 1973, in *Miami Herald Publishing Co.* v. *Tornillo,* the Florida Supreme Court was a bit more cynical about retractions, noting that the law had been used with no apparent adverse effect on newspaper publishers, "but indeed, this statute has been utilized to their financial advantage."[32]

Of the 33 states with retraction laws, Florida probably has

30. FLA. STAT. ANN. § 770.01–.02 (1984).
31. 48 So. 2d 412 (Fla. 1950).
32. 287 So. 2d 78, 91 (Fla. 1973).

gone the furthest in interpreting the mandatory notice clause to the benefit of the newspaper. The *Ross* decision upheld the retraction notice section in 1950, saying that to construe the statute otherwise would be to defeat the objective of the legislature in enacting the law.[33] Several years later the Florida Supreme Court stated that to meet the requirements of the statute, notice should specify "with particularity" the statements alleged to be false or defamatory.[34] In a 1963 case, the plaintiff's notice did not specifically identify the article in question by its headline.[35] A Florida district court of appeal held that it was not enough to give the date of the article, the publication name, and the statements alleged to be libelous. The court held that notice must also give the type of article, whether a news story or an editorial, as well as the headline and the page. In this particular case, failure to identify the article by headline resulted in a dismissal.

In *Gannett* v. *Montesano,* the newspaper *Cocoa Today* ran an article accusing a service station operator of faulty repair work.[36] Five months after the article was published, the station operator's lawyer wrote a letter to the newspaper. The notice contained the same information suggested by *American Jurisprudence Legal Forms,* a lawyer's guidebook to uniform documents and forms. The lawyer also attached a copy of the article to the notice. A Florida circuit court holding that the notice was sufficient was reversed by the district court of appeal. The appeal court said the notice itself did not specify the article, nor did it specify the statements alleged to be false. Attachment of the article to the notice did not meet the requirements of specificity. The case was reversed and remanded with instructions to enter a judgment for the newspaper.

A more recent case involved television station WCKT in Mi-

33. 48 So. 2d 412.

34. Adams v. News-Journal Corp., 84 So. 2d 549 (Fla. 1955).

35. Hevey v. News-Journal Corp., 148 So. 2d 543 (Fla. Dist. Ct. App. 1963).

36. 308 So. 2d 543 (Fla. Dist. Ct. App. 1975).

ami.[37] The plaintiff's notice contained the date of the defamatory broadcast as well as the time, but the information was too broad. The notice referred to "statements to the effect that our clients had committed the felony of extortion and bribery with regard to their dealings with a firm." The notice continued with a request to retract "any allegations, innuendoes, or intimations of criminal conduct." The court held that the notice failed to specify the exact statements used in the television report that insinuated criminal conduct. The case was dismissed.

When sufficient notice is made, the law does not require the media to retract. In *Brown* v. *Fawcett Publishers,* the Florida Supreme Court held in 1967 that the failure of the defendant to print a retraction within ten days of notice would be "some evidence of actual malice on the part of the defendant."[38] In *Brown,* the editor refused to retract after having been notified twice. The court said the editor deliberately spurned the request to retract, figuratively "thumbing its nose" at the defendant. The refusal was seen to constitute malice. It is doubtful that such a rule would prevail today considering the amount and quality of evidence needed to prove actual malice.

Common Law Defenses against a Libel Suit

In the effort to balance the right to reputation with the rights of a free press, the courts have developed defenses or justifications for the media when they defame someone. Some of these common law defenses date back to the sixteenth century. They provide the courts a means of determining, case by case, whether the public's need for information to further the public good outweighs the individual's right of redress for an injured reputation. Common law defenses include truth, fair comment, and qualified privilege.

37. Hulander v. Sunbeam Television Corp., 364 So. 2d 845 (Fla. Dist. Ct. App. 1978).

38. 196 So. 2d 465, 473 (Fla. 1967).

Truth

While defending a statement by its truth is the media's best defense, the truth of a charge is often the most difficult element to prove. This defense finds its roots in the contention that no person should be held liable for publishing the truth. Obviously, the truth can be injurious, and many persons have tried to bring suits based upon true information they allege injured their reputation.

In most personal injury actions, the complaining party has the burden of proving the accusation. However, in common law libel, the case always began with a presumption that the defamatory speech was false. Therefore, the burden fell on the defendant to prove the material was true. In actuality, the burden of proof only comes into play when the evidence is so contradictory that a finding of truth or falsity cannot be made. In such cases, the rule of common law stated that the defendant had failed to carry the burden of proof and the decision must be rendered for the plaintiff. Therefore, in libel cases that were a "toss-up," the media usually lost.

This aspect of common law libel was found by the U.S. Supreme Court to be unconstitutional in *Philadelphia Newspapers* v. *Hepps.*[39] The Court stated that the common law presumption that defamatory speech was false could no longer pass constitutional muster. "The scales must be tipped in favor of the defendant," thus shifting the burden of proof to the plaintiff.

Truth does not have to be literal, only substantial. William L. Prosser, in the fourth edition of his *Handbook of the Law of Torts,* states that it is sufficient to show that the imputation is substantially true rather than prove the literal truth in every detail. For example, if a reporter, in a hurry to meet a deadline, writes that John Doe has been charged with stealing a motorcycle and $500 from a store, but in reality Doe stole only a moped and $300, the court will likely accept the defense of substantial truth. However, to accuse someone of a felony when the offense was

39. 475 U.S. 757.

only a misdemeanor will not be looked upon as substantial truth, since a misdemeanor is not considered a demeaning offense. For example, it would not be substantial truth to report that someone was charged with driving while intoxicated when in reality the person was ticketed only for exceeding the speed limit.

Fair Comment

The defense of fair comment first became an accepted justification in libel actions in the early 1800s. Fair comment allows the media to avoid liability when they express an opinion, sentiment, conviction, or viewpoint that damages someone's reputation. Such opinion is considered privileged if made fairly and without ill will or personal malice. Fair comment will protect editorial opinions concerning subjects of public interest and reviews or critiques of restaurants, galleries, plays, music, movies, books, and other artistic works and performances. This defense, however, will not protect false and defamatory statements of fact. The rationale for fair comment was best stated in *Gertz* v. *Robert Welch, Inc.:* "Under the First Amendment there is no such thing as a false idea. However pernicious an opinion may seem we depend for its correction not on the consciences of judges and juries but on the competition of other ideas."[40]

A typical fair comment case occurred in 1977 in *Early* v. *Palm Beach Newspapers.*[41] Plaintiff Lloyd Early was the Palm Beach County superintendent of public instruction. He was criticized severely and repeatedly during a 14-month period by two Palm Beach newspapers. The newspapers had embarked on what the Florida Supreme Court termed "a concerted campaign admittedly designed to bring about the removal of Mr. Early." Hundreds of news articles and editorials and several political cartoons were aimed at Early. The alleged defamatory remarks were that the plaintiff was "unfit" for public office and was inept, incompetent,

40. 418 U.S. 323, 339–340.

41. 334 So. 2d 50 (Fla. Dist. Ct. App. 1976), *cert. denied,* 354 So. 2d 351 (Fla. 1977).

and indecisive; that "the school board had been cheated by Mr. Early's lack of leadership"; and that "Mr. Below sits on the sideline doing what he can when Mr. Early's fingers aren't in the pot." A jury found the remarks were defamatory and were made with knowledge that they were false. The jury awarded Early $1 million in damages. However, a district court of appeal reversed, stating that while the remarks were hostile, slanted, and mean, they were nevertheless opinion, not fact, and therefore protected as fair comment. The court explained that the word "cheated" was used to imply indecisiveness, not criminal fraud, and the term "fingers in the pot" did not mean thievery, only incompetent intervention.

In a case that grew out of the lengthy political argument in Clearwater over the presence of the Church of Scientology in that community, the Fifth Circuit upheld the Clearwater mayor's right to voice his harsh opinions about the church.[42] The Church of Scientology bought the old Fort Harrison Hotel in downtown Clearwater for its headquarters in the summer of 1975. This purchase spurred extensive media coverage as Mayor Gabriel Cazares became an outspoken critic of the church's presence. The mayor said, among other things, that the Scientologists practiced "ruthless tactics," engaged in "questionable schemes," undertook assaults on the community, and promoted a "helter-skelter" world. The court said the church was a public figure, and the mayor's comments were protected as fair comment.

Editorial cartoons are often subject to libel suits but more often than not can be defended as statements of opinion. In *Keller* v. *Miami Herald Publishing Co.*, the newspaper ran an editorial cartoon depicting three men, dressed as gangsters and carrying money bags, standing in a dilapidated room.[43] The words "Krestview Nursing Home" were written on a wall and a posted sign read, "Closed by Order of the State of Florida." The caption read, "Don't worry, Boss, we can always reopen it as a Haunted

42. Church of Scientology v. Cazares, 455 F. Supp. 420 (D. Fla. 1978), *aff'd,* 7 Media L. Rep. 1668 (5th Cir. 1981).

43. 778 F.2d 711 (11th Cir. 1985).

House for the Kiddies." The cartoon referred to an ongoing investigation of the nursing home by numerous local and state agencies that eventually resulted in the home being closed. The Eleventh Circuit Court of Appeal ruled that the cartoon was a statement of opinion that was not capable of being interpreted as a defamatory statement of fact. The evidence showed Krestview was in poor condition and that the owner had pocketed a great deal of money at the expense of the home and its patients. The court also noted that the medium of the editorial cartoon also signaled that the comments were opinion.

The court cited a Ninth Circuit opinion that proposed the following guidelines for determining whether a statement is opinion: (1) construe the statement in its totality; (2) consider the context of the statement; (3) consider all the words used, not particular words or phrases; and (4) consider cautionary terms used in the statement as well as the medium and the audience.[44]

In one of the last decisions of its 1989 session, the U.S. Supreme Court reversed and remanded a case that had been decided based on the above guidelines. *Milkovich* v. *Loraine Journal* was a warning to the media that audience, medium, totality, context and cautionary terms will not turn a factual statement into an opinion.[45] In *Milkovich,* a sports columnist implied that a high school wrestling coach had lied under oath. In fact, the columnist wrote that the plaintiff "lied at the hearing." The headline read: "Maple [High School] beat the law with the 'big lie.'" The lower court found the column protected as a statement of opinion, arguing that it was labeled as a column, contained cautionary words, and appeared on the sports page, which is traditionally considered to be more opinionated than the news pages. But the U.S. Supreme Court ruled that the only question to be addressed was whether the assertions were capable of being proven

44. *Id.,* citing Information Control Corp. v. Genesis One Computer Corp., 611 F.2d 781 (9th Cir. 1980). *See* Hay v. Independent Newspapers, Inc., 10 Media L. Rep. 1928 (Fla. Dist. Ct. App. 1985); Shiver v. Apalachee Publications, 424 So. 2d 1173 (Fla. Dist. Ct. App. 1983).

45. 50 S. Ct. Bull. (CCH) B3834 (June 21, 1990).

as true or false. "Draping a statement in terms of opinion doesn't dispel the factual implications contained in the statement." However, if a statement is not capable of verification, then it is protected.

Of course not all fair comment cases deal with matters of political interest. A recent Florida fair comment case involved a restaurant review.[46] The *Jacksonville Journal* published a restaurant review titled "It Wasn't a Fancy Meal." The reviewer wrote that his "scrawny" steak "appeared to have been cooked in a blast furnace" and that his wife's prime rib "had a strange, unpleasant flavor" and lacked color as if cooked in a microwave. The circuit court, relying heavily on *Early* and a restaurant review case from Louisiana, held that the review was clearly an expression of opinion about an establishment that actively engaged in seeking commercial patronage and therefore was protected. Plaintiffs in this case appealed all the way to the U.S. Supreme Court, each time being rebuffed. Anyone who places his product or talent before the public for its patronage and acceptance leaves himself wide open for criticism that can be caustic and damaging.

It must be pointed out that if the factual statements supporting an opinion are false, the defense of fair comment will fail. The rationale was well presented in an early District of Columbia case: "To state accurately what a man has done, and then to say in your opinion such conduct was disgraceful or dishonorable, is comment which may do no harm, as everyone can judge for himself whether the opinion is well founded or not. Misdescription of content, on the other hand, only leads to the one conclusion detrimental to the person . . . and leaves the reader no opportunity for judging for himself the character of the conduct condemned."[47]

In a 1978 New Jersey case, the *New York News* ran an editorial criticizing the way police handled the arrest of a teacher at a

46. Ihle v. Florida Publishing Co., 5 Media L. Rep. 2005 (Fla. Cir. Ct. 1979), *aff'd,* 399 So. 2d 136 (Fla. Dist. Ct. App. 1980), *Petition for review dismissed,* 392 So. 2d 1375 (Fla. 1980), *cert. denied,* 450 U.S. 1031 (1981).

47. DeSavitsch v. Patterson, 159 F.2d 15, 17 (D.C. Cir. 1946).

middle school.[48] The police arrested and handcuffed the teacher at the school after receiving a complaint charging assault and battery. A cartoon accompanying the editorial portrayed the policeman wearing a dunce cap and carrying handcuffs. A caption read, "Classroom arrest of teacher." The cartoon was in error in that the arrest did not occur in a classroom. The judge granted a motion to dismiss the libel suit by the policeman as fair comment. The judge characterized the mistake as "minor" and as one that was unimportant and unrelated to the "gist or sting" of the comment.

Absolute and Qualified Privilege

Considering the nature of today's news, the working reporter will find the defense of qualified privilege a greater asset than he will the defense of fair comment. Qualified privilege gives the media great latitude in reporting false information received from public officials or in privileged settings such as a city council meeting.

It is accepted in a democracy that certain persons at certain times should be able to say whatever they feel or think, whether the statements are true or false, in order that discussion and debate may be as full and open as possible. Persons holding this absolute privilege include not only congressmen; the public at large is also protected when talking about the government. The Speech and Debate Clause of the U.S. Constitution provides that no congressman may be held liable for remarks made on the floor of either house. This clause has been extended to statements that are ancillary to a congressman's duties. This same type of privilege extends to state legislators; anyone appearing in a legislative forum; anyone appearing before a court of law, a grand jury, or an administrative agency; and any city council member, mayor, high administrator, and judicial officer. Statements to the media by lower public officers, however, are likely to carry only qualified privilege. Regardless of how persons in a privileged forum malign others, knowingly lie, or disparage character, no action for libel or slander can be brought against them.

48. LaRoca v. New York News, 383 A.2d 451 (N.J. Sup. Ct. 1978).

In 1970, a Florida city prosecutor was held to enjoy absolute privilege. In *Hauser* v. *Urchisin,* the Deerfield Beach city prosecutor issued a public statement to the press after his dismissal.[49] He stated that the move was politically motivated by a city commissioner who carried a personal vendetta against him because the city prosecutor had once tried to have the commissioner removed from office. The commissioner responded publicly, "Urchisin's respect for truth is not famous." The city prosecutor sued. The Florida Supreme Court held that the prosecutor's and the city commissioner's statements were made in connection with their public duties and were protected by absolute privilege.

Absolute privilege may even be extended to a reporter—albeit rarely. In an unusual libel and conspiracy case against the *Miami Herald,* reporter Hank Messic had been given two false affidavits that accused the sheriff of Dade County of accepting $25,000 in illegal election contributions.[50] Messic, not knowing the affidavits were false, presented them to the governor, but nothing was done. He then presented them to the Dade County grand jury, which in turn subpoenaed the original sources. Again the witnesses gave false testimony, and the sheriff was indicted for perjury and eventually removed from office. At his trial, the sheriff was acquitted after it was discovered that the information in the affidavits was false. The sheriff then brought a criminal conspiracy charge against the reporter. A district court of appeal held that anyone who cooperates with or procures testimony for a grand jury is immune from liability.

Another time when the media enjoys absolute privilege occurs when a broadcaster gives a political candidate use of his facilities to exercise his rights under the Federal Communications Commission's Equal Time Rules. In such an instance, the broadcaster is immune from liability resulting from the candidate's remarks. Since a broadcaster may not censor the comments of a candidate,

49. 231 So. 2d 6 (Fla. 1970).

50. Buchanan v. Miami Herald Publishing Co., 206 So. 2d 465 (Fla. Dist. Ct. App. 1968).

he therefore cannot be held liable for those same comments, according to a 1959 Supreme Court decision.[51]

Generally, the media enjoy only conditional or qualified privilege while reporting public proceedings. The concept of qualified privilege was explained in a 1906 Florida case, *Abraham* v. *Baldwin.*[52] The Florida Supreme Court stated in that case that a communication is privileged if made in good faith, if the communicator and receiver have an "interest, right, or duty" in the information, and if the communication is made on an occasion and under circumstances that properly serve such rights and duties. If the communication is known to be false when made, malice will be inferred, thus destroying privilege. Accordingly, the requirements for qualified privilege are good faith, accuracy, proper interest on the part of the communicator and the receiver, and a proper occasion and purpose. The terms proper "interest, right, or duty" generally refer to matters of public interest that the public has a right to know about. Privileged proceedings may even include news conferences as well as remarks made during a campaign. For example, during a gubernatorial campaign, pollster Joe Abram stated that candidate Brailey Odham "appears to be slipping badly" and was in second place.[53] The *Florida Times-Union* published Odham's reply: "Joe Abram is a phony and his poll is a phony." Abram sued both Odham and the *Times-Union.* The Florida Supreme Court held that Odham was absolutely privileged to make the comments because he was running for office and the statement was made during the political campaign. The newspaper, continued the court, had a qualified privilege to publish the fair and accurate account of those remarks because they were matters of public interest and were made in a privileged setting (a campaign).

Qualified privilege flows from absolute privilege. If a public official has the absolute privilege to say something, then report-

51. Farmers Educ. and Coop. Union of America v. WDAY, 360 U.S. 525 (1959).

52. 42 So. 591 (Fla. 1906).

53. Abram v. Odham, 89 So. 2d 334 (Fla. 1956).

ers have the qualified privilege to report it fairly and accurately. Also, if anyone speaking in a privileged setting, such as a court, city council, campaign rally, or a legislative hearing, says something defamatory, it may be accurately and fairly reported by the media.

The law is fairly lenient in applying both absolute and qualified privilege to legislative, judicial, and administrative proceedings, activities, and records. However, because some law enforcement activities are more complex, they have created problems for journalists. Is the report of a defamatory statement made by a policeman or detective during a preliminary investigation before any arrests or charges are made protected by qualified privilege? What about a written confession released by the police? Is it a public document that can be reported on? Who on a police force has absolute privilege to comment about a case? A desk sergeant? A patrolman? A detective? A sheriff? A chief of police? A public information officer? These are questions any police reporter encounters daily and there are no clear answers.

The problem is further confounded because Florida courts have dealt with only a few cases in this area. In *Patterson* v. *Tribune Co.*, a Hillsborough circuit court granted summary judgment to the defendant after finding that an article based on information disseminated by the sheriff's office during an official briefing was an accurate summary of information and was protected by the privilege of reporting on official actions.[54]

On the question of police reports, a district court of appeal decision held that police reports are privileged. In *O'Neal* v. *Tribune Co.*, the *Tampa Tribune* and *Tampa Times* falsely reported that parents of an infant had accused the owner of a nursery and kindergarten with beating their eighteen-month-old daughter.[55] The information came from an offense report filed by the investigating officer. The report stated that the child had several

54. 9 Media L. Rep. 2192 (Fla. Cir. Ct. 1983).
55. 176 So. 2d 535.

bruises on her body, that the child had stayed at the nursery all day, and that the investigating officer had concluded the offense was an assault on a minor. No one was charged with the offense, no mention was made of any suspects, no claim or complaint was brought, and the parents made no accusations against the nursery. Later it was determined that the child had received the bruises during a fall at her home. The court ruled that a newspaper has qualified privilege when reporting accurately and fairly the factual contents of an offense report. However, some statements in the article were not privileged because they went beyond the information in the report and accused the nursery owner of assault.

In reaching the decision in this last case, the court reviewed over a half-dozen persuasive cases from other states because Florida had no precedent that could be relied upon. The following general guidelines from these other jurisdictions and from the more recent *Restatement of Torts* may help clarify the difficult problem of reporting law enforcement proceedings (also, refer to chapter 6 for information about public police records):

1. Statements from a sheriff or a chief of police are privileged as long as the statements are within that person's public duty.
2. Statements made orally by a patrolman, sergeant, or detective should not be equated with a written report or complaint and, therefore, are not privileged.
3. Information taken from an offense report, arrest docket, log book, or other public document required by statute or rule is privileged as long as no implication of guilt is made. (Privilege will attach to such reports whether or not any arrest, charges, or proceedings ever come about.)
4. Unofficial reports such as interviews, news releases, and hot-line telephone reports (one-way, prerecorded messages from police to media) by an investigating officer or patrolman are not privileged.

Judicial proceedings also create problems for the reporter, particularly since the procedures and technicalities surrounding our legal system are so complex. Generally, privilege applies to any statements made in any judicial procedure: a grand jury indictment, the questioning of jurors, reading of formal charges, arguments by attorney, testimony of witnesses, and verdicts, opinions, orders, and other pronouncements by a judge. This privilege is also applicable to any other proceeding of a judicial nature, such as extradition proceedings, hearings before administrative agencies, bar association disciplinary hearings, and trials or hearings before legislative bodies.

At what point privilege attaches itself in a judicial proceeding is unclear since the traditional understanding is that some official action is necessary to put privilege into effect. In Florida, pretrial filings, such as complaints, answers, pleadings, and depositions, are public documents. However, while public, is information taken from them privileged when no official action has been taken? In Florida that question is unsettled, but other jurisdictions seem to hold that until some official action is taken on a complaint no privilege is attached.

It is also unclear whether privilege attaches in those hearings that are closed to the public: paternity hearings, juvenile proceedings, and portions of a trial where a minor will be on the stand.

Several Florida cases demonstrate how inaccurate reporting of judicial proceedings will not be protected by privilege. In one case, a newspaper covered the 1931 murder trial of three defendants and reported that all three would die in the electric chair if the judge's instructions to find them guilty were carried out by the jury.[56] Actually, the judge had instructed the jury to find two of the defendants guilty and the verdict was so rendered. The innocent defendant sued the newspaper and won because the report of the judge's instructions was inaccurate, leading the reader to believe the defendant was guilty of murder.

56. Shiell v. Metropolis Co., 136 So. 537 (Fla. 1931).

Two cases demonstrate how ignorance of the law may lead to a false report. *Time, Inc.* v. *Firestone,* decided by the U.S. Supreme Court in 1976, involved the report of a divorce suit in which millionaire industrialist Russell Firestone sued his wife, Mary Alice, for divorce on the grounds of adultery.[57] A Florida circuit court granted the divorce, not on the basis of adultery, but because neither party was "domesticated." *Time* magazine ran, in its "Milestones" section, a short squib stating inaccurately that Russell Firestone had been granted a divorce on grounds of extreme cruelty and adultery. The magazine also reported that Firestone was ordered to pay Mrs. Firestone $3,000 a month in alimony. In Florida, alimony cannot be awarded when a wife is found to be adulterous. The divorce decree was extremely complex; yet, had the reporter checked the state's divorce laws, the mistake probably would have been avoided.

In another example, a newspaper was found liable after incorrectly reporting the contents of a mortgage foreclosure complaint.[58] The reporter, who was filling in for the newspaper's regular court reporter, read the complaint and mistakenly identified the defendant as the owner of a health studio being sued for foreclosure. The court hearing the libel case stated that any experienced reporter would not have made the mistake. The court held that although the reporter had not reported the information knowing it was false, nor had he reason to doubt his understanding of the document, he still was negligent.

Qualified privilege has even been extended to protect the fair and accurate reports of lawyers who comment publicly on the state of a pending action. In *Huszar* v. *Gross,* a lawyer for the Florida comptroller's office told a reporter that an attorney who refused to sign an agreement for her client was acting in an "unethical" manner and the comptroller's office was taking steps to force her to take action.[59] The district court of appeal ruled

57. 424 U.S. 448 (1976).

58. Cape Publications v. Teri's Health Studio, 385 So. 2d 188 (Fla. Dist. Ct. App. 1980).

59. 468 So. 2d 512 (Fla. Dist. Ct. App. 1985).

that the qualified privilege to make fair and accurate reports of judicial and quasi-judicial proceedings extended to protect the remarks of counsel reporting on the status of a lawsuit.

The greater the number of privileged sources used, the greater is the chance of the media being granted summary judgment. In *Ortega* v. *Post-Newsweek Stations,* a Florida district court of appeal held that a story based on statements made by Florida Department of Law Enforcement agents, public records, a real estate analyst, and the transcript of testimony before a congressional subcommittee was a fair and accurate report of official proceedings.[60] The court also noted that it made no difference whether some of the privileged information came from secondhand sources, provided it was fair and accurate.

Within the past ten years, there has been a blurring of the line between what the courts traditionally labeled as official sources and nonofficial sources. By erasing that line, there could be an end to the difficulty of judging whether a situation is privileged. The defense of neutral reporting, first set forth by the Second Circuit in *Edwards* v. *National Audubon Society,* is an extension of the traditional defense of qualified privilege.[61] The theory behind neutral reporting parallels that of qualified privilege in that much social and political debate is carried on by persons who are not public officers or by public officers who are not performing requisite duties. Nonetheless, they are responsible spokespersons, and statements from them should be reported by the media with the same vigor and the same immunity as privileged comments and activities.

In *Edwards,* the National Audubon Society magazine, *American Birds,* carried an editorial accusing pro-DDT scientists of making "false" and "misleading" statements about the effects of DDT on birds. The distortions, said the editorial, were "for the

60. 510 So. 2d 972 (Fla. Dist. Ct. App. 1987). *See also* Jamason v. Palm Beach Newspapers, 450 So. 2d 1130 (Fla. Dist. Ct. App. 1984) (reporter's sources were two assistant state attorneys).

61. 556 F.2d 113 (2d Cir. 1977), *cert. denied,* 434 U.S. 1002 (1977).

most self-serving of reasons." The scientists, who were all connected with the chemical industry, were "being paid to lie," said the editorial. The scientists had stated that the Audubon Society's annual Christmas Bird Count was proof that bird life was thriving despite the use of DDT. The truth, said the editorial, was that more birds were counted because there were more birders who were better equipped and more knowledgeable about species identification.

The *New York Times* ran an article quoting the editorial, naming the scientists, and reporting the denials of three. Three of the named scientists sued the *Times* for libel in a U.S. district court. The jury found that although the *Times* reported its information accurately, it had acted recklessly by printing the article after the three scientists had denied the charges. Such denials, said the court, should have left serious doubts in the reporter's mind about the truth of the charges. The jury returned a verdict against the *Times*.

The Second Circuit reversed the judgment and suggested the adoption of a new defense it termed neutral reporting. The court reasoned that "when a responsible, prominent organization like the National Audubon Society makes serious charges against a public figure, the First Amendment protects the accurate and disinterested reporting of those charges, regardless of the reporter's private views regarding their validity." The court further reasoned that the public interest that swirls around sensitive issues demands that the press be afforded the freedom to report such charges without assuming responsibility for them. A reporter should not be forced to withhold a story until a full-scale investigation is completed. Thus the court was attaching qualified privilege to a situation where the source was not a public official and the situation was not a public meeting or record.

The neutral reporting defense has been adopted in numerous Florida courts. In the Twelfth Circuit, a judge ruled that reporting statements made by parties to a public dispute (the administration of a local hospital) is protected by the defense of neutral reporting.[62] In *Bair* v. *Palm Beach Newspapers,* an outpatient counselor was dismissed from a drug abuse treatment program. According to an article in the Palm Beach *Post and Daily News,* the director had stated that the counselor's academic credentials "looked more impressive than they actually were" and were a "misrepresentation" of his qualifications.[63] The court ruled that because the executive director had made the statements "in connection with a controversy about which the media has a privilege to report, the accurate reporting of the statements is protected by the First Amendment."

Since the defense of neutral reporting does not fit snugly into the traditional defense of qualified privilege, most state and federal courts are understandably reluctant to adopt it. However, courts have based their decisions on neutral reporting precedents in situations where the sources of the false information were the victim of a police shooting, the president of an airline, a basketball player, a government attorney, and a television news anchor.[64] Sources not considered responsible spokespersons for the purpose of the neutral reporting defense have included rumors and an alleged alcoholic with a grudge.[65]

The Constitutional Defenses

The common law defenses to a charge of libel served both the plaintiff and the defendant well for many years. As long as libel

62. Gadd v. News-Press Publishing Co., 10 Media L. Rep. 2362 (Fla. Cir. Ct. 1984); *see also* Smith v. Taylor City Publishing, 8 Media L. Rep. 1294 (Fla. Cir. Ct. 1982); Wade v. Stocks, 7 Media L. Rep. 2200 (Fla. Cir. Ct. 1981); Hatijioannou v. Tribune Co., 8 Media L. Rep. 2637 (Fla. Cir. Ct. 1982).

63. 8 Media L. Rep. 2028 (Fla. Cir. Ct. 1982).

64. Orr v. Lynch, 401 N.Y.S.2d 897 (N.Y. App. Div. 1978); Dixon v. Newsweek, 562 F.2d 626 (10th Cir. 1977); Barry v. Time, Inc., 584 F. Supp. 1110 (D.C. N. Cal. 1984); J. V. Peters v. Knight-Ridder, 10 Media L. Rep. 1576 (Ohio Ct. App. 1984); Woods v. Evansville Press Co., 11 Media L. Rep. 2201 (D.C. Ind., 1985), *aff'd,* 791 F.2d 480 (7th Cir. 1986).

65. Martin v. Wilson Publishing Co., 497 A.2d 322 (R.I. 1985); Davis v. Keystone Printing Serv., 507 N.E.2d 1358 (Ill. App. Ct. 1987).

suits were brought primarily by private citizens and did not involve millions of dollars in damages and reporters acted responsibly in covering routine matters, more protection was not needed. However, as reporters gained greater access to reports and information and more investigative stories were published, more public officials and public figures began bringing suits that demanded half a million dollars and upward in damages. The result was that the media were losing more cases than ever, particularly when they were covering stories involving charges of graft, unethical conduct, conspiracy, and fraud—where the truth is elusive. It was the liberal-minded Court of Chief Justice Earl Warren that first recognized that without more protection newspapers would be unwilling to cover important stories, thus slowing the flow of information. This "chilling effect" theory was the basis for the first constitutional defense, actual malice, which put greater burdens upon public officials and public figures in libel cases. Ten years later the chilling effect theory was used to set forth the second constitutional defense, negligence, when a libel involved a private citizen.

Actual Malice and Public Libel

In 1964, the U.S. Supreme Court in *New York Times Co.* v. *Sullivan* set about establishing a new defense to a complaint of defamation.[66] This defense, known as the *Sullivan* rule, the actual malice rule, or the constitutional defense, grew out of the Court's concern that common law libel as applied in the majority of states allowed the media to be punished with large judgments even when the defamation was unintentional. "The pall of fear and timidity imposed [by the fear of large damage awards] upon those who would give voice to public criticism is an atmosphere in which the First Amendment freedoms cannot survive," said the Court.

Under common law, as explained earlier, the mere existence of a libel per se presumed malice, and such a presumption was suf-

66. 376 U.S. 254 (1964).

ficient for awarding damages of virtually unlimited amounts. The Court compared these civil judgments to the criminal fines allowed under sedition laws and found that such judgments could be one hundred to one thousand times greater than the maximum fine provided by criminal libel. "Would-be critics of official conduct may be deterred from voicing their criticism, even though it is believed to be true and even though it is in fact true, because of doubt whether it can be proved in court or fear of the expense of having to do so."[67]

To combat this common law rule that "dampens the vigor and limits the variety of debate," the Court held that no public official may recover "damages for a defamatory falsehood relating to his official conduct unless he proves that the statement was made with 'actual malice'—that is, with knowledge that it was false or with reckless disregard of whether it was false or not."[68] The *Sullivan* rule grew out of a case in which the *New York Times* carried a paid editorial advertisement containing misstatements of fact about civil rights demonstrations in Montgomery, Alabama. The plaintiff, L. B. Sullivan, Montgomery city commissioner in charge of the police department, claimed the ad defamed him. The paid political advertisement was signed by 64 persons, many of whom were well known either in politics, religion, entertainment, or union activities. The *New York Times,* relying upon the reputation of the signers, published the advertisement without checking its accuracy. The Supreme Court held that the failure to check the facts in the ad was not sufficient proof that the newspaper knew the material to be false or that the *New York Times* demonstrated reckless disregard for the truth.

Although the *Sullivan* decision was hailed as one of the most important First Amendment cases of the twentieth century, its immediate application was limited. The Court left many questions that would have to be answered in future cases. And it was not long before those cases appeared on the dockets. Between

67. *Id.* at 279.
68. *Id.* at 279–280.

1964 and 1971, the U.S. Supreme Court and lower federal and state courts expanded the rule to former public officials as long as the activity reported concerned the official's former public duties, to candidates for public office, to public figures who placed themselves in the vortex of a public concern, and to public figures who by virtue of their position were figures of public interest. In case-by-case application, the court defined the term "public official," pulling in a wide range of public servants from a university student body president to a patrolman. The courts also stretched the *Sullivan* rule outside the bounds of civil libel to apply it where a state had imposed a charge of criminal libel, where a school board wanted to fire a public school teacher who made false statements in a letter to the editor, and to invasion of privacy suits based on false statements.[69]

Then in 1971, the Supreme Court made the final stretch, applying the actual malice rule in a libel action brought by a private individual. In *Rosenbloom* v. *Metromedia, Inc.,* the Court recognized that all of the libel cases considered by the Courts since 1964 had involved events of "public or general concern."[70] The obvious conclusion, therefore, was to erase the artificial distinctions between public and private plaintiffs and to establish the actual malice defense for any report of a matter of public or general interest. The *Rosenbloom* decision is classified as a plurality opinion because only three of the five majority justices agreed with the "public or general concern" test. In this plurality decision the Court managed to alter the *Sullivan* decision to state that no plaintiff could receive damages in a libel suit relating to his involvement in any event of public concern unless he could prove actual malice. Since almost all defamation suits arise out of stories of public concern, and since actual malice is almost impossible for private plaintiffs to prove, the *Rosenbloom* case virtually shut off all redress for private plaintiffs, at least temporarily.

In the 1974 case of *Gertz* v. *Robert Welch, Inc.,* Justice Lewis

69. *See* Garrison v. Louisiana, 379 U.S. 64 (1964); Pickering v. Board of Education, 391 U.S. 563 (1968); Time, Inc. v. Hill, 385 U.S. 374 (1967).
70. 403 U.S. 29 (1971).

Powell's opinion for the Court reviewed the *Sullivan* rule as it had been expanded and modified through the uncertain *Rosenbloom* decision.[71] Then Powell set the groundwork for overturning *Rosenbloom.* He stated unequivocally that while the news media's need to avoid self-censorship carries with it a high societal value, it is not absolute. Any absolute protection for the media would require a total sacrifice of the competing values served by libel laws. In order to balance the needs of both the press and the individual, the Court returned to its former distinctions between public and private plaintiffs. However, the Court maintained, as it did in *Sullivan,* that the common law of libel was much too harsh since it allowed juries to award substantial sums as compensation for presumed damage to reputation. "The largely uncontrolled discretion of juries to award damages where there is no loss unnecessarily compounds the potential of any system of liability for defamatory falsehood to inhibit the vigorous exercise of First Amendment freedoms." To reconcile the common law of libel with the need for robust and uninhibited expression, the Court in *Gertz* established new rules for private plaintiffs. Before a private plaintiff can receive compensation for actual monetary loss, loss of reputation, humiliation, and personal anguish, there must be some finding of fault or negligence on the part of the media. No longer may damage be presumed from the mere existence of defamatory content; any damage award must be supported by evidence that injury did occur. The Court left to the states the problem of determining what standard of fault, short of presumed negligence, would be used. Also, no longer will punitive damages be allowed unless the plaintiff can establish actual malice as defined in *Sullivan.* Punitive damages, which are awarded as a punishment against the media, have traditionally been excessive and consequently were used selectively to punish expressions of unpopular views.

As is true with every decision reached by the U.S. Supreme Court, every jurisdiction in the country is bound to abide by the

71. 418 U.S. 323.

Sullivan and *Gertz* precedents. Although the interpretation of those cases may be divergent from court to court and state to state, the questions being asked are the same.

Who Is a Public Official?

In *Sullivan,* the Court remarked that it had no occasion "to determine how far down into the lower ranks of government employees the 'public official' designation would extend for purposes of this rule, or otherwise to specify categories of persons who would or would not be included."[72] No precise lines were drawn, and it has been for succeeding cases at all judicial levels to specify who is and who is not a public official. Generally, the determination of whether a plaintiff is or is not a public official is up to the judge and not the jury.

Two years after *Sullivan,* the Court set forth a definition of public official which was all-encompassing. In *Rosenblatt* v. *Baer* the Court said, "It is clear, therefore, that the 'public official' designation applies at the very least to those among the hierarchy of government employees who have, or appear to the public to have, substantial responsibility for or control over the conduct of government affairs."[73] Those officials who without a doubt fall under this definition of public official include all elected officials from the president of the United States down to a school board member. In Florida, elected officials include the governor, lieutenant governor, legislators, county commissioners, county sheriffs, judges, mayors, city council members, and school board members. A second classification of public official is those persons appointed to their positions, such as cabinet officers, first-term supreme court justices, administrative agency heads, school superintendents, city and county administrators, college presidents, and various state, county, and city inspectors. The third classification of public official is those public employees who are neither elected nor appointed but are "hired" as civil service

72. 376 U.S. 254, 283 n.23.
73. 383 U.S. 75 (1966).

workers to carry substantial responsibility or control over the conduct of a governmental activity. Public employees considered public officials are those who hold positions that invite greater public scrutiny than normally brought to government employees during the performance of their duties. Thus, not all public employees are public officials. "That conclusion would virtually disregard society's interest in protecting reputation," said *Rosenblatt.*[74]

States have been unable to agree on just what jobs fall under this last category of public official. The job most states agree on is that of policeman. Policemen at all ranks carry a substantial amount of responsibility and invite greater public scrutiny than most government employees.

The Second District Court of Appeal reversed a trial court's directed verdict when it found that a coordinator of an adult congregate living facility operated by the Florida Department of Health and Rehabilitative Services was not a public official.[75] The counselor was accused of allegedly abusing residents at a boarding home. The court stated that a public official is one whose position invites public scrutiny totally apart from the particular controversy that has gained public attention. The coordinator, concluded the court, had only a minimal control over the boarding home and was only a midlevel employee.

One measure of whether a person is a public or private plaintiff is that person's access to forums for rebuttal. A schoolteacher, a computer operator, or a workmen's compensation case reviewer does not have as easy access to the media to rebut false charges as does an election supervisor, school superintendent, or cabinet head.

The definition of a public official requires that the defamation be limited to anything that might touch on that person's fitness for office.[76] In *Monitor Patriot Co.* v. *Roy,* a New Hampshire news-

74. *Id.* at 86 n.13.

75. Wilkinson v. Florida Adult Care Center, 450 So. 2d 1168 (Fla. Dist. Ct. App. 1984).

76. Garrison v. Louisiana, 379 U.S. 64.

paper carried the syndicated "Washington Merry-Go-Round" column that accused one of the Democratic candidates for U.S. senator of being a "former small-time bootlegger."[77] Although the trial judge instructed the jury that the plaintiff was a public official, the jury also was instructed that the charge of "bootlegger" could be found to lie in the private sector of the plaintiff's life rather than in his public life. The U.S. Supreme Court disagreed and reversed the $20,000 verdict. The Court held that "a charge of criminal conduct, no matter how remote in time or place, can never be irrelevant to an official's or a candidate's fitness for office."

But what if the charge is false because a newspaper confused names? This was the question the Court approached in a 1971 Florida case, *Ocala Star-Banner* v. *Damron.*[78] In *Damron,* the newspaper had printed a story falsely accusing Leonard Damron, mayor of Crystal River and candidate for county tax assessor, of being charged with perjury in a federal court. In fact, the charge of perjury had been entered against the plaintiff's brother James. Two weeks after the story appeared, the plaintiff lost the election for tax assessor. It appeared at trial that the plaintiff's name had been so much on the mind of the editor because of recent election stories that when a reporter called in the story and identified the defendant in the perjury charge as James Damron, the editor inadvertently changed the name to Leonard Damron. At trial, the jury was instructed to award damages as if Damron were a private plaintiff. He was awarded $22,000, but that judgment was reversed by the U.S. Supreme Court and the case remanded for a new trial. The Court stated that Damron must be treated as a public official under the *Sullivan* rule. Using arguments from the *Monitor Patriot* case, decided on the same day as *Damron,* the Court stated that any charge of perjury is relevant to the fitness of the plaintiff for office, and liability must be based on a finding of actual malice.

77. 401 U.S. 265 (1971).
78. 401 U.S. 295 (1971).

Who Is a Public Figure?

Drawing more controversy than the question of who is a public official is the question of who is a public figure. The controversy and confusion stem in part from the changing definitions that have been offered by the courts since 1964.

It was not long after the *Sullivan* decision that state and lower courts began forwarding the proposition that some constitutional privilege exists to protect the media against libel suits by private persons who are of public interest. In 1967, the Court officially sanctioned the application of a higher standard of liability where public figures were involved. In *Curtis Publishing Co.* v. *Butts* and its tandem case *Associated Press* v. *Walker,* the Court defined a public figure as one who commanded a substantial amount of public interest either by position alone or by purposefully thrusting himself into the "vortex" of a public controversy.[79] The Court, however, did not require the same standard of liability for public figures as it did for public officials. Rather than apply the rule of actual malice, Justice John Harlan's opinion set a standard based on "highly unreasonable conduct constituting an extreme departure from the standards of investigation and reporting ordinarily adhered to by responsible publishers." This "unreasonable conduct" standard received the vote of only four justices. Three justices would have adopted the rule of actual malice; Justices William O. Douglas and Hugo Black would have abandoned any standard as wholly inadequate to prevent the press from being destroyed by libel judgments. The unreasonable conduct standard was rarely, if ever, applied in libel cases involving public figures because it was too much like the reasonable man standard when being used by some states in suits involving private plaintiffs. Most jurisdictions simply adopted the rule of actual malice when the plaintiff was a public figure, and allowed evidence of unreasonable conduct to be one of several factors a jury could use to determine liability.

The next case to tackle the problem of distinguishing between

79. 388 U.S. 130 (1967).

the private plaintiff and the public figure resulted in a temporary abandonment of the "artificial" distinctions. In *Rosenbloom,* the Court interpreted this country's dedication to robust and wide-open discussion as hinging not on who the participant was or what his status was but on the conduct of that participant and whether "the content, effect, and significance of the conduct" was of public and general concern.[80] For the next three years, the common understanding was that the *Sullivan* rule of actual malice would be the standard when a defamatory falsehood related to a private person who was either voluntarily or involuntarily a party to a matter of general or public interest. The *Rosenbloom* decision, however, is classified as a plurality opinion, with the majority voting for the result but only three justices concurring with the general and public concern test.

One Florida case, *Nigro* v. *Miami Herald Publishing Co.,* exemplifies the application of this test.[81] The case was brought against both the *Miami Daily News* and the *Miami Herald* by eleven men accused of being members of the Mafia. In March 1969, the *Daily News* ran a major news item about "ten members of the Mafia" and "Cosa Nostra men" who, on arriving from Missouri, had been handed subpoenas at the Miami airport. The paper explained that these men were coming to Miami to take over from the late Mafia boss, Vito Genovese. The article named eleven other men who also arrived and "were friends and business associates of known midwest Mafia figures." The same day, the *Miami Herald* identified the eleven as "Cosa Nostra members and associates" and "henchmen." The district court of appeal stated that the plaintiffs had to prove actual malice because organized crime was in the news. The court stated emphatically that law enforcement activities related to organized crime are issues of general and public concern. No actual malice could be established since the source of the information was an officer in the U.S. Justice Department's Task Force on Organized Crime.

80. 403 U.S. 29.
81. 262 So. 2d 698 (Fla. Dist. Ct. App. 1972).

Rosenbloom's general and public concern test was soon doomed as it became evident to the Court that the test failed to strike the proper balance between the need for full public discussion and the need to protect an individual's reputation. In 1974, Chicago attorney Elmer Gertz succeeded in having the *Rosenbloom* test overturned in a libel suit that he brought against the John Birch Society magazine, *American Opinion.*[82] The magazine had accused Gertz, a prominent and well-respected criminal attorney, of being a "communist fronter," a "Leninist," a "Marxist," and the architect of a frame-up against a policeman who shot and killed a black youth. Gertz had no part in the policeman's murder trial; he only acted as counsel for the boy's family in a civil suit that resulted in virtually no publicity. The U.S. Supreme Court reversed the *Rosenbloom* plurality opinion and reinstated the distinction between a private and public plaintiff to balance better the interests involved. The Court attempted to clarify the definition of a public figure by narrowing the term's application. The Court stated that a person could become a public figure by being a person who has achieved "such pervasive fame or notoriety that he becomes a public figure for all purposes and in all contexts." Or, more commonly, a person could become a public figure in a limited range of issues by voluntarily injecting himself or being drawn into a particular public controversy and engaging the public's attention in an attempt to influence the outcome.

The test, emphasized the Court, was to look at the nature and extent of the individual's participation in a controversy. "An individual should not be deemed a public personality for all aspects of his life" unless he does have pervasive fame or notoriety in the community. As for attorney Gertz, the Court said that while he was well known in some circles, particularly those having to do with his professional affairs, he was not known widely in the community. In fact, none of the prospective jurors called at the trial had ever heard of Gertz before the suit was brought and publicized. Also, Gertz had never discussed with the press either

82. Gertz v. Robert Welch, Inc., 418 U.S. 323.

the criminal or civil litigation involving the youth's death. The Court held that a lawyer does not assume the role of a public figure when he represents a client in a civil suit.

To determine whether a plaintiff is a public figure who must prove actual malice, a court generally must decide (1) whether the story is one of general and public concern, and (2) at what level the individual is involved in the affair.

The first determination requires that the story be more than a matter of public interest; instead, it must be a genuine public controversy. The District of Columbia Court of Appeals defined a public controversy as one in which persons other than those involved would feel the impact of its outcome. "If the issue was being debated publicly and if it had foreseeable and substantial ramifications for non-participants, it was a public issue."[83]

In *Lerman* v. *Flynt Distributing Co.*, the Second Circuit said a public controversy was any topic upon which sizable segments of society have different and strongly held views.[84]

In 1976, two years after the *Gertz* decision, the U.S. Supreme Court looked at the question of what is a public controversy. The case grew out of the Florida libel suit by Mary Alice Firestone, the wife of Russell Firestone. *Time* magazine falsely accused Mrs. Firestone of adultery in its "Milestones" column. She won a $100,000 libel judgment from a Florida circuit court. The Florida Supreme Court affirmed the judgment and defined a public controversy as one that invokes "common and predominant public activity, participation, or indulgence, and cogitation, study and debate. . . ."[85]

The U.S. Supreme Court also agreed with the lower courts, reasoning that although the plaintiff was prominent in the social affairs of Palm Beach society, she was not prominent in any particular public controversy.[86] The Court refused to equate public

83. Waldbaum v. Fairchild Publications, 627 F.2d 1287, 1297 (D.C. Cir. 1980), *cert. denied,* 449 U.S. 898 (1980).

84. 745 F. 2d 123, 138 (2d Cir. 1984).

85. Time, Inc. v. Firestone, 271 So. 2d 745, 749 (Fla. 1972).

86. Time, Inc. v. Firestone, 424 U.S. 448.

curiosity about the divorce of an extremely wealthy person with genuine public interest in a public issue. The Court stated that the dissolution of a marriage through divorce is not voluntary because one must go to court in order to obtain legal release from the marriage.

In *Friedgood* v. *Peters Publishing Co.*, a daughter tried to conceal evidence in her father's murder trial. A circuit court noted that the fact that the case gained public attention was not sufficient to make the defendant a public figure.[87] However, because the trial resulted in significant legislation that altered traditional medical practice, the case was raised above the level of curiosity. Also, in *Arnold* v. *Taco Properties,* the controversy involved the licensing of a private school, which the court ruled was of consumer interest, not merely of public interest.[88]

On the second determination, the extent of the plaintiff's involvement, the following clues have been used by various courts:

1. Did the individual voluntarily inject himself or herself into a public issue in an effort to affect its outcome?
2. Was the individual heavily involved in an area of high community concern?
3. Has the individual achieved a broad community reputation involving the activity upon which the libel suit is based?
4. Has the individual actively sought attention from the media or the public?
5. Has extensive public debate thrust the individual into the limelight?

If the answer to any of these questions is yes, then the individual will probably be considered a public figure.

In the case where the daughter of a man accused of killing his wife allegedly tried to conceal evidence, the court said the

87. 15 Media L. Rep. 1479 (Fla. Cir. Ct. 1986).
88. 427 So. 2d 216 (Fla. Dist. Ct. App. 1983).

daughter's status as a public figure rested on several factors: She was involved in a highly visible criminal trial that resulted in medical reforms; she voluntarily chose to conceal the evidence; she was the star witness in the trial; and she had ready access to the media during the trial to counteract negative information.[89]

Because a south Florida charter air service was involved in aspects of the Iran-Contra investigations, a circuit court ruled that the company was a limited-purpose public figure.[90] Southern Air Transport, which had provided charter services for the CIA, was considered a public figure because of the great public debate that revolved around the national debate over the Iran-Contra situation and because the airline had thrust itself into the forefront of the issue by hiring a public relations firm to respond to queries from the media.

In the *Firestone* case, the plaintiff did not voluntarily publicize her marital problems. However, she did hold press conferences during the divorce to answer questions from reporters. The Court held that that fact did not convert her into a public figure since the issue was still not a genuine public controversy. This holding seems to contradict the *Gertz* requisite that a person who seeks the public eye by inviting public attention through the media or otherwise is a public figure.

The *Firestone* case was the first indication that persons who use the courts for redress or who are involuntarily thrust into a judicial proceeding will not automatically be considered public figures. In 1979, the Court specifically omitted this classification of individuals from the status of public figures. In *Wolston* v. *Reader's Digest,* the plaintiff was identified in the book *KGB: The Secret Work of Soviet Secret Agents* as a Soviet agent during the 1950s.[91] The plaintiff had pleaded guilty in 1958 to a criminal contempt

89. Friedgood v. Peters Publishing Co., 15 Media L. Rep. 1479; *see also* Della-Donna v. Gore Newspapers, 489 So. 2d (Fla. Dist. Ct. App. 1986); Arnold v. Taco Properties, 427 So. 2d 216 (Fla. Dist. Ct. App. 1983).

90. Southern Air Transport v. Post-Newsweek Stations, 15 Media L. Rep. 2429 (Fla. Cir. Ct. 1988).

91. 443 U.S. 157 (1979).

charge after he failed to appear before a special grand jury investigating espionage. The U.S. Court of Appeals for the District of Columbia held that Wolston became a public figure when he failed to appear before the grand jury. The U.S. Supreme Court disagreed with this reasoning and held that Wolston was not a public figure. Persons do not become public figures, said the Court, by the simple fact that they attract media attention. "A libel defendant must show more than mere newsworthiness to justify application of the demanding burden of [actual malice]."

The following have been held to be public figures for limited issues: a college student leader, a real estate agent, an attorney who volunteered services, a court-appointed attorney, a public stock corporation, and a high school teacher. The reason all these persons were held to be public figures was not because of who they were but because of the public issue they were involved in.[92]

What Is Actual Malice?

In Florida, a finding of actual malice is necessary if a public official or a public figure is to win damages. According to *Gertz,* actual malice is also required if a private person involved in a matter of public concern is to win punitive damages or special damages. There are two parts to the definition of actual malice. The first, knowledge of falsity, has only rarely been found to exist on the part of the news media. The second, a finding of reckless disregard, is the most commonly used part of this definition because it is open to so many interpretations.

Knowledge of falsity means that the defendant is aware the material is false but publishes it anyway. Proof of knowledge of falsity must be "convincingly clear." One libel case charging knowledge of falsity has been heard by the U.S. Supreme Court. In *Greenbelt Publishing* v. *Bresler,* a newspaper had characterized as "blackmail" the plaintiff's negotiations with the city council

92. *See, e.g.,* Klahr v. Winterble, 418 P.2d 404 (Ariz. 1966); DeLuca v. New York News, 7 Media L. Rep. 1302 (N.Y. Sup. Ct. 1981); Basarich v. Rodeghero, 321 N.E.2d 739 (Ill. App. Ct. 1974).

to rezone some of his property in return for selling the city land for a high school.[93] Bresler contended that the use of the term "blackmail" (used in the article without quotation marks) charged him with a crime and that the defendant newspaper knew that he had not committed any crime. The Court ruled that the term "blackmail" in the article was not being used to accuse the plaintiff of a crime but was being used to characterize his wholly legal, yet controversial, negotiating position with the city. The term was no more than "rhetorical hyperbole" or a "vigorous epithet" and therefore was not libelous.

What constitutes reckless disregard is difficult to determine because there is no one definition of negligence. It is probably easier to assess from the cases what is not reckless disregard than what is. For example, in *Butts* and *Sullivan* the Court said that unless the defendant had a high degree of awareness of probable falsity, a plaintiff who was a public official could not collect. In *St. Amant* v. *Thompson* the Court said, "There must be sufficient evidence to permit the conclusion that the defendant in fact entertained serious doubts as to the truth of the publication" and such evidence must be "convincingly clear."[94] "Serious doubt as to the truth" can be established where the defendant doubts the veracity of the informant or the accuracy of the information. In states like Florida that have adopted the neutral reporting defense, part of this holding may not stand up because the whole concept behind neutral reporting is to give reporters the opportunity to report doubtful material if the source is a reliable and responsible person or organization.

The standard adopted in determining recklessness is not whether professional standards of journalism have been adhered to. Failure to investigate does not in itself establish bad faith. Likewise, a reporter's belief, with good reason, that the sources of information are reliable often is sufficient to rebut a charge of reckless disregard. Nor is it evidence of recklessness to rely on a

93. 398 U.S. 6 (1970).
94. 390 U.S. 727 (1968).

source that the reporter knows is somewhat biased. In *New York Times Co.* v. *Connor,* the Fifth Circuit held that while verification of facts remains important, a reporter without a high degree of awareness of probable falseness may rely on a single source even though he knows that source reflects only one side of the story.[95]

In a libel suit brought against the *St. Petersburg Times* by a Hernando County judge, a district court of appeal held that the reporter's failure to verify information completely by unsuccessfully trying to contact the plaintiff was not reckless disregard.[96]

A major Florida case, *Cape Publications* v. *Adams,* suggests that reliance on severely biased sources when other sources are available is indeed sufficient for a finding of actual malice.[97] Plaintiff Don Adams was a building official of Vero Beach and Indian County. The bureau chief of *Cocoa Today* wrote several stories charging that Adams had solicited a bribe from a construction supervisor and on another occasion had attempted to persuade the mayor of Indian River Shores to pay $2,400 for work he had done and already had been paid for. The information came from a contractor who, the reporter knew, had a running feud with Adams. The reporter went to all the individuals involved in the charges and received denials from all. As for the overcharging, the mayor of Indian River Shores not only denied the statements but told the reporter where to get the correct information. The reporter also went to the Florida East Coast Chapter of the General Contractors of America, which investigated the charges and found nothing illegal. The district court of appeal concluded that the reporter had acted with reckless disregard because all accusations were denied and the reporter knew his source of information had a feud with Adams. The reporter was on notice to question the source's credibility. In addition, witnesses said the source of the information had threatened to "get Adams" and put him in jail. There was clear and convincing support for a find-

95. 365 F. 2d. 567 (5th Cir. 1966).

96. Times Publishing Co. v. Huffstetler, 409 So. 2d. 112 (Fla. Dist. Ct. App. 1982).

97. 336 So. 2d 445 (Fla. Dist. Ct. App. 1979).

ing of reckless disregard because the newspaper published the story in spite of a high degree of awareness of probable falsity. The jury's verdict of $114,000 in compensatory damages and $100,000 in punitive damages was upheld. The U.S. Supreme Court refused to hear an appeal.

A recent libel decision from the U.S. Supreme Court sheds some light on the media's obligations to investigate conflicting information when there *is* a high degree of awareness of probable falsity. In *Harte-Hanks* v. *Connaughton,* the newspaper published charges that a candidate for municipal judge had promised a woman and her sister a job, a trip to Florida, and a place of business for their parents in exchange for their cooperation in the investigation of a municipal court employee charged with bribery.[98] The article also quoted the candidate's denials and his version of the events.

There was a sharp conflict between the versions of the story; however, when the paper began investigating the events, it made several serious errors that led the jury, the appeals court, and the U.S. Supreme Court to conclude that the paper had acted with reckless disregard. First, no reporter interviewed the woman's sister, who was the most important witness to the offers. The Court called this failure to confirm or discredit the woman's evidence "utterly bewildering" in light of the resources the paper was expending on the investigation. Second, six other witnesses were interviewed; all consistently and categorically denied the charges. Third, the newspaper never listened to tape recordings made at the time of the alleged offers, although the tapes were made available by the plaintiff. The Court noted that it was reasonable to infer that the decisions not to interview the sister and not to listen to the tapes were motivated by a concern that such investigations would raise questions about the informant's veracity.

In conclusion, a unanimous Court found that there were obvious reasons for the paper to doubt the honesty of the informant

98. 109 S. Ct. 2678 (1989).

and that the purposeful avoidance of the truth resulted in a finding of actual malice.

A Florida case demonstrates the danger of relying on anonymous sources. In *Holter* v. *WLCY,* a reporter received several anonymous calls from persons who said that Redington Beach Mayor Charles Holter had resigned under strong suspicion that he was implicated in embezzlement and extortion of moneys from private contractors.[99] Although the reporter did not know who the callers were, the television broadcast began, "According to reliable sources . . ." and ended with the warning ". . . but this has not been confirmed." The reporter did try to verify the information with the attorney general's office and the auditor general's office. He was able to confirm that Holter was resigning in January. Following the first broadcast, several more anonymous calls were received. One caller identified herself as an elected official of Redington Shores. She said the auditor general was making an investigation in that community, but she was surprised to hear Holter's name broadcast since he was mayor of neighboring Redington Beach. Holter also called station WLCY and told the reporter the information was false, that he was resigning for personal reasons, and that he knew nothing about the investigation. The story was rebroadcast unchanged at 11 P.M. The next day WLCY radio, both AM and FM, broadcast the story on their hourly news from 7 A.M. to 3 P.M., although the mix-up between the mayor of Redington Beach and Redington Shores had been clarified by the reporter during an early morning interview with Holter.

The district court of appeal stated that when an anonymous tipster gives information, "one would be hard put not to have serious doubts about the authenticity of the tip." In this case, the reporter had little or no reason to deem the source reliable and should have verified the charges before airing them. The court found that the broadcast station had acted with reckless disregard in all of the broadcasts because the reporter had relied on anony-

99. 366 So. 2d 445 (Fla. Dist. Ct. App. 1979).

mous tips for the first broadcast and after that first broadcast was given sufficient cause (the calls from the Redington Shores official and Holter) to believe the charges were false.

Distorting information received from reliable sources is also sufficient cause for a finding of actual malice. The leading case in this area is *Goldwater* v. *Ginzburg,* decided in 1969 by the Second Circuit.[100] Ralph Ginzburg, the editor of left-learning *Facts* magazine, published an article titled "The Unconscious of a Conservative: A Special Issue on the Mind of Barry Goldwater." The article was prepared by selecting, out of context, derogatory statements about Goldwater from various newspaper and magazine articles as well as books; by mailing a biased and invalid questionnaire to psychiatrists; by citing sources whom the defendant could not name later at trial; by editing and changing the content of answered questionnaires; and by removing from these questionnaires all favorable comments and distilling others. After considering these various reportorial methods, the trial court reached a verdict in favor of Goldwater because it found that Ginzburg had published the material with a predetermined and preconceived plan to malign Goldwater's character and had done so knowing the material was false. In upholding the verdict, the Second Circuit stated that while reliance on newspaper articles, books, campaign literature, and letters and questionnaires is not in and of itself actionable, it becomes actionable when the defendant knows the information is false or inherently improbable, or when the defendant distills, misplaces emphasis, exaggerates, distorts, adds innuendoes, or quotes other statements out of context. The Second Circuit upheld the jury's award of $1.00 in compensatory damages and $75,000 in punitive damages.

The burden of proving actual malice falls upon the plaintiff. The presence of knowledge of falsity or reckless disregard can be established only by examining the defendant's actions or inactions prior to the publication of the article. Thus, the plaintiff's

100. 414 F.2d 324 (2d Cir. 1969), *cert. denied,* 369 U.S. 1049 (1970).

lawyer must have access to the reporter, the reporter's sources, and the reporter's notes. At least that is the contention of lawyers representing plaintiffs. The media, however, buttressing themselves with the First Amendment, have challenged the right of the plaintiff to depose reporters for information or identification of sources.

In a 1972 libel case, *Cervantes* v. *Time, Inc.*, the Eighth Circuit ruled that compelled disclosure of sources for an article could only be upheld if there is "concrete demonstration" that the disclosure would lead to persuasive evidence on the issue of malice.[101] In *Cervantes,* information had already been entered showing that a substantial editorial effort had been expended to get independent corroboration of charges that a mayor was linked with the criminal underworld.

In Florida, the issue of reporter's privilege in libel cases was addressed in *Gadd County Times* v. *Horne.*[102] A pretrial discovery order was issued compelling a reporter to reveal her confidential source for a story alleging that a former state senator was under federal investigation. The trial judge stated that the plaintiff had a right to the reporter's testimony since knowing the identity of the source had a direct bearing on the issue of actual malice. A district court of appeal quashed the discovery order. The court held that reporters have a qualified privilege against compelled disclosure of confidential sources. But that privilege must yield if the information is relevant, if it can be obtained from alternative sources, and if there is a compelling need for the information.

If testimonial privilege not to reveal sources during a libel trial is granted, it is absolute. In other words, a reporter would have to refuse to answer any question relevant to the confidential source, such as how the information was received, whether it was given in confidence, and whether the source was reliable. The

101. 464 F. 2d 986 (8th Cir. 1972); *see also* Bruno & Stillman, Inc. v. Globe Newspaper Co., 633 F. 2d 583 (1st Cir. 1980); Miller v. Transamerican Press, Inc., 621 F. 2d 721 (5th Cir. 1980).

102. 426 So. 2d 1234 (Fla. Dist. Ct. App. 1983).

defense cannot use the privilege as both a shield to protect the reporter and as a sword to defend against evidence of negligence and malice.[103]

The question of whether a defendant in a libel suit must disclose material that falls outside of objective information and sources was finally answered in *Herbert* v. *Lando.*[104] The *Lando* case involved an allegedly defamatory broadcast of CBS's "60 Minutes." The program insinuated that the plaintiff, Lieutenant Colonel Anthony Herbert, had lied about allegations he made regarding war crimes in Vietnam. During the discovery stage of the suit, the plaintiff tried to question "60 minutes" reporter Mike Wallace and producer Barry Lando. While Lando gave almost 3,000 pages of depositions regarding what he knew or learned, he refused to answer questions in several areas about what he "believed." He refused to testify about his decisions to pursue certain leads, about his belief in the truthfulness of his sources, about his decision to include or exclude certain information, and about conversations between himself and Wallace. Lando claimed that he did not have to answer questions in these areas because the First Amendment protected against intrusion in the editorial process of the media.

A U.S. district court in New York ordered Lando to testify; however, the Second Circuit stated that Lando did not have to testify about how he made his decisions. In spring 1979, the U.S. Supreme Court overturned the appeals court decision, basing its reasoning on the fact that to offer absolute immunity to the media in a libel case would substantially enhance the burden of proving actual malice, if not make it impossible. Actual malice can only be proven by looking at why a defendant acted or did not act rather than looking only at the objective circumstances of the actual publication. The Court cited in a footnote almost 40 libel cases where courts had uniformly admitted evi-

103. *See* Laxalt v. McClatchy, 116 F.R.D. 438 (D.C. Nev. 1987); Daloney v. NBC, 129 A.2d 673 (N.Y. App. Div. 1987); Liberty Lobby v. Rees, 13 Media L. Rep. 1487 (D.C. Cir. 1986).

104. 441 U.S. 153 (1979).

dence of conduct, motive, and editorial decision making when it benefited either the plaintiff or the news media. The Court also noted that often it is the media that first present evidence about the editorial process in order to establish good faith and lack of malice. "It may be that plaintiffs will rarely be successful in proving awareness of falsehood from the mouth of the defendant himself," said the Court, "but the relevance of answers to such inquiries . . . can hardly be doubted. To erect an impenetrable barrier to the plaintiff's use of such evidence . . . is a matter of some substance particularly when defendants themselves are prone to assert their good-faith belief in the truth of their publications. . . ."[105] The Court did issue one caveat, stating that editorial discussions or exchanges do have some constitutional protection from casual inquiry or examination where the purpose is to satisfy a curiosity or a public interest. However, this protection does not extend where there is a specific claim of injury arising from a publication that is alleged to have been knowingly or recklessly false.

Negligence and Private Libel

As explained earlier, the *Gertz* decision created a new problem area for lawyers dealing with libel cases, particularly cases with private plaintiffs. Common law libel allowed recovery by private plaintiffs without any showing of injury and without any showing of negligence or fault on the part of the media. The Court in *Gertz,* realizing that damages awarded in private libel cases can be just as confiscatory as those awarded in public libel cases, established that private plaintiffs must prove their injury and must prove that the newspaper was, at minimum, negligent.

Since *Gertz,* a number of cases involving private plaintiffs have questioned whether negligence is the most appropriate standard of fault. After some contradictory opinions in Florida's lower courts, the state supreme court handed down two decisions in 1984 that answered the question of what standard is appropriate

105. *Id.* at 170.

when a purely private plaintiff is involved in a story of general and public concern. In *Miami Herald* v. *Ane* and *Tribune Co.* v. *Levin,* the court ruled that ordinary negligence was the proper standard for the award of actual damages; actual malice was still the standard for an award of special or punitive damages.[106] Private persons have a right to expect newspapers to act with reasonable care, said the court. Such a standard encourages responsible reporting while allowing room for mistakes.

At this point it is difficult to generalize about the type of reportorial activity that might be considered negligent. Listed below are some specific activities that have been considered negligent where private plaintiffs were involved:

1. Failure to check with the sources appropriate to the subject matter of the story
2. Publishing a defamatory headline over a nondefamatory story
3. Failure to verify statements, particularly when they come from persons known to be biased about the subject matter
4. Misinterpretation of court records or proceedings by a reporter

Summary Judgment

In *Lando,* Lando's depositions took over a year and filled 26 volumes, totaling 3,000 pages and 240 exhibits. The time required to take depositions and the legal fees were enormous for both parties. One way to control such costs is by urging judges to limit depositions to what is relevant and necessary.

Another way to avoid lengthy legal battles and exorbitant fees is to seek summary judgment. More and more courts are granting summary judgment in cases where there is no genuine dis-

106. 458 So. 2d 239 (Fla. 1984); 458 So. 2d 243 (Fla. 1984).

pute about the material facts.[107] The judge will examine pleadings for such deficiencies as failure to allege specific injury, failure to establish with "convincing clarity" the existence of actual malice, or failure to establish falsity, identification, or publication. This screening process will more than likely result in summary judgment for the media.

In 1979, the U.S. Supreme Court hinted in a footnote to *Hutchinson* v. *Proxmire* that perhaps summary judgment is too widely practiced.[108] Chief Justice Warren Burger noted that since proof of actual malice depends upon questioning a defendant's state of mind, such cases do not readily lend themselves to summary judgment. Nevertheless, summary judgment continues to be the rule rather than the exception in defamation cases.

Damages

The damages awarded in a defamation suit fall into two broad categories. In Florida, the first category is termed actual or compensatory damages. These damages are awarded the plaintiff who can prove injury, the requisite degree of negligence, and a lack of privilege in the defaming material. Compensatory damages are to repay the plaintiff for loss. There are two types of compensatory damages: general and special. General damages compensate for the actual reputation lost, the hurt feelings, physical pain, inconvenience, and emotional distress. According to *Gertz,* such losses cannot be presumed; they must be proven in court. Special damages compensate for the actual monetary loss experienced by the plaintiff as a result of the defamation, such as the loss of a job, loss of clients, or loss of a contract.

The second category of damages is all-inclusive. Punitive damages, also known as exemplary damages, are not awarded as compensation, and the plaintiff has no constitutional right to receive

107. *See* Anderson v. Liberty Lobby, 477 U.S. 242 (1986).

108. 443 U.S. 111 (1979).

punitive damages. Punitive damages are awarded to the plaintiff to punish the defendant for gross misconduct and to warn the defendant and other would-be defendants against such action. The Court in *Gertz* defined punitive damages as "private fines levied by civil juries to punish reprehensive conduct and to deter its future occurrence . . . juries assess punitive damages in wholly unpredictable amounts bearing no necessary relation to the actual harm caused." With the possibility of unbridled punitive fines, the Court limited the awarding of punitive damages to cases where actual malice has been proven.

In the past, damages could be reduced by the introduction of special mitigating evidence such as retraction, innocent mistake, or reliance on a reliable source. Today, few lawyers look to mitigating circumstances to reduce damage awards. Chances are that these various factors, particularly innocent mistake and reliance on a reliable source, are the pleadings that will completely negate a finding of negligence or actual malice. Retraction also has been considered of some help in persuading a judge that no actual malice existed. So rather than being the last line of defense, what used to be mitigating factors have become important evidence often defeating a finding of actual malice or negligence.

In the early 1980s, it became a popular tactic of plaintiffs to sue for both libel and intentional infliction of emotional distress in hopes that if they lost on the libel count, the latter would succeed. Under the common law of intentional infliction of emotional distress, there is no requirement for a finding of falsity or actual malice. According to the *Restatement of Torts,* recovery requires a showing that the content is so extreme and outrageous as to be beyond all possible bounds of decency and that the action is intentional and reckless.[109] Since much of American political rhetoric could fall under this definition, such a claim would be easy to win.

However, the 1988 Supreme Court decision in *Hustler Maga-*

109. RESTATEMENT (SECOND) OF TORTS § 46 comments d,h.

zine v. *Falwell* put a virtual end to the use of the claim of intentional infliction of emotional distress.[110] The Court stated that when it came to the content of speech, the state had no interest in protecting public figures from emotional distress absent a showing of falsity and actual malice.

Criminal Libel

As do many other states, Florida retains on its books several criminal libel laws. Although any challenge to these laws will probably render them unconstitutional, they are still worth noting. Laws making it a criminal offense to publish defamatory information came out of the yellow journalism period when newspapers printed hoaxes in order to boost their circulations. Readers of the *New York Sun* in the late 1800s devoured stories about the astounding discovery by an eminent South African scientist that there was indeed life on the moon. In 1917, H. L. Mencken wrote a fake newspaper article about how America fought against the introduction of the bathtub. He related the dubious anecdote about how one president ordered a tub taken out of the White House after he became stuck in it.

Those days are over for the newspapers, but the criminal libel laws still remain. The criminal libel laws of Florida are summarized below.[111]

1. No person may publish any charges of immorality unless the name of the person charged is set out fully.
2. Any publisher who permits an anonymous defamation to appear in his publication will be guilty of a misdemeanor.
3. Anyone who publishes maliciously anything that is derogatory to the financial condition or solvency of a financial institution shall be guilty of a misdemeanor.

110. 108 S. Ct. 876.
111. *See* Fla. Stat. Ann. ch. 836 (1981).

4. It is unlawful to publish anonymously anything that tends to expose any individual or any religious group to hatred, contempt, or ridicule.

There is also a criminal retraction statute that states that if a retraction is run within ten days of receiving notice from the defamed, all criminal charges will be dropped. Any cases interpreting these various criminal statutes are either between private citizens or are media cases that are too old to be of any consequence today.

Summary

When the Supreme Court in *New York Times Co.* v. *Sullivan* held that the harsh judgments allowed by the common law of libel ran counter to the guarantees in the First Amendment, the law of libel was turned upside down. However, Florida courts have joined other states in trying to right the law. This process has been difficult as it involves a delicate and controversial balance between the right of the press to report the news and the individual's right to maintain his or her reputation. In public libels, the balance favors the media by requiring a finding of actual malice. In private libels, however, a balance appears to have been struck to accommodate both interests by requiring a finding of negligence.

The *Sullivan* decision did not overturn the use of commonly accepted defenses such as truth, qualified privilege, and fair comment. In fact, recent decisions indicate that neutral reporting may join the traditional defenses. Many libel defendants may also rely on Florida's retraction law to help mitigate some damages.

The next decade probably will see a refining of the rule of actual malice, clearer definitions of negligence, and better distinctions between public and private figures. These refinements may be accompanied by confusion and contradictions at all levels, and the results may not always benefit the press.

Chapter Three

Invasion of Privacy

In contrast to libel, the tort of invasion of privacy is relatively new. Consequently, the number of invasion of privacy suits in Florida as well as in other states is small.

The right to sue for an invasion of privacy implies that individuals enjoy a right of privacy just as they enjoy a right to their reputation. The right to be secure in one's reputation has not been questioned for many centuries, yet the right to enjoy one's privacy is not settled. Some states, such as Nebraska, deny that any such right exists. The Constitution of the United States does not directly establish a right of privacy, nor do many state constitutions or statutes. In fact, the first law dealing with privacy was not passed in this country until 1903 in New York, and even that law touches only indirectly upon the right to be left alone or the right to be free of unwarranted publicity.

The idea that persons do enjoy some freedom from intrusive behavior by others can be traced as far back as the Middle Ages, when trespass was introduced into civil law to protect property rights, but little progress was made in assuring an individual's privacy until the 19th century. A discussion of the background of privacy cannot be complete unless mention is made of the 1890 *Harvard Law Review* article by two young Boston lawyers, Samuel Warren and Louis Brandeis, titled "The Right to Privacy."[1] In that

1. 4 HARV. L. REV. 193 (1890).

article, the pair presented a cogent argument for the legal recognition of the right to be let alone. They proposed that courts recognize that citizens should have the right to go to court and receive monetary redress whenever anyone, particularly the media, publishes information of a private nature about a named individual. The Warren and Brandeis article focused primarily upon invasion by publication of private information. It dealt only indirectly with the intrusive behavior of the press through trespass or through the publication of false information that is not defamatory. It did not consider that an invasion of privacy could occur when someone's name or likeness is used without consent for trade purposes. All of these areas now make up what legal scholars label as invasion of privacy.

The Warren and Brandeis article created much interest among lawyers and the courts. Since 1890, the law of privacy has expanded not only to cover intrusive behavior by the media but also to protect a person's associational rights, familial rights, decisional rights, and disclosural rights. These various privacy rights grew out of a series of cases in the 1960s that dealt with specific questions over the right to confidentiality in personal associations, in the use of contraceptives, in personal decisions about religion and politics, and over the right to be free from unlawful searches and seizures.

While the Constitution does not specifically state a right of privacy, the U.S. Supreme Court has interpreted several clauses of the Bill of Rights to include such a right. The Court called these *penumbral zones*. These clauses are the First Amendment, which guarantees freedom of worship and freedom of association; the Fourth Amendment, which guarantees against unreasonable search and seizure; the Fifth Amendment, which guarantees against self-incrimination; the Ninth Amendment, which allows that the listing of rights in the Bill of Rights is not all-inclusive; and the Due Process Clause of the Fourteenth Amendment, which calls for states to guarantee life, liberty, and property against encroachment.

Presently, some 40 states recognize a right of privacy: five by statute; the rest, like Florida, through common law or constitutional amendment.[2]

A discussion of the various types of invasion of privacy is traditionally organized around the four torts of privacy set out by Dean William Prosser in his *Handbook of the Law of Torts.* These four torts are (1) invasion by publication of false information (false light); (2) publication of private facts; (3) intrusion into one's solitude; (4) appropriation of a person's name, likeness, or personality for commercial or trade purposes. Before the courts began recognizing a legal right to privacy, the four torts of privacy had been lodged inside more traditional torts. For example, false light publication had been covered satisfactorily under defamation; publication of private information had been handled under the very broad tort of mental distress and inconvenience; appropriation was handled in some states by laws against restraint of trade or illegal trade practices; and intrusion was dealt with through the ancient trespass laws. During the twentieth century these concerns for privacy have been pulled together under the rubric of invasion of privacy. These torts of privacy are personal in nature and can be maintained only by a living person whose privacy is invaded.[3]

FALSE LIGHT—PUBLICATION OF FALSE INFORMATION

The privacy tort of false light parallels in many ways the tort of defamation, with the exception that the plaintiff's reputation need not be harmed. The story, while not harmful to reputation under the common law understanding of defamation, may be hurtful or place someone in a false light. For example, to state falsely that someone has committed a misdemeanor, while not defamatory, might be cause for a false light suit. The line be-

2. Cason v. Baskin, 20 So. 2d 243 (Fla. 1944); FLA. CONST. art. 1, § 23.

3. RESTATEMENT (SECOND) OF TORTS, § 6521 (1977); *see also* 32 FLA. JUR. TORTS, § 10 (1976 Supp.)

tween a false light case and a libel case is often so fine that it is indistinguishable, and the plaintiff's complaint will often plead defamation as well as invasion of privacy.

False light cases can be classified as those where false material is introduced on purpose or those where false information is a result of an unintentional error. The former, purposeful inclusion of false information, is also referred to as *fictionalization*.[4]

There are no reported false light cases in Florida, so it is important to examine some of the persuasive cases from other jurisdictions as well as the important U.S. Supreme Court cases that have emerged in this area.

The defendants in fictionalization suits are usually writers who dramatize true events by adding dialogue, altering characterizations, changing a setting, switching the sequence of events, or adding events for impact. The courts seem to be split over how such fictionalization should be handled. For example, in a 1958 case, NBC televised a true account about how a passenger on an airplane saved the lives of many of the passengers after a crash landing.[5] Obviously, the writer was not present during the actual disaster, so the dialogue had to be made up. The writer characterized the hero, a naval officer, as a religious man who prayed a lot and who chain-smoked during the incident. The officer sued NBC after the drama was aired, claiming he was placed in a false light. The officer won his privacy suit because the court ruled that the false information created a fiction.

Other courts, however, have stated that the fictionalization must be substantial to constitute an invasion of privacy. One of the oft-quoted cases of false light involved an unauthorized biography of baseball pitcher Warren Spahn.[6] The book contained numerous inaccuracies, distortions, and "fanciful passages." A New York court said that minor errors in a biography are protected under the First Amendment except when the errors are intentional.

4. *See* D. Pember, Privacy and the Press (1972).
5. Strickler v. NBC, 167 F. Supp. 746 (D. N.Y. 1958).
6. Spahn v. Julian Messner, Inc., 233 N.E.2d 840 (N.Y. Sup. Ct. 1967).

The U.S. Supreme Court has heard two false light cases. The first, *Time, Inc.* v. *Hill,* established the requirement of actual malice in privacy cases.[7] In that case, *Life* magazine ran a photo-review of a 1955 play appearing on Broadway called *The Desperate Hours.* The play was taken from a novel with the same title. *Life* magazine stated that the drama was a reenactment of the ordeal that the James Hill family had been through in the early 1950s when they were held captive by escaped convicts for almost 24 hours. For the photo-review, the Broadway actors were taken to the Hill family's former home and photographed as they enacted scenes from the play. The book and the play, however, depicted a violent situation where the father and son were beaten and the daughter subjected to verbal insults. No violence occurred during the Hill family's captivity; in fact, the convicts had treated the family courteously and had used no violence or abusive language.

The Hills sued *Life* magazine in 1955, complaining that the article was intended to give the impression that the play mirrored the Hill family's experience—an impression the magazine knew was false. The complaint also contended that the falsification was purposeful in order to advertise the play and to increase the circulation of the magazine. The U.S. Supreme Court held that because the opening of the play was a newsworthy event rather than just entertainment, the family would have to prove the defendant published the report knowing it was false or with reckless disregard of the truth. "Exposure of the self to others in varying degrees is a concomitant of life in a civilized community," said the Court. "The risk of this exposure is an essential incident of life in a society which places a primary value on freedom of speech and press." The case was remanded for a new trial; however, since the Hills had been fighting this case for almost 12 years, a new trial was never requested.

The second false light case heard by the U.S. Supreme Court

7. 385 U.S. 374 (1967).

involved knowing fictionalization.[8] The case centered on a feature story written for the *Cleveland Plain-Dealer's* Sunday magazine. The article was written by reporter Joe Eszterhas, who has since become recognized as a follower of the New Journalism style of nonfiction. Eszterhas was assigned to write a follow-up story about a small town in West Virginia that had been through a terrible tragedy—a bridge collapse that had killed almost all of the men in the small community. Eszterhas went to the town, talked to a few people, absorbed the emotional atmosphere, and returned to write about the suffering from the viewpoint of one family, the Cantrells. In the story, Eszterhas included some fictionalized descriptions of Mrs. Cantrell and some fictionalized quotes from her although he never saw or talked to the woman. The U.S. Supreme Court held that Eszterhas knew the statements in the story were untrue and were calculated falsehoods; thus, the story was reported in a false light.

Unlike the law of libel as retranslated in *Gertz* v. *Robert Welch, Inc.,* the Court has not yet made a distinction between private plaintiffs and public plaintiffs for the purpose of assigning a different standard of liability in privacy suits.[9] It appears that if a private person, whether voluntarily or involuntarily, is thrust into a story of legitimate public interest, then he will have to prove actual malice in order to win a privacy case. Aside from the defense offered by the rule of actual malice, the media may also plead truth as in a libel case.

Embarrassing Facts—Publication of Private Material

The traditional notion of a right to privacy has developed out of the common law recognition that individuals need to be protected against unwarranted and embarrassing publicity of personal affairs. If the information is of an intimate personal nature,

8. Cantrell v. Forest City Publishers, 419 U.S. 245 (1974).
9. 418 U.S. 323 (1974).

truth does not justify its public exposure. For instance, if an editor publishes truthfully that his neighbor is having an affair with another married woman, the truth of the affair will not stand as a defense if the court determines that the editor had no reason to publish the story other than to pass around gossip. A good example of this is *Harms* v. *Miami Daily News.*[10] In that case, a reporter wrote, for some undetermined reason, "Wanna hear a sexy voice? Call [phone number given] and ask for Louise." The upshot for Louise, a receptionist at a local business office, was a flood of calls. A district court of appeal explained that Louise was not a public person just because she worked in a business office; the story was not about the business; nor was there any public benefit to be gained through the information. In essence, then, the journalist can be held liable for publishing truthful, intimate information if it carries no legitimate public interest. Obviously, this opens the door for the court to judge what is of public interest and what is of private interest.

Since truth cannot be a defense, the media's only recourse in embarrassing facts cases is to show that the private information is of public interest and concern or that the information comes from a public record. Newsworthiness has proven to be the strongest defense in such cases, resulting in judgments for the defendants in almost eight out of every ten cases brought.

Cason v. *Baskin,* the first privacy case reported in Florida and the case in which privacy was first acknowledged as a right in this state, sets out with great authority the limitations in embarrassing facts cases.[11] Although similar cases have come before Florida courts, *Cason* is always cited at length to explain the law in this state. *Cason* is also historically significant because of the defendant—Marjorie Kinnan Rawlings, author of the American classic *The Yearling.*

In 1942, Rawlings, whose married name was Baskin, pub-

10. 127 So. 2d 715 (Fla. Dist. Ct. App. 1961).
11. 20 So. 2d 243.

lished her autobiography, *Cross Creek*. The book was an instant success, selling even more copies than *The Yearling*. In the book, Rawlings recounted her life in north central Florida, around Island Grove in Alachua County. One section describes how Rawlings became familiar with the area by traveling on horseback with a county census taker named Zelma. Several pages of the book describe the census-taking rounds. Zelma is described as a sometimes profane woman and as "an ageless spinster resembling an angry and efficient canary." The total picture is of a "fine, strong, rugged character, highly intelligent and efficient, with a kind of sympathetic heart, and a keen sense of humor." Although the book identifies the woman only by her first name, testimony was entered at trial to leave no doubt that the woman was indeed Zelma Cason, a resident of Island Grove, who had taken Rawlings along on part of her census rounds in 1930. Cason objected to the picture drawn of her and sued the author for "wrongfully and maliciously intending to injure and aggrieve her by bringing her notoriety, by destroying her comfort, peace and tranquility and bringing unwarranted and undesired publicity."

To arrive at the conclusion that an individual can maintain an action for invasion of privacy in this state, the Florida Supreme Court looked to the state constitution, which reads, in part, that every citizen has due process for any injury to "land, goods, and person." The word "person," said the court, referred to all aspects of a person's physical as well as mental well-being. Hence an invasion of privacy suit could be maintained. However, the invasion must be of such a nature that a responsible person could foresee that it would cause mental distress and injury to a person of ordinary sensibilities. The exception would be if the material were of legitimate public or general interest and not just of curiosity. The Florida Supreme Court remanded the case to the jury to determine whether there was a legitimate public interest in Cason. The guideline to be followed was whether the person "by his accomplishments, fame, mode of life, profession, or calling" gave the public a legitimate interest in him.

What followed was a "warfare of pleadings" in which the plaintiff entered 18 pleas and 4 amended pleas and the defendant entered 62 interrogatories and 40 witnesses. After an eight-day trial, judgment was rendered for Rawlings. Extensive evidence was entered about the public interest in Rawlings. One witness testified that when his ship was sinking during a battle in the Pacific, he ran back to his bunk to grab a copy of *Cross Creek* before he jumped into the life raft. Despite the volumes of evidence about the literary ability of the author, the popularity of her works, and the interest in her as a public figure, the Florida Supreme Court reversed the trial court and dismissed all of the information as irrelevant to the question of whether Cason, the census taker, was of legitimate public concern.[12] Because there was no legitimate interest in Cason, there was an invasion of privacy requiring a judgment for the plaintiff. However, Cason had proven no injury, no mental anguish, and no malice; she was awarded $1.00 plus $1,050.10 in costs. The case was in the courts four and one-half years.

Despite the outcome in *Cason,* it can still be said that the courts have usually been generous in their interpretation of legitimate public concern or newsworthiness. Undoubtedly, information about a public figure or a public official, although personal in nature, will be privileged. For example, in 1977, the student newspaper at the University of Maryland published articles stating that six of the university's basketball players were having academic problems that threatened their eligibility for the team.[13] The article revealed that four of the players were on academic probation. The information was obtained from university records through a "gratuitous source." The six players filed a $72 million suit against the student newspaper and the *Washington Star,* which also picked up the story. The circuit court granted the defendants' motion for summary judgment based upon the

12. 30 So. 2d 635 (Fla. 1947).
13. Bilney v. Evening Star, 4 Media L. Rep. 1924 (Md. Cir. Ct. 1978).

reasoning that the team members were public figures who had generated much media interest throughout their high school and college careers. Additionally, college sports generate considerable public interest.

A more typical case in Florida involved the wife of a convicted murderer in Jacksonville Beach.[14] A detective magazine, *Detective Cases,* published an account of the murder, and the wife sued for invasion of her own privacy. The court stated that the murder was a matter of wide public interest since the accused had also been charged with murdering two other persons and because the wife's testimony had been instrumental in the defendant's conviction for murder.

The real problem occurs when the subject of the report is not a public figure but has involuntarily become the subject of a story. According to court rulings in Florida as well as other jurisdictions, it is not the person's status that rules the outcome but the status of the event. The Alabama courts provide a good example of an event that is not newsworthy, even by a stretch of the most demanding editor's imagination.[15] The case did not involve a story, but a photograph. A mother and her two children attended a country fair where they entered a fun house that had an array of mirrors, gravity rooms, and various surprises for the fair-goers. At the exit was a grating under which an air jet was located. As the mother exited the building, the rush of air blew her skirt over her head, exposing her from the waist down. A photographer from the local paper, who apparently had stationed himself at the exit, snapped the woman's picture at the instant her skirt flew up. The picture appeared as a feature photo in the Sunday edition publicizing the fair. Although the mother's face was covered by her skirt, her children were identifiable in the picture and the connection easily could be made. She sued the paper and won because the court held that the picture was not

14. Nelson v. Globe, 45 Fla. Supp. 48 (1976).
15. Daily Times Democrat v. Graham, 162 So. 2d 474 (Ala. 1964).

newsworthy and that the picture was about as intimate a revelation as could be made in public, causing the woman a great deal of embarrassment.

When can such intimate and private photographs ever be newsworthy enough to balance off the embarrassment? Several years ago a camera crew from an Idaho television station went to the scene of a dispute where a man had threatened a woman with a shotgun.[16] The cameraman filmed the police taking the nude plaintiff from the house. The film, used on the evening newscast, showed the man's buttocks and genitals for less than a second. The television station argued that the event was newsworthy. The Idaho Supreme Court agreed with the station and reversed an earlier decision and remanded for a new trial. The court stated that the station had the privilege to report truthfully all details of a newsworthy event as long as the broadcast was not made to embarrass or humiliate the person or with reckless disregard as to whether it would result in embarrassment.

A similar case in Florida involved a plaintiff who was wearing a T-shirt and briefs when arrested. A local television crew filmed the arrest from 30–40 feet away. The incident happened at night and the suspect was lying on the ground surrounded by police. A circuit court found that the story was newsworthy and no private facts were revealed.[17]

When Mrs. Hilda Bridges was abducted at gunpoint from her job by her estranged husband and taken to his apartment, she was beaten and forced to undress.[18] As police gathered outside the apartment, the husband shot himself. Police entered the apartment and escorted Mrs. Bridges to a waiting police car; she was covered only by a small hand towel. A photographer from *Cocoa Today* took pictures of the woman as she ran seminude from the apartment to the police car. The pictures were published widely by the Gannett News Service and Associated Press. Mrs.

16. Taylor v. KTVB, 525 P.2d 984 (Idaho 1976).

17. Spradley v. Sutton, 9 Media L. Rep. 1481 (Fla. Cir. Ct. 1982).

18. Cape Publications v. Bridges, 423 So. 2d 426 (Fla. Dist. Ct. App. 1982), *cert. denied,* 464 U.S. 898 (1982).

Bridges sued the photographer and the various media that carried the photographs. The jury found that the newspaper had cropped the photo to provide the most sensational angle, and the publication had invaded Bridges's privacy. She was awarded $1,000 in compensatory and $9,000 in punitive damages. The verdict and judgments were reversed on appeal by a Florida district court of appeal, which said that "[j]ust because the story and photograph may be embarrassing or distressful to the plaintiff does not mean the newspaper cannot publish what is otherwise newsworthy."

Another difficult problem in this area arises when plaintiffs are involuntarily drawn into a newsworthy event without any notice. A Florida case, *Jacova* v. *Southern Radio and Television Co.*, addressed this problem over 35 years ago.[19] In *Jacova,* a Miami television station showed footage on its news show of a gambling raid on a Miami Beach restaurant followed by another raid on a hotel cigar shop. John Jacova was at the cigar shop buying a newspaper when the second raid occurred. According to testimony, he was pushed against a wall and was questioned about running a gambling establishment. On the news show that evening, the film of the police talking to Jacova was shown while the announcer reported that a raid had been made on the cigar shop where a bellboy was arrested and that the police had arrested another man at an apartment. Jacova, an innocent bystander, sued the station for invasion of privacy. The Florida Supreme Court stated that Jacova became involved in a newsworthy event. Although he was thrust into the public eye by mistake, it was neither unreasonable nor unwarranted invasion of privacy.

One of the better defenses available to the media in embarrassing facts cases is qualified privilege—the privilege to report accurately information from a public record or proceeding. In 1975, the U.S. Supreme Court acknowledged this defense in privacy cases, stating that laws that restrict the printing of information from judicial records are unconstitutional. In *Cox Broad-*

19. 83 So. 2d 34 (Fla. 1955); *see also* Stafford v. Hayes, 327 So. 2d 871 (Fla. Dist. Ct. App. 1976), *cert. denied,* 336 So. 2d 604 (Fla. 1976).

casting v. *Cohn,* a Georgia television station broadcast the name of a 17-year-old rape and murder victim.[20] Georgia law prohibits the publication of the name or identity of any female who has been raped or who has been assaulted with intent to commit rape. The girl's father sued for invasion of privacy and for violation of the law. The Court held that the media cannot be held liable for the accurate publication of information obtained from judicial records that are open to public inspection. "Once true information is disclosed in public court documents open to public inspection, the press cannot be sanctioned for publishing it. In this instance as in others, reliance must rest upon the judgment of those who decide what to publish or broadcast." The Court struck down Georgia's law as unconstitutional.

The *Cox* decision emphasized that a state may exempt from public view certain records. "If there are privacy interests to be protected in judicial proceedings, the states must respond by means which avoid public documentation or other exposure of private information." Florida has over 275 laws that make certain records and proceedings confidential and exempt from public scrutiny, including medical and abortion records, tax records, unemployment compensation records, juvenile records of various types, grand jury records, and sexual battery records.

Most exemption laws are written to prohibit the publication of information obtained from records. This does not prohibit a reporter from publishing the same information if it comes from other sources. For example, a *Pensacola News-Journal* reporter wrote about the adoption of Angela Jordan.[21] The parents sued for invasion of privacy under the adoption law, claiming that the purpose of the law, which makes adoption proceedings confidential, was to protect the adopted person from embarrassment, humiliation, and offensive publicity.[22] A district court of appeal

20. 420 U.S. 469 (1975).
21. Jordan v. Pensacola News-Journal, 314 So. 2d 222 (Fla. Dist. Ct. App. 1975).
22. FLA STAT. ANN. §§ 63.022(1)(j); 63.162 (1988).

held that since the reporter had not received the details and facts from court files, or files of the state welfare board, or files kept by licensed adoption agencies, the law had not been violated. The articles were written from information obtained during interviews with persons involved in the proceedings. The court stated that the statute did not intend to prohibit all publication of information relating to an adoption proceeding.

In *Gardner* v. *Bradenton Herald,* the newspaper wanted to publish the names of persons subject to a wiretap although Florida law prohibits such publication.[23] A circuit court ruled that although the state was not obligated to provide access to such information, it also could not restrain its publication.

Another case in Bradenton involved the televising of a rape trial where the victim's name and testimony were broadcast.[24] The district court of appeal ruled that because the trial was open to the public and the state never sought to close the proceedings, the television broadcast was a truthful account of a newsworthy event. And in *Williams* v. *New York Times Co.,* the *Lake City Reporter* not only identified a rape victim but also quoted her on the outcome of her assailant's trial.[25] Summary judgment for the newspaper was upheld by the district court of appeal because the story was an accurate account of the public trial testimony.

Several cases on this issue have been heard by the U.S. Supreme Court since *Cox.* In *Landmark Communications* v. *Virginia,* the Court declared unconstitutional a law making it a crime to publish information regarding a confidential proceeding before a judicial review board.[26] And in *Smith* v. *Daily Mail,* the newspaper learned the name of a juvenile offender from a police radio transmission and from a state's attorney.[27] The Court held that

23. 8 Media L. Rep. 1251 (Fla. Cir. Ct. 1982).

24. Doe v. Sarasota-Bradenton Florida Television Co., 436 So. 2d 328 (Fla. Dist. Ct. App. 1983).

25. 462 So. 2d 38 (Fla. Dist. Ct. App. 1984).

26. 435 U.S. 829 (1978).

27. 443 U.S. 97 (1979).

when prohibited information comes from "routine newspaper reporting techniques," a state cannot punish for the truthful publication of lawfully obtained information.

Cox, Landmark, Smith, and the Florida cases suggest that if the media lawfully obtain truthful information about a matter of public interest, the state cannot punish the publication of that information.

A recent Florida case reaffirmed these precedents. In *Florida Star* v. *B.J.F.*, the Jacksonville weekly newspaper published the name of a rape victim, contrary to a state law that prohibits publication in any mass medium of the identity of any victim of a sexual offense.[28] The information came from the incident report available from the sheriff's office. The trial court found the newspaper negligent and awarded the plaintiff $95,000. The verdict and judgment were eventually reversed by the U.S. Supreme Court in 1989. The Court held that the information was (1) lawfully obtained and truthful, (2) made available by the police, and (3) a matter of public significance. Therefore, the newspaper could not be held liable for its publication. The Court warned that the decision should not be read to hold that any truthful publication is automatically protected or that a state may never punish for the publication of the identity of a sexual offense victim.

INTRUSION—PHYSICAL INVASION OF SOLITUDE

According to most First Amendment advocates and theorists, the right to publish the news implies another basic right—the right to gather news. However, beginning with a 1965 case that denied a tourist a passport to visit Cuba and through recent cases denying newspersons access to jails and prisons, the Supreme Court has consistently denied such a corollary right to gather news: "The right to speak and publish does not carry with it the

28. 499 So. 2d 883 (Fla. Dist. Ct. App. 1986), *rev'd,* 109 S. Ct. 2603 (1989).

unrestrained right to gather information."[29] This attitude has frustrated newspersons when they enter a private home, office, or quasi-public place to gather news and when they photograph newsworthy persons or use tape recorders to gather information.

A person who invades another's property may be sued either for trespass or intrusion. Until recently, such cases were handled primarily through trespass law. Trespass is the physical entry into or onto someone's property without consent. Trespass may be a civil or a criminal action and may only be brought by the person who actually possesses or controls the property. Intrusion takes trespass a bit further and actually requires some invasion of personal privacy beyond the physical invasion. Prosser's *Handbook of the Law of Torts* explains that intrusion may be upon a person's physical solitude or seclusion. Also, the intrusion must include some objectionable or offensive form such as peeking through curtains or hiding in a closet, or using a hidden camera, tape recorder, or telephoto lens. There must also be some private or personal thing intruded into such as a personal conversation or a private activity.

Most of the cases discussed in this section are not Florida cases; however, as intrusion and trespass suits against the media increase, it is important to understand how other jurisdictions have dealt with the problem. The media may become defendants in an intrusion or trespass case even if the material gathered is never published. It is not the publication that is the basis of the complaint but the intrusive activity itself. One of the most popular cases to deal with intrusion by news gatherers is *Dietemann* v. *Time, Inc.*, a 1971 California case.[30] In *Dietemann,* two reporters for *Life* magazine preparing a story on the practice of quackery posed as a husband and wife to gain entrance to the healer's home. Antone Dietemann, who claimed to heal with herbs and clays, examined the "wife," who complained of a lump in her breast. Dietemann, after waving a wand around her and fiddling

29. *See* Zemel v. Rusk, 381 U.S. 1 (1965); Pell v. Procunier, 417 U.S. 817 (1974).

30. 449 F.2d 245 (9th Cir. 1971).

with some gadgets, diagnosed the lump and said that she had eaten some rancid butter 11 years, 9 months, and 7 days prior to the visit. The "husband," using a hidden camera, took several pictures of Dietemann during the examination. The entire conversation was recorded with a small recorder in the woman's purse and transmitted to a car outside. A month later, Dietemann was arrested on charges of practicing medicine without a license. Several weeks thereafter, *Life* magazine ran a photo story on quackery that included two photographs of Dietemann.

Dietemann sued *Life* magazine, claiming an invasion of privacy by intrusion. An award of $1,000 was affirmed by the Ninth Circuit. *Life* magazine claimed that the First Amendment immunized it from liability because it was gathering newsworthy information and that news gathering depended upon being able to use the "indispensable" tools of news gathering, namely cameras and tape recorders. The Ninth Circuit disagreed, stating "the First Amendment has never been construed to accord newsmen immunity from torts or crimes committed during the course of news gathering. The First Amendment is not a license to trespass, to steal or to intrude by electronic means into the precincts of another's home or office."

A Kentucky court found an exception to *Dietemann*.[31] The *Louisville Courier-Journal* was informed by a woman charged with two criminal counts that she could "buy her way out of her trouble" if she paid her lawyer $10,000. Two reporters began investigating the possibility of bribery in the judiciary. They provided the woman with a tape recorder and instructed her to return to the lawyer's office and ask specified questions. They agreed to provide her with the $10,000 should the lawyer agree to fix the charges against her. When the woman began asking the questions, the lawyer asked if she had a tape recorder; she denied it and he continued the conversation. The conversation did not reveal any bribery but did produce information about

31. McCall v. Courier-Journal, 6 Media L. Rep. 1112 (Ky. Ct. App. 1980), *rev'd on other grounds,* 7 Media L. Rep. 2118 (Ky. 1981).

possible unethical behavior of a lawyer toward a client. After the newspaper ran its article, the lawyer sued for intrusion and trespass. The Kentucky court of appeals stated that intrusion did not occur because nothing offensive, private, or personal was learned by the intrusion—only information about the woman's legal problems and how the lawyer proposed to resolve them. As for the trespass charge, the court ruled that the woman did not trespass because she was in the lawyer's office at his tacit invitation to discuss business. Once he suspected that the woman was carrying a tape recorder, he should have asked her to leave rather than continue the conversation. Because the woman had not trespassed, the newspaper could not be held liable for causing the woman to trespass.

The lawyer knew who the woman was, and when he suspected that she had a tape recorder, he did nothing. The failure to act implied consent. Dietemann, however, did not know the patient was really a reporter, nor did he have any suspicion that a tape recorder or camera had been spirited into his living room/office. The fact that Dietemann invited the reporters into his home, rather than into an office, may also be distinguishing. And finally, the media did not make the entry in the Kentucky case; in *Dietemann,* the reporters did make the entry.

Surreptitious entry into a private citizen's home or office is not a daily occurrence for the news media. Entry into homes usually occurs only after a crime has been committed or after some crisis, such as a fire. Several jurisdictions, including Florida, have dealt with the question of what status a news reporter holds when accompanying police or other public officials into a home.

In *Florida Publishing Co.* v. *Fletcher,* the Florida Supreme Court ruled that in certain circumstances the media do have a right to enter private homes.[32] The 1975 case involved a news photographer who was invited into a burned home by police and fire officials. In the living room of the Jacksonville home, firemen found the body of a 17-year-old girl. The fire marshal asked a photog-

32. 340 So. 2d 914 (Fla. 1975), *cert. denied,* 431 U.S. 930 (1977).

rapher from the *Florida Times-Union* to take a clear picture of the silhouette left on the floor after the girl's body was removed. The picture was developed, given to the investigators, and also run in the next day's newspaper. The girl's mother, the owner of the house, was in New York when the fire occurred and did not know about the facts surrounding her daughter's death until she read the newspaper story and saw the photograph. She sued the newspaper for trespass and invasion of privacy.

The Florida Supreme Court held that newspersons may enter the premises as long as it is a reasonable entry and if it is custom and practice for the media to enter such areas. The decision was based upon the long-standing common law notion of implied consent. Under this doctrine, a person may legally enter premises without express consent from the custodian (owner) of the property if it is common usage and practice to enter the property and if entry is made peaceably and without objection. In the *Fletcher* case, the owner was not present to object; the police invited the photographer and news reporters into the house and they entered quietly and reasonably. Numerous affidavits were filed by the media attesting that it was common custom and usage for newspersons to enter private property under such circumstances. Law officers also testified that the presence of the media is often helpful in developing leads.

At the time *Fletcher* was making its way through Florida courts, a similar case was beginning its trek. The case involved a police raid on a private institution for mentally and physically handicapped youths.[33] Police had evidence of drug and child abuse at the home. They invited the media, including television camera crews, to accompany police during the raid. The television cameras filmed the raid and the condition of the home—filthy bathrooms, dirty beds, closets used for detention, cattle prods used for behavior modification, and dozens of bottles of drugs. The film of the raid was shown on television news. Evi-

33. Green Valley School v. Cowles Florida Broadcasting, Inc., 327 So. 2d 810 (Fla. Dist. Ct. App. 1976).

dence in court indicated that much of the film was staged for the benefit of the cameras. The district court of appeal, not yet having the benefit of the *Fletcher* ruling, upheld the trespass charges. As for the charges of staging, the court held that the state was without jurisdiction in such matters; only the Federal Communications Commission could deal with the broadcaster when charges of staging news were made. The case was eventually overturned because of the *Fletcher* holding.

Implied consent or common custom and usage vanish if the owner of the property tells the media not to enter. However, it is not always the owner of the property who files the trespass and intrusion charges against the media. For example, when reporters entered the apartment of accused murderer David Berkowitz (Son of Sam) in Yonkers, New York, police arrested them and charged them with criminal trespass.[34] The police had obtained a search warrant to search the apartment and had placed a sign on the door marked "Do Not Enter, Crime Scene." When photographers and reporters arrived at the apartment, no police were present but the door was unlocked. They entered, took pictures, but were arrested as soon as the police returned. The police claimed that as long as the search warrant was in effect, the police had legal possession and control of the property and had authority to grant entrance to the apartment. A Yonkers city court judge dismissed the criminal trespass charges. The judge said that the police did not have possession of the apartment; only David Berkowitz or the landlord maintained possession. The police only had a privilege, by virtue of their official activity, to be in the apartment; therefore, the police could not maintain a complaint of criminal trespass against someone else's property. The judge, however, did not close all avenues against the reporters. Calling their action "reprehensible," the judge stated that the entry was "not rightful" and that the police department could bring some other charge, such as obstruction of evidence or willful disobedience of a police order.

34. People v. Berliner, 3 Media L. Rep. 1942 (Yonkers City Ct. 1978).

If a state or agent of the state is in possession of property, then criminal trespass charges can be brought successfully against the news media. In an Oklahoma case, seven news reporters were arrested on criminal trespass charges after following demonstrators onto a nuclear power plant construction site.[35] After the trial, defendants moved to dismiss the charges. An Oklahoma district court refused to dismiss and a judgment of guilty was entered. The court found that the Public Service Company of Oklahoma was an agent of the state. The reporters argued that by virtue of being a state agent, the utility company had denied the reporters their First Amendment rights as guaranteed by the Fourteenth Amendment. While the court agreed that constitutional rights were in question, it did not agree that those rights had been abridged. Citing numerous U.S. Supreme Court decisions that have refused to recognize a right to gather news, the court held that newspersons have no constitutional right of access to scenes of crimes or other crises when the general public is excluded. The court concluded that the balance had to be weighted in favor of the right of the company to be secure in its property and the power of the state to maintain order and enforce criminal statutes.

Unlike a home, office, or other controlled public property, business property cannot be too strictly controlled. For example, a grocery store or a department store must be accessible to the public. They are considered *quasi-public* places—"quasi" because they are public only for the use for which they are intended. While an owner may not discriminate as to whom he allows into his establishment, he may regulate entrance with reasonable rules and may discharge persons who do not intend to use the property for its normal purposes. These notions appear reasonable on their face, but when applied to the media covering a newsworthy event, the owner's prerogatives over her property can

35. Oklahoma v. Bernstein, 5 Media L. Rep. 2313 (Okla. Dist. Ct. 1980).

get in the way. A 1978 New York case points out the problem. In *LeMistral* v. *CBS,* the owner of a Manhattan restaurant sued television reporters for entering his business without his permission.[36] The New York City Health Department had cited several Manhattan restaurants for various health violations. The restaurants were told to make the necessary adjustments within six weeks. At the end of the grace period, a CBS news reporter and camera crew visited one of the restaurants to see if it had indeed made the changes. The television crew did not get permission to enter the restaurant nor did it call ahead. The crew entered the restaurant unannounced with cameras rolling and lights blazing. Patrons waiting to be seated left; others left without paying; and others hid behind napkins and tablecloths. The manager ordered the crew to leave and tried to push them out into the street—cameras still rolling. A New York appeals court, hearing the trespass action against CBS, stated that although the restaurant was a place of "public accommodation," the crew had no intention of taking advantage of the accommodations. Citing *Dietemann,* the court stated that the "First Amendment is not a shibboleth before which all other rights must succumb." The court upheld a jury award of $1,200 in compensatory damages.

As noted earlier, intrusion is not always into some physical property but can be into someone's solitude or "life space." Photographers may find that the pictures they are taking in a public place are of such an intrusive nature that they may be ordered by the courts to "back off." The major case of photographic intrusion involved Jacqueline Onassis and photographer Ronald Galella.[37] Galella is what the Italians call a *paparazzo* or a gadfly—one who makes his living by buzzing about famous people and shooting their picture at every turn. One of Galella's most popular subjects has been the Onassis family. His photographic efforts eventually resulted in his arrest by Secret Service agents assigned to protect

36. 61 App. Div. 2d 491 (N.Y. Sup. Ct. 1978).
37. Galella v. Onassis, 457 F.2d 986 (2d Cir. 1973).

the children and Jackie. Galella filed a countersuit against Jackie, claiming false arrest, interference with his trade, and malicious prosecution. In testimony it was revealed that Galella had jumped out from behind trees, frightened the children, and had entered the school yard where the children were playing. He also had come dangerously close in a powerboat to where Jackie was swimming. The Second Circuit ruled in 1973 that Galella had no First Amendment right to invade the privacy of the family. The court did not ban Galella's right to photograph Jackie and the children; instead, the court entered orders specifying how the photographer could reasonably cover the family's activities. The orders specified distances Galella was to remain from the family.

Reporters depend not only on the camera but also rely on the tape recorder for accuracy of information. Despite the fact that tape recorders are an essential reportorial tool, their use is restricted in Florida. Federal law requires that only one of the parties consent to recording. However, Florida law prohibits the tape recording of any communication unless all parties to the communication have given prior consent.[38] This prohibition does not apply to public communications or to recordings legally conducted to obtain evidence of criminal activity.

On October 1, 1974, the very day that the Florida law was amended, *Fort Myers News-Press* reporter Fran Williams was secretly recording a telephone conversation from a woman who had information about a recent homicide.[39] Two days later, the reporter used a hidden tape recorder in her car to tape a conversation between two of her sources while she was not in the car. Following her standard practice, the reporter used the tapes to write the story, then erased them, preparing them for reuse. An indictment was brought against her and the newspaper for tampering with evidence and destroying evidence in a homicide investigation. The district court of appeal ruled that both of the

38. FLA. STAT. ANN. § 934.03 (2)(d) (Fla. Supp. 1988).

39. Florida v. News-Press Publishing Co., 338 So. 2d 1313 (Fla. Dist. Ct. App. 1976).

recordings obtained by the reporter were illegal under the new law. However, the court also ruled that the erasing of the tapes was not destruction of evidence since the reporter had no way of knowing that they might be used as evidence.

The Florida media have challenged the law without success. The *Miami Herald* and WCKT-TV, Miami, filed a complaint stating that the law severely restricted and impaired news gathering activities in violation of the First Amendment.[40] The media offered arguments and evidence as to the importance of concealed recordings in investigative stories. While a circuit court judge found the arguments persuasive, the Florida Supreme Court did not. The state high court refused to declare the law unconstitutional, citing U.S. Supreme Court precedents *Pell* v. *Procunier* and *Houchins* v. *KQED,* which denied unrestrained access to prisons and jails for news gathering.[41]

A unanimous Florida Supreme Court held that while news gathering is an integral part of news dissemination, hidden tape recorders are not indispensable tools of that function. The law, explained the court, does not restrict what the press may publish, nor does the law command that the press publish what it prefers to withhold. The law does not intrude on speech or assembly, nor does it prevent sources from talking to the press. "First Amendment rights do not include a constitutional right to corroborate news gathering activities when the legislature has statutorily recognized the privacy rights of individuals." The U.S. Supreme Court refused to review the Florida court's decision.

Oftentimes, the media do not do their own trespassing or intruding but instead receive information from others who have done the misdeed. To what extent are the media liable in such cases? One of the early intrusion cases involved just this question. In *Pearson* v. *Dodd,* employees of Connecticut Senator Thomas Dodd copied documents out of Dodd's office files and

40. Shevin v. Sunbeam Television Corp., 351 So. 2d 723 (Fla. 1977), *cert. denied,* 435 U.S. 920 (1978).

41. 417 U.S. 817; 438 U.S. 1 (1978).

gave them to Drew Pearson, "Washington Merry-Go-Round" columnist.[42] Pearson was found not liable for trespass or invasion of privacy because he had not actually participated in the intrusive activity. Dodd also brought charges of conversion against Pearson. Conversion is the converting of another's property to one's own use. The U.S. Court of Appeals for the District of Columbia did not find any conversion since Pearson had not received the original documents, only copies. Also, the information held no market value.

The distinction made in *Dodd* between an original and a copy is weak. A 1973 California case probably states the law more accurately.[43] Two reporters for the *Los Angeles Free Press* received copies of a list of narcotics agents from a person who they believed was a government employee and who they believed had a right to be in possession of the document. After the list was published, they were charged with possession of stolen goods and found guilty by a trial court. However, they were freed by the state supreme court when it was clear that there was insufficient evidence to prove that the reporters knew the list was stolen. Had the evidence been stronger, the conviction would have been upheld. Here the court made no distinction between holding the original or a copy.

Appropriation—Commercial Usage

Florida's only right of privacy statute protects against invasion of privacy by the commercial appropriation of a person's name, personality, or likeness.[44] This statute resembles New York's privacy law, the first privacy statute passed in this country. However, unlike New York's law, Florida's has seen little litigation. The Florida law prohibits the use of a person's name, portrait, photograph, or other likeness for commercial or trade purposes un-

42. 410 F. 2d 701 (D.C. Cir. 1969).
43. People v. Kunkin, 107 Cal. Rptr. 184 (1973).
44. Fla. Stat. Ann. § 540.08 (1978).

less written or oral consent has been given. If consent is not obtained, then the person may stop the publication or sue for recovery of damages. Recoverable damages include any royalty that would have been earned as well as any punitive damages.

The law does not protect against the use of photographs or pictures of a person who represents a member of the public at large and is not named or otherwise identified in connection with the usage. For example, if a brochure by the City of Orlando uses a picture of a group of people sitting in a park, no individual in that group can sue since no individual is being used for trade purposes. Nor does the law affect the use of a person's name or likeness in a bona fide news report of an event of public and legitimate concern. Because appropriation involves advertising and trade usage, rather than use by the news media, the study of this tort will be brief. Only those cases that tangentially affect the news aspects of the doctrine will be examined.

Although appropriation was the earliest form of invasion of privacy recognized in this country, it is not truly a privacy question but a property rights question. The plaintiff in such cases is not being compensated for mental distress, embarrassment, humiliation, or general discomfort, but for the proprietary interest a person has in his own self. Appropriation means theft, and in this tort the theft of a person's likeness or name to make money creates grounds for an action at law. Some would argue that appropriation should not be classified as a right of privacy action but as a right of publicity action.

In Florida, consent to use a person's name or likeness for trade purposes may be given either by the individual; by any firm or corporation authorized in writing by that person to use his name or likeness; or, if the person is dead, by his family or any firm or corporation previously authorized by the deceased or by the family. Unless the rights to a person's name and likeness are legally assigned to the surviving family on death of the individual, no right of publicity will survive beyond a person's own life.

While consent is the best defense in an appropriation case, it is not always possible to get consent, nor is it always the best way of covering news events. Numerous attempts have been made by plaintiffs to argue that the appearance of their name or picture in a story or in a magazine helps sell the magazine, and therefore their appearance on the pages is for trade purposes. The courts have not agreed with that argument. The U.S. Supreme Court in *Time, Inc.* v. *Hill* stated clearly that although publishing and broadcasting are businesses, their publications (excluding fiction and entertainment programming) are produced primarily for information rather than for trade or advertising.[45]

Often the fine line between newsworthiness and commercial exploitation is difficult to draw. In *Zacchini* v. *Scripps-Howard Broadcasting Co.*, a television camera crew visited the Ohio State Fair where it filmed a rehearsal for a performance by the Florida circus daredevil Hugo Zacchini, who shoots himself out of a cannon.[46] The television station showed the entire 15-second performance on its evening news. The Ohio Supreme Court upheld the broadcast as a newsworthy event protected by the First Amendment. On appeal, the U.S. Supreme Court reversed, reasoning that the broadcast station took away Zacchini's right to earn money from the performance. "If the public can see the act for free on television, they will be less willing to pay to see it at the fair," said the Court. The effect of the broadcast was to prevent Zacchini from charging an admission fee. The Court also saw no social purpose in allowing the television audience to get for free what it would normally pay to see. In other words, the performance was not seen by the Court as a newsworthy event.

When is commercial use not considered commercial use? That question was asked in a famous case that involved the well-known actress Shirley Booth.[47] *Holiday* magazine used Miss Booth's picture in advertisements that promoted the magazine. The photograph pictured Miss Booth in the water up to her neck

45. 385 U.S. 374.
46. 433 U.S. 562 (1977).
47. Booth v. Curtis Publishing Co., 15 A. 2d 343 (N.Y. App. Div. 1962).

and wearing a colorful straw hat. The picture had been taken earlier, with Miss Booth's knowledge, for a feature story about a Jamaican resort hotel. However, when the photograph appeared in an advertisement for *Holiday* magazine in the *New Yorker* and *Advertising Age,* Miss Booth sued under New York's appropriation statute. The photograph was accompanied by copy that indicated that the type of pictures and coverage represented by Miss Booth's picture was the type of fare the reader would get in the magazine. The advertisement was not a testimonial. According to a New York court, the appropriation statute did not prohibit the incidental advertising of the news medium itself. It was not the name or likeness of Miss Booth that was being used, but an example out of the magazine itself. "It stands to reason that a publication can best prove its worth and illustrate its content by submission of complete copies or of extractions from past editions." The court noted that it was common for publications to reproduce miniatures of its covers in advertisements when these covers were of famous and not-so-famous persons.

Public figures can expect little privacy from those who would write about them, but they do retain their publicity rights. In one case, *Playgirl* magazine ran a very realistic watercolor cartoon depicting Muhammad Ali sitting nude in the corner of a boxing ring.[48] Although *Playgirl* argued that Ali's status as a public figure immunized the publication from any liability, a U.S. district court disagreed. The court said that although the boxer may have very little protection when he injects himself into newsworthy activities, he still must be free from commercial exploitation at the hands of others. The court enjoined further distribution of the publication and ordered *Playgirl* to return all plates of the picture to Ali.

The consent form and model release are the photographer's and journalist's best defense against appropriation actions. In one Florida case, nude photographs taken from a model's portfolio

48. Ali v. Playgirl Publishing Co., 447 F. Supp. 723 (D. N.Y. 1978).

were given without consent to a magazine by an advertising agency to use in an ad in the magazine.[49] The jury awarded the plaintiff $500,000 for wanton, intentional, and malicious disregard for privacy. However, the verdict was overturned on appeal because there was no evidence the magazine knew the photos were offered without consent; the magazine assumed that the ad agency had permission, as it did with all advertising art.

Various types of consent forms are available from lawyers who deal with commercial usage. Some forms are specific about the use that will be made of the photograph; others are broad, giving unrestricted usage of the material. If the contract is broken by the user, then the consent no longer exists. For example, if a photograph is used for purposes outside the limits of the contract, then consent no longer applies. It is possible for someone to withdraw consent, but only if there has been no exchange of money and if it creates no extraordinary inconvenience for the other party. Consent cannot be withdrawn after the agreed usage. Also, if a picture or likeness is altered, it is no longer the same portrait or photograph and a new consent form must be signed. The change must be substantial enough to alter the context, emphasis, or situation.[50]

Summary

Invasion of privacy suits are brought primarily by private persons since public figures or officials will rarely be able to win such suits. Even persons who place themselves either willingly or unwillingly before the public may find that the private or embarrassing details of their lives receive little protection from the courts.

The past several years have seen an increase in the number of

49. Genesis Publications v. Gross, 437 So. 2d 169 (Fla. Dist. Ct. App. 1983).

50. Russell v. Marboro Books, 183 N.Y.S.2d 8 (1959).

intrusion cases as reporters seek access to private places to gather news. The ruling law, which is unlikely to change in the near future, is that the press has no First Amendment right to invade a person's life space beyond that allowed the ordinary citizen. On the decline are false light complaints, which are so similar to libel suits that courts are often confused by the narrow differences. The confusion is further augmented by the requirement that actual malice be proven in false light cases.

Chapter Four

Reporter's Privilege

In Citrus County, a newspaper photographer was ordered to produce photographs taken of an accident that occurred at a road construction site. The Fifth District Court of Appeal ruled that the photographs were relevant, necessary, and critical because they were the "unique and best method" to establish the condition of the road at the time of the accident.[1] However, in a similar case a Hillsborough County circuit judge held that videotapes made in the course of news gathering were protected from disclosure in a personal injury suit although the tapes were the only visual evidence of the accident.[2]

Until 1987, it was fairly well settled in Florida that the qualified privilege not to reveal information applied to published and unpublished as well as confidential and nonconfidential information. However, recent cases, including the two above, in various courts indicate a significant difference of opinion developing among the districts. Until that controversy is settled by the state's high court, reporters and attorneys should be aware of how courts in their part of the state view the breadth and reporter's privilege.

1. Carroll Contracting v. Edwards, 15 Media L. Rep. 2121 (Fla. Dist. Ct. App. 1988).

2. Damico v. Lemen, 14 Media L. Rep. 1031 (Fla. Dist. Ct. App. 1987).

CONTEMPT

Whenever a reporter is faced with the choice of whether or not to disclose information on demand, one of the factors to be considered is the penalty for disobeying a court order. That punishment falls under the broad category of contempt.

The contempt power is an awesome, yet dangerous, tool that has been used for many years against reporters who refuse to testify before courts, grand juries, Congress, and state legislatures. Contempt in Florida takes two forms—criminal and civil. (See chapter 5 for a fuller discussion of contempt.) Civil contempt occurs when someone refuses to obey a judge's order or to follow a judge's ruling. The person may be jailed and fined until he or she complies with the order. The contemptuous action usually occurs after a trial is over and is seen as a dispute between the defendant and the judge rather than between the defendant and the court. The fine and/or jail sentence are seen as coercive rather than punitive.[3]

Criminal contempt occurs when a person defies the authority or integrity of the court by doing something during a proceeding that cannot be undone or by continual or willful disobedience of an order. A journalist's refusal to testify is treated as criminal contempt. Cases of direct criminal contempt are witnessed by the court and are handled by summary judgment.[4] Indirect or constructive criminal contempt occurs away from the court and requires notice and hearing.[5]

In addition to being found guilty of contempt of court, reporters may also be found guilty of contempt of grand jury. The grand jury votes to find a witness in contempt and a hearing is held in the district court of appeal that convened the grand jury. A reporter may be found guilty of either criminal or civil contempt of grand jury.

In 1975, reporter Mary Jo Tierney wrote a story based on secret

3. *See generally* 17 CJS, *Contempt,* §§ 1–7 (1963).
4. FLA R. CRIM. P. § 3.830 (1989).
5. *Id.* 3.840.

testimony before a Brevard County grand jury.[6] The grand jury offered Tierney immunity if she would reveal her source's identity. She refused twice and was sentenced first to six hours and then 30 days in jail and $500. On appeal, a district court of appeals held that she could not be found guilty twice because only one contempt was committed by repeated refusal to answer the same questions at different times.[7] The second sentence was vacated, but the court suggested that criminal contempt could have been brought when it became obvious at the end of the grand jury session that Tierney was not going to comply.

Testimonial Privilege

When reporters refuse to testify or produce evidence gathered in their capacity as professionals, they do so because they believe that revealing information abridges their First Amendment rights. Their argument is simple and straightforward: News gathering is only one step in the process of informing the public. If a reporter is forced to reveal sources of information, those sources and others will be hesitant to provide information the next time. Often, the kind of information received by confidential sources is of high public interest. If reporters know they may be subpoenaed because of certain coverage, they may decide the safest course is not to investigate the subject at all. However the chill comes, the end result is that the public will be less well informed about important matters.

The American press has always tried to maintain an independent position as the Fourth Estate or the "watchdog" for the public. If the press were forced to reveal confidential or unpublished information, that independence would dissolve and the media would be perceived as convenient informers for law enforcement. From an even more practical viewpoint, the journalist who does

6. *In re* Tierney, 328 So. 2d 40 (Fla. Dist. Ct. App. 1976).
7. *Id.*

succumb without a court fight and reveals information will be branded as unethical and unprofessional by fellow journalists.

In short, the claim is that a journalist and his or her source should enjoy the same testimonial privilege offered in common law to such relationships as physician and patient, clergyman and penitent, lawyer and client, or husband and wife. But, while the latter privileges have been acknowledged in common law and in statute, the journalist and source privilege has not.

Over the years the courts have developed some minimum protections for both journalists and ordinary citizens when forced to disclose information. These protections are aimed at preventing abuses by overzealous legislators or lawyers. Generally, no one can be forced to disclose information if questions are not relevant to the investigation, are not made in good faith, or are meant to harass. In *Branzburg* v. *Hayes,* the only reporters' privilege case heard by the U.S. Supreme Court, a 5–4 majority held that the Constitution does not grant greater testimonial privilege for the press than it does for the average citizen.[8] The Court then restated the above protections.

The Court did not completely shut the door to relief. The opinion, written by Justice Byron White, did suggest that legislatures could pass a statutory reporter's privilege "as narrow or broad as deemed necessary . . . and to refashion those rules as experience from time to time may dictate." Even more pertinent to the Florida experience was the Court's admission that it is "powerless to bar state courts from responding in their own way and construing their own constitutions so as to recognize a newsman's privilege, either qualified or absolute."

Justice Potter Stewart's dissent in *Branzburg* denounced the hard-line approach of the Court as a "crabbed view of the First Amendment" that would impair not only the performance of the press but the administration of justice. He would offer constitutional protection by requiring the state (1) to demonstrate probable cause in believing the information was relevant to a specific

8. 408 U.S. 665 (1972).

offense, (2) to show that the information cannot be obtained by alternative means, and (3) to demonstrate a compelling interest in the information. Justice Stewart's dissent, which was taken from an opinion he wrote 14 years earlier while a judge on the Second Circuit court, was to prove valuable to state courts seeking to support journalists' claims.[9] Although Florida has not passed shield legislation, its courts have designed a constitutional shield following Justice Stewart's dissent that provides more protection than most statutes in other states.

Florida courts have not always respected a constitutional claim from reporters for confidentiality. In 1951, the Florida Supreme Court said, "Members of the journalistic profession do not enjoy the privilege of confidential communication, and are under the same duty to testify . . . as any other person."[10] The case arose after the editor-publisher of *Miami Life,* a daily newspaper, printed a detailed story about a grand jury investigation. Editor Reubin Clein's story included questions and answers from the secret proceedings as well as information only the grand jury members knew. The material could not have been from the grand jury's report because none had been issued. Clein was subpoenaed but twice refused to reveal his source. He was found guilty of contempt and sentenced to 30 days in jail. On appeal, the Florida Supreme Court said Clein's position as an editor carried no special privileges and the First Amendment played no part in cases where crimes were being investigated.

The *Clein* case was the last such case reported in Florida for 22 years. But following the U.S. Supreme Court's 1972 *Branzburg* decision, courts throughout the country were flooded with reporters' privilege cases and these courts began to fashion their own protection. Florida decided early that, despite the U.S. Supreme Court's ruling, reporters in this state did hold a broad qualified privilege against compelled testimony.[11] The Florida

9. Garland v. Torre, 259 F.2d 545 (2d Cir. 1958), *cert. denied,* 358 U.S. 910 (1958).

10. Clein v. State, 52 So. 2d 117, 120 (Fla. 1951).

11. Spiva v. Francouer, 39 Fla. Supp. 49 (Fla. Cir. Ct. 1973).

guidelines for determining whether a compelling state interest exists have been strong enough in the majority of reported cases for subpoenas to be quashed.

Florida's experience with privilege in criminal and civil courts reveals that the refusal to identify a confidential source has not been the problem. The cases seem to deal primarily with the refusal to reveal nonconfidential, yet unpublished, information. This distinction has created a difference in the quality of protection although a U.S. district court said, "[T]he compelled production of reporters' resource materials is equally as invidious as the compelled disclosure of his confidential sources."[12] In all privilege cases involving grand juries, reporters have been subpoenaed to reveal the names of persons who leaked grand jury information.

Most news personnel have been involved in privilege cases, including newspaper photographers, columnists, and broadcast journalists. As to photographers, a circuit court judge in Broward County said, "[T]he assertion that a photographer is entitled to less protection than a reporter or editor has no constitutional justification."[13] However, recent cases indicate that the "memory" of a photograph or videotape often subjects such evidence to compelled disclosure.

Civil Litigation

When reporters are subpoenaed in civil cases, most Florida courts have been reluctant to see any overriding need for the journalist's information. In a 1973 case, the *Miami Herald* ran an editorial criticizing irregularities in issuing harbor pilot licenses after the licensing board had rejected the license application of two pilots. A suit was brought by the pilots in Dade County.[14] The rejected seamen issued a subpoena to the *Miami Herald* for all documents

12. Loadholtz v. Fields, 389 F. Supp. 1299, 1303 (M.D. Fla. 1975).

13. State v. Miller, 45 Fla. Supp. 137 (Fla. Cir. Ct. 1976); *see also* Schultsie v. Weyer Bros., 6 Media L. Rep. 1661 (Fla. Cir. Ct. 1980).

14. Spiva v. Francouer, 39 Fla. Supp. 49.

involving the situation. The circuit court quashed the subpoena, saying that civil litigants can obtain the same information by their own investigation and by the discovery process. The First Amendment far outweighed the inconvenience of the plaintiff to conduct his own investigations, said the judge.

In 1974, *Palatka Daily News* reporter Clarence Prevatt was subpoenaed to testify at a deposition and produce all notes of interviews he had with Palatka attorney Alan Fields, who had filed a countersuit against Putnam County Sheriff Thomas Loadholtz.[15] Prevatt refused to produce his notes or to answer any questions. Loadholtz then filed a motion in U.S. district court to compel Prevatt to comply with the subpoena. The court denied the motion and stated that reporters have a First Amendment right to refuse to testify or produce notes in civil cases, regardless of whether or not confidential sources are involved. The judge ruled that the plaintiff had shown no compelling reason to force disclosure and the information could be gleaned from other sources. The judge refused to apply the *Branzburg* decison, saying, "This Court has neither been cited nor has found any subsequent case which has extended the *Branzburg* case holding beyond the limited confines of the criminal justice system."

Most subpoenas issued in civil cases are quashed because the burden of proof—by a preponderance of evidence—is less demanding than that for criminal cases—beyond a reasonable doubt. The impediments to proof and the loss of monetary redress do not, in most judges' estimates, constitute a "compelling" or "paramount" state interest that outweighs the First Amendment. For example, a Palm Beach judge quashed a subpoena served on a reporter during a divorce and child custody case.[16] The reporter had interviewed the husband, musical star Ted Nugent. The wife alleged that the information would bear

15. Loadholtz v. Fields, 389 F. Supp. 1299.

16. Nugent v. Nugent, 49 Fla. Supp. 119 (Fla. Cir. Ct. 1979); *see also* Harris v. Blackstone Developers, 41 Fla. Supp 176 (Fla. Cir. Ct. 1974); Schwartz v. Almart, 42 Fla. Supp. 165 (Fla. Cir. Ct. 1975).

on the fitness of Nugent to have custody of the children. The judge quashed the subpoena, saying that the unrestricted flow of information outweighed the interests of the wife in the proceeding.

The courts, however, have not granted newspersons an absolute privilege in civil cases because there may be a rare instance where the court does find that compelling interest, such as in the case of *St. Petersburg Times* reporter Jane Baumann.[17] The members of the John 3:16 Mission had asked for an emergency hearing at 7:45 A.M. on a motion for a temporary injunction to prohibit John Cook from selling church property. Because Cook had left for Oklahoma, the members did not know when the sale would take place. Ms. Baumann was the only person who had spoken to Cook and who had firsthand confirmation that he was planning to sell the mission to pay off creditors. The judge ordered Baumann to testify about a phone conversation she had had with Cook. She refused and asked to consult her attorney. The judge refused her request and threatened her with contempt if she did not testify. Baumann then testified. Several weeks later a district court of appeal quashed the order to testify. According to the district court of appeal, the judge erred by not following the procedure of notice and hearing after Baumann refused to reveal her information the first time.

In another civil case, a photographer was subpoenaed to produce unpublished photographs after an automobile accident. The Second District Court of Appeal quashed the subpoena and ruled that unpublished photographs "stand on the same footing as any other information gathered by a news-gatherer."[18] And in *Damico v. Lemen,* a Hillsborough County judge quashed a subpoena for videotape of an auto accident.[19] Although all of the footage had

17. Times Publishing Co. v. Burke, 375 So. 2d 297 (Fla. Dist. Ct. App. 1979).

18. Johnson v. Bentley, 457 So. 2d 507 (Fla. Dist. Ct. App. 1984).

19. 14 Media L. Rep. 1031; *see also* Overstreet v. Neighbor, 9 Media L. Rep. 2255 (Fla. Cir. Ct. 1983).

been broadcast, the judge stated the qualified privilege protects any reporter's work product—whether confidential or not and whether published or not. The only way that privilege can be overcome, said the judge, was to show that all alternative sources for the information (e.g., evidence from the case and accident site, police reports, etc.) had been completely exhausted. Only after such a showing would the judge address the other two criteria—relevancy and compelling need.

In 1988, the Fifth District Court of Appeal ignored the above cases, saying there was no accurate substitute for photographs and they were obviously relevant and critical to the outcome of the personal injury suit.[20] An off-duty photographer for the *Citrus County Chronicle* took pictures immediately after an accident that occurred at a road construction site. The accident victim sued the road contractor, claiming that the company failed to warn motorists of the hazardous conditions of the road. The district court of appeal held that people's memories are poor and less accurate than a photograph, which is unique and is the best record of the condition of the road. The court noted that all the requirements for overcoming the privilege—relevancy, alternative sources, and compelling need—had been met.

In *Woods* v. *Lutheran Inner-City Center,* a Duval County circuit court judge quashed that part of a subpoena that sought videotape that was not broadcast.[21] But if relevancy could be shown, videotape that was broadcast as well as materials, records, and testimony concerning identification, inception, and custody of tapes could be subpoenaed.

However, a Hillsborough County judge quashed a subpoena sought by the Florida Bar for videotapes of interviews with an attorney being investigated.[22] The judge said that all tapes, whether broadcast or not, were protected.

20. Carroll Contracting v. Edwards, 15 Media L. Rep. 2121.

21. 11 Media L. Rep. 1775 (Fla. Cir. Ct. 1985).

22. *In re* Confidential Proceedings, 13 Media L. Rep. 2071 (Fla. Cir. Ct. 1987).

Criminal Trials

The Florida Supreme Court has not heard a case involving a reporter's refusal to reveal information in a criminal trial. However, criteria for determining whether a qualified privilege exists were first enunciated in *State* v. *Stoney* in 1974, and they have appeared in almost every reporters' privilege case since then.[23] The criteria are an expansion of the guidelines suggested in Justice Stewart's *Branzburg* dissent. *Stoney* involved *Miami Herald* reporter Bea Hines who wrote a feature article about a rape victim named "Lisa." Hines had conducted the interview of the woman in the presence of State Representative Elaine Gordon. At the trial of the alleged rapist, Hines was subpoenaed to bring all notes, memoranda, and unpublished information relating to her story. Apparently, Gordon's deposition contradicted the testimony of the rape victim, and the defendant wanted Hines's material in order to substantiate Gordon's testimony should the state try to impeach it. The circuit court judge quashed the subpoena, reasoning that subpoenas issued to the media inhibit a reporter's movements and news gathering conduct.

The court said that to ensure against this inhibition, the state must show a compelling interest in the material by proving that (1) the material or testimony is relevant to the offense charged or to the defense; (2) the information is not available from alternative sources; (3) if the information is available elsewhere, all alternative means of securing the information have been unsuccessful; and (4) the nonproduction of the information will result in a violation of defendant's Sixth Amendment right to a fair trial.

In *Tribune Co.* v. *Green,* the Second District Court of Appeal condensed the *Stoney* criteria to the same three-part test used in civil cases: (1) Is the information relevant to the charges? (2) Have alternative sources been exhausted? (3) Is there a compelling need for the information?[24]

23. 42 Fla. Supp. 194 (Fla. Cir. Ct. 1974).
24. 440 So. 2d 484 (Fla. Dist. Ct. App. 1983).

To determine relevancy, a judge will examine the reporter's evidence in light of its admissibility; whether the reporter had direct knowledge of the crime; whether the reporter's source appears to have direct knowledge of the crime; or whether the subpoena is simply an attempt to harass the reporter. The purpose of the second guideline requiring that the subpoenaing party exhaust alternative sources is to ensure against using reporters as investigative arms of the police or against duplicating existing testimony. The final test for compelling need asks whether the reporter's relevant and exclusive testimony is necessary to prevent a miscarriage of justice. In other words, the judge must determine whether the reporter has evidence upon which the indictment or verdict will turn, or evidence which might result in a reduction of the charges or affect the final sentence. Of course, a judge would have to make these determinations without actually hearing or seeing the reporter's evidence.

In most instances, an alternative source is available when the subpoena calls for nonconfidential unpublished information. That source might be another witness (like Representative Gordon), the defendant himself, or an officer of the court. For example, a *Miami Herald* reporter was present when a criminal defendant made self-incriminating statements to a state's attorney. The defendant subpoenaed the reporter to reveal unpublished information that would show the statements were made involuntarily. The circuit court quashed the subpoena on the basis that the state's attorney was an alternative source for the information.[25]

In *Tribune Co.* v. *Green,* a district court of appeal quashed a subpoena because the state had not taken any steps to obtain testimony from the "first hand players" in the case.[26]

Several recent cases indicate that there may be certain kinds of information or evidence that are more prone to disclosure because of their compelling nature than are other types. In *CBS* v. *Cobb,*

25. State v. Miller, 45 Fla. Supp. 137.
26. 440 So. 2d 484.

the Second District Court of Appeal required the disclosure of a videotape interview with convicted murderer Bobby Jo Long.[27] After Long was convicted and given the death sentence, the Florida Supreme Court reversed the conviction and ordered a new trial. Between trials, a television reporter interviewed Long, who stated, "I've probably destroyed about a hundred people." The state obtained the broadcast interview and planned to use it in the retrial, over Long's objection. Long's attorney subpoenaed the station to release the entire tape of the interview, including outtakes. The station's motion to quash was denied.

The district court of appeal, applying the three-part test, held that the videotape was relevant. If the state can introduce a portion of the tape, the defendant may also introduce any portion of the same tape. The alternative source was Long himself, who admitted he did not remember everything said or the order of the questions. The court agreed that memories are often poor and possibly fallible. The evidence was also considered compelling since the state was basing much of its case on the broadcast statement. Long had the right to examine the whole tape to see whether the segment in question was edited properly, understood in its proper context, or was distorted. The court concluded that the balance was in favor of the defendant since "Long is, literally, fighting for his life."

The same court also required disclosure of a confession by Dr. Robert P. Rosier, who admitted in a television interview killing his terminally ill wife.[28] After his admission was aired, a grand jury indicted him. During the pretrial stage, the state subpoenaed the station to turn over the tape of the interview. The motion to quash was denied. The court stated that the confession was relevant and that there was no alternative means of getting the information. The tape was also found to be compelling as a major tool for discovering the truth.

At least in criminal cases, there appears to be no distinction

27. 15 Media L. Rep. 2229 (Fla. Dist. Ct. App. 1988).

28. Waterman Broadcasting v. Reese, 523 So. 2d 1161 (Fla. Dist. Ct. App. 1988).

between confidential and nonconfidential information. In *U.S.* v. *Blanton,* a federal district court quashed a subpoena issued to a *Miami Herald* reporter whose nonconfidential interview with a person indicted on drug charges was sought in order to verify that certain statements were in fact made.[29] The court said that the distinction between confidential and nonconfidential information is irrelevant to the qualified privilege against compelled disclosure.

Often a subpoena is so broad that it would be virtually impossible to comply with it. In the federal trial of Judge Joseph Gersten on various charges under the federal antiracketeering law, the defendant subpoenaed the news director of WTLV-TV in Jacksonville to produce all tapes, scripts, stories, notes, etc., on the defendant.[30] Gersten had been in the news for years, and the station had many films on the judge. The station moved to quash the subpoena since it was not specific as to the items needed, and compliance would have been impossible since materials were filed chronologically rather than by subject matter. The circuit court judge granted the motion to quash in part, holding the subpoena to require only film already broadcast that related specifically to the charges brought, court proceedings, and other charges against the other defendants. Since the material was neither confidential nor unpublished, the subpoena was not viewed as having a chilling effect on the media.

It must be stressed that no protection is available to the reporter who witnesses a crime. In *Branzburg,* the defendant Paul Branzburg had observed two persons processing marijuana. The Court was adamant in providing no protection for any reporter who wants to conceal knowledge of a crime.

In *Miami Herald Publishing Co.* v. *Gross,* a reporter was an eyewitness to the arrest and search of a suspected drug dealer at Miami International Airport.[31] In pretrial motions, the defendant sought to suppress evidence gained during the search. The

29. 534 F. Supp. 295 (S.D. Fla. 1982).
30. United States v. Gersten, 5 Media L. Rep. 1334 (S.D. Fla. 1979).
31. 15 Media L. Rep. 1834 (Fla. Dist. Ct. App. 1988).

defendant subpoenaed the reporter to testify about what he witnessed. The Third District Court of Appeal stuck closely to the *Branzburg* precedent, saying that a reporter's qualified privilege "has utterly no application when the reporter is an eyewitness to an event that is subsequently at issue in a court proceeding."

Grand Jury Subpoenas

The grand jury is an investigative arm of the court system; it uses citizens to hear evidence and make reports. In Florida, a grand jury is required in criminal cases only when the accused is charged with an offense punishable by death. Also, grand juries may investigate the conduct of public officers or employees regardless of whether criminal or irregular conduct is being charged.[32] All grand jury proceedings are secret.

The first privilege case in Florida, *Clein* v. *State,* involved an editor who refused to name the person who leaked detailed testimony and deliberations that occurred before a Dade County grand jury.[33] The editor was forced to reveal his source or spend 30 days in jail.

However, the case that received the most publicity involved former *Pasco Times* reporter Lucy Ware Morgan.[34] Morgan fought against disclosure for almost three years before the Florida Supreme Court finally quashed the subpoena. In November 1973, Morgan wrote an article summarizing the contents of a sealed grand jury presentment. The grand jury was investigating alleged corruption in Pasco County. When a grand jury report does not bring an indictment, the law allows the report to be sealed 15 days to give persons mentioned unfavorably a chance to institute motions to suppress or expunge.[35] It was during this stipulated period that Morgan obtained information about the report. The attorney general of Florida, on his own behalf, questioned

32. Fla. Stat. Ann. § 905 (1981).
33. 52 So. 2d 117.
34. Morgan v. State, 337 So. 2d 951 (Fla. 1976).
35. Fla. Stat. Ann. § 905.28 (1981).

Morgan about the leak; she refused to answer questions and was sentenced to five months in jail. On appeal, the conviction was eventually reversed. Then the grand jury itself subpoenaed Morgan. She again refused to answer questions and was sentenced to 90 days in jail. The conviction was affirmed by a Florida district court of appeal.

Three years after the contempt conviction, the Florida Supreme Court reversed the second conviction. The court held that the preservation of the integrity of grand jury proceedings was not a substantial enough governmental interest to require the forfeiture of First Amendment rights. The grand jury was not investigating a specific crime; therefore, release of the information did not harm the administration of justice. Relying on the *Branzburg* decision, the court ruled that the only purpose served by the subpoenas and subsequent convictions was to harass Morgan.

Morgan is not the only reporter to be convicted twice for contempt after refusing to identify a grand jury leak. Mary Jo Tierney twice refused to answer questions put to her by a Brevard County grand jury.[36] She was sentenced to six hours in jail for her first refusal and 30 days and $500 for the second refusal. On appeal, a Florida district court of appeal overturned the second conviction, based on lower court error. However, the first conviction was affirmed. The court cited *Branzburg* at length on the subject of maintaining the grand jury's integrity. The First Amendment did not give reporters any privilege beyond that offered other citizens to answer questions relevant to a good-faith grand jury criminal investigation. Since revealing what goes on in the secret proceedings is a misdemeanor, a reporter has no privilege to conceal the criminal conduct of the source. Also, a grand jury is fully empowered to investigate breaches of its own security in order to protect its "sanctity and integrity." The court remained true to the *Branzburg* decision, finding relevancy and good faith present in the subpoena. Both *Morgan* v. *State* and *In*

36. *In re* Tierney, 328 So. 2d 40.

re Tierney indicate that reporters refusing to reveal sources of grand jury leaks will not receive the same broad protection offered their counterparts in criminal and civil trials held in Florida.

A recent Florida Supreme Court case involving reporter's privilege had to do with refusal to reveal information to an assistant state attorney.[37] A *Tampa Tribune* reporter wrote that a Hernando County resident had filed a complaint against two county commissioners with the Ethics Commission. The complaint was filed but eventually dropped. Florida law prohibits the disclosure of an intent to file an ethics complaint or of the existence of a complaint.[38] In an effort to identify the reporter's source, the assistant state attorney subpoenaed the *Tribune* reporter, who moved to quash the subpoena. The motion was denied and the reporter was found guilty of civil contempt for refusing to cooperate with the investigation. The district court of appeal affirmed the contempt citation.

The Florida Supreme Court found that the state's interest in protecting the reputation of public officials was not great enough to outweigh the significant First Amendment interest in informing the public. Chief Justice Boyd dissented, arguing, as did the lower courts, that the reporter had actually been a witness to a crime when he received the information, and therefore he was not protected by qualified privilege.

Procedural Safeguards

Florida Courts

Whenever a reporter is subpoenaed to give a deposition or to testify in a Florida court, that procedure is carefully cloaked with judicial safeguards which recognize that reporters do have some qualified privilege. Once a subpoena is received (it must be served on the reporter personally), the reporter is allowed to enter

37. Tribune Co. v. Huffstetler, 489 So. 2d 722 (Fla. 1986).
38. Fla. Stat. Ann. § 112.317(6) (1985).

a motion to quash the subpoena. Once this motion is filed or even made orally during a proceeding, the court may not compel the testimony until adequate notice has been given and a hearing held. No information should be disclosed to the attorney seeking the information, for that disclosure may be deemed a waiver of First Amendment rights to confidentiality. Also, the reporter should never contact the attorney involved; that is the responsibility of the editor or the media's lawyer.

If only eyewitness testimony, without notes or names of sources, is wanted, a motion to quash should still be entered on the ground that even the very presence of the reporter on the witness stand can foreclose future stories and can taint the reporter's objectivity in the future. Should a court still require a reporter to testify after rejecting a motion to quash, the reporter can move for a protective order. Under Florida Rules of Civil Procedure, a court may issue an order to protect any witness from "annoyance, embarrassment, oppression, or undue burden" during testimony.[39] The court can order that attorneys not question a reporter on certain specified matters or can order that attorneys, while questioning the reporter, limit their scope of questions to certain matters. The protective order is sought when it is clear that the judge is going to require some testimony from the reporter.

However, if a reporter is harassed by unsupported or numerous subpoenas, a court can issue a protective order. For example, in *Florida* v. *Lee,* a reporter for the *Lake City Reporter* was granted a protective order against the issuance of any subpoena in a case arising out of a particular murder investigation.[40]

Florida precedent requires the judge to hold a hearing on any motion to quash. At this hearing, the reporter is allowed to have an attorney and any witnesses in her favor.[41] The hearing is held before the same judge who authorized the subpoena, and that judge will determine whether the state's compelling need has

39. FLA. R. CIV. P. § 1.280 (1987).
40. 14 Media L. Rep. 1863 (Fla. Cir. Ct. 1987).
41. Times Publishing Co. v. Burke, 375 So. 2d 297.

been demonstrated or not. The burden of proof is with the state. Because reporters' privilege involves vital First Amendment questions, a reporter may appeal all the way to the U.S. Supreme Court after all state remedies have been sought.

Federal Courts

Most federal courts of appeals have adopted the three-part test when dealing with subpoenas of reporters in both civil and criminal cases. In addition, if federal prosecutors are seeking the disclosure in criminal cases, they must follow the Department of Justice guidelines.[42] The guidelines incorporate the three-part test and also require prosecutors to negotiate in good faith with reporters and their lawyers.[43]

Search and Seizure in Newsrooms

Until 1981, if a district attorney or county prosecutor felt that a subpoena for information and material would eventually be quashed, he could obtain a search warrant authorizing police to search the newspaper's office and seize the material he wanted. The case that approved this tactic was *Zurcher* v. *Stanford Daily.*[44] A warrant was issued to search the newsroom of the *Stanford Daily* for photographs and film that might identify students who injured policemen in a demonstration at the Stanford University Hospital.

In a 5–3 decision, the U.S. Supreme Court upheld surprise search warrant raids against innocent third parties. Justice Byron White, the same justice who wrote the *Branzburg* opinion, said such warrants are constitutionally permissible as long as there is

42. 28 C.F.R. § 50.10 (1988).

43. Baker v. F & F Investment, 470 F. 2d 778 (2d Cir. 1972), *cert. denied,* 411 U.S. 966 (1973); Loadholtz v. Fields, 389 F. Supp. 1299; United States v. Cuthbertson, 651 F.2d 189 (3d Cir. 1981); United States v. Horne, 11 Media L. Rep. 1312 (N.D. Fla. 1985); United States v. Paez, 13 Media L. Rep. 1973 (S.D. Fla. 1987).

44. 436 U.S. 547 (1978).

probable cause to believe the information sought is held by the news media, the material sought is specified in the warrant, and the search and seizure process is carried out in an orderly manner so as not to disturb the routine of the news office. "Surely a warrant to search a newspaper premises . . . carries no realistic threat of prior restraint or of any direct restraint whatever on the publication of the [newspaper] or on its communication of ideas," said White.

Justice Stewart countered in his dissenting opinion that "it seems to be self-evident that police searches of newspaper offices burden the freedom of the press" because of "the possibility of disclosure of information received from confidential sources or of the identity of the sources themselves."

Both Congress and state legislatures reacted immediately with a flurry of bills to protect individuals as well as the media from unannounced searches unless they are suspected of criminal activity.

In October 1980, Congress passed the Privacy Protection Act of 1980.[45] The law requires government agents (federal or state) to obtain a subpoena when seeking evidence from reporters. The exceptions to the law allow seizure without subpoena if the person holding the material has committed or is committing a crime, if seizure is necessary to prevent death or bodily injury, or if there is reasonable cause to believe that a subpoena would result in the destruction, alteration, or concealment of the material. If a search warrant is issued, news media can challenge it in court. The law became effective January 1, 1981.

Summary

The U.S. Supreme Court ruled in 1972 that reporters' privilege to withhold information from a court does not exist under the Constitution. However, the Court did not foreclose the right of state legislatures or courts to establish such a right for its jour-

45. 42 U.S.C. § 200aa (Supp. 1981).

nalists. Greater protection could be allowed as long as the state's interest in protecting the fair administration of justice was not defeated. Florida's courts accepted the Court's challenge and developed a qualified reporter's privilege.

Florida precedent has established that a subpoena cannot stand unless a hearing is held at which it must be determined (1) whether the information goes directly to the defense or to the offense, (2) whether alternative sources are available, and (3) whether the information is necessary for a fair trial. For the most part, Florida's circuit courts have followed the precedent. In the event a judge does not quash a subpoena, the media may apply immediately to a district court of appeal for a stay.

There will always be judges who, knowing a subpoena is invalid, will nevertheless enforce it for immediate purposes. The only way to demonstrate that such tactics are repugnant is for reporters to face contempt convictions willingly rather than give in to a subpoena.

Chapter Five

Reporting the Courts

In December 1916, a Florida newspaper editor published an editorial charging the Florida Supreme Court with hostility toward lawyers, "stubbornness, partiality, ignorance of the law, and partisanship." [1] The editor was found in contempt of court for the publication of a libel against the court. This is the first reported case dealing with contemptuous action by a journalist in this state. Apparently, the court had made a controversial decision upon a point of evidence in a criminal case. The supreme court did not appreciate the editor's comments, calling him a "pseudo-Journalist" who dipped his pen in the ink of morbid thoughts. Other epithets were also used: "enemy of his people," "disloyal," and "traitor."

While publishers have the right to bring to public notice the conduct of the system, said the court, this notice must be a true account and "fair in spirit." The liberty of the press is subordinate to the independence of the judiciary. To allow the media the privilege to "scatter abroad suspicion and distrust is not only an insult to the public, but it impairs the efficiency of the courts." The court prayed that the good sense of the people would restrain the "impulsive and ill-natured words of those among us who seem to be so alert to suspect and ready to condemn and that proceedings of this nature may not be necessary in the future to

1. *In re* Hayes, 73 So. 362 (Fla. 1916).

restrain the vicious tendencies . . . which lead [the media] to attacks upon the integrity and authority of our institutions."

Needless to say, this was not the last time the media would attack the integrity and authority of the courts. Nor was it the last time that the media would be chastised for doing so by the judiciary. While editors today rarely experience the type of problem that the editor in the above situation faced, they are still encountering problems, but of a different nature: the closing of courts and court records as well as the gagging of trial participants.

The Contempt Power

Historically, a judge has enjoyed great power within his courtroom, including the prerogative to act as witness, accuser, judge, and jury in contempt cases. This awesome power can be abused, but more often than not, this power is wielded by a judge who genuinely feels, rightly or wrongly, that he is the only one who can protect the fair trial rights of the defendant.

The contempt power grew out of ancient Anglo-Saxon law when a judge was a substitute for the king. Just as the king would have absolute power if he were reigning over the court, so too would his proxies, the judges. Out of this system has grown the traditional formality that accompanies any court procedure—the black robes, the bench (usually set above the rest of the room), calling the judge "Your Honor," and the ceremony of rising upon the judge's entry and exit.

The law of contempt as it has developed in British and American court systems recognizes several different classifications of a contemptuous act. First is civil contempt, which normally involves a refusal to do something, such as a refusal to obey a court order or to abide by a court ruling or judgment. A civil contempt is handled in a summary procedure in Florida courts and any fine assessed or jail sentence imposed lasts until the individual agrees to obey the court. Usually, civil contempt is not used to punish those who create a threat to the administration of justice but to punish those who would affront administered justice. For example, if a court orders an individual to repay certain moneys to another and he refuses, then a civil contempt action can be brought and the person jailed or fined until he agrees to pay the amount. Media are rarely involved in civil contempt actions.

The second classification is criminal contempt. Florida law recognizes two types of criminal contempt: indirect (or constructive) and direct. Direct criminal contempt is a contemptuous act that occurs in the presence of the court or "so near thereto" that it affects the judicial proceedings in progress.[2] For example, if a reporter, once on the stand, refuses to testify about his source of information, he may be held in contempt of court. Criminal contempt is punished summarily if the judge witnesses the contempt. The judge merely recites the facts, informs the defendant of the accusations, orders the defendant to show cause why he should not be held in contempt, gives the defendant opportunity to present evidence of the circumstances, signs and enters the judgment of the court, and pronounces sentence. The maximum sentence for direct criminal contempt in Florida is one year or $500. If the sentence is six months or more, the judge must impanel a jury to hear and decide on the facts, unless the defendant waives a jury trial.

Indirect criminal contempt is the type of contempt most often adjudged against newspersons. This is conduct that occurs away from a court but which the judge feels presents a clear and present danger to the administration of justice. The two typical causes for indirect contempt actions against the media are reporting of information from closed proceedings and refusing to appear to give testimony. Indirect contempt is handled in Florida as a summary proceeding but with notice and hearing.[3] The procedure set down by law is as follows: The judge first signs and issues an order stating the facts giving rise to the contempt action

2. Fla. R. Crim. P. § 3.830 (1989).
3. *Id.* § 3.840.

and orders the defendant to appear at a hearing where the defendant must show why he or she should not be held in contempt. If the defendant does not enter a plea of guilty, then a hearing will follow the arraignment. At the hearing, the defendant may have his lawyer and any witnesses for his side. At the conclusion of the hearing, the judge enters his judgment at which time the defendant can produce any mitigating evidence. Sentence is then pronounced. If a contemptuous act directly involves a judge, the judge must disqualify himself from the proceedings. The defendant may be fined or may be placed in jail and remain there for the duration of the original proceedings. Because of the indefinite length of any trial or proceeding, the law does not specify a maximum jail sentence. However, if a judge can reasonably foresee that a proceeding before him will last more than six months, he must grant the contempt defendant the right to a jury trial.[4]

When Congress passed the Judiciary Act of 1789 that established the federal court system, it authorized federal judges to punish at their discretion any contempts of judicial authority before them. However, it became clear that judges were interpreting the term "judicial authority" much too broadly, and Congress passed another law in 1831 to limit the use of the contempt power. The new law said that summary contempt proceedings should be used only when contemptuous activity occurred in the presence of the judge or "so near thereto" as to obstruct justice. Because of the pervasiveness of the media and the interest of the public in court news, the term "so near thereto" eventually received broad interpretation. In *Toledo Newspaper Co.* v. *United States,* an editor criticized a judge who was taking an inordinately long time deciding the constitutionality of a rate fare change for city streetcars.[5] The *Toledo News-Bee* was found in contempt of court. The newspaper argued that the editorial, written and published miles from the judge's court or chambers, was not "so near

4. Bloom v. Illinois, 391 U.S. 194 (1968).
5. 247 U.S. 402 (1918).

thereto," and hence the newspaper could not be punished. The U.S. Supreme Court disagreed and held that any action that has a "reasonable tendency" to obstruct justice was near enough. The case was eventually overturned in 1941 when Justice William O. Douglas held that federal judges must limit their contempt power to activities that take place either within the courtroom or geographically near it.[6]

While federal judges were limited in their use of contempt power, state courts were operating unrestricted. State courts had held for almost a century that legislatures could not limit judges' powers because that power was inherent in the very existence and creation of the court system. This notion, forwarded in an 1855 Arkansas case, *State* v. *Morrill,* became the ruling precedent until the 1940s.[7] *In re Hayes,* the case described at the opening of this chapter, demonstrates this assumed power. In that case, the Florida high court stated that "the liberty of the press is subordinate to the independence of the judiciary." And it was common for temperamental judges to cite newspapers for contempt whenever an editorial or story offended them.

Beginning in the 1940s, the U.S. Supreme Court began pulling some of this power from state judges, particularly when that power was being used against the news media. In a series of cases from Florida, Texas, and California, the Court acknowledged that contempt citations against the press for editorial comment and opinion before and after trials were unconstitutional, unless the judge could establish that such comment presented a "clear and present danger to the administration of justice." These three cases, all very similar in their attacks on judges, were the first step in promoting open discussion of the judiciary in this country.

The first decision, *Bridges* v. *California,* is actually two cases, the tandem case being *Times-Mirror Co.* v. *Superior Court.*[8] Both cases involved comment upon cases before separate courts. The

6. Nye v. United States, 313 U.S. 33 (1941).
7. 16 Ark. 384 (1855).
8. 314 U.S. 252 (1941).

comments, while capable of being characterized as criticism, were not critical of the judges as much as they were critical of the decisions being made. Both defendants were cited for contempt of court. The U.S. Supreme Court stated that the judges' fears of being intimidated were not sufficient reason to punish the comment. The contempt citations were issued at the precise time when public interest in the matters discussed would naturally be at its height. The ban, said the Court, is likely to fall not only at a critical time, but upon the most important topics of discussion. The only time a curtailment of expression can be justified is when the expression might cause "a serious substantive evil of unfair administration of justice." Such an evil was not found and the contempt convictions were overturned.

The second case came five years later when the Court heard *Pennekamp* v. *Florida,* the first Florida First Amendment case to be heard by the Court.[9] *Pennekamp* involved two editorials published in the *Miami Herald* that criticized the circuit court judges in Dade County for allowing the courts to be "subverted into refuges for lawbreakers." The editorials cited recent cases before the courts to demonstrate that judges were using "obstructing technicalities" to ensure that criminal defendants were getting "delay when wanted and prompt decision when requested." The editorials were based upon false information. The U.S. Supreme Court stated that while courts must have the power to protect the interests of prisoners and litigants before them, "freedom of discussion should be given the widest range compatible with the requirement of justice." The test to be used in determining the constitutionality of a contempt citation such as this was whether "the editorials are a clear and present danger to the fair administration of justice in Florida." The Court reversed the contempt citation and suggested that if the false information amounted to a defamation, any of the judges could sue for libel.

The third case in this series was *Craig* v. *Harney,* in which the *Corpus Christi* (Tex.) *Caller-Times* severely criticized a lay judge

9. 328 U.S. 331 (1946).

for "arbitrary action," "travesty of justice," and a "gross miscarriage of justice."[10] The judge, concluding that the editorial was designed to portray falsely the proceedings and to prejudice the court, cited the newspaper for contempt. The U.S. Supreme Court stated on appeal that no matter how vehement or unfair the criticism, the comment is protected unless there is a threat to the administration of justice. "That danger must not be remote or even probable; it must immediately imperil."

This series of cases in the 1940s virtually ended the use of the judge's contempt power to punish newspapers who commented upon and criticized the actions of a judge. However, still left were large areas of contempt, such as gagging the press before or during a trial, restricting access to judicial records, excluding the media from a courtroom during proceedings, and restricting access to court or trial participants.

Traditional Safeguards for a Fair Trial

Trials, particularly criminal trials, draw a great deal of public attention and publicity. It is this publicity that creates the tension between a defendant's right to a fair trial and the press's right to cover that trial. The concern of judges and lawyers alike is that the defendant's Sixth Amendment right to a "speedy and public trial by an impartial jury" does not become less important than the public's right to be informed by the press of the judicial process. The constitutional mandate of an "impartial" juror makes it incumbent upon the judge in any trial to assure that those who will sit in judgment of an accused will be open-minded and able to render a verdict after fair consideration of the testimony. Open-minded does not mean ignorant; it means only that the juror be free from any deep impressions and influences that will distort his ability to weigh information clearly and fairly.

The legal system has developed a set of six procedures to safe-

10. 331 U.S. 367 (1947).

guard this impartiality. Four of these safeguards are aimed at making sure those influenced by publicity do not serve on a jury, and two are to prevent a seated jury from being influenced by publicity during a trial. These traditional safeguards date back to the seventeenth and eighteenth centuries, and because they deal with the influence of publicity rather than the publicity itself, they have raised few First Amendment problems. Nevertheless, the journalist must be aware of these traditional safeguards for two important reasons. First, the traditional safeguards protect not only the defendant but also the public. If any one of these safeguards is abused by the court, the defendant would not receive a fair trial and any conviction could later be overturned and a new trial required—all at a cost to the state and taxpayers. Journalists should be constantly vigilant over the court system for the protection of both the guilty and the innocent. Second, Florida courts require that before any restraints can be placed upon media coverage of a trial, the court must prove that the existing safeguards were not sufficient to guarantee a fair trial. The journalist must look after himself and report laxity or abuses of the traditional safeguards in order to avoid being the victim of restrictions upon his own coverage. For example, it is more convenient and less costly to exclude a reporter from a courtroom than to sequester a jury. Journalists must be constantly vigilant of the system to ensure that convenience and necessity are not confused. The failure to use these safeguards properly has resulted in convictions being overturned. These traditional safeguards are voir dire (to speak truthfully), continuance, change of venue, change of venire, admonition, and sequestration.

Voir Dire

The process of jury selection is a tedious one, often lasting as long or longer than the trial itself. Yet it is probably the best technique for ensuring that those who will hear and try a case will be the least influenced by information they have read or heard about a crime.

Criminal lawyers are specially schooled in the fine art of juror selection, using sociology, psychology, religion, and numerous other social sciences to ferret out those jurors who may not only be prejudiced by the facts in the case, but who also may be unfriendly to one side or another for various reasons. Each attorney is given an unlimited number of chances to reject a prospective juror "for cause." A challenge for cause is based upon some obvious prejudice in the juror. All the attorney must do is convince the judge that whatever prejudice the individual holds will make him incapable of serving as an impartial juror. Typical challenges for cause are exercised when a prospective juror states that he or she is unable to be impartial, when the juror is found to be racially prejudiced against the accused, or when the juror is an acquaintance, relative, or business associate of the accused.

In addition to challenges for cause, each attorney is given a limited number of peremptory challenges. The number is determined by the law and the gravity of the crime. In Florida, ten peremptory challenges are allowed if the defendant is tried on charges punishable by death or by life imprisonment, six for other felony charges, and three for misdemeanors.[11] The judge does not have to be informed of the reason for the challenge, nor may the judge refuse the challenge. Peremptory challenges are often used to challenge jurors the judge refused to dismiss during a challenge for cause. In cases where the judge suspects that prospective jurors might have been overly exposed to extensive pretrial publicity about the case, the judge has the discretion to increase the number of peremptory challenges. A lawyer is often rated by how effectively he uses the limited number of peremptory challenges.

Numerous studies have been conducted since the mid-1960s to learn just what the impact of pretrial publicity is on a jury. The results are varied but seem to indicate that persons can be prejudiced by extensive pretrial publicity and that the voir dire process can only be as effective as the honesty of the juror or the

11. FLA. R. CRIM. P. § 3.350 (1989).

intensity of the questioning. The failure of a judge to oversee the voir dire process properly or the failure of the lawyers to question prospective jurors carefully can be a cause for reversing a conviction.

In 1975, the U.S. Supreme Court heard an appeal from Florida for reversal of a conviction for robbery. *Murphy* v. *Florida* involved the notorious Robin Hood of Dade County, "Murph the Surf."[12] Murphy was convicted of breaking and entering with intent to commit robbery and of assault with intent to commit robbery. He had broken into a Miami Beach home but was apprehended while fleeing. Extensive media attention was brought on Murphy because of his flamboyant lifestyle and because of other criminal charges, including murder, theft of the Star of India sapphire from a New York museum, and conspiracy to transport stolen securities in interstate commerce. At first, he was committed to a hospital after being declared mentally incompetent to stand trial for the robbery. He was then indicted in the securities case and then convicted on the murder charge, all before he was tried for the Miami Beach robbery. During the jury selection process, 78 prospective jurors were questioned. Thirty of those were excused for personal reasons, 20 were excused for prejudice, 20 were excused peremptorily, leaving eight to serve. Murphy's lawyer moved to dismiss the remaining eight because they were aware of Murphy's previous convictions. That motion was denied and Murphy was convicted.

The U.S. Supreme Court upheld the conviction, saying that just because jurors have information about prior criminal records does not presume prejudice on their part. The Court could not go along with the proposition that juror exposure to information about a defendant's prior convictions for crimes necessarily deprives the defendant of due process. Evidence indicated that none of the jurors had any hostility toward Murphy. Some had only a vague recollection of the robbery, and each had some knowledge about one or more of his past convictions. In fact, during the

12. 421 U.S. 794 (1975).

voir dire process, one juror did not know of the theft conviction for the Star of India until Murphy's attorney told him. Another did not know of the murder conviction until told by the defense attorney. Another was informed about the securities case for the first time during the voir dire questioning.

Continuance

Continuance means postponing a trial until a time when the community's attention is no longer riveted to the facts of the case. Continuance makes the assumption that time is the best way of retarding memory as well as prejudice. The only problem with the assumption is that once a delayed trial begins, the media will pick up and rewrite all of the old stories, retelling the information in as much detail as before. Thus, for crimes which originally receive a great deal of coverage, continuance is probably not an effective legal safeguard. However, for trials with only temporary interest, a continuance may be the best solution.

Change of Venue

Although expensive, moving a trial from one county to another has been seen as a moderately effective way of reducing jury prejudice. In change of venue, the judge, defendant, witnesses, defense attorneys, and court personnel move to another community from which a jury is selected. It is hoped that prospective jurors in the new community will not have been exposed to as much publicity as have persons in the original community. Change of venue is effective in large states such as Florida that have dispersed concentrations of population, where circulation of newspapers is intensive rather than widespread, and where radio and television coverage is limited geographically. For example, the first murder trial of Theodore Bundy, accused of several murders in and out of this state, was moved from Tallahassee, where he allegedly killed two college women, to Miami. Later, his trial on charges of killing a Lake City girl was moved from that town to Orlando. While most Floridians knew of the charges against

Bundy, those in cities such as Orlando and Miami had not been exposed to the intense and in-depth coverage by the newspapers in the northern part of the state.

Two Florida cases and one from Indiana point out the problems encountered when a change of venue is not considered. *Shepherd* v. *Florida* dealt with the murder conviction in 1950 of four young black men in Lake City who were found guilty of raping a 17-year-old white girl at pistol point.[13] The incident created a serious confrontation in the small town: Mobs burned several homes of black families, several families were removed from town by police to prevent midnight lynchings, and other families fled the town. The National Guard and the 116th Field Artillery from Tampa were called out. Newspapers reported that a confession had been given police, yet no confession was ever offered at trial. The information about the confession came from a press release written by the sheriff. During the grand jury deliberations, a newspaper ran an editorial cartoon depicting four electric chairs with the caption "No Compromise—Supreme Penalty." The Florida Supreme Court, in refusing to overturn the convictions, reasoned that the inflamed public sentiment was against the crime and not the race of the young defendants. There was evidence that the judge did try to control the courtroom by searching all persons who entered. But as Justice Robert Jackson said in his concurrence to the U.S. Supreme Court's reversal, the "very need for this type of security reflected the prejudicial atmosphere which permeated the trial." Although the defense attorney entered motions for continuance and change of venue, they were denied. The U.S. Supreme Court's per curiam reversal was not based upon the atmosphere and the racial prejudice that engulfed the community but on the manner in which the all-white grand jury had been selected. Justice Jackson's concurrence said that the prejudicial influences were brought to bear upon the jury with such force "that the conclusion is inescapable that

13. 341 U.S. 50 (1951).

defendants were prejudged guilty and the trial was but a legal gesture to register a verdict already dictated by the press and the public opinion which it generated."

The U.S. Supreme Court has consistently placed its stamp of approval upon the use of change of venue as a proper means of trial management. In *Irvin* v. *Dowd,* the defendant's conviction in southern Indiana on six counts of murder was reversed because the judge not only had failed to exercise his prerogatives during the voir dire process, but he also had not appropriately used his power to grant a second change of venue.[14] Leslie Irvin was arrested in Evansville and charged with six murders. The newspaper, radio, and television coverage was extensive and vitriolic, detailing former convictions, AWOL charges during the war, parole violation, a confession, police lineup identification, and running extensive interviews with the sheriff. Irvin's lawyer moved for a change of venue, which was granted to the adjoining county where publicity had been just as rampant. Ninety percent of the prospective jurors from that county said they entertained some opinion as to Irvin's guilt. The lawyer sought another change of venue to a county sufficiently removed from Evansville, but the second motion was denied because Indiana law allowed only one change of venue.

The state called 430 prospective jurors. Over half were excused for stated prejudice, 103 were excused because they did not believe in the imposition of the death penalty, and 30 were challenged peremptorily. Of the ten seated, eight said they had an opinion about the defendant's guilt but felt they could be impartial. The U.S. Supreme Court, reversing the conviction, found that a pattern of deep and bitter prejudice existed that was brought about by extensive media publicity. The Court chastised the judge for not taking the proper measures to ensure that an impartial jury was selected and for not granting a change of venue the first time to a place removed from the furor of the public and the media.

14. 366 U.S. 717 (1961).

In *Murphy,* Florida judges were given a test for determining when to grant a change of venue.[15] The state supreme court required a determination to be made as to whether the general state of mind of the citizens is so infected by knowledge of the incident and the accompanying prejudice, bias, and preconceived opinions that jurors could not possibly put these matters out of their minds and try the case solely on the evidence presented in the courtroom. A 1979 case did not properly apply that test. In *Manning* v. *State,* Derrick Manning was found guilty and sentenced to death for the murders of two sheriff's deputies in Columbia County.[16] Following Manning's arrest, publicity was intense, inflammatory, and contradictory. Manning's attorney filed a motion for change of venue, citing the inordinate publicity, pronounced prejudice, and hostility toward the accused. The motion was denied and a jury was seated that knew of the crimes through the local media accounts and community discussion. The Florida Supreme Court reversed and granted a new trial based on a finding that the "inhabitants of Columbia County were so infected by knowledge of the incident and accompanying prejudice that jurors from the community could not possibly try the case solely on the evidence presented in the courtroom . . . the general atmosphere in this rural community was sufficiently inflammatory to require the trial court to grant a change of venue. . . ."

Change of Venire

The Sixth Amendment states that a jury shall be selected from the district wherein the alleged crime occurred. However, some states hold that a judge may select jurors who do not live in the same county where the crime occurred and still hold the trial in that county. It may be less expensive to house a foreign jury than to transport the court and all of its personnel to another county. Change of venire is also used whenever it would be impossible to

15. 421 U.S. 794.
16. 378 So. 2d 274 (Fla. 1979).

change venue because of the stationary character of evidence. For example, change of venue would be impractical if it were necessary that jury members actually visit the site of the crime, perhaps several times.

Admonition

Once a jury is impaneled, it is always a fear of judges and lawyers that jury members will read or listen to accounts of their own deliberations and the court's activities reported in the media. This is particularly so in Florida where television cameras are allowed to film court proceedings. More than one critic of Florida's cameras in the courtroom policy has said that jurors, intrigued by seeing themselves on television, will be hard put not to turn on the television set and watch themselves.

Admonition is probably the weakest safeguard against such exposure. An admonition is a simple warning by the judge not to read or watch anything about the trial nor to talk about or discuss the case with anyone. If a juror does receive information during the process, he may be penalized by contempt of court if the information was obtained purposefully. However, if the information came about by accident, the juror may be requestioned by the attorneys to determine the effect the information had on the individual's ability to keep an open mind. If prejudice has occurred, a mistrial may be declared or the juror will be replaced with an alternate.

Sequestration

Sequestering of the jury is the most effective way of preventing prejudicial influence from the press. Jurors are housed together, eat together, and are transported to and from the court together. Visitation with families is restricted and so is exposure to the media. It is not uncommon for a police officer to be assigned the job of cutting out of the paper any stories that might be prejudicial before delivering the paper to the jurors. Most judges avoid the use of sequestration when they know the trial will be a long one. However, with the presence of cameras in Florida's courtrooms, sequestration, although very costly to the state, is being used more often.

The case that points out how one judge abused his discretion to initiate any one of these traditional safeguards, particularly sequestration, and that opened the door for other types of questionable safeguards is *Sheppard* v. *Maxwell.*[17] In that case, Dr. Samuel Sheppard, a Cleveland osteopath, was charged in 1954 with murdering his wife. Despite denials by Sheppard and testimony that he struggled with someone in the home and was hit over the head, the Cleveland media did not believe him and called for his immediate arrest. The reports were unimaginable in light of today's professional attitude toward reporting sensational crimes. Various forms of trial mismanagement that resulted in "an orgy of sensationalism" included the following: No change of venue was granted; jurors were not sequestered; cameras with hot lights and snaking cables were allowed into the courtroom; police, prosecutors, and witnesses were given free rein to publicize their sentiments about the guilt or innocence of the defendant; the coroner's hearing was held in a school gymnasium and broadcast to the city; the judge and district attorney, who were up for reelection, held daily press conferences after the proceedings. The U.S. Supreme Court refused to hear Sheppard's first appeal for a reversal. Five years later, a young criminal lawyer, F. Lee Bailey, repetitioned the Court to review the case. In 1966, the conviction was reversed. On remand, Dr. Sheppard was acquitted during a relatively quiet trial.

In reversing the conviction, the Court chastised the judge for his mismanagement of the trial and for allowing the media to take over the courtroom. The judge was scolded for not considering and using the traditional means of safeguarding Sheppard's fair trial rights, such as sequestration and change of venue. "We conclude that these procedures would have been sufficient to guarantee Sheppard a fair trial and so do not consider what sanctions might be available against a recalcitrant press." The Court

17. 384 U.S. 333 (1966).

went on to say that the "carnival atmosphere" could easily have been avoided by adopting stricter rules governing the use of the courtroom by the media. Specifically, the justices suggested that access to the courtroom by the media could be limited by selecting only a representative number of reporters to cover the trial. Second, the Court suggested that the judge should have restricted statements and opinions from witnesses, police, lawyers, and other court personnel. Third, the judge should have admonished all of the media to report only material that was entered at trial and to be more careful about checking the accuracy of rumor. The latter suggestion raised many eyebrows among the legal profession as well as among the media. The Court in *Sheppard* did not say the judge could restrict the publication of prejudicial information, nor did the Court say the judge could not restrict such publication. The Court merely took the middle ground—admonition—and applied it to the specific facts of the Sheppard trial.

Restrictive Safeguards

Restrictive Orders—Prohibiting Publication

The *Sheppard* case and several other sensational trials in the late 1950s and early 1960s prompted the American Bar Association to interpret the Supreme Court to mean that if judges felt a defendant's rights could be prejudiced, they could do whatever was in their power to preserve the decorum of the trial—even if it meant restricting what the media could publish. In 1968, the ABA made its recommendations in what has been historically referred to as the Reardon Report, but which is more accurately called the ABA's *Standards Relating to Fair Trial and Free Press.*[18] This report, which has since been revised, sanctioned the use of restrictive orders against the press. Specifically, the report suggested that if anyone willfully publishes information that goes

18. ABA Project on Minimum Standards Relating to Fair Trial and Free Press (1968).

beyond the public records and that threatens the outcome of the trial, the judge may use his contempt power to punish that person. Additionally, any person who willfully disobeys a judge's restrictive order could also be held in contempt of court.

Although the Reardon Report was not law but only a guideline for judges to follow, it had the practical effect of telling judges that restrictive orders were permissible. However, not all legal groups were telling the judges the same thing. While the Reardon Report was being passed by the ABA, the Judicial Conference of the United States also formulated recommendations in its *Report of the Committee on the Operation of the Jury System, Free Press-Fair Trial Issue.*[19] This report, called the Kaufman Committee Report, took two years to prepare. It is an inventory of the various methods available to a judge to protect the defendant's fair trial rights. Unlike the controversial Reardon Report, the Kaufman Committee Report made no specific suggestions for controlling the content of the news. Only two suggestions touched on the media: (1) seating of media representatives so as to minimize disruption and (2) warning against the disruptive nature of television or still photographers.[20]

Between 1964 and 1976, restrictive orders against the media and sources were almost daily occurrences. Media were restricted in their coverage of major civil disobedience trials during the late 1960s and early 1970s. Judge John Sirica of the U.S. District Court in Washington, D.C., issued dozens of restrictive orders during the Watergate trials of the mid-1970s.

During the 1972 Republican National Convention in Miami, eight young antiwar activists, later designated the "Gainesville Eight," were arrested and charged with conspiring to disrupt the convention. Before the pretrial proceedings began, a federal district court judge issued an order prohibiting the media from sketching in the courtroom. CBS artist Aggie Whelan obeyed the judge's order and did not bring any sketching materials into

19. 45 F.R.D. 391 (1968).

20. *Id.* § 3(c)(1), at 409–411; *and* Local Rule 10—Subjects of Special Order.

the courtroom; instead, she observed what transpired in the courtroom and went into the hall to do the sketches. After hearing of this affront, the judge ordered CBS reporters into his chambers, confiscated the drawings, and issued another order that no sketches were to be made of the proceedings in the courtroom "or its environs." The next day, Whelan did not go to the courthouse but sketched the trial participants from memory. Four of the sketches were shown on the CBS morning news. CBS was found guilty of defying the order. The judge issued another order, this time prohibiting the publication of sketches regardless of where they were made. CBS appealed the order.[21] The Fifth Circuit said sketching is not intrusive and can be done quietly or even away from the court. As for publication, the Fifth Circuit held that a total ban on the publication of sketches was far too broad and too remotely related to the danger sought to be avoided. Only when there has been a showing that the sketching is obtrusive and disruptive can a court prohibit it.

Since CBS was found guilty of disobeying the judge's second order, the network did not defy the third order but challenged it by appealing. In an earlier case, the Fifth Circuit warned the media that if they feel a judge's restrictive order or any order is unconstitutional, they should challenge the order first, rather than break it.[22] A court order is considered constitutional until held otherwise. Unless an order is "transparently invalid" or "patently frivolous," it must be obeyed until reversed by orderly review or until it is withdrawn. The court reasoned that a deliberate refusal to obey an order of the court without testing its validity through established processes requires further action by the judiciary and therefore directly affects the judiciary's ability to discharge its duties and responsibilities. As for CBS, it was ordered to pay the fine assessed for the contempt conviction although the Fifth Circuit ruled that the sketching bans were too broad. A general warning is that reporters should not break or-

21. United States v. CBS, 497 F.2d 102 (5th Cir. 1974).
22. United States v. Dickinson, 465 F.2d 496 (5th Cir. 1972).

ders but acquaint themselves with the law so they can successfully challenge unconstitutional orders.

It was not until 1976 that the U.S. Supreme Court heard a gag order case. In *Nebraska Press Association* v. *Stuart,* a Nebraska judge had issued a far-reaching restrictive order against publishing information about the murder trial of Edwin Simants, accused of murdering six members of one family.[23] The judge's order followed the guidelines voluntarily adopted by members of the state bar association and the state's news media. Between October 22 and December 12, 1975, the media tried to have the order vacated by the state courts and twice by the U.S. Supreme Court.[24] Each time the order was appealed it was modified, until it prohibited only the reporting of confessions and admissions and any other information "strongly implicative of the accused as the perpetrator of the slayings." Still not satisfied, the media applied to the U.S. Supreme Court for a third time to stay the order. The Court agreed to hear the appeal but denied motions to expedite review or to stay the order. The Court's opinion was not handed down until June 30, 1976, the last day of the Court's 1975 session and almost six months after Simants was convicted of murder and sentenced to death.

Despite the delays and frustrations, the Nebraska media received a decision that would virtually end the use of gag orders against the media. The Court stated that while most restrictive orders against the press are unconstitutional, there are certain extraordinary circumstances that might justify such restrictions. To help judges determine whether such circumstances exist, the Court set down a three-prong test that has since been labeled the *Nebraska* guidelines. The guidelines state that before issuing a restrictive order, a judge first should examine the nature and extent of the pretrial publicity to assess what probable effect it would have on prospective jurors. Second, the judge should exhaust all other measures, such as sequestration, continuance, voir

23. 424 U.S. 539 (1976).
24. 423 U.S. 1319 (1975).

dire, and change of venue, that would likely mitigate against the effects of the pretrial publicity. Third, the judge should not enter an order unless the gag is the only way of ensuring a fair trial.

In 1977, the Florida Supreme Court adopted the *Nebraska* guidelines in *Florida ex rel. Miami Herald* v. *McIntosh.*[25] In that case, six stockbrokers were charged with securities fraud and were scheduled for trial in a Palm Beach circuit court. Before trial, the defendants moved to prohibit the reporting of any testimony or evidence made outside of the presence of the jury until it was made a part of the public record or public trial. The motion also barred participants from commenting on the case. The judge granted the motion and entered the order. The media sought a revocation of the order and a hearing was scheduled. At the conclusion of the hearing, the judge refused to withdraw the order, saying that it was his assessment that publicity would injure the defendants' right to a fair trial.

On appeal, the Florida Supreme Court stated that without a fair trial, freedom of press could not exist and without freedom of press, fair trials could not be assured. "We firmly reject any suppression of news in criminal trials except in those rare instances such as national security and where a news report would obviously deny a fair trial. . . . News delayed is news denied." The court cited the *Nebraska* guidelines as the standard to be used in Florida to determine whether publication would "obviously deny a fair trial." Additionally, if a judge feels he has met the *Nebraska* guidelines, he must give the media reasonable notice and an opportunity to challenge before enjoining publication.

Only once since the *Nebraska* decision has the U.S. Supreme Court upheld a gag order. In *Seattle Times* v. *Rhinehart,* the newspaper was the defendant in a libel suit brought by a religious group, the Aquarian Foundation, and its leader.[26] During the discovery process, the newspaper sought and was granted access to a list of donors and members of the Aquarian Foundation.

25. 340 So. 2d 904 (Fla. 1977).
26. 467 U.S. 20 (1984).

However, the court issued a protective order prohibiting publication of the information. The Supreme Court upheld the order, stating that a litigant does not have an unrestrained right to disseminate information that has been obtained through pretrial discovery. The order, concluded the Court, was narrowly drawn to further the interest of privacy and freedom of religion and association. Although the newspaper was prevented from taking advantage of its position as a party in the case, the Court did say that publication of the same material, if learned from other sources, could not be restrained.

Many states, including Florida, have a variety of laws that prohibit publication of certain types of information from judicial proceedings. However, it is apparent from several U.S. Supreme Court decisions that such laws have little effect if the media use legal means to obtain the information. In *Smith* v. *Daily Mail Publishing Co.,* a Charleston, South Carolina, newspaper learned from witnesses and police the name of a 14-year-old boy who shot and killed a schoolmate.[27] State law prohibited the publication of the identity of juvenile offenders. The Court ruled that when prohibited information comes from "routine newspaper reporting techniques," the state cannot punish the truthful publication of lawfully obtained information.

In *Landmark Communications* v. *Virginia,* the newspaper published a story identifying a judge against whom a complaint had been brought before the state judicial review commission.[28] According to a Virginia law, which is similar to one in Florida, the publication of the fact that a complaint has been filed or publication of the complaint's contents is prohibited. The newspaper was found in contempt and fined $500. Although the Supreme Court was sympathetic to the need to protect the reputation of judges and the judicial system, to protect complainants, and to prevent publication of groundless charges, the Court did not feel there were compelling enough reasons to punish the truthful

27. 443 U.S. 97 (1979).
28. 435 U.S. 829 (1978).

publication of information about a public official. A state legislature cannot declare that every such publication is a clear and present danger to the judicial system. Instead, a court must decide, case by case, whether there is a compelling need to prohibit such publication.

A federal district court in Florida used the *Landmark* ruling to invalidate a Florida Bar Rule that allowed grievances brought before the Bar to be confidential.[29] A client filed a complaint with the Bar against his former lawyer, charging deceit and fraud. The charges were found to be true, and the attorney received a private reprimand. The client was under penalty of contempt not to reveal any information about the complaint, the findings, or the punishment. The confidentiality was forever, according to the rule. However, the district court held that the rule was unconstitutional because it suppressed truthful information without a compelling need. The Bar's interests—protecting complainants, protecting lawyers from frivolous complaints, and protecting the integrity of the Bar—could be dealt with by less drastic means. Suppression of truthful information, said the federal court, will not enhance or protect the integrity of lawyers or the Bar, and secrecy certainly does not foster confidence in the profession. The court suggested that laws against perjury and filing false reports were a less drastic means of dealing with false or frivolous complaints.

Florida has several laws prohibiting publication of information resulting from judicial proceedings. Some of those closed records include adjudicatory hearings for dependency involving unwed mothers, custody, sexual abuse, or permanent custody. Also, records of all adoption proceedings and presentencing investigation reports are closed.

In *Oklahoma Publishing Co.* v. *District Court,* a judge opened the trial of a juvenile but ordered the media not to publish information they learned.[30] The U.S. Supreme Court ruled that if a trial

29. Doe v. Florida Supreme Court, 17 Med. L. Rep. 1405 (S.D. Fla. 1990).

30. 430 U.S. 308 (1977).

is public, so is the information. If the judge did not want information published, he should have closed those portions of the trial where sensitive information was revealed.

A case involving the *St. Petersburg Times* serves as a warning to reporters to consult their lawyers before agreeing to any conditions a judge might place on their presence in the courtroom. In *Mayer* v. *Florida,* a judge, unsure of his discretion to close a child custody hearing, allowed a reporter to stay in the hearing as long as she agreed not to publish information learned at the hearing if the judge subsequently decided the case should have been closed.[31] At noon, the judge determined that the hearing should have been closed and he informed the reporter's editor. Although the editor told the reporter not to publish the story and the judge told her twice that the information was restricted, she managed to get the story into the next day's edition. The reporter was found in contempt, fined $200, and given a ten-day suspended jail sentence. The contempt conviction was affirmed on appeal. The district court of appeal stated that the reporter agreed to the original conditions and then deliberately and contemptuously violated orders not to print. Since Florida law allowed the hearing to be closed, the information was not public.[32]

Press Remedies

Gag orders are less common today than they were in the 1960s and early 1970s; however, it is not improbable that a circuit court judge may attempt to issue such an order to freeze information immediately. For that reason, it is important to understand the legal procedures that protect against such orders.

If a reporter is in a courtroom when a judge issues a verbal or written order restricting publication of information, or if the reporter receives a copy of the order before the court is in session, the reporter should move immediately for a hearing on the order.

31. 15 Media L. Rep. 2039 (Fla. Dist. Ct. App. 1988).

32. FLA. STAT. ANN § 63.022 (1988); statute held valid in *In re* Adoption of H.Y.T., 458 So. 2d 1127 (Fla. 1984).

If there is time, the reporter should call the media's lawyer to appear and make the motion. Many Florida media have made available to their reporters wallet cards that carry the words of such a motion. Reporters are instructed to deliver the motion to the judge or to stand up in court and be noticed by the judge and then to read from the card. Below is a suggested motion for Florida reporters covering trials in this state:

> Your Honor, my name is ______. I am a working journalist representing ______. As regards this court's order(s) not to publish (broadcast) certain information, I wish to move that this court convene a hearing without delay in order that my newspaper (station) may challenge this court's order(s). I request that any further proceedings in this case be postponed until such time as I can contact our organization's lawyer, who can appear on our behalf to challenge the order. According to the state supreme court, it is the court's duty to convene a hearing and to hear arguments for and against any motion to invalidate such an order.

Once this motion is made, the judge should set a hearing date and time at which the media's lawyers should appear to address all the legal arguments for invalidating the order. If the judge refuses to hold such a hearing or if the judge continues to uphold his order after such a hearing, the media may seek a stay of the order and a review from the district court of appeal.

In 1978, the Florida Supreme Court passed a rule that permits "quick" appeals from court orders that impinge on the freedom of the press.[33] The rule allows the media, once an order is issued, to appeal the order's constitutionality and to seek a stay of the proceedings pending a review.

An example of such a process is found in *Sarasota Herald-Tribune* v. *J.T.J.*[34] In that case, a juvenile shot and killed his

33. Fla. R. App. P. § 9.100(d) (1985).

34. 13 Media L. Rep. 2039 (Fla. Dist. Ct. App. 1987).

brother. The case received considerable publicity, and the name of the juvenile and the victim were published in all the local media. Immediately prior to the defendant's adjudicatory hearing, the judge issued an oral order prohibiting the photographing of the defendant and the publication of the names of parties in the case. There was no notice of the order, nor was there a hearing at which the media could present argument. The district court of appeal quashed the order because it was issued without proper notice and hearing.

This appeals process may be carried to the state supreme court and, if necessary, to the U.S. Supreme Court. If time is of the essence and the media feel a resolution is necessary immediately, it is possible to petition a member of the U.S. Supreme Court responsible for the Eleventh Circuit Court of Appeal to stay the order pending a full review by the Court.

When an application for the stay of an order is made to a single U.S. Supreme Court justice, that justice may stay the enforcement only if the following four elements are present: (1) irreparable harm will occur if the stay is not granted; (2) reasonable probability exists that four justices will find the issue sufficiently substantial to grant certiorari; (3) a fair prospect exists that the majority of the Court will reverse the decision of the lower court; and (4) "balance of equities" to parties and the public favors issuance of the stay.

Although a case may be moot by the time the appeals process has begun, the court may still hear arguments and reach a decision. It is a rule of American courts that a case must be a concrete controversy and "ripe" for adjudication. There are exceptions to the mootness doctrine because some cases and controversies simply do not have a long enough life span to still be "ripe" by the time all appeals have been pursued. For example, by the time the U.S. Supreme Court heard the *Nebraska* case, Simants had been found guilty. The Court has noted that many cases by their very nature evade review as actual controversies; however, the situations are capable of repetition. Under such circumstances, appeals courts may still hand down decisions, although these resemble advisory opinions rather than actual holdings. From a legal standpoint, the rule allowing such review of a moot case is obviously a good one, but it does the reporter who is trying to give his readers information about an ongoing trial little good if the orders remain in effect for the duration of the trial.

Exclusionary Orders—Closing the Courtrooms

With the virtual demise of restrictive orders in 1976, judges and attorneys were forced to be more resourceful in finding ways to safeguard defendants' rights without the inconvenience associated with traditional safeguards such as continuance, change of venue, or sequestration. This resourcefulness turned up a little-used tactic that most courts had dismissed long ago as being contrary to common law: the closing of the courtroom to the public and press. The judge, knowing he could not prohibit publication of information, found that restricting the ability of the media to gather that information was just as effective. Exclusionary orders, orders to exclude the press from the courtroom, were issued not only for the trial itself but also for pretrial and posttrial hearings in criminal and civil cases.

After criminal charges are brought, either by way of a grand jury indictment or an information, the defendant may begin a trek through a labyrinth of pretrial hearings. These hearings may be held on motion of defense or prosecution before or after the preliminary hearings for probable cause. Typical pretrial hearings include suppression hearings, in which the admissibility of evidence or confessions is determined; fitness and competency hearings, where the fitness of the defendant to stand trial is examined; and jurisdictional hearings, which determine a court's jurisdiction over the offense. An addition to these common pretrial hearings is the preliminary hearing (probable cause hearing), at which the judge reviews the facts, listens to testimony, acts on motions, and determines whether there is reasonable and probable cause to bind the defendant over for trial. The most common posttrial hearing is a sentencing hearing.

It is well understood that a judge has the discretion to control his courtroom in order to maintain order and decorum. Exclusionary orders have been found valid and necessary to preserve the order of the courtroom, to protect the identity of undercover agents or sources, to protect minors, and to preserve the confidentiality of vital investigative material. However, when none of these extraordinary circumstances exist, courts had adopted the common law rule of open proceedings even in civil trials.

Beginning in 1977, closure orders became more common. Some of these orders were sustained on appeal and others rescinded, creating uncertainty among state and federal jurisdictions about the status of such orders.

Early closure cases in Florida involved civil litigation and produced contradictions about a judge's prerogative to close courts and about the remedies available to challenge such orders. Closure is common in civil trials. In fact, Florida statutes either allow or require closure in certain sensitive proceedings such as paternity suits and adoption or juvenile hearings. Otherwise, parties in litigation must seek an administrative order from a judge to close the courtroom.

Augustin Collazo was shot by a Miami policeman during a burglary investigation and was paralyzed.[35] He filed a civil suit against the city, but before final settlement, all parties agreed that the terms would not be made public. The terms were decided in closed proceedings and the settlement records were sealed. The *Miami Herald* filed a petition for reconsideration of the order, but the petition was denied. The district court of appeal reversed the closure and sealing orders, stating that no justification was given except a preference for closure and an unsupported fear that there would be adverse effects on other pending litigation. The court ruled that a trial, in the absence of an immediate threat to the administration of justice, is a public event that "takes place on public property and over which the judiciary possesses no special editorial, censorial, or suppression powers."

35. Miami Herald Publishing Co. v. Collazo, 329 So. 2d 333 (Fla. Dist. Ct. App. 1976).

Divorce proceedings in Florida are not required to be closed, but they have been closed whenever both parties agreed. The press was excluded from the divorce proceedings of comedian Jackie Gleason at the request of both parties.[36] Also, the transcripts of the proceeding were ordered sealed. A news reporter sought and was granted a writ of prohibition from the district court of appeal. The court explained that the power to exclude does exist, particularly where an open trial would inhibit testimony necessary to a fair trial, where testimony would be offensive to young persons, or where there is a question of the safety of witnesses. However, in civil cases, closure can be granted only "for the most cogent of reasons." The court found no such reasons in the Gleason proceeding. It was not enough to want a proceeding held away from prying eyes: "[T]he right to one's privacy is secondary to public access especially when public figures are of public interest. . . . Access to the courthouse is and should be through the front door and not the rear door." The court also found the writ of prohibition a proper remedy for press challenges.

That decision was overturned two years later by the Florida Supreme Court in *English* v. *McCrary* because the writ of prohibition was held not to be the proper remedy.[37] In that case, a reporter for the *Tallahassee Democrat* was barred from the divorce hearing of a state attorney. The newspaper then sought a writ of prohibition from the district court of appeal, which was denied.[38] A writ of prohibition theoretically is used only to prohibit or prevent a court from exceeding its jurisdiction, not to correct a lower court's action. In this case, the reporter had already been barred and the dissolution proceedings were finished. The district court of appeal said that since the circuit court judge had jurisdiction in the divorce proceeding, he also had the discretion to determine whether the hearing should be closed. The

36. State *ex rel* Gore Newspaper Co. v. Tyson, 313 So. 2d 777 (Fla. Dist. Ct. App. 1975).

37. 348 So. 2d 293 (Fla. 1977).

38. 328 So. 2d 257 (Fla. Dist. Ct. App. 1977).

Florida Supreme Court agreed, specifically recognizing a trial judge's discretion to close or restrict access in civil proceedings no matter who was involved.[39] The court also ruled that where prohibited proceedings have been completed, as they were in this case, a writ of prohibition may not be used to establish precedent for future cases. Hence, the proceeding must be dismissed where the issue has become moot. The court in *English* was in effect leaving the media without a legal remedy once closure had been carried out despite the Florida Constitution's prohibition against dismissing any case just because improper remedy was sought.

While *English* was going through the Florida courts, the U.S. Supreme Court held that any time a state attempted to restrain full enjoyment of the First Amendment, process must be available for immediate review or for a stay pending review.[40] This opinion plus the *English* decision made it imperative that the Florida judiciary devise a process for quick review of cases that touched upon First Amendment rights. In October 1977, the Florida Supreme Court adopted a revision of the Florida Rules of Appellate Procedures that was to take effect March 1, 1978. Two months later, on reconsideration of the rules, the Florida court agreed to a last-minute addition—Rule 9.100(d)—to meet the appellate aspects of the problem confronted in *English*.[41]

The rule allows the media to petition for the review of any order excluding them from any proceeding, any part of a proceeding, or from any access to judicial records, as long as the proceedings or records are not confidential by law. The petition for review may be filed as soon as an order has been issued. The appeals court must immediately consider the petition and determine whether a stay of the proceedings in the lower court is appropriate. The rule also allows oral arguments on the petition to review the restrictive order.

By 1978, closure orders were still a new idea in Florida courts,

39. 348 So. 2d 293.

40. National Socialist Party v. Skokie, 432 U.S. 43 (1977).

41. *In re* Proposed Florida Appellate Rules, case 50,409 (1977); FLA. R. APP. § 9.100(d) (1985).

and judges had no substantive or procedural guidelines to rely on in order to avoid making arbitrary decisions. Late in 1978, a district court of appeal judge in Miami proposed that the three-pronged guidelines used in *Nebraska* for determining the constitutionality of gag orders be used for determining the validity of closure orders as well. That case, *Miami Herald Publishing Co.* v. *State,* involved international jewel thief Peter Salerno, who was convicted of burglary and grand larceny.[42] Almost a year after the conviction, the judge closed the posttrial proceedings and sealed the transcript of the sentencing hearing. No hearing on the closure order was held; a hearing on the sealing order was held after the fact. The press was invited back into the courtroom to hear the sentence pronounced. The district court of appeal looked at both *Nebraska* and the Florida Supreme Court's decision on gag orders in *McIntosh* and ruled that although those cases did not involve access to courtrooms, "the distinction is one of form rather than substance, inasmuch as the end result in both cases is a withholding of the publication of a court proceeding." The court ruled that closure must be preceded by a hearing, and the judge must show that no less-restrictive alternatives are available and that closure is the only way to guarantee a fair trial.

In a series of cases beginning in 1978, the U.S. Supreme Court dealt with the constitutional status of exclusionary orders. The first case was in 1979. *Gannett* v. *DePasquale* held that the Sixth Amendment's guarantee of a public trial was a right that belonged solely to the defendant and not to the public.[43] *Gannett* involved closing a pretrial suppression hearing in which lawyers argued the admissibility of certain evidence in a murder trial. The Court's opinion, however, spoke only of "criminal trials" without making any distinction between actual jury trials and other types of pretrial and posttrial hearings. Also, the Court based its decision solely upon its interpretation of the Sixth Amendment, purposefully shunning any First Amendment ar-

42. 363 So. 2d 603 (Fla. Dist. Ct. App. 1978).
43. 443 U.S. 368 (1979).

guments. The Sixth Amendment, said the Court, required only that a judge find a "reasonable probability of prejudice" before closing a courtroom. The Court rejected the presumption that the three-pronged *Nebraska* guidelines applied to closure, explaining that the guidelines were to prevent prior restraints on information already held by the media. Since closing a courtroom does not prevent publication, it is not a prior restraint, reasoned the Court. This reasoning is contrary to that used by the Florida court of appeal in *Miami Herald* v. *State,* which argued that there was no difference between restricting access to information and restricting publication of material the media already has.

A year later, in *Richmond Newspapers* v. *Virginia,* the Court held that jury trials are required by the Constitution to be open but that no such requirement needs to be made of other types of hearings.[44] The decision overturned a Virginia court ruling that permitted a two-day murder trial to be closed. The opinion stated that "[a] presumption of openness inheres in the very nature of the criminal trial under our system of justice." After reviewing the history of open courts, Chief Justice Warren Burger held that the "explicit, guaranteed rights to speak and to publish concerning what takes place at a trial would lose much meaning if access to observe the trial could . . . be foreclosed arbitrarily."

The Court found that although public attendance at criminal trials was guaranteed, such a right was not absolute. A court could be closed if a judge found an "overriding interest" in closure. The opinion did not specify how overriding interest would be determined but did note that various alternatives are available to satisfy the demands of fairness.

The Court did not overturn its *Gannett* decision, explaining that pretrial hearings remain closed at the discretion of the judge. The court also did not require openness in civil proceedings, although Burger's opinion noted that openness is a tradition in civil as well as criminal cases.

During the year between *Gannett* and *Richmond Newspapers,*

44. 448 U.S. 555 (1980).

much confusion developed over just what types of proceedings were covered and what effect *Gannett* would have on existing state precedents regarding pretrial hearings. In 1982, the Florida Supreme Court attempted to resolve some of the issues in *Miami Herald Publishing Co.* v. *Lewis,* which involved the trial of a 14-year-old boy charged with rape and murder.[45] After a motion for change of venue was denied, the defendant's attorney moved to close a suppression hearing at which the admissibility of a confession was to be determined. The media were notified of the motion and the judge held a hearing after which he ordered the suppression hearing closed. After the suppression hearing, the judge also ordered the records of the hearing sealed until the trial began. A contingent of Florida media appealed the orders, stating that at the hearing to determine closure, the judge was given no evidence to support his decision for closure.

The Florida Supreme Court established a modified set of guidelines that, it said, "provide the best balance between the needs for open government and public access . . . and the paramount right of a defendant to a fair trial before an impartial jury." The *Lewis* three-part test provided as follows: (1) closure is necessary to prevent a serious and imminent threat to the administration of justice; (2) no alternatives are available, other than change of venue, that would protect the defendant's rights; and (3) there is substantial probability that closure would be effective in protecting the accused without being more restrictive than necessary to accomplish the purpose.

The court told judges to begin any hearing on a motion for closure with the assumption of openness since the court is the only place the public has to learn about police conduct. The decision explained that the factors to be considered in determining serious and imminent threat are the extent of the hostile publicity, the probability that issues at pretrial will further aggravate adverse publicity, and whether traditional safeguards can satisfactorily insulate the jury. As for the use of alternative means of

45. Miami Herald Publishing Co. v. Lewis, 426 So. 2d 2281 (Fla. 1982).

preventing prejudice, the court said that change of venue does not have to be considered as an alternative, and warned judges not to resort to alternatives that would "unduly burden" expeditious disposition of the case.

The *Lewis* decision was applied to a pretrial hearing where the admissibility of similar fact evidence was challenged. In *Florida* v. *Jarrell,* the defendant was charged with sexual battery of two teen-agers.[46] The state served notice that it intended to introduce evidence of similar crimes by the defendant against other victims. A hearing was held to determine whether a pretrial hearing on the admissibility of the evidence should be closed. Using the *Lewis* factors, the judge noted that there had hardly been any pretrial publicity in the case and there was no evidence that release of the information would result in any notoriety. Because the jury was to be selected from Duval County, less-restrictive alternatives such as individual voir dire, change of venire, and additional peremptory challenges would adequately protect the defendant. The judge determined that there was no perceived harm to the defendant by keeping the hearing open.

In 1986, the U.S. Supreme Court adopted the "substantial probability of prejudice" test for dealing with pretrials, effectively overturning the earlier *Gannett* decision. In *Press Enterprises* v. *Superior Court (II),* the Court ruled that "reasonable alternatives to closure" of pretrials must be sought, and any pretrial closure must be narrowly tailored.[47]

The U.S. Supreme Court also heard a series of cases in the 1980s involving jury trials that eventually led to the adoption of guidelines similar to those already adopted by Florida in *Lewis.* In *Globe Newspapers* v. *Superior Court,* a judge closed the trial of a rapist whose victim was a minor.[48] According to Massachusetts law, any trial involving a victim who is a minor can be closed. The Court held that the state's interest in protecting the privacy of the victim was not sufficient to require closure of the entire

46. 11 Media L. Rep. 2012 (Fla. Cir. Ct. 1985).
47. 478 U.S. 1 (1986).
48. 457 U.S. 596 (1982).

trial. Instead, any closure should be narrowly tailored only to those parts of the trial where the victim is on the stand.

The same "narrowly tailored" closure was required in *Press Enterprises* v. *Superior Court (I),* where the judge had closed the entire voir dire proceeding.[49] The Court ruled that jury selection must be open unless there is (1) an overriding interest that closure is essential to a fair trial, (2) orders are no broader than necessary to protect interests, (3) reasonable alternatives are considered, and (4) reasons are specific and explained fully by the court.

In *Globe, Press Enterprises,* and *Waller* v. *Georgia,*[50] the Court also established procedural safeguards to protect reporters' First Amendment rights. Any closure motion must be followed by a notice to the media and by a hearing at which the media can present arguments against closure. If the judge grants the closure motion, the reasons must be specific and written in order for there to be a reviewable record when the order is appealed.

Press Remedies

As stated earlier when discussing gag orders, it is imperative that reports covering the courts know what due process rights they have when they encounter any administrative order from a court.

If a closure order is moved when the media are not present, Florida precedent requires that reasonable notice must be given the media. If such is the case, a written copy of the order should be picked up at the courthouse. If there is enough time to notify a lawyer, then do so.

If a motion for closure is made in the presence of a reporter, that reporter should object immediately with a statement similar to that used in gag order cases. The objection is really a motion for a hearing at which the media's lawyer will do the actual arguing. A typical statement might read:

49. 464 U.S. 501 (1984).
50. 467 U.S. 39 (1984).

> Your Honor, my name is ______. I am a working journalist representing ______. I challenge the motion to close this hearing. I move that a hearing be held on the motion at which time a lawyer representing my newspaper (station) will be present to make the proper legal arguments. The closing of a trial is a clear violation of the First Amendment rights of the public and the press. Court precedent in this state, particularly *Miami Herald* v. *Lewis,* established that before such a motion can be granted, reasonable notice and a full hearing must be granted to those who oppose it. I move that such a hearing be held to determine the constitutionality of this order.

If a reporter arrives when a closed hearing is already in session, a written objection similar to the above but with an additional request for access and for a stay of the proceedings should be sent to the judge. A police officer or any court employee should give the written objection to the judge. The written objection should also be filed with the court clerk under the case being tried.

If the judge refuses to grant the motion for a hearing, the reporter should not leave the courtroom until ordered to do so. It is not advisable to leave voluntarily, nor is it advisable to refuse to leave when ordered.

Whether a hearing is granted or not, the media should proceed to appeal the order and seek a stay of the order under Appellate Rule 9.100(d). If the appeal should fail to stay the circuit court's order, the appeals process may continue through the court system to the Florida Supreme Court and to the U.S. Supreme Court, time and resources allowing.

Protective Orders—Sealing Court Records

The *Lewis* case had a significant impact on the ability of the media to cover preliminary hearings and trials in Florida. In fact, since that decision in 1982 there have been very few cases involving access to courtrooms. The same cannot be said, however, of access to discovery materials.

Every civil and criminal case is accompanied by a discovery process whereby attorneys seek to learn as much as possible about evidence and witnesses before the trial. One major tool of discovery is the taking of depositions. According to the Florida Rules of Civil and Criminal Procedures, sworn depositions are sealed until filed with the court in which the action is pending. Once the clerk receives the deposition, it is opened and made part of the public record, available to anyone for a reasonable charge. This is the normal procedure unless a protective order has been entered sealing certain records "for good cause."[51] A motion for a protective order is not entered solely to prevent pretrial publication of information that will eventually be entered into court records. Like evidence, depositions may contain information that is inadmissible. A deposition does not automatically become evidence; it must first be ruled admissible by the court. In a criminal trial, depositions are limited in their actual use to impeaching the testimony of the deponent when being questioned as a witness in the courtroom or introducing testimony when a witness cannot be present at the trial.[52] Therefore, much of what is contained in depositions will not be used in the trial.

Because so much information is revealed in depositions, reporters see them as a valuable source while covering cases. In numerous cases before 1984, many Florida judges ruled that the taking of depositions constituted a pretrial judicial proceeding and therefore the closure or the sealing of deposition transcripts could only be accomplished if there was a proven compelling need.[53] However, in 1984, the U.S. Supreme Court held in *Seattle Times* v. *Rhinehart* that "pre-trial depositions and interrogatories are not public components of a civil trial."[54] Recognizing

51. Fla. R. Crim. P. § 3.220 (1989); Fla. R. Civ. P. § 1.280 (1989).

52. *Id.* § 1.330 (1981).

53. *See, e.g.,* News-Press Publishing Co. v. State, 345 So. 2d 865 (Fla. Dist. Ct. App. 1977); Bundy v. State, 455 So. 2d 378 (Fla. 1984); Sentinel Star Co. v. Booth, 372 So. 2d 100 (Fla. Dist. Ct. App. 1979); Cazares v. Church of Scientology, 6 Media L. Rep. 2109 (Fla. Cir. Ct. 1980).

54. 467 U.S. 20, 34 (1984).

the conflict between Florida's judicial history in such cases and the high court's ruling, the Florida Supreme Court agreed to review the question of access to depositions.

In *Palm Beach Newspapers* v. *Burk,* the court upheld a lower court judge who had denied the press the right to attend pretrial discovery depositions or to have copies of depositions that had not been transcribed or filed with the court.[55] Basing its decision on *Seattle Times,* the court stated that discovery depositions are not judicial proceedings. There is no judge present, nor are there any rulings or adjudications made at depositions. Consequently, liberal discovery produces information that may be irrelevant, inadmissible, and prejudicial, and which, if publicly released, could also be damaging to a person's privacy. The process, explained the court, must be free of any chilling influences in order for a lawyer to explore all matters that may be of use to the case. "Providing access to unfiled depositions . . . would not only present serious constitutional concerns, . . . it would also undermine effective advocacy. . . ."

Discovery information becomes part of the public record only after it has been given to the accused and admitted into the trial record. Even after discovery information becomes part of the public record, access is not always guaranteed if a judge finds that publication of the material will jeopardize the defendant's right to a fair trial.

In *Florida Freedom Newspapers* v. *McCrary,* a newspaper reported that prisoners in the county jail were being mistreated.[56] Eventually, two jailers were charged with criminal mistreatment of prisoners. The two defendants successfully prevented public access to pretrial discovery information that was given to the defendants by the state attorney's office. The information would be made public only after a jury was selected and sequestered.

Under Florida's Rules of Criminal Procedure, a prosecutor is required to furnish to the accused the identity of persons with

55. 504 So. 2d 378 (Fla. 1987).
56. 520 So. 2d 32 (Fla. 1988).

relevant information as well as any statement made by those persons. And according to Florida's Public Records Law, such information becomes public record when it is given to the accused.[57] However, the court in *McCrary* argued that it is the job of a judge to balance the right of public access against the defendant's right to a fair trial. In this case the trial court, using the *Lewis* guidelines, found that there had been prior prejudicial publicity, that public disclosure would further aggravate the prejudicial publicity, and that the only measure available to the court was to cut off further prejudicial publicity until a jury could be selected. The Florida Supreme Court upheld the use of *Lewis* in determining whether public access to judicial public records should be allowed.

Sometimes the discovery material being sought is evidence such as photographs or videotapes. In a Jacksonville child-selling case, a judge denied a local television station access to a videotape.[58] The tape had been released to the defendants and thus was considered public record. However, a Florida circuit court judge ruled that if the tape were shown, the effect on the prospective jurors would be so great that change of venue would be required. However, according to *Lewis,* the accused cannot be forced to select a change of venue as the only alternative to access to a tape. The media would have to wait until the tape was introduced in court.

Press Remedies

Usually a reporter will encounter the protective order when asking the clerk for the records in a particular case. If the clerk denies access based on a judge's order, then a written request for access should be made to the judge. The reporter should state the materials he wishes to inspect but should not offer any rea-

57. FLA. STAT. ANN. § 119.011(3)(c) 5 (1988); FLA. R. CRIM. P. § 3.220 (1989).

58. Florida *ex rel.* Harte-Hanks v. Austin, 9 Media L. Rep. 1170 (Fla. Cir. Ct. 1983).

sons for wanting to see the documents. If the request is denied, then the reporter should follow the same appeals procedures suggested for challenging closure orders.

Gagging Participants

In *Sheppard* v. *Maxwell,* the Supreme Court held that proper trial management could include restricting trial participants, court officers, and jurors from talking about the case. Until recently, there had been little reason to challenge this gagging of participants; but, with an increasing number of courtrooms and court records being closed, the only alternative sources of information for the reporter are often the participants in the trial. In *Sentinel Star* v. *Edwards,* the court gagged all participants in a hearing called to determine whether the jury had acted illegally.[59] Since the only purpose of the gag was to protect the privacy of jury deliberations, and the persons interviewed during the hearing were not jurors, the gag was lifted.

In *McCrary*, the Florida Supreme Court upheld not only the denial of media access to pretrial discovery information but also the gagging of attorneys and police.[60] The court noted that prohibiting comment is an acceptable alternative to prior restraint, and such a prohibition did not prevent the media from talking to other parties in the case.

Cameras in the Courtroom

In 1935, the ABA adopted Canon 35 of the Canons of Judicial Ethics, prohibiting photography and radio broadcasting in a courtroom. In 1952, Canon 35 was amended to prohibit television cameras as well. Only two states, Colorado and Texas, did not adopt the canon as part of their judiciary's rules. When the Florida Supreme Court, in April 1979, amended Canon 3A(7) of

59. 387 So. 2d 367 (Fla. Dist. Ct. App. 1980).
60. 520 So. 2d 32.

the Code of Judicial Conduct to authorize camera coverage of courts on a permanent basis, this state's judiciary was making an affirmative statement about openness in the judicial system. It was also paving the way for the U.S. Supreme Court to rule that the presence of cameras in a courtroom is not unconstitutional.

The question of whether cameras in the courtroom present a clear and present danger to the administration of justice was first heard by the U.S. Supreme Court in *Estes* v. *Texas* in 1965.[61] The trial of Billie Sol Estes received national attention because of the widespread political tie-ins that Estes had. Estes was charged with inducing farmers to buy nonexistent fertilizer tanks and to sign over to him the mortgage on the property. During the pretrial hearing, 12 cameras squeezed into a small courtroom in Tyler, Texas. Cables and wires were run across the aisles, and microphones were placed to pick up every noise in the courtroom. When it was obvious that the distraction of the bright lights and bulky cameras would be unavoidable, the judge ordered a partition built in the back of the room. Holes were cut out of the partition through which the camera lenses could protrude. Estes appealed his conviction on the ground that the presence of the television cameras had created an atmosphere in which a fair trial was impossible. The Court agreed: "Television in its present state and by its very nature reaches into a variety of areas in which it may cause prejudice to an accused." After enumerating various ways television could prejudice the jury, witnesses, lawyers, judges, and defendants, the Court reversed Estes's conviction. The decision did not say the presence of cameras would always be a denial of a fair trial, noting that the "ever-advancing techniques of public communications and the adjustment of the public to its presence may bring about a change in the effect of telecasting upon the fairness of criminal trials."

By the early 1970s, the "ever-advancing techniques" of television had reached the stage where cameras were less intrusive because they were smaller, noiseless, and required no special light-

61. 381 U.S. 532 (1965).

ing or extensive electrical hookups. In 1972, the ABA revised Canon 35 to take into account these new advances. The new Canon 3A(7), while still prohibiting television cameras in the courtroom, acknowledged that television was a viable tool that the court system should not overlook. It suggested that television could be used to make a permanent record of a trial, to provide educational tapes for law classes, and to broadcast closed-circuit to adjoining rooms for the press, spectators, or even a defendant.

In 1976, Alabama and Washington were the first states to amend their judicial rules to allow broadcasting with the consent of both parties. These two states were followed by others, including Florida, which instituted one-year experiments to determine the feasibility of cameras in the courtroom.

Florida's one-year experiment with cameras was the most widely publicized experiment in the country, for it was during the experimental phase that the murder trial of 15-year-old Ronny Zamora was televised from a Miami courtroom. Florida's emergence into the era of cameras in the courtroom began in January 1975, when television stations belonging to the Post-Newsweek chain filed a petition with the Florida Supreme Court either to adopt a substitute for Canon 3A(7) or to reexamine the canon for purposes of making the court's own revision.[62] The court granted the latter portion of the petition in May and began to review information on the subject, including a review of tapes made in Washington where that state was in the middle of its experiment. A year later, the court agreed to conduct its own limited experiment. It chose to televise one civil and one criminal trial in the Second Circuit in Tallahassee if it could find parties who would agree. After failing to get consent from persons on trial in that circuit, the court expanded the experiment to the Fourth, Eighth, and Ninth Circuits.[63] Still, consent was impossible to obtain and the initial experiment was termed a failure. In April 1977, the court, by interlocutory decree, mandated a

62. *In re* Petition of Post-Newsweek Stations, 327 So. 2d I (Fla. 1976).

63. *In re* Petition of Post-Newsweek Stations, 337 So. 2d 804 (Fla. 1976).

one-year experiment beginning July 1, 1977, when the electronic media would be permitted to cover all court sessions without participant permission pursuant to rules of conduct and technology set out by the court.[64] By June 30, 1978, when the experiment ended, over 2,750 persons had been involved in trials covered by television cameras.

To determine whether cameras would become a permanent fixture in Florida's courtrooms, the state supreme court conducted a survey to determine what effects, if any, cameras had on various participants. All participants except the actual litigants were surveyed. Responses to the survey indicated that cameras did not create any undue stress, embarrassment, distraction, nervousness, lack of concentration, or flamboyance. The court concluded that "on balance there is more to be gained than lost by permitting electronic media coverage of judicial proceedings." Canon 3A(7) was amended to permit permanent camera access to Florida courtrooms effective May 1, 1979.[65]

The amended canon now reads:

> Subject at all times to the authority of the presiding judge to (i) control the conduct of proceedings before the court, (ii) ensure decorum and prevent distractions, and (iii) ensure the fair administration of justice in the pending cause, electronic media and still photography coverage of public judicial proceedings in the appellate and trial courts of this state shall be allowed in accordance with standards of conduct and technology promulgated by the Supreme Court of Florida.

During the one-year experiment, several challenges were made to the constitutionality of the experiment and to the presence of cameras. The first challenge came in the first month of the ex-

64. *In re* Petition of Post-Newsweek Stations, 347 So. 2d 402 (Fla. 1977); FLA. R. CRIM. P. Experimental Rules § 3.110 (1977), *repealed by In re* Petition of Post-Newsweek Stations, 370 So. 2d 764 (Fla. 1979).

65. *In re* Petition of Post-Newsweek Stations, 370 So. 2d 764.

periment. Jules Briklod sought a temporary injunction in federal district court to stop the use of television and still cameras in the first of several conspiracy and grand larceny trials.[66] The federal court agreed to hold an emergency hearing on the motion for a temporary injunction. Normally, a defendant must exhaust all of his state remedies before appealing to a federal district court. The federal court agreed to review the case because there was some question whether the cameras rule was "patently unconstitutional," one acceptable reason for going directly to a federal court before going through all the state courts. The federal court found that while the U.S. Supreme Court opinion in *Estes* expressly prohibited television cameras, the majority of the justices did not find cameras unconstitutional in all cases. The court denied the injunctive relief, saying that the experiment was not "patently and flagrantly unconstitutional."

The second challenge during the experiment took the question of the constitutionality of cameras in the courtroom all the way to the U.S. Supreme Court, where, in January 1981, the Court ruled that the presence of cameras in the courtroom did not per se create a threat to a fair trial.[67] This case involved the convictions of two former Miami policemen. The policemen, Noel Chandler and Robert Granger, were charged and convicted on four counts—burglary, grand larceny, possession of burglary tools, and conspiracy to commit a felony. Their trial began in December 1977, halfway through the year-long camera experiment. Before and during the trial, defendants filed various motions to exclude the cameras and entered several challenges to the constitutionality of the amended canon. They appealed their convictions based on several errors by the trial court, including the judge's refusal to prohibit the cameras. The district court of appeal ruled that there was no error in allowing the cameras to remain in the courtroom during the trial. The defendants were unable to bring evidence that the cameras caused any difficulty

66. Briklod v. Rivkin, 2 Media L. Rep. 2258 (S.D. Fla. 1977).

67. Chandler v. Florida, 366 So. 2d 64 (Fla. Dist. Ct. App. 1978), *petition for rev. denied,* 376 So. 2d 1157 (Fla. 1979), *aff'd,* 449 U.S. 560 (1981).

in the preparation or presentation of the case, nor that the cameras deprived them of an impartial jury. The Florida Supreme Court denied the petition for appeal and the U.S. Supreme Court granted certiorari. In an 8–0 opinion, the court ruled that cameras may be allowed into a courtroom as long as they are carefully monitored so as not to produce prejudice against the defendant. The decision was not based upon a constitutional right of access by the media but upon the Sixth Amendment and the Florida Supreme Court's authority to supervise its court system. Also, the decision was not to be interpreted as a mandate requiring access, only as an affirmation that under carefully controlled situations, cameras may be allowed. The Court did not issue guidelines to help a judge determine when camera coverage might create a clear and present danger to the administration of justice.

It was unclear during the experimental phase just what discretion a judge had over the cameras since the Florida rules mandated their presence. For example, the widow of a murder victim moved to prohibit cameras when she was to appear as a witness.[68] The trial judge overruled her claim to privacy. During the same trial, a prison inmate refused to testify for fear of reprisals from fellow inmates and was held in contempt. The judge apparently did not realize that discretion reposed in him to grant the objections by these two witnesses. In *Time Publishing Co.* v. *Hall,* the presiding judge in the trial of Wilfred Bannister considered but refrained from prohibiting electronic media coverage of the testimony of a sixteen-year-old rape victim.[69] However, the district court of appeal did hold that if such an order were entered, notice and hearing must be given the media.

Obviously, there are times when the electronic media can be prohibited from filming court proceedings. The Florida Supreme Court, in amending the canon, noted that cameras could be prohibited during child custody proceedings or when a witness is

68. State v. Herman, No. 77-1236 (15th Jud. Cir. 1977).

69. 357 So. 2d 736 (Fla. Dist. Ct. App. 1978).

under protection of anonymity or threatened with reprisal, if a witness is the victim of sexual battery, is a relative of the victim, or is a confidential informant. The Florida Supreme Court adopted the following standard for judges. "The presiding judge may exclude electronic media coverage of a particular participant only upon a finding that such coverage will have a substantial effect upon the particular individual which would be qualitatively different from the effect on members of the public in general and such effect will be qualitatively different from coverage by other types of media."

Determining the "qualitatively different effect" can be difficult. For example, in *Green* v. *Florida,* a lawyer appealed her conviction on two counts of embezzlement because she claimed that the television coverage of her trial had rendered her incompetent to assist with her defense.[70] Adelita Green had been under psychiatric care several months after being found mentally incompetent to stand trial. After psychiatric counseling, a second competency hearing was held at which she was found competent to stand trial. None of the testimony at this second hearing dealt with the effect television coverage might have on her "fragile mental condition." Before trial began, the defendant's lawyers filed a motion to exclude television. Arguments were heard, but again, no testimony was heard about the effect of television's presence. When Green's trial began and several times throughout, the defense repeatedly moved to exclude the cameras, and each motion was denied without hearing. The district court of appeal reversed and remanded for a new trial with another competency hearing. The court said that public exposure through a televised trial is almost certain to create a greater level of anxiety in a defendant than if the trial were not televised. This increased anxiety may render a mentally disturbed, but technically competent, defendant unable to consult with counsel or unable to

70. 377 So. 2d 193 (Fla. Dist. Ct. App. 1979), *aff'd,* 395 So. 2d 532 (Fla. 1981), *on remand,* 7 Media L. Rep. 1885 (Fla. Cir. Ct. 1981).

understand the proceedings. Two years later, an evidentiary hearing was held, and a circuit court judge found that camera coverage of Green's trial would deny her a fair trial.

The protection of witnesses for personal safety reasons was an issue in a case involving murder charges against a prison inmate.[71] A grand jury indicted Arthur Sekell for first-degree murder in the torching death of fellow inmate William Wright. The state filed a pretrial motion requesting that the court prohibit the filming of two state witnesses who were inmates at Lantana Correctional Institute. The state based its motion on the fear that television coverage would subject the witness to prison reprisals by inmates who were friends of Sekell's. The circuit judge held a hearing on the motion, at which time the state gave the judge sealed affidavits from the witnesses which said they would not testify, on pain of contempt, if television coverage were allowed. The media were not allowed to see the contents of the affidavits. Also, the state said it could produce a prison officer to testify about the possibility of danger and reprisals. The prison officer was not asked to testify. The circuit judge granted the motion, which also barred the sketching of the two witnesses. The names of the witnesses were not restricted.

The district court of appeal, on petition for review of the order, said that this situation might fall under the exceptions recognized by the Florida Supreme Court, and the refusal to testify on pain of contempt could well be a "qualitatively different effect." However, the court ruled that the trial judge's order was based only upon the subjective fears of the state and not upon objective facts. The court ordered the trial judge to hold a hearing at which time he must make the affidavits available to the media and must hear the testimony of the prison official. "To require less would result in an automatic exclusion of the media upon any witness simply by advising the court that he harbored some uncertainty about his safety should he be exposed to the media

71. Palm Beach Newspapers v. State, 378 So. 2d 862 (Fla. Dist. Ct. App. 1979), *aff'd,* 395 So. 2d 544 (Fla. 1981).

while testifying." This ruling was affirmed by the Florida Supreme Court, which warned that evidence of a "qualitatively different effect" must be open to the public.

After the trial of Ronny Zamora was televised, Zamora's codefendant in the slaying of an 84-year-old Miami woman moved to have charges dropped against him and his case discharged because of the publicity that had surrounded the Zamora trial.[72] He contended that the broadcast and rebroadcast of the Zamora trial created conditions under which a fair trial for him would be impossible. Darrell Agrella had pled nolo contendere to charges of murder, robbery, and burglary but argued that his case should be discharged because of the publicity that surrounded the televised trial. The circuit court denied the motion to discharge and the district court of appeal agreed. There was no evidence to prove prejudice, no jury had been selected, and there was as yet no trial. Agrella appealed all the way to the U.S. Supreme Court, which refused to review the case.

Grand Jury Coverage

State Grand Juries

Historically, grand jury proceedings have always been closed to the public and their reports closed until opened by order of a court. Closure of a grand jury proceeding has never been challenged as an abridgment of the First Amendment; however, the sealing of indictments and presentments and the gagging of witnesses have been challenged on several occasions.

The grand jury is an arm of the judiciary; its responsibility is to determine whether there is sufficient information and evidence to bring a person to trial. Grand juries in Florida range in size from 18 to 25 members, depending on the size of the county, and they are appointed for the six-month term of the court. Grand juries in Florida fulfill two major functions: (1) to bring

72. Agrella v. State, 372 So. 2d 487 (Fla. Dist. Ct. App. 1979), *cert. denied,* 450 U.S. 910 (1981).

indictments against those being accused of a capital offense and (2) to act as an investigative arm of the courts to study the performance of public offices and officers. In determining probable cause in a criminal action, the grand jury is charged with returning either a true bill (indictment) or a no bill. Indictments are sealed by law until the indicted person has been taken into custody.[73] In investigative sessions, the grand jury may issue an indictment, or it may return a report or presentment that criticizes but does not indict.

Florida law requires the confidentiality of all grand jury deliberations and of all votes of a grand jury. Until recently, testimony before a grand jury could not be disclosed outside the grand jury until and unless the testimony became part of a court proceeding. In *Butterworth* v. *Smith,* the U.S. Supreme Court held that the Florida law prohibiting witnesses from disclosing their own testimony violated the First Amendment's guarantee of freedom of speech.[74] In that case, a reporter who had testified before a grand jury wanted to write a story about the case. Had the story revealed information he had disclosed to the grand jury, he would have been subject to criminal prosecution. The court reasoned that interests advanced by Florida, namely confidentiality and privacy, were not sufficient to overcome the First Amendment right to make truthful statements regarding information persons acquire on their own.

Of more concern than the actual grand jury proceedings are presentments or indictments that include names of persons not indicted. Florida law provides that any grand jury report must remain sealed until unindicted persons have been furnished a copy of the report and have been given 15 days to file for repression or expunction of the report.[75] Also, a court may repress any portion of a grand jury report that is "improper or unlawful."

After a Broward County grand jury filed its interim report on an investigation of the fatal shooting of J. W. Nimmo by two

73. FLA. STAT. ANN. § 905.27 (1982).
74. 110 S. Ct. 1376 (1990).
75. FLA. STAT. ANN. § 905.28 (1987).

Florida highway patrolmen, the defendants filed motions to repress certain portions of the report. Following a hearing, the judge ordered all but one page of the report released, holding that the repressed portion was "improper and unlawful" and not a "fair report." The *Miami Herald* moved to set aside that order.[76] The repressed section stated that the officers did not possess the qualities required of law officers and recommended that they be dismissed following an administrative hearing. The Florida Supreme Court found nothing improper or unlawful about the recommendation since the patrolmen were public officials. The high court held that a repression cannot be based upon the highly subjective standard of "fairness" but must be based on a finding that the report had no factual foundation or that the recommendations were not germane to the scope of the proceedings for which the grand jury was convened. The case was remanded to the trial court to determine repression based on impropriety and unlawfulness rather than unfairness.

Generally, once the 15-day period has passed, such presentments become public record. In a case involving the *Tampa Tribune,* the contents of a presentment were leaked to the newspaper sometime within the 15-day expunction period. When the newspaper wanted copies of motions to expunge, the court said it made no difference whether leaks occurred; there would be no access to the contents of the presentment or to the motions to expunge until the 15-day period had passed.

When an indictment or true bill is handed down by a grand jury, the 15-day rule does not apply. However, a court still has the authority to seal such records if, after applying the *Lewis* rules, it finds that release will affect the due process rights of the accused.

Federal Grand Juries

Federal grand juries operating in Florida have a different function than state grand juries. First, the Fifth Amendment requires that

76. Miami Herald Publishing Co. v. Marko, 352 So. 2d 518 (Fla. 1977).

before suspects can be tried for a felony under federal law, they must be indicted by a grand jury. The only type of investigative power resting in a federal grand jury concerns organized crime or recommendations for removal of a public official because of non-criminal misconduct or misfeasance involving organized crime.[77]

The secrecy of federal grand juries is similar to that of state grand juries with the exception that witnesses are free afterward to disclose whatever they hear, see, or say in the hearing. As in Florida, indictments are usually kept sealed until the defendant is in custody.[78]

The disclosure of a federal grand jury report has been an issue only twice in Florida. In a 1977 case, a federal grand jury in Miami filed a nonindicting report with the federal district court regarding an investigation into the Internal Revenue Service.[79] The report condemned allegations made by certain newspapers including the *Miami Daily News.* Because the report was nonindicting, the district court did not make the report public until all parties named in the report had a chance to file for repression. The only party to file a motion to stay the disclosure of the unexpunged portions of the report was the *Daily News.* The court granted the motion and ordered the report sealed until an appeal was decided by the Fifth Circuit. However, two days later, the *New York Times* published an article quoting verbatim portions of the sealed report. The *Miami Daily News*'s motion to stay the disclosure had become moot.

In *United States* v. *Gurney,* the media petitioned to quash a federal district judge's order prohibiting the disclosure of Gurney's grand jury testimony.[80] The media wanted "unlimited" access to the senator's testimony, but the district court judge refused, stating that the media could obtain transcripts from the court reporter of only those portions read to the jury. The media

77. 18 U.S.C. § 3333 (1982).

78. FED. R. CRIM. P. § 6(e) (1978).

79. *In re* Disclosure of Grand Jury Report, 2 Media L. Rep. 1225 (S.D. Fla. 1977).

80. 558 F.2d 1202.

were not satisfied; they wanted a transcript of the original grand jury testimony, including the portions not read to the trial jury. The Fifth Circuit said Federal Rules of Criminal Procedure make portions not read to the jury confidential. Also, the Fifth Circuit held the district court was justified in refusing to deliver an unexcised grand jury transcript to the media; the trial transcript showing only those portions of the testimony read to the jury was sufficient.

SUMMARY

The Sixth Amendment guarantee of a fair trial and the First Amendment guarantee of freedom of the press come head to head in the context of a criminal trial, and the balancing of these rights has not been easy. When too much information is released by the press about an upcoming trial, there is a fear that an impartial jury will not be found. Although a court can protect against such prejudice by using traditional safeguards such as voir dire, change of venue, continuance, or sequestration, courts often contend that these methods are costly and inconvenient. The result has been to restrain the press from publishing information, to close courtrooms, to seal court records, and to gag participants.

In 1976, the U.S. Supreme Court declared that, except in highly unusual circumstances, restricting the publication of information before and during a trial was unconstitutional, thus virtually ending the use of gags against the press. In the 1980s, the Supreme Court held that criminal pretrials and jury trials must be open unless there is some overriding interest in keeping them closed. The *Lewis* case has had a significant impact on the opening of judicial proceedings and records. This openness is complemented by the 1981 U.S. Supreme Court decision in *Chandler* v. *Florida* to allow cameras in courtrooms as long as the defendant's interest in a fair trial was not overlooked.

Chapter Six

Reporting Public Agencies

The right of access to governmental information and the public's right to know about governmental affairs are becoming increasingly important as the media make more clear every day that those who run the government are just as fallible as those who elect the government. It is the duty of the press to provide the public with information through intensive searching, questioning, and reporting in order that the public may exercise its duty knowledgeably at the polls. Oftentimes, however, reportorial diligence clashes with government's persistence to act in secret as well as with individual privacy rights. Since the early 1960s, numerous laws have been passed at both the federal and state levels to increase public access to governmental affairs, specifically to records and meetings. The two major federal statutes dealing with access are the Freedom of Information Act and the Federal Government in the Sunshine Law. Other statutes dealing with public access include the Privacy Act of 1974, the Buckley Amendment to the Family Educational Rights and Privacy Act, and the Law Enforcement Assistance Administration Act (LEAA Guidelines).

On the state side, Florida's open meeting law is the Government in the Sunshine Law passed in 1967. The state's Public Records Law, passed in 1909, was amended in 1975 to provide better access to state records. The Government in the Sunshine Law is the legislature's affirmation of openness in government. There are several statutory exceptions to the law, but the great majority of cases before the courts have interpreted the open meetings law in favor of openness. The Public Records Law, on the other hand, is weak, allowing over 275 statutory exemptions.

In 1978, the Office of the Attorney General of Florida first published *Florida's Government-in-the-Sunshine Manual* through a grant from the New York Times Affiliated Newspaper Group of Florida. The manual, updated annually, is a compilation of all major court and attorney general opinions concerning the state Public Records Law and the Government in the Sunshine Law. The manual is available from the attorney general's office in Tallahassee. This chapter attempts to summarize major opinions in the area of access, emphasizing major cases and opinions.

This chapter also will look at governmental business carried on in institutions, particularly state prisons. In recent years, as the public's interest has been focused on the death penalty, journalists have been attempting to gain access to state prisons in order to give the public a look inside these institutions.

Florida's Government in the Sunshine Law

Florida's Government in the Sunshine Law is brief and to the point. For this reason, there has been little opportunity for the courts or the attorney general's office to interpret the law negatively. The following examination of the law is brief and deals primarily with interpretation that has come from the courts and the attorney general. It should be remembered that attorney general opinions are only advisory to the state and are not law; they quickly can be deemed uncontrolling by a court.

Scope

"All meetings. . . ." Normally a meeting occurs whenever two or more members of an agency gather to discuss agency business. However, there have been many attempts by governmental bodies to frustrate the system of public exposure by holding meetings at luncheons, by memorandum, or at cocktail parties. The

attorney general's office has consistently warned against such ruses, stating that such private meetings could have a "chilling" effect upon the public's willingness or desire to attend open meetings.[1] The rule adopted by the courts to test whether such meetings must be open is: "Will discussion occur involving matters on which foreseeable action could be taken by the board represented?"[2]

In *Bigelow* v. *Howze,* a district court of appeal dealt with the problem of out-of-state or out-of-town inspection trips.[3] The court stated that in order for the meeting to be public, the board must give advance notice to the public and give a reasonable opportunity for the public to attend.

Obviously, internal meetings of an agency cannot be opened to the public. Staff meetings, employee conferences, and casual conversations are not included within the intent of the Sunshine Law. In *Occidental Chemical Co.* v. *Mayo,* the Florida Supreme Court rejected the idea that meetings between county commissioners and their staff must be held in public.[4] However, the use of staff members as intermediaries to carry messages among agency members for the purpose of circumventing the requirements of the law is a violation.

In January 1979, the Orange County School Board was faced with the sensitive question of whether or not to close a junior high school in order to meet redistricting demands.[5] To avoid "dysfunctional or disruptive stress or distress" over the various alternatives, the superintendent set up a series of private meetings, one after the other, with each of the school board members. After 11 separate office visits, the board met publicly to announce its decision. A district court of appeal ruled that the se-

1. AGO 071–159.

2. Board of Public Instruction of Broward County v. Doran, 224 So. 2d 693 (Fla. 1969).

3. 291 So. 2d 645 (Fla. Dist. Ct. App. 1974).

4. 351 So. 2d 336 (Fla. 1977).

5. Blackford v. Orange County School Bd., 375 So. 2d 578 (Fla. Dist. Ct. App. 1979).

cret sessions were de facto meetings of two or more members at which official action was taken. The court ordered the entire redistricting problem rediscussed in public.

". . . of any board or commission or any state agency or authority or of any agency or authority of any county, municipal corporation, or any political subdivision. . . ." In 1969, a district court of appeal held that "any board or commission" referred to every board or commission over which the municipal, county, or state government has dominion or control.[6] Such bodies have included a district mental health board, a board of governors of a municipal country club, a police complaint review board, a regional planning council, and the board of regents of the State University System. It makes no difference whether the board is elected or appointed, nor does it make any difference whether the individuals attending the meeting are elected, appointed, or are only members-elect.[7]

The "dominion or control" test also encompasses private consulting firms and advisory boards that act merely as advisors to a government entity or are paid for their work. In *Town of Palm Beach* v. *Gradison,* the Florida Supreme Court said an agency cannot conduct the public's business in secret through advisory boards or private consultants.[8] In that case the Palm Beach Town Council met in closed session to appoint a citizens' advisory zoning committee. The committee subsequently met with professional planning consultants in meetings that were closed to the public and at which no minutes were taken. The committee made zoning recommendations to the town council. The town subsequently adopted a comprehensive zoning plan during public meetings. The zoning plan was attacked in court by citizens who claimed that its adoption was invalid because of the non-

6. Times Publishing Co. v. Williams, 222 So. 2d 470 (Fla. Dist. Ct. App. 1969).

7. Hough v. Stembridge, 278 So. 2d 288 (Fla. Dist. Ct. App. 1973).

8. 296 So. 2d 473 (Fla. 1974).

public nature of the advisory group's deliberations. A district court of appeal invalidated the zoning ordinance. The Florida Supreme Court affirmed in an opinion which observed that "the taxpayer deserves an opportunity to express his views and have them considered in the decision-making process." The news media, said the court, have made citizens aware of governmental problems by their continual reporting of community affairs.

A case from Jacksonville, however, indicates that some consulting firms can bypass openness. In *Shevin* v. *Byron, Harless, Schaeffer, Reid and Associates,* the Jacksonville Electric Authority hired a consulting firm of management psychologists to find a director for JEA.[9] The firm interviewed prospects from all over the country before narrowing its list to four or five individuals. When prospects were interviewed, the firm promised confidentiality. However, when a Jacksonville television station asked to look at the consultants' papers regarding the final selections, the firm and JEA refused. A district court of appeal agreed with the refusal. Although the consulting firm was acting on behalf of JEA and was therefore an "agency" of the state and although the records were "received in connection with the transaction of official business," the privacy interests of the prospects were found to outweigh the public interest. The fact that the firm had promised confidentiality gave the prospects a legitimate expectation of privacy, and no state interest could be found that was compelling enough to deprive the individuals of that expectation.

The television station appealed the ruling to the Florida Supreme Court, which ruled that the public must be given access to all of the information except the personal notes of the consultants.[10] According to the court, "If the purpose of the document is to perpetuate, communicate, or formalize knowledge, then it is an open public record. If it is circulated for review, comment, or information, it is a public record." Although the case dealt

9. 360 So. 2d 83 (Fla. Dist. Ct. App. 1979), *rev'd,* 379 So. 2d 633 (Fla. 1980).

10. 379 So. 2d 633.

with records rather than meetings, its holding is applicable to the Sunshine Law.

The case falls in line with *Krause* v. *Reno,* in which a citizens' committee was appointed by the city manager of Miami to review approximately 165 applications for the position of chief of police.[11] The committee's first meeting, at which the list was narrowed to 15 or 18 prospects, was held without notice, behind closed doors, and without any minutes taken. A reporter for the *Miami Daily News* demanded the right to attend the meetings but was denied. The city manager argued that the committee was simply doing what he would have to do himself: screening applicants, evaluating them, and making a selection. Because such process is purely administrative, he argued that the committee was not acting as an agency, board, or commission. The district court of appeal disagreed, stating that it is the substance of the deliberation rather than its form that determines whether a meeting is open. Screening, interviewing, and evaluation are integral parts of the decision-making process and the advisory committee was acting on the city manager's behalf. As such, the committee was an agent of the municipality. Since the city manager is within the dominion and control of the city commission, then so too is any agent of the city manager.

In many states, quasi-judicial hearings in which personnel matters are discussed are closed. However, in Florida there is no exception in the law for such deliberations. At such hearings, personnel records are assessed, and facts or claims of competency, misconduct, or malfeasance are brought forward. In 1969, in *Times Publishing Co.* v. *Williams,* a district court of appeal stated emphatically for the first time that "personnel matters are not sacred, nor legally privileged, nor do they enjoy any insulation from legislative control."[12] In 1973, the Florida Supreme Court held that there is no quasi-judicial exception to the Sunshine

11. 366 So. 2d 1244 (Fla. Dist. Ct. App. 1979); *see also* News-Press Publishing Co. v. Cape Coral Medical Center, 6 Media L. Rep. 1157 (Fla. Cir. Ct. 1980).

12. 222 So. 2d 470.

Law.[13] Although a district court of appeal said two years later that a Career Service Commission deliberation was exempt from the law since it was quasi-judicial,[14] the attorney general's office has refused to acknowledge this latest aberration.[15] Therefore, until the Florida Supreme Court recedes from its 1973 holding, there is no such exception.

The question of quasi-judicial hearings has not been completely answered, particularly in light of a case the Florida Supreme Court refused to hear in 1977. In the case of *Gainesville Sun Publishing Co.* v. *Marston,* the district court of appeal held that the University of Florida Honor Court was not required to hold student disciplinary hearings in public.[16] The University of Florida argued that since the board of regents had authority under law to promulgate regulations concerning the release and custody of "limited access" records maintained on students, it could also promulgate rules limiting access to meetings where such records might be introduced. The district court agreed, in effect allowing an exception to the Public Records Law to act also as an exception to the Sunshine Law.

By not hearing the case on appeal, the Florida Supreme Court refused to deal with the continuing problem of just what types of meetings on a university campus are open. According to a University of Florida press secretary, "The University of Florida is not affected by the Sunshine Law." The argument is that under the Administrative Procedures Act only the office of the university president must hold public meetings when rules affecting constituencies are being decided.[17] All other meetings on a campus are seen as advisory since the president is the sole policy-

13. Canney v. Board of Public Instruction of Alachua County, 278 So. 2d 260 (Fla. 1973).

14. Department of Pollution Control v. Florida Career Serv. Comm'n, 320 So. 2d 846 (Fla. Dist. Ct. App. 1975).

15. AGO 077–48.

16. 341 So. 2d 783 (Fla. Dist. Ct. App. 1976).

17. FLA. STAT. ANN. ch. 120 (1988); 2 FLORIDA FREEDOM OF INFORMATION CLEARING HOUSE NEWSLETTER 4 (August 1978).

making authority. However, as mentioned earlier, the courts have always considered advisory bodies to be covered by the Sunshine Law. The difference, argue universities, is that administrative advisory boards are composed internally, such as a council of deans, rather than externally, such as a city's commission on the status of women.

One circuit court dealt with internal advisory boards on campus. The case involved the University of Florida College of Law search committee for a new dean. The circuit court judge held that meetings of the search committee must be opened under the Sunshine Law.[18] The court refused to find that the Administrative Procedures Act overrode the Sunshine Law's mandate for openness. Attorney general opinions also have said that advisory search committees and ad hoc advisory committees on operations were to be open.[19]

In 1979, a law was passed to exempt from the Sunshine Law search committees screening applicants for chancellor. But attempts to close search committees for university or community college presidents have failed.

If the Florida Legislature wishes to make exceptions to the Sunshine Law, it may do so by passing special acts. This occurred in 1969, when the Florida Legislature passed a special act applicable only to Hillsborough County.[20] The law states that before a probationary teacher is dismissed, charges must be filed with the board of public instruction, notice and hearing must be provided, and the teacher must be given the option of a public or private hearing. The *Tampa Tribune* and several other newspapers sought access to a closed disciplinary hearing but were denied access.[21] The newspapers challenged the law, stating that it left the question of public access up to an individual rather than to a governing agency. The Florida Supreme Court, basing its deci-

18. Wood v. Marston, 6 Media L. Rep. 1326 (Fla. Cir. Ct. 1980).

19. AGO 074–267.

20. 1969 Fla. Laws ch. 1146.

21. Tribune Co. v. Hillsborough County School Bd., 367 So. 2d 627 (1978).

sion solely upon the special act, held that the legislature knew what it was doing when it passed the law, and the court declared it a valid exception to the Sunshine Law. The test used by the court was that if there was an unresolvable conflict between a general law such as the Sunshine Law and a special act, the special act would be seen as a more specific expression of legislative will and would be given effect over the general law.

There are other statutory exceptions to the Sunshine Law, including (1) certain proceedings of the Commission on Ethics, (2) certain proceedings of the Elections Commission, (3) certain types of collective bargaining negotiations, (4) certain deliberations of the Public Employees Relations Commission, (5) hearings held to challenge material found in records of public school students, (6) certain hearings in dependency cases, (7) search committees for selection of a board of regents chancellor, (8) certain disciplinary proceedings of governing bodies of hospital or ambulatory surgical centers, and (9) certain meetings of the Human Rights Advocacy Committee.[22] In 1978, the Florida Supreme Court acknowledged another exception, that of meetings of the Judicial Nominating Commission. According to the court, the commission is executive in nature and cannot be limited by legislative action through the Sunshine Law.[23]

Exceptions also exist within the interpretation of the law itself. For example, the law covers only state agencies, not federal meetings. Also, just because a public official serves on a federal or private body, that body does not become subject to the Sunshine Law. Private organizations that receive public funding are not considered to fall under the "dominion or control" of the legislative branch of government.[24]

The Florida law does not acknowledge common types of exceptions found in other states' laws, such as negotiations for pur-

22. FLA. STAT. ANN. §§ 112.324(1) (1985); 106.25(5); 447.605; 447.205(10); 228.093(3)(d) (1984); 39.408(1)(c), 240.209(2) & (3) (1988).

23. Kanner v. Frumkes, 353 So. 2d 196 (Fla. Dist. Ct. App. 1977); FLA. CONST. art. 5, § 11.

24. AGO 074–22, 071–191.

chasing real estate, investigative hearings, or conferences with lawyers. Several cases, including *Wait* v. *Florida Power and Light Co.*, held that the legislature waived the attorney-client privilege for all public agencies when it passed the Sunshine Law.[25] The statutory exception for labor negotiations, found in the Public Employees Collective Bargaining Act, is very narrow and provides that discussions between the chief executive officer of the public employer and the legislative body of the public employer relative to collective bargaining are exempt.[26] For example, a meeting between a mayor and a city council about collective bargaining is immune from public scrutiny; however, negotiations between a mayor and a local firefighters union or between the union and the city council are open.

". . . at which official acts are to be taken. . . ." According to *Board of Public Instruction of Broward County* v. *Doran,* a meeting encompasses all phases of all deliberations where decisions affecting the public are being made, whether the action is foreseeable or is immediate.[27] In other words, it is the entire decision-making process that the legislature intended to protect against secrecy. "Every step in the decision-making process, including the decision itself, is a necessary preliminary to formal action. It follows that each such step constitutes an 'official act,' an indispensable requisite to 'formal action' within the meaning of the act."[28] As a result of this broad application of the term "meeting," the attorney general's office has held the following types of gatherings to be meetings under the law: workshops, planning sessions, fact-finding discussions, work sessions prior to a formal meeting, and executive sessions prior to hearings on personnel matters.

The law does not specify that the actual voting on an issue must be open. However, through attorney general opinions and

25. 372 So. 2d 420 (Fla. 1979).
26. FLA. STAT. ANN. § 447.605(1) (1984).
27. 224 So. 2d 693.
28. Times Publishing Co. v. Williams, 222 So. 2d 473.

court decisions it has been established that casting votes in secret or casting coded votes is in violation of the law because the secrecy of the voting can be interpreted to mean that the meeting was not open to the public at all times and that public scrutiny was denied.[29] It is also not considered to be an open meeting when the discussion is carried out in codes or references to section numbers of documents not available to the public.[30] For example, in a public meeting the Board of County Commissioners of Lee County had voted to place a warning of possible termination in the personnel file of a county department head.[31] The employee was never referred to by name during the meeting; instead, the commission referred to the individual by a pseudonym. The Florida Supreme Court held that "[t]he policy of this state as expressed in the public records law and the open meetings statute eliminates any notion that the commission was free to conduct the county's personnel business by pseudonyms or cloaked references. We cannot allow the purpose of our statutes to be thwarted by such obvious ruses."

A circuit court judge in *State ex rel. Crago* v. *Hunter* entered an injunction requiring a school board to conduct collective bargaining negotiations in such a manner that a person of reasonable intelligence and reading ability could comprehend what was transpiring.[32] The school board had been conducting the public sessions through written proposals and references to documents that were not available to the public.

Although the law requires openness at all times, the deliberating body can issue reasonable rules and policies regulating attendance as long as those rules are for the purpose of ensuring orderly conduct and do not act as restrictions on openness. Obviously, before a meeting can be considered to be open, the public must know about it. The Sunshine Law does not specify that

29. Marks v. Board of Pub. Instruction of Broward County, 36 Fla. Supp. 175 (Cir. Ct. 1971).

30. *Id.*

31. News-Press Publishing Co. v. Wisher, 345 So. 2d 646 (Fla. 1977).

32. Case No. 75-515 (Cir. Ct., Indian River County 1975).

notice be given to the public; however, in *Hough* v. *Stembridge,* a district court of appeal held that in order for a meeting to be public, "reasonable notice thereof" is mandatory.[33] The lack of a notice provision is probably the weakest aspect of the Florida law.

Violation

". . . and no resolution, rule, regulation or formal action shall be considered binding except as taken or made at such meeting." The law provides that any action taken in an illegally closed meeting is invalid. However, the most recent court rulings on the question of voidness state that when an action is taken in violation of the Sunshine Law, it may be possible to sanitize the action by holding an open public vote. In *Tolar* v. *School Board of Liberty County,* the school board met in secret to discuss and vote on the elimination of the position of director of administration.[34] Later a public meeting was held at which the matter was discussed and a formal vote taken. The director of administration brought suit against the school board, saying that the deliberations must be voided because they were in violation of the statute. A district court of appeal said that while the closed meetings were "unquestionably a technical violation of the statute" and "an illegal prior action," the open vote at the open meeting did not have to be voided. The Florida Supreme Court had upheld this idea several years earlier in a case where the School Board of Palm Beach met in secret and elected a school board chairman, then ratified its action later by voice vote in an open meeting.[35] The court held that the voice vote, although the "fruit of an illegal prior action," was valid. "In this particular instance, any initial violation by secret written ballot was cured and rendered 'sunshine bright' by the corrective open, public vote which followed."

33. 278 So. 2d 288.
34. 363 So. 2d 144 (Fla. Dist. Ct. App. 1978).
35. Bassett v. Braddock, 262 So. 2d 425 (Fla. 1972).

"The minutes of a meeting of any such board shall be promptly recorded and such records shall be open to public inspection." The law is very clear on the keeping of minutes. They must be recorded and made available to the public as soon as possible. Although taped minutes may be made, they are not required.[36]

Jurisdiction

"The circuit courts of this state shall have jurisdiction to issue injunctions to enforce the purposes of this section upon application by any citizen of this state." Once a meeting is convened and there is a showing that the law has been violated, then the circuit court may issue an injunction against the offending board or agency.

The courts have made it easier for citizens to obtain injunctive relief by requiring only a showing that there has been a violation rather than a showing of irreparable injury. A court may also enjoin future violations if it appears that an agency will continue closing open meetings. Any allegation of violation must be specific as to who met where, when, and why.

A state agency has an added privilege that the citizenry in general does not have. Any agency wanting to know whether a meeting should be opened or closed may request an opinion from the attorney general. The attorney general acts as legal advisor to state agencies. However, such opinions are merely advisory and are not binding on the courts.

The Sunshine Law was amended in 1978 to provide for the payment of attorney fees.[37] Any government unit found in violation of the statute, even if the action was found to be in good faith, will be assessed attorney fees unless legal advice of its attorney was sought and followed. This also applies to an appeal that affirms a lower court finding of a violation. Also, if any member is subsequently acquitted of charges of violating the statute, he or she must be reimbursed attorney fees by the agency or board.

36. AGO 075–45.
37. 1978 Fla. Laws ch. 365.

Penalty Provision

"Any person . . . who knowingly violates the provisions of this section . . . is guilty of a misdemeanor of the second degree. . . ." A second-degree misdemeanor is punishable by imprisonment in the county jail not to exceed 60 days, a $500 fine, or both. Before such punishment may be rendered, there must be proof of scienter, or knowledge that the individual was acting against the law.[38] The initial action to open a meeting is through the injunction process. Once the court has rendered a decision about the openness of the meeting, criminal charges are rarely pursued by the state. The major problem in implementing the penalty section is the difficulty of proving that a member of a board or agency knew enough about the Sunshine Law to know that the meeting should have been open in the first place. However, the law was amended in 1985 to provide for civil penalties. "Any public officer who violates any provision of this section is guilty of a non-criminal infraction punishable by fine not to exceed $500."

THE FLORIDA PUBLIC RECORDS LAW

Although the Public Records Law is much more detailed than the Sunshine Law, it has far more exceptions. The law states that it is public policy that all state, county, and municipal records are open for public inspection. Records are defined as "all documents, papers, letters, maps, books, tapes, photographs, films, sound recordings or other material regardless of physical form or characteristics, made or received pursuant to law or ordinance or in connection with the transaction of official business by any agency."[39] Each agency head is designated as custodian of records and is responsible for establishing reasonable regulations for the inspection, examination, and copying of the records.

38. Board of Pub. Instruction of Broward County v. Doran, 224 So. 2d 693.

39. FLA. STAT. ANN. § 119.011(1)(1985).

Public documents are held not only by state agencies but may also be held by private agencies or businesses if they receive any public funds or act on behalf of a public agency. Any documents or records pertaining to any payment by a public agency to a private agency are public. The law is interpreted to cover advisory boards, ad hoc committees, consulting groups, independent contractors, or committees of private citizens.

Records include not only final copies but also drafts and tentative proposals that are circulated within and without an agency. These "work products" are considered open if they "perpetuate, communicate or formalize knowledge."[40] The Public Records Law does make an exception for some work products of an agency's attorney. Those documents include those that reflect an impression, conclusion, litigation strategy, or legal theory. The document, however, becomes a public record once the litigation has ended. There are other exceptions to the work product rule. For example, work products coming out of collective bargaining negotiations, the Public Employees Relations Commission, or the auditor general's office are exempt from disclosure.

Aside from work products, the following have at one time or another been considered by the attorney general's office to be open records: complaints by private citizens to a health board, poll lists, correspondence from a state senator to a division head, operating budget of a university athletic department, personnel files of a hospital, license plates of law enforcement officers, inspection reports, job applications, salaries of public employees, and itineraries and plane reservations of public officials. Personnel records of state employees also are open for inspection.

As mentioned earlier, there are more than 275 statutory exceptions to Florida's Public Records Law. While it is not feasible to list all of the exemptions, the general categories under which these statutory exemptions fall are student records and evaluative records on university personnel, records of parolees and inmates, certain medical records, tax records, unemployment compensa-

40. Shevin v. Byron, Harless, Schaeffer, Reid and Assocs. 360 So. 2d. 83.

tion records, certain juvenile records, adoption records, grand jury records, collective bargaining records, sexual offense records, certain criminal investigative records, and exemptions required by federal law.

There are also certain constitutional exemptions. For example, the Florida Constitution provides that records of the Judicial Nominating Commission and the Judicial Qualifications Commission are closed. Also, the Sixth Amendment to the U.S. Constitution allows a judge to close court records in an effort to ensure a fair trial.

Until recently, many agencies also had assumed that the common law provided exceptions to the Public Records Law. The law reads, "All public records which are presently provided by law to be confidential . . . shall be exempt. . . . " Many argued that "law" was not restricted to statutory law and therefore courts may determine exceptions in the name of public policy. For example, in *News-Press Publishing Co.* v. *Wisher,* the Lee County commissioners placed a reprimand in the file of one of the county's department heads but did not identify the individual publicly.[41] The *Fort Myers News-Press* asked to see the personnel files of department heads so that it could determine for itself the identity of the individual. The county refused access, citing privacy considerations. For many years, courts have acknowledged a common law right of privacy. The county's argument was that although the Public Records Law does not specify privacy as an exception, court decisions on privacy rights in general do support such an exception. The circuit court ordered the files open to public inspection, but that decision was reversed on appeal. The district court of appeal held that personnel files were exempt from disclosure. The Florida Supreme Court disagreed. In a narrowly drawn opinion, which failed to discuss the broad issue of access to personnel files, the court ruled that the documents in this particular case must be made public because the documents

41. 345 So. 2d 646; *see also* News-Press Publishing Co. v. Gadd, 388 So. 2d 276 (Fla. Dist. Ct. App. 1980).

sought were the result of an open meeting by a public agency at which the individual's performance was discussed and the warning was agreed to. "No policy of the state protects a public employee from the embarrassment which results from his or her public employer's discussion or action on the employee's failure to perform his or her duties properly."

Article I of the Florida Constitution was amended in 1980 to protect citizens from governmental intrusion into private areas. The amendment, however, does not limit the public's access to records and meetings under the governance of the Public Records Law or the Sunshine Law.

Another case that proposed that the common law right of privacy was a valid exception to openness came out of demands for access to a report critical of a police chief. In December 1975, the mayor of Anna Maria announced the findings of an investigation of the town's police chief, Conrad Justice.[42] The report, prepared by a three-person committee, claimed that Justice had used official equipment for personal use and had used funds in a questionable and capricious manner. The mayor suspended Justice, who later resigned. After the summary of the report was issued, reporters sought access to the full report and to the testimony before the committee. Access was denied on the basis that the material included personnel records and involved an inhouse investigation of possible criminal activity. The committee that prepared the report claimed it was not subject to the open meeting or open records laws because its members had been "deputized as special policemen." The reporters appealed to the circuit court judge, who ruled that the documents were public records and ordered the mayor to release them. The judge rejected the mayor's argument that disclosure might embarrass some Anna Maria residents, explaining, "The public's right to know far outweighs any damage resulting from the issuance of the document." The judge also ruled that the closed committee meeting violated the open meetings law. The mayor appealed,

42. *See* 10 PRESS CENSORSHIP NEWSLETTER 99 (1976).

but the district court of appeal upheld the lower court's ruling without opinion.

One of the arguments made by the mayor in the above case was that the material requested was part of an ongoing criminal investigation and thus was not public. This was not an illegitimate claim. For years, records dealing with the detection, apprehension, and prosecution of criminals were considered by courts to be confidential although such exceptions were not provided for by law.

In 1979, the Public Records Law was amended to allow the sealing of all "active" criminal investigatory information.[43] "Active" means related to an ongoing investigation where there is an anticipation of an arrest or prosecution in the foreseeable future. Also closed is information that reveals the identity of confidential sources and undercover personnel, surveillance techniques, addresses and telephone numbers of police officers, information about spouses and children of police officers, and any information received in confidence from another state or country. The media may still obtain basic arrest information about a crime, such as time, date, place, and nature of the crime; name, sex, age, address, and occupation of the suspect and victims (except victims of sexual or child abuse); and court informations and unsealed indictments.

When the *Fort Lauderdale News* learned that money taken into police custody was missing, the paper sought access to the property custody records from the Sunrise Police Department but was denied.[44] The police claimed an investigation was under way, although only information recorded on one date was considered important to the investigation. Also, the investigation was upgraded to an active one only after the newspaper filed the petition for a writ of mandamus to gain access. A circuit court ruled that the records must be made public with the exception of the infor-

43. 1979 Fla. Laws ch. 187.

44. Zadell v. Ramputti, 5 Media L. Rep. 2531 (Fla. Cir. Ct. 1980); *see also* Times Publishing Co. v. Pinellas County, 7 Media L. Rep. 1091 (Fla. Cir. Ct. 1981).

mation recorded on that one date that the police claimed was sensitive.

Unlike the federal government's Freedom of Information Act, the Public Records Law establishes no detailed process for securing records. Each agency head is required to set reasonable rules for inspection and copying of the documents. According to *Tribune Co.* v. *Cannella,* the only delay permitted in filling a records request is the limited reasonable time it takes for the custodian to retrieve the record and delete the exempted portions, if any.[45]

While a custodian may not charge a fee for search, retrieval, and oversight, he may charge for the actual cost of any duplication. If a person is denied the right of inspection, he may begin a civil action in the circuit court to compel compliance with the law. The law does not specify how long a person must wait between a request for a record and an appeal to the circuit court. Also, there is no provision for appealing from a division to an agency head before a court suit is filed. After a court orders compliance, the agency must allow inspection within 48 hours unless that court's order is stayed on appeal.

The penalties for violating the Public Records Law are similar to those for violating the Sunshine Law. Noncriminal infraction is punishable by a fine not exceeding $500; knowing and willful violation is punishable as a first-degree misdemeanor.

If a civil action results in a finding that an agency has unlawfully refused access to a public record, the court shall assess costs and attorney fees against the agency. An example of how costly an unlawful refusal can be was demonstrated in *Jones* v. *Miami Herald Publishing Co.*[46] The newspaper was categorically refused access to the files of a completed police internal review. The court held that the refusal was not only in violation of the law but was also unreasonable. Attorney fees were assessed against the agency for over $70,000 to both the *Miami Herald* and *Miami Daily News,* and $2,988 in court costs were imposed.

45. 438 So. 2d 516 (Fla. Dist. Ct. App. 1983), *quashed,* 458 So. 2d 1075 (Fla. 1984).

46. 8 Media L. Rep. 2108 (Fla. Dist. Ct. App. 1982).

Public inspection is not limited to any one individual or group expressing a special interest. Documents may be inspected by any person. Any request for a written statement of purpose should be ignored. Nor must a person specify with particularity the records desired as long as enough information is furnished for a competent agency employee to locate the document. However, a person who is engaged in litigation with an agency may not be able to obtain documents from that agency under the Florida Evidence code.[47]

Readers wishing more information about exemptions to the Public Records Law should refer to the latest *Government-in-the-Sunshine Manual,* published by the First Amendment Foundation.

THE FLORIDA ADMINISTRATIVE PROCEDURES ACT

In addition to the Sunshine Law and the Public Records Law, Florida also has another statute that provides access to rules, orders, instructions, and forms of state (not county or municipal) agencies and county school boards. The Administrative Procedures Act (APA) was passed in 1974 and states that any rule (an agency statement of general applicability or policy) or order (a final agency decision resulting from some formal proceeding) must be available for public inspection. Also, such rules and orders must be indexed for user ease.[48] Not only are the rules and orders available to the public, but so are deliberations at which such orders and rules are formulated, amended, or repealed. Anyone requesting to be notified about such decisions must receive information on a specific intended action, an explanation of the purpose and effect of the action, the legal authority, the economic impact, and a statement of where the text of the rule and the economic statement are available.

47. State *ex rel.* Davidson v. Crouch, 156 So. 2d 297 (Fla. 1934); FLA. STAT. ANN. § 90.502 (1979); Aldredge v. Turlington, 378 So. 2d 125 (Fla. Dist. Ct. App.), *cert. denied,* 383 So. 2d 1189 (Fla. 1980).

48. FLA. STAT. ANN. ch. 120 (1985).

The APA came into play in an appeal by the *St. Petersburg Times* of an emergency rule by the Department of Corrections (DOC) banning press interviews with death row inmates whose death warrants had been signed.[49] Two inmates, Charles Proffitt and Robert Sullivan, were scheduled to be executed June 17, 1979. On June 11, the DOC issued a 90-day emergency rule that canceled all interviews with death row inmates until the death warrant was stayed or executed. The APA allows such emergency rules to be promulgated if the rule is necessary to protect the public interest and if the agency specifies facts and reasons for finding an immediate danger. The media immediately challenged the emergency ruling because the DOC failed to specify the facts and reasons behind the rule, stating only that it was necessary to maintain security during execution periods.

The Second District Court of Appeal in Lakeland struck down the emergency rule because the explanation of the specific facts and reasons was not given. Three weeks later, the DOC promulgated an identical emergency rule. Again, the media appealed, citing an insufficient reason for the rule. The First District Court of Appeal heard the second appeal and ruled that the DOC had upgraded its statement of facts and reasons, but the court found that there was no demonstrated danger in allowing access at least to those prisoners whose death warrants were issued.[50] The court stated, "Those whose electrocution is imminent are in a class apart from others [on death row] because . . . the reported interviews of those prisoners are uniquely of interest to a public which continues to debate the morality of capital punishment." That portion of the emergency rule held to be valid was to be effective only until September 9, 90 days from the issuance of the first emergency rule. After the expiration of the emergency rule, the DOC adopted a permanent rule regulating news media interviews with death row inmates. According to the APA, interested

49. Times Publishing Co. v. Florida, 375 So. 2d 304 (Fla. Dist. Ct. App. 1979).

50. Times Publishing Co. v. Florida, 375 So. 2d 307 (Fla. Dist. Ct. App. 1979).

parties must be given the opportunity to respond to any proposed rule. The new rule allows a one-hour interview by ten reporters designated by DOC and scheduled two days before an execution. Individual interviews with the persons scheduled to be executed or with any other death row inmates are prohibited.

ACCESS TO JAILS AND PRISONS

In neither of the above appeals by the media did the newspapers argue that the First Amendment provided a right of access to prisoners beyond that already acknowledged by the DOC. This claim could not be made because the U.S. Supreme Court has repeatedly held that the media do not enjoy any extraordinary right to gather news. As explained in the chapter on privacy, the news media have no more right of access to places or events than does the ordinary citizen.[51] This same First Amendment philosophy extends to places that are under state control, such as prisons and jails.

In 1974, the U.S. Supreme Court heard two companion cases on the right of access to prisoners. *Pell* v. *Procunier* involved access to state prisoners, and *Saxbe* v. *Washington Post* involved access to federal prisoners.[52] The Court ruled that the security and the unusual atmosphere within prisons and the purposes of imprisonment were sufficient to restrict access to prisoners for interviews by the press. In both cases, reports sought to interview specified inmates but were barred by broad rules that prohibited the press from interviewing individual inmates even when the inmates requested the interview. The Court upheld the broad rules, noting that other types of access were available, such as group interviews, tours of the facilities, brief "conversations" with random inmates, and correspondence with individual inmates.

This holding was later extended to county jails.[53] However, a

51. Zemel v. Rusk, 381 U.S. 1 (1965).
52. 417 U.S. 817 (1974); 417 U.S. 843 (1974).
53. Houchins v. KQED, 438 U.S. 1 (1978).

1974 ruling by a Broward County circuit court intimates that reporters in Florida may have greater access to prisoners being held in county jails than the First Amendment requires. In December 1974, Richard Croll was arrested and charged with conspiracy to commit murder. After his arrest, the *Fort Lauderdale Sun-Sentinel* asked to interview Croll. While Croll and his attorney agreed to the interview, the sheriff refused to allow it. The rule at the jail was that no inmate could be interviewed while awaiting trial but could be interviewed after conviction. The newspaper brought suit seeking access to the inmate. Florida has no law regulating access to inmates for interviews. The circuit court judge held that there was no showing that the interview would create any problems with security or privacy. The judge permitted the interview as long as the sheriff's department did not eavesdrop or interfere in any way other than to maintain security during the interview.[54]

With the 1976 execution of Gary Gilmore in Utah, the first execution in the United States since 1967, debate on capital punishment has become more widespread than at any other time in our history. One result of the intense interest has been the increase in the number of requests by the media to witness executions. A federal district court in Utah denied the *Salt Lake Tribune*'s request to witness Gilmore's execution, upholding a state law that prohibited media and the public from witnessing executions because of security and privacy aspects.[55] Meanwhile, a federal district judge in Dallas ruled that broadcasters have as much right to film and record an execution as the newspaper reporter has to take notes at an execution. This ruling was overturned by the Fifth Circuit, which stated that a ban on audio and visual recording of executions did not violate the First Amendment rights of broadcasters since access to the execution was allowed.[56]

54. *See* 7 PRESS CENSORSHIP NEWSLETTER 60 (1975).

55. Kearns Tribune v. Utah Board of Corrections, 2 Media L. Rep. 1353 (D. Utah 1977).

56. Garrett v. Estelle, 556 F.2d 1274 (5th Cir. 1977).

Most states, such as Utah, prohibit the press or the public from witnessing executions. Florida, however, allows representatives of the media to be present when a death warrant is carried out.[57]

Summary

Florida's Government in the Sunshine Law, one of the strongest in the country, requires all meetings of any governmental body or agency to be open and the minutes recorded. If reporters wish to challenge the closing of a meeting, they may petition for an injunction in a circuit court. If a public agency wants to know whether a meeting should be closed, it may get an advisory opinion from the Florida attorney general. Any decisions made at a meeting held in violation of the law will be void. Any person found guilty of knowingly violating the law is subject to fine or imprisonment. By interpretation, the law also requires reasonable notice to the media of a public meeting. The law has several very narrow exceptions. The rule of thumb used by the attorney general's office is: "When in doubt, open the meeting." One stumbling block in the path of full implementation of the law is the Administrative Procedures Act, which some state officials, especially university presidents, use to avoid the Sunshine Law.

Unlike the Sunshine Law, the Florida Public Records Law has over 275 statutory exceptions. This law remains very weak despite a state supreme court decision that refused to acknowledge any common law exceptions to the law. Media access to public institutions, such as jails and prisons, is also restricted according to several decisions by the U.S. Supreme Court.

57. Fla. Stat. Ann. § 922.11(2) (1982).

Appendix A

The Florida Libel Statute

770.01 Notice condition precedent to action or prosecution for libel or slander

Before any civil action is brought for publication or broadcast, in a newspaper, periodical, or other medium, of a libel or slander, the plaintiff shall, at least 5 days before instituting such action, serve notice in writing on the defendant, specifying the article or broadcast and the statements therein which he alleges to be false and defamatory.

770.02 Correction, apology, or retraction by newspaper or broadcast station

(1) If it appears upon the trial that said article or broadcast was published in good faith; that its falsity was due to an honest mistake of the facts; that there were reasonable grounds for believing that the statements in said article or broadcast were true; and that, within the period of time specified in subsection (2), a full and fair correction, apology, or retraction was, in the case of a newspaper or periodical, published in the same editions or corresponding issues of the newspaper or periodical in which said article appeared and in as conspicuous place and type as said original article or, in the case of a broadcast, the correction, apology, or retraction was broadcast at a comparable time, then the plaintiff in such case shall recover only actual damages.

(2) Full and fair correction, apology, or retraction shall be made:

(a) In the case of a broadcast or a daily or weekly newspaper or periodical, within 10 days after service of notice;

(b) In the case of a newspaper or periodical published semimonthly, within 20 days after service of notice;

(c) In the case of a newspaper or periodical published monthly, within 45 days after service of notice; and

(d) In the case of a newspaper or periodical published less frequently than monthly, in the next issue, provided notice is served no later than 45 days prior to such publication.

770.03 Civil liability of broadcasting stations

The owner, lessee, licensee, or operator of a broadcasting station shall have the right, except when prohibited by federal law or regulation, but shall not be compelled, to require the submission of a written copy of any statement intended to be broadcast over such station 24 hours before the time of the intended broadcast thereof. When such owner, lessee, licensee, or operator has so required the submission of such copy, such owner, lessee, licensee, or operator shall not be liable in damages for any libelous or slanderous utterance made by or for the person or party submitting a copy of such proposed broadcast which is not contained in such copy. This section shall not be construed to relieve the person or party or the agents or servants of such person or party making any such libelous or slanderous utterance from liability therefor.

770.04 Civil liability of radio or television broadcasting stations; care to prevent publication or utterance required

The owner, licensee, or operator of a radio or television broadcasting station, and the agents or employees of any such owner, licensee or operator, shall not be liable for any damages for any defamatory statement published or uttered in or as a part of a radio or television broadcast, by one other than such owner, licensee or operator, or general agent or employees thereof, unless it shall be alleged and proved by the complaining party, that such owner, licensee, operator, general agent or employee, has failed to exercise due care to prevent the publication or utterance of such statement in such broadcasts, provided, however, the exercise of due care shall be construed to include the bona fide compliance with any federal law or the regulation of any federal regulatory agency.

770.05 Limitation of choice of venue

No person shall have more than one choice of venue for damages for libel or slander, invasion of privacy, or any other tort founded upon any single publication, exhibition, or utterance, such as any one edition of a newspaper, book, or magazine, any one presentation to an audience, any one broadcast over radio or television, or any one exhibition of a motion picture. Recovery in any action shall include all damages for any such tort suffered by the plaintiff in all jurisdictions.

Appendix B

Florida's "Quick" Appeals Rule (Florida Appellate Rules)

Rule 9.100 Original Proceedings

(d) Exception; Orders Excluding Press or Public.

(1) A petition to review an order excluding the press or public from access to any proceeding, any part of a proceeding, or any judicial records, if the proceedings or records are not required by law to be confidential, shall be filed in the court as soon as practicable following rendition of the order to be reviewed, if written, or announcement of the order to be reviewed, if oral. A copy shall be furnished to the person (or chairperson of the collegial administrative agency) issuing the order, and to the parties to the proceeding.

(2) The court shall immediately consider the petition to determine whether a stay of proceedings in the lower tribunal is appropriate, and on its own motion or that of any party the court may order a stay on such conditions as may be appropriate.

(3) If requested by the petitioner or any party, or on its own motion, the court may allow oral argument.

Appendix C

Florida's Government in the Sunshine Law

286.001 Reports statutorily required of executive agency or officer; filing, maintenance, retrieval, and provision of copies

(1) Unless otherwise specifically provided by law, any agency or officer of the executive branch of state government required by law to make reports periodically shall be construed to have fulfilled such requirement upon filing a notice of filing, as scheduled by law, with the Executive Office of the Governor and with the person or agency to which the report is to be directed, which notice of filing provides indexing information and an abstract of the contents of such report no more than one-half page in length. The actual reports shall be retained by the reporting agency or officer, and copies of the reports shall be provided to interested parties upon request, in accordance with guidelines established by the Executive Office of the Governor under subsection (2).

(2) With respect to reports statutorily required of agencies or officers within the executive branch of state government, it is the duty of the Executive Office of the Governor to:

(a) Receive notices of filing with respect to such reports.

(b) Index such notices of filing alphabetically by subject of report, by reporting agency or officer, and by receiving agency or officer.

(c) Establish guidelines with respect to:

1. The appropriate procedure for requesting copies of such reports.

2. The timely provision, by the reporting agency or officer, of copies of such reports, upon receipt of a request properly made and any fee applicable to such provision.

3. The establishment of appropriate fees, based upon actual costs of materials, handling, and postage, which fees may be charged by reporting agencies or officers for providing such copies.

4. The exemption from fee provisions of agencies or officers to whom reports are required by law to be directed.

(d) Regularly compile and update index information on such reports and publish such information, together with a summary of the guidelines established under paragraph (c), for distribution as provided in paragraph (e).

(e) Provide for quarterly or semiannual distribution of published indexes on reports:

1. To agencies and officers within the executive, legislative, and judicial branches of state government, free of charge; and

2. To other interested parties, upon request, properly made and upon payment of an appropriate fee for such provision, which fee, based upon actual costs incurred, shall be determined by the office.

(3) As soon as practicable, the administrative head of each executive agency required by law to make reports periodically shall assure that those reports are created, stored, managed, updated, and retrieved through electronic means.

286.0105 Notices of meetings and hearings must advise that a record is required to appeal

Each board, commission, or agency of this state or of any political subdivision thereof shall include in the notice of any meeting or hearing, if notice of the meeting or hearing is required, of such board, commission, or agency, conspicuously on such notice, the advice that, if a person decides to appeal any decision made by the board, agency, or commission with respect to any matter considered at such meeting or hearing, he will need a record of the proceedings, and that, for such purpose, he may need to ensure that a verbatim record of the proceedings is made, which record includes the testimony and evidence upon which the appeal is to be based. The requirements of this section do not apply to the notice provided in § 200.065(3).

286.011 Public meetings and records; public inspection; penalties

(1) All meetings of any board or commission of any state agency or authority or of any agency or authority of any county, municipal corporation, or political subdivision, except as otherwise provided in the Constitution, at which official acts are to be taken are declared to be public meetings open to the public at all times, and no resolution, rule, or formal action shall be considered binding except as taken or made at such meeting.

(2) The minutes of a meeting of any such board or commission of any such state agency or authority shall be promptly recorded, and such records shall be open to public inspection. The circuit courts of this state shall have jurisdiction to issue injunctions to enforce the purposes of this section upon application by any citizen of this state.

(3)(a) Any public officer who violates any provision of this section is guilty of a noncriminal infraction, punishable by fine not exceeding $500.

(b) Any person who is a member of a board or commission or of any state agency or authority of any county, municipal corporation, or political subdivision who knowingly violates the provisions of this section by attending a meeting not held in accordance with the provisions hereof is guilty of a misdemeanor of the second degree, punishable as provided in § 775.082, § 775.083, or § 775.084.

(4) Whenever an action has been filed against any board or commission of any state agency or authority or any agency or authority of any county, municipal corporation, or political subdivision to enforce the provisions of this section or to invalidate the actions of any such board, commission, agency, or authority, which action was taken in violation of this section, and the court

determines that the defendant or defendants to such action acted in violation of this section, the court shall assess a reasonable attorney's fee against such agency, and may assess a reasonable attorney's fee against the individual filing such an action if the court finds it was filed in bad faith or was frivolous. Any fees so assessed may be assessed against the individual member or members of such board or commission; provided, that in any case where the board or commission seeks the advice of its attorney and such advice is followed, no such fees shall be assessed against the individual member or members of the board or commission. However, this subsection shall not apply to a state attorney or his duly authorized assistants or any officer charged with enforcing the provisions of this section.

(5) Whenever any board or commission of any state agency or authority or any agency or authority of any county, municipal corporation, or political subdivision appeals any court order which has found said board, commission, agency, or authority to have violated this section, and such order is affirmed, the court shall assess a reasonable attorney's fee for the appeal against such board, commission, agency, or authority. Any fees so assessed may be assessed against the individual member or members of such board or commission; provided, that in any case where the board or commission seeks the advice of its attorney and such advice is followed, no such fees shall be assessed against the individual member or members of the board or commission.

(6) All persons subject to subsection (1) are prohibited from holding meetings at any facility or location which discriminates on the basis of sex, age, race, creed, color, origin, or economic status or which operates in such a manner as to unreasonably restrict public access to such a facility.

(7) Whenever any member of any board or commission of any state agency or authority or any agency or authority of any county, municipal corporation, or political subdivision is charged with a violation of this section and is subsequently acquitted, the board or commission is authorized to reimburse said member for any portion of his reasonable attorney's fees.

286.0111 Legislative review of certain exemptions from requirements for public meetings and recordkeeping by governmental entities

The provisions of § 119.14, the Open Government Sunset Review Act, apply to the provisions of law which provide exemptions to § 286.011, as provided in § 119.14.

286.012 Voting requirement at meetings of governmental bodies

No member of any state, county, or municipal governmental board, commission, or agency who is present at any meeting of any such body at which an official decision, ruling, or other official act is to be taken or adopted may abstain from voting in regard to any such decision, ruling, or act, and a vote shall be recorded or counted for each such member present, except when, with respect to any such member, there is, or appears to be, a possible conflict of interest under the provisions of § 112.311, § 112.313, or § 112.3143. In such cases said member shall comply with the disclosure requirements of § 112.3143.

Appendix D

The Florida Public Records Law

119.01 General state policy on public records

(1) It is the policy of this state that all state, county, and municipal records shall at all times be open for a personal inspection by any person.

(2) All agencies shall establish a program for the disposal of records that do not have sufficient legal, fiscal, administrative, or archival value in accordance with retention schedules established by the records and information management program of the Division of Library and Information Services of the Department of State.

119.011 Definitions

For the purpose of this chapter:

(1) "Public records" means all documents, papers, letters, maps, books, tapes, photographs, films, sound recordings or other material, regardless of physical form or characteristics, made or received pursuant to law or ordinance or in connection with the transaction of official business by any agency.

(2) "Agency" means any state, county, district, authority, or municipal officer, department, division, board, bureau, commission, or other separate unit of government created or established by law and any other public or private agency, person, partnership, corporation, or business entity acting on behalf of any public agency.

(3)(a) "Criminal intelligence information" means information with respect to an identifiable person or group of persons collected by a criminal justice agency in an effort to anticipate, prevent, or monitor possible criminal activity.

(b) "Criminal investigative information" means information with respect to an identifiable person or group of persons compiled by a criminal justice agency in the course of conducting a criminal investigation of a specific act or omission, including, but not limited to, information derived from laboratory tests, reports of investigators or informants, or any type of surveillance.

(c) "Criminal intelligence information" and "criminal investigative information" shall not include:

1. The time, date, location, and nature of a reported crime.

2. The name, sex, age, and address of a person arrested or of the victim of a crime except as provided in § 119.07(3)(h).

3. The time, date, and location of the incident and of the arrest.

4. The crime charged.

5. Documents given or required by law or agency rule to be given to the person arrested, except as provided in § 119.07(3)(h), and, except that the court in a criminal case may order that certain information required by law or agency rule to be given to the person arrested be maintained in a confidential manner and exempt from the provisions of § 119.07(1) until released at trial if it is found that the release of such information would:

a. Be defamatory to the good name of a victim or witness or would jeopardize the safety of such victim or witness; and

b. Impair the ability of a state attorney to locate or prosecute a codefendant.

The exemptions in this subparagraph are subject to the Open Government Sunset Review Act in accordance with § 119.14.

6. Informations and indictments except as provided in § 905.26.

(d) The word "active" shall have the following meaning:

1. Criminal intelligence information shall be considered "active" as long as it is related to intelligence gathering conducted with a reasonable, good faith belief that it will lead to detection of ongoing or reasonably anticipated criminal activities.

2. Criminal investigative information shall be considered "active" as long as it is related to an ongoing investigation which is continuing with a reasonable, good faith anticipation of securing an arrest or prosecution in the foreseeable future. In addition, criminal intelligence and criminal investigative information shall be considered "active" while such information is directly related to pending prosecutions or appeals. The word "active" shall not apply to information in cases which are barred from prosecution under the provisions of § 775.15 or other statute of limitation.

(4) "Criminal justice agency" means any law enforcement agency, court, or prosecutor. The term also includes any other agency charged by law with criminal law enforcement duties, or any agency having custody of criminal intelligence information or criminal investigative information for the purpose of assisting such law enforcement agencies in the conduct of active criminal investigation or prosecution or for the purpose of litigating civil actions under the Racketeer Influenced and Corrupt Organization Act, during the time that such agencies are in possession of criminal intelligence information or criminal investigative information pursuant to their criminal law enforcement duties.

119.0115 Videotapes and video signals; exemption from chapter

Any videotape or video signal which, under an agreement with an agency, is produced, made, or received by, or is in the custody of, a federally licensed radio or television station or its agent is exempt from this chapter.

119.012 Records made public by public fund use

If public funds are expended by an agency defined in subsection 119.011(2) in payment of dues or membership contributions to any person, corporation, foundation, trust, association, group, or other organization, then all the financial, business and membership records pertaining to the public agency from which or on whose behalf the payments are made, of the person, corporation, foundation, trust, association, group, or organization to whom such payments are made shall be public records and subject to the provisions of § 119.07.

119.02 Penalty

A public officer who knowingly violates the provisions of § 119.07(1) is subject to suspension and removal or impeachment and, in addition, is guilty of a misdemeanor of the first degree, punishable as provided in § 775.082 or § 775.083.

119.021 Custodian designated

The elected or appointed state, county, or municipal officer charged with the responsibility of maintaining the office having public records, or his designee, shall be the custodian thereof.

119.031 Keeping records in safe places; copying or repairing certified copies

Insofar as practicable, custodians of vital, permanent, or archival records shall keep them in fireproof and waterproof safes, vaults, or rooms fitted with noncombustible materials and in such arrangement as to be easily accessible for convenient use. All public records should be kept in the buildings in which they are ordinarily used. Record books should be copied or repaired, renovated, or rebound if worn, mutilated, damaged, or difficult to read. Whenever any state, county, or municipal records are in need of repair, restoration, or rebinding, the head of such state agency, department, board, or commission, the board of county commissioners of such county, or the governing body of such municipality may authorize that such records be removed from the building or office in which such records are ordinarily kept for the length of time required to repair, restore, or rebind them. Any public official who causes a record book to be copied shall attest it and certify on oath that it is an accurate copy of the original book. The copy shall then have the force and effect of the original.

119.041 Destruction of records regulated

Every public official shall systematically dispose of records no longer needed subject to the consent of the records and information management program of the Division of Library and Information Services of the Department of State in accordance with § 257.36.

119.05 Disposition of records at end of official's term

Whoever has the custody of any public records shall, at the expiration of his term of office, deliver to his successor or, if there be none, to the records and information management program of the Division of Library and Information Services of the Department of State all records, books, writings, letters, and documents kept or received by him in the transaction of his official business.

119.06 Demanding custody

Whoever is entitled to the custody of public records shall demand them from any person having illegal possession of them, who shall forthwith deliver the same to him. Any person unlawfully possessing public records shall upon demand of any person and within 10 days deliver such records to their lawful custodian unless just cause exists for failing to deliver such records.

119.07 Inspection and examination of records; exemptions

(1)(a) Every person who has custody of a public record shall permit the record to be inspected and examined by any person desiring to do so, at any reasonable time, under reasonable conditions, and under supervision by the custodian of the public record or his designee. The custodian shall furnish a copy or a certified copy of the record upon payment of the fee prescribed by law or, if a fee is not prescribed by law, upon payment of the actual cost of duplication of the record. The phrase "actual cost of duplication" means the cost of the material and supplies used to duplicate the record, but it does not include the labor cost or overhead cost associated with such duplication. However, the charge for copies of county maps or aerial photographs supplied by county constitutional officers may also include a reasonable charge for the labor and overhead associated with its duplication. Unless otherwise provided by law, the fees to be charged for duplication of public records shall be collected, deposited, and accounted for in the manner prescribed for other operating funds of the agency.

(b) If the nature or volume of public records requested to be inspected, examined, or copied pursuant to this subsection is such as to require extensive use of information technology resources or extensive clerical or supervisory assistance by personnel of the agency involved, or both, the agency may charge, in addition to the actual cost of duplication, a special service charge, which shall be reasonable and shall be based on the cost incurred for such extensive use of information technology resources or the labor cost of the personnel providing the service that is actually incurred by the agency or attributable to the agency for the clerical and supervisory assistance required, or both. "Information technology resources" shall have the same meaning as in § 282.303(8).

(c) When ballots are produced under this section for inspection or examination, no persons other than the supervisor of elections or his employees shall touch the ballots. The supervisor of elections shall make a reasonable effort to notify all candidates by telephone or otherwise of the time and place of the inspection or examination. All such candidates, or their representatives, shall be allowed to be present during the inspection or examination.

(2)(a) A person who has custody of a public record and who asserts that an exemption provided in subsection (3) or in a general or special law applies to a particular public record or part of such record shall delete or excise from the record only that portion of the record with respect to which an exemption has been asserted and validly applies, and such person shall produce the remainder of such record for inspection and examination. If the person who has custody of a public record contends that the record or part of it is exempt from inspection and examination, he shall state the basis of the exemption which he contends is applicable to the record, including the statutory citation to an exemption created or afforded by statute, and, if requested by the person seeking the right under this subsection to inspect, examine, or copy the record, he shall state in writing and with particularity the reasons for his conclusion that the record is exempt.

(b) In any civil action in which an exemption to subsection (1) is asserted, if the exemption is alleged to exist under or by virtue of paragraph (e), paragraph (f), paragraph (g), paragraph (m), paragraph (o), or paragraph (r) of subsection (3), the public record or part thereof in question shall be submitted to the court for an inspection in camera. If an exemption is alleged to exist under or by virtue of paragraph (d) of subsection (3), an inspection in camera will be discretionary with the court. If the court finds that the asserted exemption is not applicable, it shall order the public record or part thereof in question to be immediately produced for inspection, examination, or copying as requested by the person seeking such access.

(c) Even if an assertion is made by the custodian of a public record that a requested record is not a public record subject to public inspection and examination under subsection (1), the requested record shall, nevertheless, not be disposed of for a period of 30 days after the date on which a written request requesting the right to inspect, examine, or copy the record was served on or otherwise made to the custodian of the record by the person seeking access to the record. If a civil action is instituted within the 30-day period to enforce the provisions of this section with respect to the requested record, the custodian shall not dispose of the record except by order of a court of competent jurisdiction after notice to all affected parties.

(3)(a) All public records which are presently provided by law to be confidential or which are prohibited from being inspected by the public, whether by general or special law, are exempt from the provisions of subsection (1).

(b) All public records referred to in §§ 199.222, 228.093, 257.261, 288.075, 624.319(3) and (4), and 655.057(1)(b), (3), and (4) are exempt from the provisions of subsection (1).

(c) Examination questions and answer sheets of examinations administered by a governmental agency for the purpose of licensure, certification, or employment are exempt from the provisions of subsection (1). A person who has taken such an examination shall have the right to review his own completed examination.

(d) Active criminal intelligence information and active criminal investigative information are exempt from the provisions of subsection (1).

(e) Any information revealing the identity of a confidential informant or a confidential source is exempt from the provisions of subsection (1).

(f) Any information revealing surveillance techniques or procedures or personnel is exempt from the provisions of subsection (1). Notwithstanding § 119.14, any comprehensive inventory of state and local law enforcement resources compiled pursuant to part I, chapter 23, and any comprehensive policies or plans compiled by a criminal justice agency pertaining to the mobilization, deployment, or tactical operations involved in responding to emergencies, as defined in § 252.34(2), are exempt from the provisions of subsection (1) and unavailable for inspection, except by personnel authorized by a state or local law enforcement agency, the office of the Governor, the Department of Legal Affairs, the Department of Law Enforcement, or the Department of Community Affairs as having an official need for access to the inventory or comprehensive policies or plans. This exemption is subject to the Open Government Sunset Review Act in accordance with § 119.14.

(g) Any information revealing undercover personnel of any criminal justice agency is exempt from the provisions of subsection (1).

(h) Any criminal intelligence information or criminal investigative information including the photograph, name, address, or other fact or information which reveals the identity of the victim of the crime of sexual battery as defined in chapter 794; the identity of the victim of the crime of lewd, lascivious, or indecent assault upon or in the presence of a child, as defined in chapter 800; or the identity of the victim of the crime of child abuse as defined by chapter 827 and any criminal intelligence information or criminal investigative information or other criminal record, including those portions of court records, which may reveal the identity of a person who is a victim of any sexual offense, including a sexual offense proscribed in chapter 794, chapter 800, or chapter 827, is exempt from the provisions of subsection (1).

(i) Any criminal intelligence information or criminal investigative information which reveals the personal assets of the victim of a crime, other than property stolen or destroyed during the commission of the crime, is exempt from the provisions of subsection (1).

(j) All criminal intelligence and criminal investigative information received by a criminal justice agency prior to January 25, 1979, is exempt from the provisions of subsection (1).

(k) The home addresses, telephone numbers, and photographs of active or former law enforcement personnel and personnel of the Department of Health and Rehabilitative Services whose duties include the investigation of abuse, neglect, exploitation, fraud, theft, or other criminal activities; the home addresses, telephone numbers, photographs, and places of employment of the spouses and children of such personnel; and the names and locations of schools and day care facilities attended by the children of such personnel are exempt from the provisions of subsection (1). These exemptions are subject to the Open Government Sunset Review Act in accordance with § 119.14.

(l) Any information provided to an agency of state government or to an agency of a political subdivision of the state for the purpose of forming ridesharing arrangements, which information reveals the identity of an individual who has provided his name for ridesharing arrangements as defined in § 341.031(6), is exempt from the provisions of subsection (1).

(m) Any information revealing the substance of a confession of a person arrested is exempt from the provisions of subsection (1), until such time as the criminal case is finally determined by adjudication, dismissal, or other final disposition.

(n) A patient record obtained by the Hospital Cost Containment Board established under § 395.503, which record contains the name, residence or business address, telephone number, social security or other identifying number, or photograph of any person or the spouse, relative, or guardian of such person or which record is patient-specific or otherwise identifies the patient, either directly or indirectly, is exempt from the provisions of paragraph (1)(a).

(o) A public record which was prepared by an agency attorney (including an attorney employed or retained by the agency or employed or retained by another public officer or agency to protect or represent the interests of the agency having custody of the record) or prepared at the attorney's express direction, which reflects a mental impression, conclusion, litigation strategy, or legal theory of the attorney or the agency, and which was prepared exclusively for civil or criminal litigation, or for adversarial administrative proceedings, or which was prepared in anticipation of imminent civil or criminal litigation or imminent adversarial administrative proceedings, is exempt from the provisions of subsection (1) until the conclusion of the litigation or adversarial administrative proceedings. When asserting the right to withhold a public record pursuant to this paragraph, the agency shall identify the potential parties to any such criminal or civil litigation or adversarial administrative proceedings. If a court finds that the document or other record has been improperly withheld under this paragraph, the party seeking access to such document or record shall be awarded reasonable attorney's fees and costs in addition to any other remedy ordered by the court.

(p) Sealed bids or proposals received by an agency pursuant to invitations to bid or requests for proposals are exempt from the provisions of subsection (1) until such time as the agency provides notice of a decision or intended decision pursuant to § 120.53(5)(a) or within 10 days after bid or proposal opening, whichever is earlier.

(q) In any case in which an agency of the executive branch of state government seeks to acquire real property by purchase or through the exercise of the power of eminent domain all appraisals, other reports relating to value, offers, and counteroffers must be in writing and are exempt from the provisions of § 119.01 and subsection (1) until execution of a valid option contract or a written offer to sell which has been conditionally accepted by the agency, at which time the exemption shall expire. The agency shall not finally accept the offer for a period of 30 days in order to allow public review of the transaction. The agency may give conditional acceptance to any option or offer subject only to final acceptance by the agency after the 30-day review period. If a valid option contract is not executed, or if a written offer to sell is not conditionally accepted by the agency, then the exemption from the provisions of this chapter shall expire at the conclusion of the condemnation litigation of the subject property. An agency of the executive branch may exempt title information, including names and addresses of property owners whose property is subject to acquisition by purchase or through the exercise of the power of eminent domain, from the provisions of § 119.01 and subsection (1) to the same extent as appraisals, other reports relating to value, offers, and counteroffers. This exemption is subject to the Open Government Sunset Review Act in accordance with § 119.14. Nothing in this section shall be construed to provide an exemption from or exception to § 286.011. For the purpose of this paragraph "option contract" means an agreement of an agency of the executive branch of state government to purchase real property subject to final agency approval. This paragraph shall have no application to other exemptions from the requirements of § 119.01 or subsection (1) which are contained in other provisions of law and shall not be construed to be an express or implied repeal thereof.

(r) Data processing software obtained by an agency under a licensing agreement which prohibits its disclosure and which software is a trade secret, as defined in § 812.081, and agency-produced data processing software which is sensitive are exempt from the provisions of subsection (1). The designation of agency-produced software as sensitive shall not prohibit an agency head from sharing or exchanging such software with another public agency. As used in this paragraph:

1. "Data processing software" has the same meaning as in § 282.303(5).

2. "Sensitive" means only those portions of data processing software, including the specifications and documentation, used to:

a. Collect, process, store, and retrieve information which is exempt from the provisions of subsection (1);

b. Collect, process, store, and retrieve financial management information of the agency, such as payroll and accounting records; or

c. Control and direct access authorizations and security measures for automated systems.

(s) A patient record obtained by the Department of Health and Rehabilitative Services pursuant to § 641.27 from a health maintenance organization or from a provider of a health maintenance organization as to subscribers treated by the provider pursuant to a provider contract with a health maintenance organization, which record contains the name, the residential or business address, the telephone, social security, or other identifying number, or a photograph of any subscriber or of the spouse, relative, or guardian of the subscriber, or which record is patient-specific or otherwise identifies the patient, either directly or indirectly, is exempt from the provisions of subsection (1).

(t) A report obtained by the Department of Insurance from a

health maintenance organization pursuant to § 641.311, to the extent that such report contains the name, the residential or business address, the telephone, social security, or other identifying number, or a photograph of any subscriber or of the spouse, relative, or guardian of the subscriber, or other subscriber-identifying information, is exempt from the provisions of subsection (1).

(u) All complaints and other records in the custody of any unit of local government which relate to a complaint of discrimination relating to race, color, religion, sex, national origin, age, handicap, marital status, sale or rental of housing, the provision of brokerage services, or the financing of housing shall be exempt from the provisions of subsection (1) until a finding is made relating to probable cause, the investigation of the complaint becomes inactive, or the complaint or other record is made part of the official record of any hearing or court proceeding. This provision shall not affect any function or activity of the Florida Commission on Human Relations. Any state or federal agency which is authorized to have access to such complaints or records by any provision of law shall be granted such access in the furtherance of such agency's statutory duties, notwithstanding the provisions of this section. This paragraph shall not be construed to modify or repeal any special or local act. This exemption is subject to the Open Government Sunset Review Act in accordance with § 119.14.

(v) All complaints and other records in the custody of any agency in the executive branch of state government which relate to a complaint of discrimination relating to race, color, religion, sex, national origin, age, handicap, or marital status in connection with hiring practices, position classifications, salary, benefits, discipline, discharge, employee performance, evaluation, or other related activities shall be exempt from the provisions of subsection (1) until a finding is made relating to probable cause, the investigation of the complaint becomes inactive, or the complaint or other record is made part of the official record of any hearing or court proceeding. This provision shall not affect any function or activity of the Florida Commission on Human Relations. Any state or federal agency which is authorized to have access to such complaints or records by any provision of law shall be granted such access in the furtherance of such agency's statutory duties, notwithstanding the provisions of this section. This exemption is subject to the Open Government Sunset Review Act in accordance with § 119.14.

(w) A patient record obtained by the Department of Health and Rehabilitative Services or its agent pursuant to § 395.035, which record contains the name, residence or business address, telephone number, social security or other identifying number, or photograph of any person or the spouse, relative, or guardian of such person or which record is patient-specific or otherwise identifies the patient, either directly or indirectly, is exempt from the provisions of subsection (1).

(x) All records supplied by a telecommunications company to a state or local governmental agency which contain the name, address, and telephone number of subscribers are exempt from the provisions of subsection (1).

(y) All information relating to the medical condition or medical status of employees of the state, which is not relevant to the employee's capacity to perform his duties, is exempt from the provisions of subsection (1). Information which is exempt shall include, but is not limited to, information relating to workers' compensation, insurance benefits, and retirement or disability benefits. All information which is exempt from subsection (1) pursuant to this paragraph shall be maintained separately from nonexempt employment information.

(z) The records of a medical review committee created pursuant to § 766.101 or former § 768.40 by the Department of Corrections or the Correctional Medical Authority, or both, are exempt from the provisions of subsection (1). This exemption is subject to the Open Government Sunset Review Act in accordance with § 119.14.

(4) Nothing in this section shall be construed to exempt from subsection (1) a public record which was made a part of a court file and which is not specifically closed by order of court, except as provided in paragraphs (e), (f), (g), (m), (o), and (r) of subsection (3) and except information or records which may reveal the identity of a person who is a victim of a sexual offense as provided in paragraph (h) of subsection (3).

(5) Nothing in subsection (3) shall be interpreted as providing an exemption from or exception to § 286.011.

(6) The provisions of this section are not intended to expand or limit the provisions of Rule 3.220, Florida Rules of Criminal Procedure, regarding the right and extent of discovery by the state or by a defendant in a criminal prosecution.

119.072 Criminal intelligence or investigative information obtained from out-of-state agencies

Whenever criminal intelligence information or criminal investigative information held by a non-Florida criminal justice agency is available to a Florida criminal justice agency only on a confidential or similarly restricted basis, the Florida criminal justice agency may obtain and use such information in accordance with the conditions imposed by the providing agency.

119.08 Photographing public records

(1)(a) In all cases where the public or any person interested has a right to inspect or take extracts or make copies from any public record, instruments or documents, any person shall hereafter have the right of access to said records, documents or instruments for the purpose of making photographs of the same while in the possession, custody and control of the lawful custodian thereof, or his authorized deputy.

(b) This section applies to the making of photographs in the conventional sense by utilization of a camera device to capture images of documents, paper, books, receipts, paper photographs, and other similar media and excludes the duplication of microfilm in the possession of the clerk of the circuit court where a copy of the microfilm may be made available by the clerk.

(2) Such work shall be done under the supervision of the lawful custodian of the said records, who shall have the right to adopt and enforce reasonable rules governing the said work. Said work shall, where possible, be done in the room where the said records, documents or instruments are by law kept, but if the same in the judgment of the lawful custodian of the said records, documents or instruments be impossible or impracticable, then the said work shall be done in such other room or place as nearly adjacent to the room where the said records, documents and instruments are kept as determined by the lawful custodian thereof.

(3) Where the providing of another room or place is necessary, the expense of providing the same shall be paid by the person desiring to photograph the said records, instruments or documents. While the said work hereinbefore mentioned is in progress, the lawful custodian of said records may charge the person desiring to make the said photographs for the services of a deputy of the lawful custodian of said records, documents or instruments to supervise the same, or for the services of the said lawful custodian of the same in so doing at a rate of compensation to be agreed upon by the person desiring to make the said photographs and the custodian of the said records, documents or instruments, or in case the same fail to agree as to the said charge, then by the lawful custodian thereof.

119.085 Remote electronic access to public records

(1) As an additional means of inspecting, examining, and copying public records of the executive branch, judicial branch, or any political subdivision of the state, public records custodians may provide access to the records by remote electronic means. The custodian shall charge a fee for remote electronic access, granted under a contractual arrangement with a user, which fee shall include the direct and indirect costs of providing such access. Fees for remote electronic access provided to the general

public shall be in accordance with the provisions of § 119.07(1). The custodian shall provide safeguards to protect the contents of public records from unauthorized remote electronic access or alteration and to prevent the disclosure or modification of those portions of public records which by general or special law are exempt from § 119.07(1).

(2) This section is repealed on October 1, 1990, and shall be reviewed by the Legislature in advance of said date. In determining whether to reenact this section, the Legislature shall consider for the time period from July 1, 1985 through July 1, 1989:

(a) The number of the remote electronic access contracts which have been entered into by records custodians.

(b) Whether the fees charged have closely approximated the costs incurred in providing remote electronic access.

(c) Whether the security of the electronic records maintained by records custodians has been breached as a result of such access.

(d) Whether the provision of such access impaired the ability of records custodians to meet other public record requests.

119.09 Assistance of the Division of Library and Information Services, records and information management program, of the Department of State

The Division of Library and Information Services, records and information management program, of the Department of State shall have the right to examine into the condition of public records and shall give advice and assistance to public officials in the solution of their problems of preserving, creating, filing, and making available the public records in their custody. Public officials shall assist the division by preparing an inclusive inventory of categories of public records in their custody. The division shall establish a time period for the retention or disposal of each series of records. Upon the completion of the inventory and schedule, the division shall (subject to the availability of necessary space, staff, and other facilities for such purposes) make space available in its records center for the filing of semicurrent records so scheduled and in its archives for noncurrent records of permanent value and shall render such other assistance as needed, including the microfilming of records so scheduled.

119.092 Registration by federal employer's registration number

Each state agency which registers or licenses corporations, partnerships, or other business entities shall include, by July 1, 1978, within its numbering system, the federal employer's identification number of each corporation, partnership, or other business entity registered or licensed by it. Any state agency may maintain a dual numbering system in which the federal employer's identification number or the state agency's own number is the primary identification number; however, the records of such state agency shall be designed in such a way that the record of any business entity is subject to direct location by the federal employer's identification number. The Department of State shall keep a registry of federal employer's identification numbers of all business entities, registered with the Division of Corporations, which registry of numbers may be used by all state agencies.

119.10 Violation of chapter; penalties

(1) Any public officer who violates any provision of this chapter is guilty of a noncriminal infraction, punishable by fine not exceeding $500.

(2) Any person willfully and knowingly violating any of the provisions of this chapter is guilty of a misdemeanor of the first degree, punishable as provided in § 775.082 or § 775.083.

119.11 Accelerated hearing; immediate compliance

(1) Whenever an action is filed to enforce the provisions of this chapter, the court shall set an immediate hearing, giving the case priority over other pending cases.

(2) Whenever a court orders an agency to open its records for inspection in accordance with this chapter, the agency shall comply with such order within 48 hours, unless otherwise provided

by the court issuing such order, or unless the appellate court issues a stay order within such 48-hour period.

(3) A stay order shall not be issued unless the court determines that there is substantial probability that opening the records for inspection will result in significant damage.

(4) Upon service of a complaint, counterclaim, or cross-claim in a civil action brought to enforce the provisions of this chapter, the custodian of the public record that is the subject matter of such civil action shall not transfer custody, alter, destroy, or otherwise dispose of the public record sought to be inspected and examined, notwithstanding the applicability of an exemption or the assertion that the requested record is not a public record subject to inspection and examination under § 119.07(1), until the court directs otherwise. The person who has custody of such public record may, however, at any time permit inspection of the requested record as provided in § 119.07(1) and other provisions of law.

119.12 Attorney's fees

(1) If a civil action is filed against an agency to enforce the provisions of this chapter and if the court determines that such agency unlawfully refused to permit a public record to be inspected, examined, or copied, the court shall assess and award, against the agency responsible, the reasonable cost of enforcement including reasonable attorneys' fees.

(2) Whenever an agency appeals a court order requiring it to permit inspection of records pursuant to this chapter and such order is affirmed, the court shall assess a reasonable attorney's fee for the appeal against such agency.

119.14 Periodic legislative review of exemptions from public meeting and public record requirements

(1) This section may be cited as the "Open Government Sunset Review Act."

(2) This act provides for the periodic automatic application of the policy of open government as provided in §§ 119.01 and

286.011 to certain exemptions from § 286.011 and chapter 119. It is the intent of the Legislature that exemptions to § 286.011 and chapter 119 shall be maintained only if:

(a) The exempted record or meeting is of a sensitive, personal nature concerning individuals;

(b) The exemption is necessary for the effective and efficient administration of a governmental program; or

(c) The exemption affects confidential information concerning an entity.

Thus, the maintenance or creation of an exemption must be compelled as measured by these criteria. Further, the Legislature finds that the public has a right to have access to executive branch governmental meetings and records unless the criteria in this act for restricting such access to a public meeting or public record are met and the criteria are considered during legislative review in connection with the particular exemption to be significant enough to override the strong public policy of open government. To strengthen the policy of open government, the Legislature shall consider the criteria in this act before enacting future exemptions.

(3)(a) On the dates specified in this subsection with respect to the chapters of law included in the titles of the Florida Statutes specified in this subsection, the provisions of §§ 119.01, 119.07(1), and 286.011 shall fully apply, notwithstanding any provisions in such chapters of law included in the titles of the Florida Statutes to the contrary, unless the application of this subsection to such chapters of law has been modified by subsequent law passed by the Legislature. The repeal dates and titles of the Florida Statutes are as follows:

a. Each exemption in chapter 119 which has not been reviewed in prior years because such exemption was not contained in those titles or because the exemption is generic in character and language and consequently applies to records created, maintained, or stored, by substantive language in two or more such titles; and

b. Each exemption which is identified as being in two or more titles of the Florida Statutes by the Division of Statutory Revision.

(b) In the year prior to the repeal of an exemption pursuant to this section, the Division of Statutory Revision of the Joint Legislative Management Committee shall certify to the President of the Senate and the Speaker of the House of Representatives, by December 1, 1985, and by August 1 of each subsequent year, the language and statutory citation of each exemption scheduled for repeal the following year which meets the criteria of an exemption as defined in this act. Any exemption which is not identified and certified to the President of the Senate and the Speaker of the House of Representatives shall not be subject to legislative review and repeal under this act. If the division fails to certify an exemption which it subsequently determines should have been certified, it shall include such exemption in the following year's certification after such determination.

(c) An "exemption" is defined as a provision of the Florida Statutes which creates an exception to § 119.01, § 119.07(1), or § 286.011 and which applies to the executive branch of state government or to local government, but shall not include any provision of a special or local law.

(d) No exemption which is required by federal law shall be subject to repeal.

(4)(a) The Legislature shall conduct a review of the exemption prior to its scheduled repeal and shall consider as part of the review process the following:

1. What specific records or meetings are affected by the exemption?

2. Whom does the exemption uniquely affect, as opposed to the general public?

3. What is the identifiable public purpose or goal of the exemption?

4. Can the information contained in the records or discussed in the meeting be readily obtained by alternative means? If so, how?

(b) An exemption shall be maintained only if it serves an identifiable public purpose. An identifiable public purpose is served when the exemption meets one of the following purposes and such purpose is considered during legislative review in connection with the particular exemption being considered to be significant enough to override the strong public policy of open government:

1. Allows the state or its political subdivisions to effectively and efficiently administer a governmental program, which administration would be significantly impaired without the exemption;

2. Protects information of a sensitive personal nature concerning individuals, the release of which information would be defamatory to such individuals or cause unwarranted damage to the good name or reputation of such individuals or would jeopardize the safety of such individuals; or

3. Protects information of a confidential nature concerning entities, including, but not limited to, a formula, pattern, device, combination of devices, or compilation of information which is used to protect or further a business advantage over those who do not know or use it, the disclosure of which information would injure the affected entity in the marketplace.

(c) No records made prior to the date of a repeal of an exemption under this act shall be made public unless otherwise provided by law. In deciding whether such records shall be made public the Legislature shall consider whether the damage or loss to persons or entities uniquely affected by the exemption of the type specified in subparagraph (b)2. or subparagraph (b)3. would occur if the records were made public.

(d) Legislation which creates an exemption which is scheduled for repeal in the year it is enacted or the year following enactment shall not be subject to this act until the next review cycle for that title.

(e) An exemption that is created or revived and reenacted shall contain uniform language which clearly states the section in the Florida Statutes from which it is exempt, chapter 119 or § 286.011. The uniform language shall also provide for the maximum public access to the meetings and records as is consistent with the purpose of the exemption. Each exemption shall also contain the statement: "This exemption is subject to the 'Open Government Sunset Review Act' in accordance with § 119.14."

(f) In the year prior to the 1995 regular session, the Legislature shall consider the necessity of conducting further reviews of exemptions.

(g) Notwithstanding the provision of § 768.28 or any other law, neither the state or its political subdivisions nor any other public body shall be made party to any suit in any court or incur any liability for the repeal or revival and reenactment of any exemption pursuant to this act. The failure of the Legislature to comply strictly with this section shall not invalidate an otherwise valid reenactment.

Table of Cases

Index

For names of newspapers and persons see Table of Cases

Analysis for Action

Nursing Care of the Elderly

Analysis for Action
Nursing Care of the Elderly

Shirley R. Good, R.N., Ed.D.
Marywood College

Susan S. Rodgers, R.N., M.S.
Community Health Nurse

Prentice-Hall, Inc., Englewood Cliffs, New Jersey 07632

Library of Congress Cataloging in Publication Data

Good, Shirley Ruth (date)
Analysis for action.

Bibliography: p.
1. Geriatric nursing–Case studies. I. Rodgers, Susan S., joint author. II. Title.
RC954.G66 610.73'65 79-21048
ISBN 0-13-032623-2

Editorial/Production Supervision and Interior Design by Lynn Frankel
Cover Design by Miriam Recio
Manufacturing Buyer: Cathie Lenard

Case II photograph by Allan S. Rodgers
Case VI photograph by Shirley R. Good
All other photographs by Howard Lake

10 9 8 7 6 5 4 3 2 1

Printed in the United States of America

Prentice-Hall International, Inc., *London*
Prentice-Hall of Australia Pty. Limited, *Sydney*
Prentice-Hall of Canada, Ltd., *Toronto*
Prentice-Hall of India Private Limited, *New Delhi*
Prentice-Hall of Japan, Inc., *Tokyo*
Prentice-Hall of Southeast Asia Pte. Ltd., *Singapore*
Whitehall Books Limited, *Wellington, New Zealand*

To our parents who taught us
the zest and value of living and aging gracefully

And

To our students past and present

Contents

Foreword

This book deals with an age-old fact, that of aging. That we seem to have recently discovered this fact perhaps accounts for the great upsurge of interest in it. The problems of the aged—social, economic, and psychological as well as physical—are beginning to receive the attention they have long deserved. Actually, the problems of the aged are only symptoms of more deep-seated problems, such as changes in the family, urbanization, housing, inadequate income, the skyrocketing costs of medical care, and failure to provide for health preservation and promotion.

The cases presented here, which are taken from real life, are both an indictment of the medical and nursing professions and a challenge, especially to the nursing profession, whose commitment is to promote health as well as to provide care for the ill. Surely in reading these cases one can readily see where both medicine and nursing have failed; equally clear, however, are the opportunities to assist these individuals, who are but a few of many, to live more healthful lives even in their declining years. In presenting these cases, all difficult and complex, the authors give students and practicing nurses an opportunity to apply the knowledge and skills that are a part of their armamentarium. The readers are provided with clues, with thoughtful questions and guides to resolving the problems of aged persons with long-term illness.

It is hoped that when nurses and physicians fully realize and appreciate the predicaments of individuals such as those presented here, preventive measures as well as treatment measures will assume their rightful importance. It is one of the successes of medical science that individuals have longer life expectancies. The concomitant challenge is now to make the longer lives of individuals more

productive, more satisfying, more healthy. It is no doubt more difficult to do this than to find new technologies, new cures, and new drugs, but that is no reason it should not be done. Here is where nursing can make its greatest contribution.

Mildred L. Montag, Ed.D. R.N.

Garden City, New York

Preface

Nurse educators are acknowledging an increased need for nursing professionals to have knowledge and skills of gerontological nursing by including courses in this area of specialization in their curricula. This book is designed primarily as a basic text utilizing the case method for an analytical approach to the solution of patient, client, and nursing problems. We believe that the content is appropriate for upper division baccalaureate and graduate nursing courses concerned with the care of the aging and aged. Since the text is diverse and relatively comprehensive, we also expect the book to serve as a valuable resource for continuing education, gerontological practitioner, and in-service programs.

Several strategies were developed to facilitate use and understanding of the case method by both students and educators. First, a philosophical frame of reference is given in the Introduction, describing the educational and personal attributes and competencies considered necessary for gerontological nurse specialists. Also included is an overview of the thinking process and of the utilization of the case method, a variant of the discussion method, as a teaching–learning strategy for developing disciplined thought before action.

As a departure from the customary case method, wherein the reader develops his or her own list of problems for analysis, general and specific study guide questions were developed. The former offer an orderly approach applicable to all cases for the development of a broad knowledge base in a relatively new field of study; the latter give focus to the unique problems of a particular clinical case.

Rather than leave students entirely to their own resources to provide substantive rationale for decisions taken, a sampling of

suggested readings and resources are included, as are diagrams depicting Erikson's developmental tasks and essential strengths, and phases of the loss process over time.

The material presented in the text reflects the problems frequently encountered by nurses. Therefore, the clinical cases are representative of segments in the lives of *real* people. To fake, embellish, or partially fictionalize an account would have been a subjective imposition. Data would have been biased, the information would have been narrowed, and no purpose would have been served. The adage "truth is stranger than fiction" served us well.

In all but one instance the case material was collected by the authors from people they cared for in acute, long-term and home settings. Each patient, client, or their significant other(s) provided informed consent with the assurance of anonymity. Consequently names, places, and dates have been changed.

The clinical studies, being segments from real life, are histories. Some are ordered and comprehensive; others are incomplete. Wherever possible, social, emotional, economic, occupational, and environmental components are included, as are the past and present health and illness states. Significant, contributory diagnostic studies for identification, corroboration, and progression of health problem(s), subsequent treatment modalities, and the actions of health care professionals are included. Each situation presented has many problems that beg for nursing solutions. As a consequence we did not order the sequence of cases according to the complexity of the problems. Nor did we attempt to develop a uniform format. All case studies begin with our entry into the patients' care milieu; observations were made and data collected actively and in retrospect.

Finally, this is not a "how-to" book. Cumulative knowledge and careful analytical reading of each case are required to meet, as we suggest, discerning judgment for responsible action in caring for elderly people.

Shirley R. Good

Susan S. Rodgers

Acknowledgments

We have been helped in preparing this book by innumerable people, including all of our students over the past twenty years, our elderly friends and patients, and various university colleagues, especially Mildred L. Montag, a sustaining friend and mentor, who read this manuscript and provided the scholarly, humane foreword. We also owe a debt of gratitude to Roberta Sligh, Librarian, who helped locate books and articles we could not have obtained without her help. And we thank editors William Gibson and Fred Henry of Prentice-Hall, Inc., who believed this book could contribute to learning about and caring for the silent minority in our society—the aging and the aged.

Shirley R. Good

Susan S. Rodgers

Introduction: Gerontological Nursing and the Case Method

By definition, members of the nursing profession are committed to, and accountable for, thoughtful action in providing innumerable health services. A concomitant obligation is to know as much as possible about the theories, principles, and applications of biological and social sciences, in order to effect positive changes in the health of the persons served or, when necessary, to dignify and ease their death.

The knowledge industry assails us with countless theories, principles, concepts, etc. No one can know and understand all that is needed for the personalism required in the cure and care of the elderly. Nor can the plethora of course offerings or a single teaching strategy lead to the integration, synthesis, and extent of knowledge requisite for thoughtful action.

Nowhere is this challenge more evident than in caring for the aging and aged, as life events are individually determined, defined, and culminated.

Before proposing answers to these concerns, other questions must be addressed: What does educational preparation for care of the elderly entail? Who is best able to apply thoughtful nursing action? What are the expected areas of competence? Each of these will be dealt with separately.

EDUCATIONAL PREPARATION

The study of aging can best be described as multidisciplinary in perspective. Within the divisions of the natural and biological sciences, social sciences, fine arts, and professional studies, numerous disciplines contribute to the knowledge of the elderly. Some of these fields are anatomy, physiology, genetics, biochemistry, psychology, human growth and development, sociology, political science, anthropology, ethnic studies, economics, history, literature, art, music, dance, languages other than English, education, recreation, home and family life, environmental studies, religion, dentistry, sex therapy, pharmacology, physical and occupational therapies, rehabilitation, and communicative disorders. Such disciplines form the basis of what is known as the science of *gerontology*. Facets of these and other fields can readily be applied to gerontology nursing, which is particulary concerned with the elderly on the health-illness continuum, and the psychological, social, economic, and legal interactive processes that affect an individual's adaptation and well-being, "the goals of which are to provide for health, longevity and independence, or the highest level of functioning possible . . . ."[1]

It becomes apparent that no first or advanced degree program can fully prepare a nurse for this specialized area of practice. This leads to the second question posed.

WHO BEST?

A ready answer to this question might be "the holistically prepared professional nurse." This connotes finality, however, when in fact, the concepts of holistic preparation and professionalism are ideals to be pursued throughout life.

Just as life is comprised of major components: the past, the

[1] L. M. Gunter and J. C. Miller, "Toward a Nursing Gerontology," *Nursing Research*, 26:3 (May–June 1977), p. 208.

present, and the future, there are identifiable components characteristic of the qualified gerontology nursing specialist.

There is ample evidence in the literature to support the contention that certain personal attributes are essential in nurses who are to effect positive care for the elderly. Some of the attributes delineated below arise from the literature; others are from personal observation. Some are quantifiable, but others are not. However, it is highly desirable that those in gerontology nursing possess these qualities:

A personal value system that incorporates the dignity and worth of the aging and aged
Sensitivity for the human condition and human rights wherever the individual is found
Ability to care for and about people
Ability to communicate in several media (language, touch, graphic and pictorial arts)
An admixture of independence and ability to collaborate with other health professionals
An adventuresome nature
Creativity
Patience (the ability to do without immediate rewards)
A sense of purpose
A sense of humor
Ability to utilize research findings and conduct research
Perseverance
Flexibility (initiates change)
Professional commitment

It is therefore concluded that the characteristics of the people best able to apply thoughtful nursing action are those who exercise judgment based on scientific principles and theories, pursue knowledge, maintain quality performance, and have the personal attributes identified as highly desirable for gerontology nursing. This, too, is a lifetime pursuit, but adds the dimension of the special areas of competence.

EXPECTED AREAS OF COMPETENCE

Gerontology nursing is moving out of its formative period and is becoming a viable field of specialization. And as in any specialty, the clinician must exhibit certain qualitative and quantitative knowledge

and certain psychosocial and motor skills gained in cumulative educational experience and practice. Quite unlike other nurse specialists, the gerontology clinician's areas of competency are not determined by the locus of practice. This clinician must be willing and able to traverse the manifold settings of the community (homes and clinics), acute, intermediate, and tertiary care centers as a health provider. Both epidemiology and demographic studies of the elderly support this contention.

Older individuals are known to be subject to more disability, to seek health care more frequently, and to have longer hospital stays than persons in younger age groups. They are second only to the under-5 age group in days of restricted activity due to acute illnesses (1,092 days per 100 persons per year),[2] and approximately one half of all the elderly people in the United States have at least one chronic condition; "the incidence of all chronic disease . . . rises steadily with advancing years . . . at age 65 there are 4,000 per 1,000 population . . . ."[3] Only 14% are thought to have no chronic conditions, diseases, or impairments (e.g., arteriosclerotic heart disease, subarachnoid and cerebral hemorrhage, chronic brain syndrome, hypertensive heart disease, osteoporosis, chronic obstructive pulmonary disease). In addition to physiological changes and more disabling and chronic diseases, the elderly are faced with economic, social, psychological, and cultural stresses and developmental adjustments. Elderly people often erroneously attribute physical, mental, and psychosocial symptoms and changes to the aging process and thus fail to seek health care. On the other hand, government officials and gerontologists repeatedly voice concern for the approximately 1,150,000 elderly currently housed in long-term care facilities (amounting to 5% of the 23 million elderly in the United States), 35–50% of whom, they suggest, could be discharged if better distribution and monitoring systems were planned and developed.

The educational preparation of health care personnel emphasizes cure models of acute diseases that occur from conception to the middle years. Such personnel have little experience with or motiva-

[2] Harvey E. Estes Jr., Health Experience in the Elderly," in *Behavior and Adaptation in Late Life*, 2nd ed., eds. Ewald W. Busse and Eric Pfeiffer (Boston: Little, Brown and Company, 1977), p. 101.

[3] Estes, "Health Experience in the Elderly," p. 101.

tion for managing the care of the aging and aged. Two observations by Estes point out the special problems of delivering health care to the elderly: "The older, declining areas of large cities and smaller towns and rural areas . . . have failed to attract new physicians. These are the same areas in which older persons are found in greater proportion . . .";[4] and ". . . the complexity of the hospital or clinic may deter the older patient from utilizing its services unless compelled to do so."[5]

The evidence suggests that there is a need for the clinical nursing specialist not only to fill the void in the delivery of care but also to assume responsibility to keep the elderly well and to provide direct and rehabilitative care to those with chronic conditions in order to maintain a high level of health and function. In fact, it can be said that nursing activities expand as the need arises.

In an attempt to clarify what "competency" means, we contend that concern is with advanced qualifications in the application of knowledge and skills. (The need for growth in these areas is implicit.) And we submit that particular fields of knowledge supportive of advanced practice include theories of aging; social and psychological events of aging; life style adaptations; normal physiological changes in aging; altered responses to pathological conditions; interactive effects of age, illness, therapeutic modalities; and nursing interventions.

The composite skills are seen as emphasizing assessment, synthesis of knowledge and information, and judgment in planning, executing, and evaluation. More specifically, the essential skill competencies are: assessing actual health status; identifying potential health problems (physical, psychosocial, economic); identification and use of the client's internal and external resources; assessing response to illness or disability and to therapeutic regimes; within legal constraints, managing and modifying treatment plans and activities of daily living; performing selected diagnostic procedures; and instituting supportive and restorative measures.

Intermingled are the skills of collaboration and consultation with other health professionals, the public, and the clients (including mutual goal setting); communication of information to the client, family, and professional colleagues about diagnosis, treatment, and nursing actions; teaching and instituting health maintenance for clients, family, and community; utilizing relevant research findings;

[4] Estes, "Health Experience in the Elderly," p. 108.
[5] Estes, "Health Experience in the Elderly," p. 108.

utilizing community resources (local, state, and federal); utilizing advocacy skills for clients and families; and vigilant evaluation of nursing actions in the light of responsibility and accountability to the public served.

Competence is viewed primarily as a positive adaptive response to new knowledge, interactions, and interventive skills. All of these contribute to high-level problem solving and thinking.

PROBLEM SOLVING AND THINKING

Few would dispute that all learning involves problems. And problem solving and thinking are interrelated processes that are basic to discussion of the Case Method as a teaching strategy.

The aim of problem solving is to stimulate creative thinking and originality in conceiving new relationships (syntheses) for application to practice. Use is made of Getzels' classification: ". . . both presented and discovered problems . . . [examining] . . . issues of what is known and what is unknown in the problem situation."[6] Of the eight types of cognitive problems delineated by Getzels, two are particularly applicable to those developed for this book. These are:

> The problem is given (is known) but no standard method for solving it is known to the problem solver or to the others.

and

> The problem itself exists but remains to be identified or discovered, and no standard method for solving is known to the problem solver or to the others . . . .[7]

Inherent in both statements is the discovery method outlined by John Dewey in *How We Think*.[8] Many variations of the five modes of thought have developed to fit the problems presented in various subject matter fields. The major determinants are whether the problems are valuative or nonvaluative. Nursing is no exception. The nursing process was introduced as a method—a way of examining problems and arriving at tentative solutions for action and subse-

[6] J. W. Getzels, "Creative Thinking, Problem-solving, and Instruction," in *Theories of Learning and Instruction*, Sixty-third Yearbook, National Society for the Study of Education (Chicago: University of Chicago Press, 1964), p. 241.

[7] Getzels, "Creative Thinking," p. 241.

[8] John Dewey, *How We Think* (Boston: D. C. Heath and Company, 1910. Revised 1933).

quent evaluation. This process is the departure from unquestioning rote learning. It enables discovery, the value of which lies in translating knowledge into action; provides positive reinforcement from successes; is a way of avoiding error; and employs the activity of logical thought.

Despite the rationality of the method, many students flounder in a seemingly pervasive fog when attempting to transfer this activity from one situation to another (e.g., from one patient care setting to another, or to colleagual interchange or to research). This leads to speculation that reflective thinking, analyzed by Dewey to reveal the interplay of deductive and inductive thought, needs to be examined from the source. Between problem identification and resolution, the five states of thinking are:

1. *Suggestions*, in which the mind leaps forward to a possible solution.
2. An intellectualization of the difficulty or perplexity that has been *felt* (directly experienced) into a *problem* to be solved, a question for which the answer must be sought.
3. The use of one suggestion after another as a leading idea or *hypothesis* to initiate the guide observation and other operations in collection of factual material.
4. Mental elaboration of the idea or supposition (*reasoning*, in the sense in which reasoning is a part, not the whole, of inference).
5. Testing the hypothesis by overt or imaginative action.[9]

Educators and students alike are often too enmeshed in the five-step process to heed Dewey's conclusion: There is no set order to the five phases; there is nothing magical about the division into *five* phases; subsets can be delineated within each; two phases may be collapsed into one, and some may be quickly dealt with; and "the burden of reaching a conclusion may fall mainly on a single phase, which will then require a seemingly disproportionate development." "No set rules can be laid down on such matters. The way they are managed depends upon the individual tact and sensitiveness of the individual."[10]

The key words in these statements are "managed" and "sensitiveness." These place on the teacher the onus of creating a climate conducive to promoting students' intellectual growth through the application of reasoned thought. And one of the best techniques to

[9]Dewey, *How We Think*, pp. 106–7.
[10]Dewey, *How We Think*, pp. 115–16.

develop student learning at this level is discussion, the wisdom of which is expressed in the old Russian proverb: one understands only after one has discussed.

The sensitivity component is relevant to identifying students' and teachers' readiness to use the discussion method, for it requires optimal teacher-student interaction. In part this is what the case method is all about.

THE CASE METHOD

The case method provides the forum for inductive thinking. Umstattd supports this position and points out:[11]

> It [the case method] is a variant of the discussion procedure in which the class begins with a common body of facts relevant to a situation and together proceed to the best solution. Relationships are studied; ideas associated; points of view challenged and defended; tentative solutions are tested by logic, argumentation, and references to authoritative sources; and gradually a synthesis is reached that reflects at least general, if not unanimous agreement."

The method is not an easy one. Thinking never is. However, in order to use the technique successfully, to provide a climate for learning, the following should be kept in mind:

1. Cases are usually complex, ill-structured, incomplete, lengthy accounts of events or situations that are laden with problems or practices typical within a field of study.
2. The use of discussion for analysis and the resolution of problems is time consuming.
3. Extensive preparation for class meetings by both teacher and students is requisite.
4. The method is highly student-centered and by implication a highly nondirective teaching approach.
5. Teachers must allow students to make mistakes as well as expecting them to make rational decisions.
6. Questions raised for discussion should focus on the facts.
7. Objectivity is absolutely essential in exploring resolutions to the problems.
8. Resolutions sought should be an exercise in judgment making and applying knowledge and supported by substantive rationale.

[11] J. G. Umstattd, *College Teaching: Background, Theory and Practice* (Washington, D.C.: University Press of Washington, D.C. and Community College Press, 1964), p. 156.

9. Tolerance of divergent points of view is essential.
10. The discussion should not disintegrate into a "rap session."

Furthermore:

1. A scholarly approach is essential in dealing with the problems presented. This includes drawing on knowledge from major disciplines; having a working acquaintance with established sources of reliable information; continuing the search for truth; and translating facts, principles, theories, and ideas into acceptable realistic interventions.
2. The realistic problems are related to recurring situations. These provide meaning for the learner and are conducive to maximizing transfer learning, developing modes of inquiry, seeing patterns, acquiring insights, and identifying relationships.
3. The skills of identifying, assessing, synthesizing, and evaluating problems serve as a cumulative learning experience that can be formalized and practiced in classrooms, by people committed to rational judgments that can be translated into discerning health care interventions.
4. The problems, method, and process contribute to future multidisciplinary communication, collaboration, and coordination.

As Hunt notes, the case method has the following outcomes: "Retained capacity to think in a subject area"; "power to analyze and to master a tangle of circumstances . . ."; "ability to utilize ideas, to test them against the facts of the problem, to throw both ideas and facts into fresh combinations . . ."; "recognize a need for new factual material or the need to apply technical skills to a problem . . ."; "ability to use later experience as a test of the validity of the ideas . . . with flexibility to revise goals and procedures as experience is deepened . . ."; "communicate their [students] thinking to others in a manner which induces thought . . ."; "use ideas in theoretical form . . ."; "attain the goal simply, completely, and without any more waste than is necessary in any thinking about an unfamiliar problem."[12]

The clinical cases and general and specific questions developed for this book are offered as a means of educating gerontology clinical nurse specialists to meet the challenges of disciplined thought for discerning application.

[12] Pearson Hunt, "The Case Method of Instruction," *Harvard Educational Review* 21:3 (Summer 1951), pp. 177–78.

Case

I

Mr. Hans Schultz: A Desperate Man

SUGGESTIONS FOR APPROACHING THE CASE

Try to imagine yourself a practitioner of nursing who is faced with developing a plan for nursing intervention. To complicate matters, no nursing history exists; consequently no behavioral outcomes were established, no plans for short- and long-term goals, and no evaluation procedures. The only data available to you are based on a medical model.

Using knowledge bases, including theories and collaborative interchange, analyze the data and plan the phases of care for this case, which has as its central problems

unresolved grief
stressors
coping behaviors
areas of deprivation

developmental tasks
unmet needs
physiological manifestations
sick role
undeveloped support systems

Further, this case encompasses a series of events that span a considerable time. Consideration should be given to what preventive measures might have been taken, at what phase, and what intervention techniques would have been appropriate.

Also examine the hospitalization period with a view to determining what could have been done differently, by whom, and what actions would effect continuity of care, rehabilitation, and health maintenance.

THE CASE

History of Present Illness

On Christmas Eve, Mr. Schultz, age 74, was brought in an automobile to a hospital emergency room by his son. During the evening Mr. Schultz had given himself several enemas until he became lightheaded and experienced syncope. He apparently did not lose consciousness and called to his son, who was spending the evening at the family home. When seen in the emergency room, Mr. Schultz was ataxic, somewhat confused, and lethargic, exhibiting left arm weakness and flaccidity with spontaneous movement. There was no sensation in the left arm, and Mr. Schultz was not aware of its location; his remarks suggested that the arm did not belong to him.

Neurological examination revealed normal function of the cranial nerves, pupils, and neck muscles. Deep tendon reflexes were 2+ and symmetrical with right plantar flexor and left plantar extensor responses. Abdominal reflexes were absent.

When questioned, Mr. Schultz's son said he was certain his father did not have a history of bowel problems and could give no reason for the current behavior. Mr. Schultz had no recollection of giving himself the enemas. His abdomen was soft and not tender. The immediate medical impression was probable right hemisphere thromboembolic infarction.

Mr. Schultz was admitted to the neurological intensive care unit for close observation.

Laboratory tests on admission:

Blood:			
pH:	7.43	O_2 saturation at 97%	
$APCO_2$:	38	HCT:	39%
APC_2:	85	HGB:	13.7%
HCO_3:	25.4	WBC:	7,600

Past Health History

This information was contributed by Mr. Schultz's younger son, age 30, three hours after his father's admission to hospital. Mr. Schultz was thought to have been healthy and active for most of his life.

A. *Family history*

Father died age 75, mother died age 96 (causes unknown).
One sister, age 68, alive and well.
One brother died at age 70 (auto accident).
No known family history of diabetes mellitus, tuberculosis, cancer, or other familial problems.
Three sons, ages 26, 30, and 32; one daughter, age 34; all living and well.
No grandchildren.

B. *Habits*

Exercise: Usually walks one mile each day with no distress or discomfort. Climbs two flights of stairs without dyspnea. Cleans his own five-room house.

Sleeping: Sleeps with one pillow. No orthopnea. Experienced no insomnia until the past year. Arouses once each night to void. Takes no sleeping medications.

Eating: Has always enjoyed food and had, until the past six months, a large appetite. Generally ate with friends or a son. Liked to eat in restaurants on occasion. Meat intake has decreased over the past two or three years. Does enjoy sweets.

Tobacco: Nonsmoker.

Alcohol: Does not drink alcoholic beverages.

Coffee: One to two cups at breakfast and lunch. Tea with the evening meal.

C. *Occupation*

Retired plumber for the past year. Youngest son took over the business.

D. *Medications at home*

Aspirin tabs. II for occasional headache.
Pepto-Bismol for "upset stomach."

E. *Personal history*

Born 1902 in the United States. Graduated from high school and became a plumber's apprentice. Eventually founded his own successful business.

F. *Social history*

Was married for 32 years, until his wife died in 1972.
Three sons and one daughter live in the vicinity.
Owns five-room home and has managed to live comfortably on savings and social security.
No longer drives a car but walks or is driven by sons or friends.
Gardened and cleaned his home until three months ago. Sons helped when they found time.
Income not known.
Health insurance: Medicare.

Previous Health and Illness

Acute Infections:	Nature of childhood diseases not known. No known history of tuberculosis, pneumonia, or influenza.
Immunizations:	Does not maintain immunizations.
Allergic Phenomena:	No known drug or food intolerance. Stated he has "hay fever" in the spring but never tested for pollen allergies. No history of blood transfusion.
Head:	Has worn glasses for reading and a hearing aid for the past five years. Adentulous but refuses to wear dentures; reason unknown. Has not visited an ophthalmologist or dentist in many years.
Neuromuscular:	No history of dizziness, tremors, weakness, ataxic gait, fainting, facial drooping, or mental confusion.
Respiratory:	Essentially unremarkable. No history of frequent upper respiratory infections, cough, dyspnea, or sputum production.
Cardiac:	No history of dyspnea on exertion. Climbs two flights of stairs without difficulty. Denies chest pain and ankle edema.
Gastrointestinal:	Occasional "stomach upset," relieved with Pepto-Bismol. Episodes not correlated with seasonal changes or foods.
Genitourinary:	Denies problems such as dysuria, pain, or polyuria. Nocturia $\times$ 1.

Emotional: Essentially stable, outgoing, active until four and a half years ago, upon death of his wife in 1972. Intermittent periods of "depression" have increased since loss of his mother six months ago. At that time he developed delusions of scabies, heart condition, and weakness in his right arm. Conversations became increasingly concerned with death and morbid topics. Communication with sons markedly decreased in frequency. More time was spent alone at home, until the week prior to Christmas holidays, when he visited his eldest son.

Physical Assessment

First day of admission

General Appearance: Mr. Schultz is a well-developed, elderly man (6 ft, 170 lb).
Lethargic but aroused by a loud voice; responding with single words to questions.
Skin color ruddy and clear; no pallor, pigmentation, jaundice, petechiae, or spider angiomata. Skin dry with little wrinkling. Turgor fair (for his age); body hair scant.
No digit clubbing or edema.
Blood pressure 130/70; pulse 80; respirations 18; temperature 99°F.

Head: Normal cephalic; no scars, deformities, or tenderness. Hair thick, white, and dry. Features symmetrical.

Eyes: Visual acuity not tested with Snellen's chart. Able to read magazine print with eyeglasses. Pupils equal and react to light and accommodation. Eyeballs: extra ocular movements through six cardinal fields within normal limits. Eye grounds: discs unremarkable; no hemorrhages.

Ears: No mastoid tenderness or discharge. Right tympanic membrane gray, shiny, and intact. Left tympanic membrane essentially absent. Patient denies trauma or infection to left ear or head.

Nose: No abnormalities in shape; no obstruction to breathing; no sinus tenderness. Turbinates dull red.

Mouth: Mucous membranes and gums pink, smooth, and moist. Tongue well papillated, noncoated, and midline. Adentulous. Throat clear, uvula midline.

Neck: No palpable masses or thyroid. No abnormal pulsation or venous engorgement. Trachea midline.

Lymph Glands: None palpable.

Spine:	No vertebral tenderness. Moderate osteoporotic kyphosis.
Thorax:	No barreling of thorax; no flared ribs.
Lungs:	Equal fremitus; no rales, rhonchi, friction rubs, or wheezes. Equal diaphragmatic excursion.
Heart:	Point of maximum impulse sixth intercostal space mid clavicular line. No clicks or murmurs. Normal sinus rhythm.
Pulses:	All present, full, and equal.
Abdomen:	Soft, scaphoid, and symmetrical. Bowel sounds decreased. No scarring or tenderness. Liver nonpalpable.
Extremities:	All present; skin warm; moderate brown pigmentation anterior lower legs; no mottling. Full range of motion all joints; no hesitancy or pain. No tremors, bruises, or scars. Does not move left arm on command. Sensation and kinesthesis absent in left arm. Muscular strength in legs equal. Nails yellow, hard, thick, and brittle.
Neurological:	Gait not evaluated. See history of present illness.
Genitalia:	Normal uncircumsized male. Evidenced lack of sphincter control.
Rectal:	Mucosa unremarkable on digital examination. Prostate moderately enlarged and soft.

First day after admission

X-rays:	Chest and skull unremarkable.
Laboratory Tests:	CBC, urinalysis, and electrolytes within normal limits. VDRL negative.
Progress (Neurological):	Afebrile. Obtunded but easily aroused verbally. Spoke occasionally and hesitantly; no dysphasia. Intermittent confusion as to person, place, and time.
Physical Parameters:	Blood pressure range 126/74–130/70. Pulse 70–84 and regular. Respirations 16–20. Temperature 98°F to 99.4°F.
Medications:	Mellaril 50 mg P.O. t.i.d. Doridan I capsule hour of sleep. Intravenous infusion 2000 cc 0.045 normal saline each 24 hours for the first two days.

On the fourth day Mr. Schultz's medical prognosis was considered stable and favorable for good recovery. He was transferred to a five-bed room.

Fifth day

Laboratory Results:	Negative for: Rheumatoid arthritis. Kidney disease.

Presence of amphetamines, opiates, methadone, and barbiturates.
Serum B_{12} level normal.
T_4: 4.9
T_3: 31
Lumbar puncture: no WBC's
RCB's: 158/mm^3
EMI: moderate cortical atrophy.

Neuromuscular Assessment by Physical Therapist: Three areas of limitation:

1. Ataxic motor control of the left upper extremity.
2. Weak left shoulder muscles.
3. Absence of sensation, left upper extremity.

Emotional Assessment by Psychiatrist: Long-term memory intact. Loss of short-term memory. Some mental confusion relative to time and place. Continued expression of preoccupation with death; when pressed for personal and social reality, talk of death decreased. Conversation generally initiated by others; responses appropriate.

Physical Status: Urinary output through Foley catheter continued approximately 75–80% of intake; amber; clear; specific gravity 1.025.
Incontinence of soft brown stool became a problem.
Night sleep pattern remained constant with periods of restlessness and requests for water.
Appetite adequate; regular pureed house diet eaten; some assistance with liquids.

Environment: Five-bed room. Four male roommates, ages 24 to 56. Bed beside window and farthest from the door. All the men were confined to bed and/or wheelchairs, a result of various neurological dysfunctions.

Awareness of Environment: Staff not recognized from one encounter to another.
Orientation to routine and surroundings presented by staff were not retained and frustration exhibited by pushing his left arm away or an object onto the floor.
Did not ask questions of staff or family.
No interaction initiated with roommates.
Watched television if someone turned it on; did not request to view; did not read magazines when they were offered.

Two weeks after admission

Neurological Assessment:

1. Angiography and brain scan:
   Major neck vessels patent.
   Right hemispheric blood flow lag.
   Vascular compromise of midcerebral artery.
   No cerebral infarction, mass, tumor, or hematoma.

2. Minnesota Test for Differential Diagnosis of Aphasia. (Administered by patient's eldest son)
   Reading ability error free at paragraph level.
   Sentence reading intact.
   Verbal retention for digits and sentences within normal limits.
   Demonstrated more awareness of surroundings and asked questions concerning physical progress.

Musculoskeletal Progress: Physical therapy daily sessions for two hours.
Emphasis:
Increasing left-side strength and kinesthetic awareness.
Transferring from bed to chair by pivoting.
Standing with assistance.

General Physical Progress: Urinary incontinence requiring external collection.
Bowel pattern alternated between constipation and diarrhea; rectal control returned intermittently. Dulcolax tab I q.d. provided some regularity.
Sleeping pattern continued to be nightly with periods of wakefulness.
Frequent requests for water and assistance in turning.

Third week

Neurological Progress: No conversation initiated; responses appropriate. Participated in patient and staff interaction when encouraged.
Left arm remained weak; movements were gross and position awareness absent.

Musculoskeletal Progress: Required assistance in activities of daily living.
Transfer from chair to bed and standing with assistance improved. Weight bearing equal.
Did not exercise left arm actively despite teaching to that effect.

General Physical Progress: Skin remained intact. Every meal eaten completely. Lungs clear. Vital signs stable. Urinary incontinence continued. Bowel elimination pattern more regular.

Family Interaction: Eldest son (Tom) and youngest son (Eric) visited each evening for two hours.
Daughter-in-law Barbara (Eric's wife) visited in the afternoon for 2–3 hours, reading newspaper to Mr. Schultz.
The middle son (Robert) and daughter (Sandra) did not visit, although they lived in the area.
Sons kept father informed daily of family events.
Communication flowed to Mr. Schultz more frequently than from him.

Eye contact maintained between Mr. Schultz and family.
Family frequently questioned staff for information about Mr. Schultz's progress.
Tom called the physician twice from Mr. Schultz's phone to have questions answered.
Barbara accompanied Mr. Schultz to physical therapy one afternoon.

At the end of the third week the medical staff felt Mr. Schultz's prognosis for rehabilitation was fair.

Family pressed for Mr. Schultz's discharge to Tom's apartment. Tom lived with a male friend and was considered by Eric and Barbara to be able to provide more of the necessary resources for Mr. Schultz's recovery. Tom agreed.

Tom, a frequently unemployed musician and writer, had more living space and time to devote to his father.

Mr. Schultz adamantly refused to consider a convalescent home for continuing rehabilitation.

Fourth week

All systems essentially unchanged.

Discharge Plans:

Medications:
Mellaril 50 mg t.i.d.
Doridan I capsule h.s.
Dulcolax I tab q.d. A.M.
Psychiatric followup weekly at our patient psychiatric clinic.
Mr. Schultz's sons expressed many concerns relative to post hospitalization care, their roles, expectations, and anxieties.
The health team did not meet with Mr. Schultz or his family to discuss Mr. Schultz's future or his problems.

Post-Hospitalization Information

Two weeks after Mr. Schultz's discharge from the acute care hospital, his eldest son visited the hospital nursing unit to thank the staff for the care they had given his father.

The son voiced concern about his father's interrupted night sleeping pattern, which wakened other members of the household. In addition Mr. Schultz had frequent episodes of weeping and out-

bursts of shouting. He continued to have periods of left hemesthetic unawareness that resulted in hematomas to the arm and hand. His appetite was poor, and he had lost interest in his surroundings. His main diversion was sitting by a window watching people pass by on the street.

Mr. Schultz had returned to the hospital psychiatric clinic for a followup conference but refused any subsequent visit.

At this time the family members were not ready to consider placing Mr. Schultz in a long-term care facility.

A month after hospitalization the social worker telephoned Mr. Schultz's son and learned the problems were unresolved. Mr. Schultz refused to exercise his extremities and refused to wear the external urinary drainage appliance. Also, bowel constipation had increased; fluid intake had decreased and sleep patterns were reversed.

On the basis of this information the social worker initiated discussion with two of Mr. Schultz's sons relative to a suitable care facility.

STUDY GUIDE QUESTIONS

1. Identify the underlying factors or events that precipitated the immediate crisis. Describe the interrelated processes.
2. Identify Mr. Schultz's unresolved basic needs.
3. Determine problems that could have been anticipated and prevented. By what measures? At what phase?
4. From the limited case data, develop a nursing history. What components are unattainable? How could a history have been obtained? What data that are essential for the elderly are not known about Mr. Schultz?
5. Analyze the effectiveness of Mr. Schultz's support systems.
6. Frequently, hospitalizations are unnecessarily long. At what point could Mr. Schultz have been safely discharged? Support your reasons. Develop a realistic, comprehensive discharge plan. When could this plan have best been implemented? Provide a timetable for the proposed events.
7. Following brain trauma, cerebral functioning such as learning ability is often significantly altered. From knowledge of physiology and location of deficit, what cognitive abilities are affected?

Retained? Utilizing theories and methods of teaching and learning, outline a realistic plan for Mr. Schultz.

8. Mr. Schultz's problems and needs will undoubtedly remain multifaceted and long-term. Develop a plan of long-term care in the community. Keep in mind cost, methods of financing, manpower, services, patient criteria, and facilities.

Case

Mrs. Rachel Bergman: Insult to Impairment

INTRODUCTION

Envision yourself a Gerontology Nurse Clinician in joint practice with an internal medicine physician, serving a suburban population of elderly clients. Your part of the practice involves patient education, assessment, treatment, consultation, and continuity of care. The settings for providing care are office practice, an acute care hospital, extended care facilities, and patients' homes. The roles with the physician are complemental, collaborative, and interdependent with maximum autonomy within the scope of nursing practice.

One of your clients is Mrs. Bergman, an elderly Jewish woman who presents these major considerations in nursing care management:

Wound healing and the impediments to it caused by aging
The infectious process and its relationship to mental status
Management of confusion in the elderly

Treatment modalities for decubitus ulcers
Dental hygiene in institutionalized elderly
Long-term institutional care:
  Selection
  Assurance of quality care
  Regulation
  Costs
Health care benefits for the elderly

Second, the role of the gerontology nurse clinician should be examined relative to

Scope of practice
Regulations, license, and certification
Reimbursement for services

The questions developed throughout and at the conclusion of the case address these problems and issues.

THE CASE

On April 2 a Gerontology Nurse Clinician received a request from Highland Nursing Home to visit Mrs. Rachel Bergman. Mrs. Bergman, age 78, had apparently become febrile and abdominally distended and refused to feed herself.

A review of office records showed Mrs. Bergman's problems to be:

Chronic renal insufficiency
Organic brain disorder
Sacral and left heel decubiti
Hypertension
Emphysema
Gallstones

Mrs. Bergman had been referred to the office six months earlier, upon admission to the nursing home from her daughter's home.

The nurse clinician arrived at Highland to find Mrs. Bergman slumped in a wheelchair, alternately screaming and calling "Ma Mama Ma." Her gray hair hung long and damp, smelled sour, partially covering her face. Her brown eyes had a vacant look. She had a foul body odor but had been heavily powdered. A round, short

woman, she was unable to bear weight and cried out when moved. An aide helped the nurse clinician lift Mrs. Bergman into bed for a physical examination.

Vital Signs:	Blood pressure 140/82. Temperature 101.6 rectally. Radial pulse 70. Respirations 18.
Head:	Essentially unremarkable.
Mouth:	Adentulous with mucosal plaques.
Thorax and Respiratory:	Anterior/posterior diameter 1:2. Few fine rales scattered at the bases and clear with coughing.
Cardiovascular:	Lower extremity pulses 1+ bilaterally. No peripheral edema or varicosities. Heart essentially unremarkable.
Abdomen:	Protuberant and round with no scars. Bowel sounds heard in all quadrants. Liver percussed at 8 cm at the MCL. No apparent tenderness throughout all quadrants. Incontinent of soft, formed stool during examination; guaiac negative.
Genitourinary:	No inflammation of urinary meatus and no discharge apparent. Indwelling catheter drained dark, foul-smelling, opaque urine.
Integument:	Dark red area 7 cm X 5 cm over the sacrum with three nearby abrasions, one 2 X 3 cm and two 3 X 5 cm with serous drainage. There was a 5 cm unruptured blister with surrounding erythematous area on left ankle.

Mrs. Bergman became fatigued, and the remainder of the examination was postponed. According to the staff, Mrs. Bergman called out continually, asking for her mother. The staff felt Mrs. Bergman was confused, paranoid, and hopelessly senile.

Current Physician's Orders:	Valium 2 mg P.O. q.h.s. Enduron 2.5 mg q.o.d. Digoxin 0.125 mg daily except Sunday. MOM 30 cc p.r.n. Fleets enema p.r.n. General diet with ground meat and eggnog supplemental feeding.

The Gerontology Nurse Clinician called the physician with whom she collaborated to report the preliminary findings and request orders for an antibiotic. Tetracycline 500 mg q.i.d. was added to the above list.

The following nursing orders were written for the nursing home staff:

Urine culture, sensitivity, and analysis
Vital signs every eight hours

Change indwelling catheter and irrigate with sterile normal saline 60 cc p.r.n.
Increase physical contact with patient
Feed patient, with encouragement to feed herself
Infrared lamp to decubitus on coccyx by physical therapy department b.i.d.
Heel cuffs at all times

The problems of abdominal distention, febrility, and urinary tract infection were added to the office records. In the progress notes the nurse discussed plans to visit Mrs. Bergman weekly to monitor her progress, to contact Mrs. Bergman's daughter, Ruth, to discuss ways of improving the care at the home, and to organize a plan of treatment with the physician.

The next day the nurse called Highland Nursing Home and was assured that Mrs. Bergman's condition was unchanged and orders were being followed.

Later that week the nurse visited Highland Nursing Home and found no report of the urine tests ordered. No one knew which laboratory the home used, and no assistance was volunteered. By searching other records, the nurse eventually obtained the name of the laboratory and called for results, which were reported as follows:

Urinalysis:

Color: Amber
Character: Cloudy
pH: 8.0
Specific gravity: 1.036
Albumen, sugar, and acetone: negative
Occult blood: moderate
WBC: 0–1
RBC: 5–10
Bacteria: 3+
Amorphous crystals: 3+
Culture: pseudomonasaerugonisia 300,000/ml
Sensitivity: Not completed

Notes were left in strategic places instructing the duty nurse to call the office and report the sensitivity results. The nurse clinician informed the staff that Vitamin C and cranberry juice were to be added to Mrs. Bergman's diet.

The nurse clinician found Mrs. Bergman still confused and calling for her mother. Urine was opaque and foul smelling.

The decubitus ulcers continued unchanged except for an increased area of erythema surrounding the left heel blister. The heel

cuffs were not in place. Mrs. Bergman was wearing scuff slippers, and one bare ankle was pressed against the wheelchair pedal.

Note: Assess the data presented above, plan nursing interventions, and provide rationale in support of the decisions made.

On April 14 the nurse clinician visited Mrs. Bergman. Mrs. Bergman had apparently been given the tetracycline and cranberry juice as ordered, but the urine pH was now 9.0 and continued to be opaque and foul smelling. A repeat urinalysis, culture, and sensitivity were ordered for two days after completion of the ten-day course of antibiotic therapy.

Mrs. Bergman's skin condition had deteriorated markedly within five days. The left heel blister was 7 cm in diameter with serous contents. There was a 4 X 2 cm blister on the dorsal medial side of the left foot and a 4 X 1 cm blister on the right lateral lower leg. Cyanosis in the coccyx area had increased to 12 cm in diameter. Over the ischial tuberosities there had developed a 14 X 3 cm indurated, inflamed area, for which infrared light and Betadine paintings were ordered, to be carried out by the physical therapist. The nurse clinician was convinced the physical therapists followed through on orders for Mrs. Bergman and the nurses did not.

Mrs. Bergman remained confused but was sleeping more and appeared increasingly lethargic. Her frequent calling for her mother annoyed the staff, and the nurse clinician was requested to meet with the administrator to discuss this problem. The administrator immediately demanded that the nurse clinician explain why Mrs. Bergman's sedation medication was not increased as requested. The administrator emphatically stated, "That woman must be sedated during the day or else she will have to go elsewhere. She is too disruptive to other patients and the staff. Her screaming gets on everyone's nerves. I think you should write an order for Haldol; that works quite well." The clinician explained that she does not prescribe medications and that the physician would not approve sedation. She attempted to explain the relationship between infections and mental confusion in the elderly. The administrator was not interested: "I don't really believe that nonsense. I want immediate treatment with sedatives, which is the only thing that will work in a case such as this. I've seen a lot of senility in my time, so I am well able to recognize it." The clinician tried again to describe the impli-

cations of such medications for aging physiology and suggested a mild analgesic instead. Her suggestion was discounted and undoubtedly ineffective.

Note: Delineate the nursing management problems; determine how you would have handled them, providing clearly supported reasons for each.

Following this encounter, the nurse clinician called Mrs. Bergman's daughter, Ruth, to inform her of recent events. Ruth was angry and discouraged, saying, "I can't handle her at home anymore, and I can't afford to move her to a more expensive place. I know the care at that nursing home isn't good; that's why I visit her every day and at least try to feed her. You know, I took care of her myself until she became so bedridden I couldn't lift her." Ruth went on to describe her mother's difficult life as a teenage immigrant from prerevolutionary Russia in 1916. "She has always worked; her whole life she worked, and now look at her. Treated like an animal, she is. She never looked for anything; never had anything except her family, which was everything to her. She had four children, but I'm the only one that survived so it's all up to me."

Two days later Ruth called the nurse clinician to say that her mother was unresponsive to anyone. That day the clinician visited Mrs. Bergman and found her obtunded and dangerously dehydrated. A conference with Ruth, the physician, and the clinician resulted in plans to hospitalize Mrs. Bergman for intravenous therapy, antibiotics, and evaluation.

Mrs. Bergman was transferred to an acute care hospital on April 17 with a temperature of 101.8°F rectally. Intravenous fluids were begun immediately on admission. Urine culture and sensitivity were ordered statim. Within 24 hours Mrs. Bergman was conscious and recognized her daughter, although she was still confused and called for her mother.

Ruth and the nurse clinician discussed plans for Mrs. Bergman's future care. Ruth felt $800 monthly was the maximum her mother's estate could afford. "I have to contribute every month as well, and being widowed with two teenagers isn't easy. My salary isn't all that good." Arrangements were made for Ruth to meet with Social Service personnel the next day to discuss Mrs. Bergman's eligibility for Medicaid.

On April 20 laboratory analysis of Mrs. Bergman's urine was found to be grossly contaminated with E. Coli not pseudomonas and resistant to tetracycline. She was immediately started on 500 mg of ampicillin every six hours intravenously. Electrocytes had been elevated on admission due to hemoconcentration from dehydration. These returned to normal limits within the first week.

After one week Mrs. Bergman's intravenous was discontinued and ampicillin was given orally. Mrs. Bergman began eating but would not feed herself. Her appetite was surprisingly good and oral fluid intake more than adequate.

Mrs. Bergman's skin condition remained poor. Although no new decubiti developed, those present showed deterioration. Foul brown material drained from the coccyx, left ischial tuberosity, and left heel. Black necrotic material had hardened in the center of the coccyx. Treatment with an enzymatic debriding agent was instituted.

After one week of enzyme debridement, surgical debridement of the sacral and hip decubiti was completed. A large abscess was discovered below the sacral eschar which drained green, purulent material. Followup treatment included irrigations with Dakin's solution and wet Dakin's packing to the wound. The enzyme debridement to the leg and feet decubiti was continued.

Mrs. Bergman continued steady physical improvement. She had gained strength and was able to sit in a wheelchair for short periods. Emotionally, she was less disturbed, with few episodes of calling for her mother. She was pleasant to others, but she did not recognize her daughter and could not remember familiar names. Responses to questions were generally inappropriate, and she was not oriented to time, person, or place.

On May 8 Mrs. Bergman developed loud generalized wheezes and an irregular respiratory pattern of alternating periods of hyperpnea and apnea without Cheyne-Stokes respiration, characteristic building quality. Concomitantly 3+ pitting pedal edema developed. The nurse clinician visited and found heel cuffs tightly applied, further obstructing circulation and resulting in cyanosis and hypothermia to the feet. Heel cuffs were loosened and feet were elevated. The clinician consulted the physican, and Lanoxin .125 mg daily was ordered.

During this time, Ruth contacted the nurse clinician for advice in selecting a safe, appropriate nursing home for her mother. She was anxious to avoid the problems encountered in the previous situation.

Ruth had investigated several recommended homes and had selected one she felt met her criteria of cost and location. She wanted a professional's opinion to reassure and confirm her decision. The nurse clinician arranged to visit the home to evaluate its appropriateness.

The nurse administrator was contacted for permission to tour the facilities. The administrator was pleasant, answered questions readily, and arranged for the clinician to tour the home. Introductions were made to all staff who would be involved with Mrs. Bergman's care, after which the nurse clinician was encouraged to look around on her own and talk to residents.

The nurse clinician reported favorably of the home's milieu to Mrs. Bergman's daughter. Ruth expressed concerns about abandoning her mother as well as her inability to care for her at home. "I never feel relaxed anymore. If anything more happens, I don't think I can cope. I'll leave town and you can deal with it."

The following day Ruth received notice from the hospital that her mother's Medicare coverage would end within twenty-four hours, necessitating immediate transfer to the nursing home. Ruth called the social worker and became abusive. The physician was notified, and he met Ruth at the hospital, at which time she threatened to sue the hospital, the physician, and the nurse clinician for prematurely removing her mother from the care she still required. She would accept no rational explanation.

Note: Delineate the problems. Explain how you would handle and offer resolutions to the problems based on facts and principles related to nursing management of the elderly.

The Social Service department personnel arranged for Mrs. Bergman's transfer to the selected nursing home the next day. Medicare had agreed to cover the cost of the first three weeks in the nursing home, but Medicaid would not become effective for three months. When informed of these plans, Ruth was sarcastic, but ultimately complied with the decision.

Mrs. Bergman was successfully transferred to the new nursing home, accompanied by the nurse clinician and Ruth.

Physician's Orders:

Lanoxin 0.125 mg daily except Sunday.
Mandelamine 1 gm q.i.d. (use suspension).
Vitamin C 500 mg q.i.d.
Dakin's solution one half strength dressings daily to left foot, coccyx, and hip ulcers.

Colace 100 mg daily.
Chloral hydrate 0.5 gm at bedtime p.r.n.
Dulcolax or glycerin suppository p.r.n.
Tap water enema p.r.n.
Irrigate indwelling catheter with sterile normal saline p.r.n.

Note: Provide rationale for the foregoing orders. Evaluate appropriateness for Mrs. Bergman. Write nursing orders. Provide rationale for those orders.

Ten days following transfer, the nurse clinician visited Mrs. Bergman.

Note: Develop a plan for assessing quality of care.

The nurse clinician found Mrs. Bergman in the dining room wearing a blue dress, shoes, and stockings. Her hair had been cut and set. She was sitting erect in a wheelchair and feeding herself. The nurse greeted Mrs. Bergman and was surprised to receive an appropriate, descriptive response. Mrs. Bergman discussed the menu and introduced her table companions. The nurse and she subsequently went to a lounge and talked for another half hour. Mrs. Bergman had patchy recall of the past months, but did remember the nurse from previous encounters and apologized for not acknowledging her on those occasions.

The nurse clinician took Mrs. Bergman to her room for a followup examination.

Findings:

Blood pressure: 120/62 right arm (sitting).
Cardiovascular:
- Rate 68 and regular.
- Holosystolic grade II–III murmur at the left sternal border in the tricuspid area not elicited previously.

Pulmonary:
- Rate 18 and shallow.
- No rales, rhonchi, or wheezes.
- Breath sounds decreased at the bases on normal inspiration.

Decubiti unchanged, but without indication of infection.
Urine: clear, yellow; no foul odor; pH 7.

At this point Mrs. Bergman's roommate, Hannah, returned, and introductions were made. Hannah, a verbose woman in her late seventies, described Mrs. Bergman's first few days there. "I don't allow Rachel to call Ma-Ma. If she wants something, she has to call me." Mrs. Bergman asked Hannah to get her a drink of water, which Hannah did with some difficulty, maneuvering her wheelchair into the bathroom. Mrs. Bergman took one sip and placed the glass on the bedside table. Hannah admonished her roommate, "I didn't go to all that work for one sip. You should drink it all." At this Mrs. Bergman smiled and finished the water.

Note: Complete a summary nursing assessment, plans for nursing intervention based on clearly supported evidence from the literature.

STUDY GUIDE QUESTIONS

1. Develop criteria for evaluation of a skilled-care facility to include:
   Physical plant, floor plan and facilities
   Emotional climate
   Safety
   Privacy
   Aesthetics
   Social interaction
   Activities
   Religious observances
   Nutrition
2. For extended care, determine criteria for accreditation and methods of regulation, review, and control of standards (state and federal).
3. Determine methods of financing long-term institutional care:
   Individual
   Third-party reimbursement
   Criteria for individual and institutional eligibility
4. Identify levels of long-term care and criteria for each level.
5. Discuss the scope of nursing practice within your state Nurse Practice Act.
   a. Formal and informal limitations and controls.
   b. Appropriateness for current nursing practice.
   c. Methods of altering the Act.

6. Discuss problems and methods of reimbursement for nursing services within the following settings:
   Institutions
   Collaboration with physicians
   Independent practice
   Health maintenance organizations

Case III

Mrs. Hattie Brown: Poor, Black, Disabled, and Aging

INTRODUCTION

Poverty is no respecter of race, creed, color, or age, nor is chronic neurologic disability. In this set of circumstances Mrs. Brown is representative of the aging, economically disadvantaged person who has a debilitating long-term health problem.

Mrs. Brown is not atypical of a Southern Black born, reared, and educated under poverty conditions who eventually moved to a large northern city (at the end of World War II) in search of a better life for herself and her family. As indicated in the title, location did not improve her living conditions. Therefore it is suggested that this case be examined in view of these concerns and other readily identifi-

In collaboration with the authors, Patricia Cemashko Canty, R.N., M.S., developed the background material for this case as part of a course assignment while a Masters student in gerontology nursing at Rush University, College of Nursing, Chicago.

able problems affecting the total health care management of Mrs. Brown.

The questions at the end of this case give focus to the resolution of the concerns and lend to active discussion. A few answers are provided, but they should not be taken as final or complete. You should elaborate them when necessary and judge them for appropriateness and conclusiveness.

THE CASE

Hattie Brown was born in Mississippi in 1918. At the end of sixth grade her formal education ended, and she went to work in a laundry to help support ten siblings. Married at age 21, she moved north ten years later with her husband and young daughter. Shortly afterward, her husband abandoned the family; Mrs. Brown remarried but left her second husband after ten years. Throughout this time Mrs. Brown worked, ironing clothes in a laundry, to support her family. When she was 50 years old and a grandmother, Mrs. Brown became the legal guardian of her 5 year-old half brother, Nathan, son of her father's second wife. The boy's mother had abandoned him, and his father had died. Since that time, she has been the sole supporter of this boy.

Hattie Brown and Nathan rent a small, two-bedroom, second-floor apartment in the southwest sector of a metropolitan city. Their furnishings are adequate and well cared for, though old. There is no air conditioning, and screens need repair. "That landlord, he don't take much notice of what needs doin'. When I asks him to fix stuff, he says he'll get to it. But mostly he don't."

The neighborhood is an ethnic mix of Black, Mexican, Polish, and Lithuanian people. Once a thriving business district, the area has deteriorated into old brick shells, most in poor repair or vacant. Street lighting is poor and the crime rate high. The few local shops are small, inadequate, and expensive. A medical center is three miles distant, but buses are infrequent and unsafe and taxi service costly.

Mrs. Brown's sole outside interest is her church. She has been active in the Spiritual Baptist Church for the past thirty years and has many friends among the membership.

Five years ago Mrs. Brown developed Parkinsonism and was forced to retire from her job in a laundry. "I guess I shook too much,

and I got too slow. I kinda miss the folks there. I worked there for twenty-five years." Upon her early retirement Mrs. Brown received no pension and had no savings. "It takes everything just to live." Her income is limited to Social Security and Public Aid with an allowance for Nathan and Medicare disability benefits. Nathan has not seen his mother in ten years and receives no support from her.

With Mrs. Brown's increasing disability, Nathan assumed responsibility for grocery shopping and heavy household chores. Mrs. Brown's daughter is married, has children, and lives fifteen miles away. "She don't come and visit much anymore. I'd like to see the children more, but she say she don't have time. At least Nat is good to me. Not trouble like some his age. He goes to high school real regular."

In January 1978, Hattie Brown's tremors had become uncontrollable, and she was admitted to a neurology unit of the medical center. A graduate student majoring in gerontology nursing chose Mrs. Brown for primary care. She found Mrs. Brown in an uncomfortable position, staring blankly at the wall with severe tremors shaking the bed. Speaking was difficult and limited to short, slow, whispered phrases. Obtaining a health history required two hours of careful listening. Mrs. Brown was a reliable historian, but because of her exhaustion, supplemental data was obtained from the neurology clinic where she had been a patient for the past ten years.

Hattie Brown is a short heavy woman 5 ft 1 in. tall and weighs 170 lb. She has short, tightly curling gray hair and smooth, dark brown skin. She is alert and maintains eye contact but does not change facial expression. Mrs. Brown claims she came to the hospital because her Parkinsonism "got worse. I walk all hunched over and clumsy. My neck get stiff at night 'cause I'm hunched over all day. I didn't think I get this Parkinson again since I been taking the medicine the doctor give me a long time ago."

Hattie Brown described herself as having been in excellent health until ten years ago, when a tremor and weakness developed in her right hand and arm. She was told she had Parkinson's disease and was treated with a medication, the name of which Mrs. Brown did not know. The symptoms gradually increased in severity, with profound total body stiffness (which impaired general movement) appearing two to three years later. Levodopa therapy was initiated, and this relieved all symptoms except a fine tremor of the right hand. However, hypotension resulted, and a regimen of Sinemet

(amount unknown), Librium 5 mg t.i.d., and Artane 2 mg t.i.d. was instituted. Tremors were controlled, but general weakness increased.

Gradually, Mrs. Brown noticed difficulty changing positions in bed and in rising from a chair, bradykinesia, difficulty ambulating, slowness in initiating ambulation, sialorrhea, frequent diaphoresis, constipation, and short-term memory loss. There had apparently been no seborrhea or speech changes and no loss of balance or falling.

Mrs. Brown showed little knowledge of Parkinson disease and felt unfortunate because she continued to "get it again and again." Exacerbations came without warning despite alleged adherence to the prescribed medication regimen and medical management. No occupational hazards had been determined in Mrs. Brown's work history. There had been no chronic exposure to carbon monoxide, heavy metals, or noxious chemicals. She had not visited Guam. There had been no history of psychiatric disorder.

Shortly after admission, it was reported that Mrs. Brown was having nightmares. Mrs. Brown was unaware of these and attributed her nocturnal confusion to change in environment, stating that it did not occur at home. Her daughter disagreed, stating that Nathan had expressed concern about the increased frequency of episodes within the past year.

Mrs. Brown recalled having the usual childhood infections. She also recalled being told she had hypertension but could not remember the medication used nor the reason for discontinuing treatment. There was no report of hypertension in the clinic's record.

Family history was sketchy, with very little known of siblings' deaths. "They all died in the South. I'm the only one that got to be old. My mother's mother had the same thing as me. I can remember her shakes." Mrs. Brown has one daughter; a son died at birth, cause unknown. Menopause occurred at age 59.

Mrs. Brown has never smoked and rarely drinks alcoholic beverages. She enjoys two cups of coffee or tea daily. She fries most of her meat, preferring chicken and pork. Favorite foods include hominy and grits, black-eyed peas, greens boiled with pork fat, and biscuits with gravy.

Following admission, Mrs. Brown's medication regimen was altered to the following:

Artane 2 mg p.o. t.i.d.
Sinemet II tabs. 10/100 t.i.d.

Dalmane 30 mg p.o. q.h.s. p.r.n.
Dulcolax 5 mg p.o. q.h.s.

On the second hospital day the graduate student assessed Mrs. Brown's physical status and systems review.

Blood Pressure:	*Right Arm*	*Left Arm*
	112/80 supine	
	110/80 sitting	110/80 sitting
	92/72 standing	
Temperature:	99°F orally	
Apical Rate:	92	
Radial Rate:	92	
Respirations:	18	
	Objective	*Subjective*
Skin:	Dark brown color Increased pigmentation around finger and toenails	Skin is dry
Nails:	Short, clear, appear brittle	Chip and break easily
Hair and Scalp:	Hair dry, coarse in texture, and lacking luster; distribution normal Scalp dry Hair absent over dorsal surfaces, hands, and lower extremities	Hair and scalp dry
Head:	Normal cephalic No lesions or abnormalities	No sinusitis Occasional headaches
Eyes:	Acuity with corrective lenses: 20/20 Right eye 20/30 Left eye Without glasses: 20/180 bilaterally Extra Occular Movement intact without nystagmus Convergence slow Accommodation normal Pupils react equally but slowly to light Anisocoria present: Left pupil = 4 mm Right pupil = 6 mm Arcus senilis present Slight edema of the upper eyelid Optic disc crisp with no hemorrhages or exudates; eye grounds darkly pigmented	Wears eyeglasses for reading Last eye exam one year Occasional redness, itching and excessive tearing (associated with hay fever season) Night blindness

Ears:	Pinna and mastoid nontender Acuity grossly intact (ticking watch) Weber and Rinne Tests normal Tympanic membrane intact Moderate cerumen	
Nose:	Symmetrical with no deviation No inflammation or lesions Sense of smell intact	Occasional hay fever symptoms
Mouth:	Lips dry Buccal mucosa pink Gingiva pink with no hyperplasia Teeth in generally good condition except lower left second molar, which is severely decayed Tongue symmetrical with no deviation or tremor Sense of taste intact	Frequent toothaches Bleeding gums Last dental examination three years ago
Neck:	Trachea midline No thyroid enlargement or nodules Good Range of Motion	Hoarseness associated with increased mucus secretion Neck pain and stiffness most pronounced in the morning
Lymph Nodes:	No enlargement	
Lungs and Thorax:	Symmetrical thorax with equal expansion and normal Anterior-Posterior meter Tactile fremitus equal bilaterally Percussion resonant too dull over Left lower lobe and Right lower lobe Diaphragmatic excursion 3 cm bilaterally Breath sounds normal with no adventitious sounds	Occasional nonproductive cough
Breasts:	Large, pendulous, symmetrical with no masses Nipples darkly pigmented	
Cardiovascular:	No lifts or heaves Point of Maximum Impulse at sixth Intercostal Space Left midclavicular line. S_1 and S_2 normal, no S_3 or S_4 No murmurs	Occasional palpitations History of hypertension, treated with medications (names unknown); treatment discontinued ten years ago by physician. Dizziness on rising

	Internal jugular distention 2 cm above sternal angle with head of bed raised to a 45° angle No hepatojugular reflex present	Murmur present when a young adult
Peripheral: Vascular:	No carotid, femoral, or aortic bruits Peripheral pulses all equal and normal Homan's sign negative No varicosities No peripheral edema	
Abdomen:	Protuberant, symmetrical abdomen with large amount of adipose tissue Musculature appears normal Umbilicus midline with no herniation, discoloration, deviation or discharge Bowel sounds present in all quadrants at 6–8 per minute Liver not palpable, percussed 8–9 cm at Right Midclavicular Line and is 2 cm below the xyphoid process No tenderness over liver No ascites Spleen not palpable with no Left Upper Quadrant tenderness Kidneys not palpable with no costal vertebral angle tenderness Bladder not percussible or palpable	Intolerance to gas-forming foods Frequent eructation Nausea after taking medications Constipation constant problem. Bowel movements occur 1–2 times per week. Feces light brown in color and very hard. Much straining and pain with each movement
Musculo-skeletal:	Normal curvature of spine No joint deformities or swelling Muscle development normal with equal strength Tone rigid, with cogwheel rigidity in wrists and elbows	Some limitation of movement and stiffness, occurring in the early morning
Genitourinary:	Unremarkable Pelvic exam omitted	Menopause symptoms of sweating and hot flashes present sporadically (1–2 times per week) Nocturia 1–2 times per night No urinary retention

Neurological:	*Cranial Nerves* 1. Smell intact 2. Visual acuity intact Ophthalmoscopic examination normal Visual fields decreased in periphery 3, 4, 6. Anisocoria Pupillary reaction to light sluggish EOM's intact without nystagmus 5. Mastication and sensation normal bilaterally 7. Motor function intact over face and forehead Taste intact 8. Hearing grossly intact Weber and Rinné normal 9. Gag reflex present No hoarseness 11. Trapezius muscle strong 12. Tongue symmetrical with no fasciculations, deviations, or atrophy	
	Reflexes Glabellar positive Snout negative Knee and ankle clonus negative Grasp negative Toe signs negative Abdominal reflexes absent Remaining reflexes present and equal bilaterally	
	Coordination Finger-to-nose performed slowly bilaterally; when the patient concentrates her tremor decreases to allow task completion Finger-to-nose and heel-to-shin slow bilaterally Patient unable to do rapid alternating movements Romberg sign negative	Right hand dominance Difficulty changing positions in bed Bradykinesia
	Gait festinating with short, shuffled steps	Gait "hunched over and clumsy"

Arms held in flexed position when ambulating Associated arm movements absent Cannot stand on one foot or tandem walk Arm drift negative	No problem with falling
Speech	
Slightly slurred Low volume Lack of inflection	
Abnormal Movements	
Severe resting tremor of upper extremities (right arm greater than left) Tremor increases with anxiety and decreases with intention Flat affect	Tremor of right hand began ten years ago, associated with generalized weakness
Sensation	
Position sense intact Vibration, pin, dull, soft sensation intact except for slight decrease of vibratory sense in feet bilaterally	
Cerebral	
Orientation to time, person, and place good Memory good (5/5 items recalled after one minute and 4/5 after five minutes) Long-term memory intact Calculations: 25 + 25 = 50 20 nickels = 1 dollar Abstraction: appropriate answer to "a stitch in time saves nine" Judgment good Response to questions and directions appropriate but delayed.	Poor short-term memory Nocturnal mental confusion
Psychological	
Patient identifies herself as anxious, depressed, with insomnia and frequent nightmares.	

Has had no sexual contacts for the past few years and did not want to comment further on her sexuality.

The physical examination exhausted Mrs. Brown, necessitating postponement of further assessment until the next day.

It was determined that Mrs. Brown's ability to perform activities of daily living would begin with basic ambulation and transference from bed to chair. This physical task required strength and coordination beyond Mrs. Brown's endurance. After five minutes of little movement, she stated she could not get out of bed herself. With the assistance of two nurses, Mrs. Brown eventually negotiated a few steps into the corridor. She was rigid, her gait festinating and gaining in momentum. She had difficulty maintaining balance and could not sit in a chair without support. Mrs. Brown was discouraged by her performance and asked to be left alone.

The next day Mrs. Brown appeared tired and depressed. She stated she had been having nightmares, which caused her to lose sleep. She expressed anxiety about Nathan. He had apparently neither called nor visited the hospital, and Mrs. Brown was concerned. "I can't talk loud enough on the phone for him to hear me. Could I ask you to call for me?" The student called Nathan, who reported being busy with school. He was eating with neighbors and felt he was managing adequately on his own.

"I get so nervous when I worries about that boy I shakes worse. Look at my arms and legs go. At least he's doing OK on his own. I hope he don't get too independent and want to leave me soon."

An examination of Mrs. Brown's joints revealed cogwheel rigidity in her wrists, elbows, knees, and ankles. She was ambulated again with assistance of two nurses; although her gait remained unchanged, dyskinesia was reduced. Mrs. Brown was pleased about being able to sit in a chair rather than being confined to bed all day. "I only wishes they wouldn't tie me in at night. The nurses say I wanders when I has those nightmares. I could find my way back to my own bed once I wakes up." The more anxious she appeared, the more her tremors increased.

The graduate student discussed the problem of nightmares with the physician; Mrs. Brown's Artane was discontinued and the Sinemet doubled. Mrs. Brown's sleep pattern showed marked improvement with decreased dyskinesia and rigidity. "I'm glad that Parkin-

son's is going away. I hope this will be it." The chronic nature of Parkinson's disease had been discussed many times with Mrs. Brown, and the need for continued medication control and medical followup had been stressed. Mrs. Brown remained unwilling to accept the chronic nature of the disease.

Mrs. Brown continued steady physical improvement. She was depressed, and her lack of emotional expression made acquiring new friends difficult. She worried about Nathan's absence. Mrs. Brown's daughter felt her mother should move to a nursing home. Mrs. Brown objected to this idea. "She just wants to get rid of me. As if she had to help me or Nathan anyway. She won't take no responsibility for that boy."

As she began to feel better and the tremors diminished sufficiently to allow adequate performance of personal hygiene, Mrs. Brown began asking to be allowed to go home. She was still too weak to walk any distance or help with household chores. Nathan refused to come to the hospital and participate in discharge planning, but he agreed to help around the home as before.

STUDY GUIDE QUESTIONS WITH SELECTED RESPONSES

1. Identify those aging processes (physical, psychological, and social) that
   a. contributed to the present disease states.
   b. will directly and/or potentially alter recovery or adaptation.
   c. will affect optimum drug therapy.
      (1) Metabolism of each drug
      (2) Utilization
      (3) Response
      (4) Excretion
      (5) Drug interaction
2. Determine, with the limited data available, Mrs. Brown's assets:
   a. Physical
   b. Psychological
   c. Sociological
   d. Environmental

   Mrs. Brown has a limited number of assets. There do not seem to be many community supports that are actively involved with her. For example, the neighbor support subsystem is not

operating in her mixed ethnic setting. She has few financial assets other than her Social Security income. Her daughter, who visits about once a month, is of little help. The half brother represents a major asset, because he is constantly present, helping when necessary. He appears to love her and care about her well-being. He provides her with someone to care about. She is motivated to attain maximum functioning level because of her feeling of responsibility to the boy. Mrs. Brown's religion provides a spiritual and emotional support upon which she relies heavily. It appears that her major asset is herself; she has learned to be independent and to accept and make the most of life.

3. On the basis of normal aging within American society, what developmental tasks would be appropriate for Mrs. Brown?

Mrs. Brown, at the age of 60 years, is in a transitional stage in her life (the late middle age period, entering the young elderly phase). The successful completion of middle age tasks will facilitate an easier adaptation to late life.

The middle age developmental tasks are "... (1) maintenance of traditional values and institutions; (2) maintenance of generational support and boundaries; (3) maintenance of interpersonal relationships both intimate and friendly, and redefining one's self" (Ebersole in Burnside, 1976: 60). Mrs. Brown appears to have achieved the first two tasks within her social and family limitations. It is uncertain whether she has achieved the maintenance of interpersonal relationships. She states that she has no intimate relationships. Her friends are limited to church groups and do not include people in the neighborhood. She has had difficulty redefining her "self" because of her role as a mother to her half brother. She had no need to redefine her role until she was no longer able to work. This precipitated questioning her role (as a newly retired individual) relative to her brother.

Mrs. Brown has been forced by her chronic disease to cope with the tasks of late life. There are three developmental components that she will have to master in late life: receptive tasks, expressive tasks, and dynamic tasks (Ebersole in Burnside, 1976: 69–79). With the loss of physical youth and health, Mrs. Brown must learn to accept her chronic disease; she has not done this yet, as indicated by denial of chronicity. She refers to her disease as something that comes and goes like a cold, not something that will always be present. Loss of short-term memory and incidents of nocturnal confusion upset Mrs. Brown. She has not accepted these events as a permanent part of her life. If disen-

gagement is included in the developmental tasks, Mrs. Brown may be closest to achieving this goal. She rarely sees anyone other than her half brother and makes no effort to change this. However, it is most likely that this behavior is due to her depression rather than disengagement from society. Mrs. Brown has not completely mastered the receptive tasks of late life.

The expressive tasks of self-transcendence frequently involve religion (Ebersole in Burnside, 1976: 74). The Spiritual Baptist religion plays a large role in Mrs. Brown's life. This will help her achieve this task. She has not started to engage in finding her place in history. She appears to be too involved in what is happening in the present to be reminiscent of the past.

Mrs. Brown is beginning to deal with the dynamic tasks of late life. She talks about death as something that happens to someone else. However, she also realizes that death is inevitable and wonders how she will die. It appears that she is beginning to cope with her own death by talking about it as something that happens in the future.

4. On the basis of the data, theories of aging, and the considerations preceding the case history, develop a list of Mrs. Brown's problems.

   Acute
   Intermittent/situational
   Long-term
   Potential

   a. Acute
      (1) Depression, nervousness, and irritability
      (2) Decreased tolerance of pharmacologic therapy
      (3) Short-term memory loss
      (4) Anorexia
      (5) Orthostatic hypotension
      (6) Insomnia and frequent nightmares
      (7) Denial of chronicity of her condition

   b. Intermittent/situational
      (1) Anorexia
      (2) Hay fever with eye irritation
      (3) Toothaches and bleeding gums
      (4) Orthostatic hypotension
      (5) Insomnia and frequent nightmares
      (6) Fear of using public transportation

c. Long-term
   (1) Depression, nervousness, and irritability
   (2) Social isolation
   (3) Menopause (with sweating and hot flashes)
   (4) Parkinsonism (with severe tremor, weakness, and stiffness)
   (5) Limited finances
   (6) Decreased tolerance of drug therapy
   (7) Short-term memory loss
   (8) Constipation
   (9) Sexuality
   (10) Overweight
   (11) Slight decrease in peripheral eye fields and night blindness
   (12) Flat affect
   (13) Poor housing
   (14) Loss of control of body, environment, income
   (15) Failure to keep medical appointments (limited access to clinic)

d. Potential
   (1) Weight loss from malnutrition
   (2) Fecal impaction from chronic constipation
   (3) Periodontal disease, with loss of teeth
   (4) Falling and fractures from orthostatic hypotension and Parkinson's disease
   (5) Chronic depression
   (6) Complete social isolation upon eventual exiting of half brother

5. a. Formulate short-term health care goals in behavioral terms.

The following goals were established between Mrs. Brown and the graduate student while Mrs. Brown was still in hospital.

(1) *Independence:* For Mrs. Brown to demonstrate increasing skill in independently performing activities of daily living. For her to seek knowledge about improved ways of performing these activities.
(2) *Medication compliance:* For Mrs. Brown to demonstrate knowledge of the purposes of her medications, dosages, schedule of administration, and common side effects.
(3) *Trust:* For Mrs. Brown to begin to express anxieties and

concerns related to problems of living with a chronic illness and to seek the companionship of other patients.

b. Develop long-term goals for Mrs. Brown upon reentering her community.

6. Formulate health care interventions:
   a. Plan nursing interventions for each problem identified, based on specific theories, the case data and knowledge gained from the foregoing questions. Make all possible use of Mrs. Brown's assets when formulating interventions.
   b. Anticipate possible difficulties in implementing your proposed interventions.
   c. Develop an evaluation tool for each intervention.
   d. Discuss the time and setting that would be most effective for evaluation of each intervention.
   e. What restrictions would be anticipated as affecting the evaluation?
   f. Project modifications for those interventions.
   g. Application of knowledge.
      (1) Provide theoretical rationale and correlate with *each* intervention developed.
      (2) Provide rationale for the evaluation process developed.

Example 1

A discussion of the decreased tolerance of pharmacologic therapy follows.

Theoretical rationale

Treatment of Parkinson's disease falls into two categories: surgical and medical. Surgical treatment of geriatric patients is often unsuccessful and has a relatively high mortality rate (Rossman, 1971: 138). Mrs. Brown, at age 60, was not considered a candidate for this treatment modality.

Medical treatment consists of anticholinergic drugs, antiviral agents, and levodopa, alone or in combination. Anticholinergic drugs are used in Parkinson's disease because they eliminate or decrease the symptoms. The decreased tremor and rigidity leads to increased mobility, coordination, and motor performance. The action of these drugs in Parkinson's disease has not been established, although it is thought that relief of symp-

toms is due to blocking of acetycholine in the central nervous system. This drug improves the patient clinically but does not change the progression of the disease (Loebl et al., 1977: 485).

Side effects of anticholinergic drugs are related to the depression of the parasympathetic nervous system. Some of these effects, such as decreased salivation, are desirable in Parkinsonism. Undesirable effects include "drowsiness, dizziness, dry mouth, blurred vision, nausea, nervousness, urinary retention, and psychic disturbances" (Fischbach, 1978: 67). Most of the side effects are related to the dose; decreasing dosage frequently decreases the side effects (Loebl et al., 1977: 485).

Levodopa reverses most of the symptoms of Parkinsonism by increasing the level of dopamine in the brain. Directly giving dopamine to a patient is not effective because it does not cross the blood brain barrier (Rossman, 1971: 138). Combining levodopa with dopa decarboxylase inhibitor (Sinemet) decreases the breakdown of levodopa to dopamine in the peripheral vascular system. This leads to a higher concentration of levodopa in the brain, thus lowering the dosage of medication needed by the patient. The resulting advantage is the occurrence of fewer and less severe side effects (Stein, 1978).

A high-protein diet should be avoided when taking levodopa because it decreases the transfer of levodopa into the brain, reducing its effect (Stein, 1978). Pyridoxine reverses the action of levodopa and thus should be restricted in patients who take levodopa. It does not have this effect with Sinemet because of the presence of dopa decarboxylase (Kastrup and Boyd, 1978: 290d). Levodopa frequently causes nausea and vomiting, which can be controlled by taking the medication with food.

Sinemet has many side effects that involve the gastrointestinal, genitourinary, neurological, respiratory, and cardiovascular systems (Fischbach, 1978: 67). The incidence of side effects is related to the dose and the individual patient. Often levodopa is given in combination with anticholinergic or antiviral agents to give the maximum relief of symptoms with the minimum of side effects (Rossman, 1971: 139).

Amantadine (Symmetrel) is an antiviral agent that also decreases the symptoms of Parkinson's disease. It acts to increase the release of dopamine from neuronal storage sites. The side effects are similar to those of anticholinergic drugs, with the addition of orthostatic hypotension, depression, edema, and congestive heart failure (Fischbach, 1978: 67).

Evaluation of pharmacologic therapy

Mrs. Brown was taking Sinemet, Artane, and Librium (dosages unknown) prior to her admission to the hospital. The Sinemet had been decreased two to three weeks prior to admission because of increased nausea and mental confusion. The adverse side effects may have been attributable to the use of Librium and Artane. Rossman (1971: 138) states that Librium does not mix well with an anticholinergic agent (Artane).

Artane is poorly tolerated by the elderly, causing many more side effects than in younger patients. It is known to cause mental disturbances, such as hallucinations, confusion, and suicidal tendencies in elderly patients (Rossman, 1971: 382). Cogentin and Disipal are recommended anticholinergic drugs for the elderly (Rossman, 1971: 138). Treatment with a combination of Sinemet and Disipal or Cogentin may have avoided Mrs. Brown's need for hospitalization.

Drug treatment during hospitalization included Artane 2 mg t.i.d.; Sinemet 10/100, seven tablets throughout the day; Dalmane 30 mg h.s. p.r.n.; and Dulcolax 5 mg h.s. Artane was discontinued on the second hospital day because of the increased incidence of mental confusion, hallucination, and nightmares. The dosage of Sinemet was increased to nine 10/100 tablets throughout the day. The first improvement seen was decreased rigidity and dyskinesia. Mrs. Brown began to walk at a slow pace with larger steps. Associated arm movements returned. Her speech remained slow and monotonous, and her tremors continued to be severe. Her positive response to treatment allowed the staff and Mrs. Brown to prepare for discharge.

Interventions and modifications

Discharge medications: Sinemet 10/100, nine tablets over 24 hours. Elavil 25 mg h.s. Pericolace I tab daily.

This change in medication occurred one day prior to discharge, allowing insufficient time for physiological or emotional adjustment to the drug under professional scrutiny. Because the nurse had not anticipated a change in medications, adequate patient teaching was impossible. A referral was therefore made for visiting nurse followup for medication instruction and monitoring of side effects.

An initial plan of instruction was developed to begin teaching Mrs. Brown the actions, potential, common side effects, and method of administration of Sinemet. She was told to take the drug with meals to minimize the side effect of nausea and to be aware that Sinemet causes darkening of urine and perspiration.

Pericolace was prescribed as a replacement for Dulcolax to avoid the use of stimulants in the control of constipation. Mrs. Brown would need reinforcement of the action of this drug, diet, fluid intake, and activity toward correcting chronic constipation. A notation to this effect was made for the visiting nurse.

In an attempt to treat Mrs. Brown's depression and insomnia at home, Elavil was prescribed. Many patients who have taken Sinemet over long periods have difficulty sleeping at night but tend to sleep better during the day. Elavil has been helpful in reversing this problem. The low dosage (25 mg h.s.) is indicated because the drug is poorly tolerated by the elderly patient. Mrs. Brown and the community health nurse will have to be aware of the possibility of the increase in Parkinson's symptoms that is sometimes caused by tricyclic antidepressants. Any return of symptoms will have to be discussed with Mrs. Brown's physician to determine whether Elavil should be discontinued.

Medication noncompliance is a potential problem in home management of the chronically ill. If Mrs. Brown omits her Sinemet for long periods, her symptoms will abruptly return. If she overmedicates, the dose-related side effects of Sinemet will present a serious problem. In an attempt to avoid these problems, Mrs. Brown assisted in developing her home medication schedule. Relating medications to routine activities may improve her compliance.

Mrs. Brown states that she always eats her breakfast between 8 and 9 A.M. Her morning medications could then be associated with her breakfast. Setting out a 24-hour medication supply is a technique that could allow her to check whether she has taken all her doses for the day. The nurse must spend time exploring with this patient methods of insuring compliance. The plan that Mrs. Brown and the nurse devise should be communicated to the community health nurse for followup, reinforcement, and evaluation.

Example 2

A brief discussion of the seventh acute problem listed above, denial of chronicity of her illness, is given here as an example.

Theoretical rationale

In American society, where youth, independence, and productivity are valued, chronic illness has no acceptable place. Little has been done to ease the problems of transportation, mobility, and isolation of those afflicted. Chronicity is often

viewed as inherent in aging, especially since there is a tenfold rise in incidence in chronic disease in people of age 65 compared with those of age 15 (Busse and Pfeiffer, 1977: 101). Therefore it is not unexpected that Mrs. Brown has not accepted her disease as chronic. She has denied the severity of Parkinson's disease and as a result denied the necessity of medication therapy.

Intervention

Encouragement to express the effects of Parkinsonism on her life and appropriate explanation of pathophysiological changes will facilitate acceptance at the cognitive level. Emphasis should be placed on her ability to control symptoms through adherence to the established medical and nursing regimen. Her asset of independence should be stressed as a positive method of coping.

Followup of the initial steps in intervention will be a role of the visiting nurse. The cyclic nature of this chronic problem requires long-term intervention and periodic evaluation.

In many instances referral to a day care center for the elderly would be an appropriate additional measure. Many large cities and universities offer group sessions for the elderly to discuss problems relative to chronic illness.

The first two home visits were made by the graduate student prior to transferring Mrs. Brown to the care of the visiting nurse.

7. Develop a method of insuring effective discharge planning for the elderly returning home with chronic disability.
8. Determine which agencies in your community are available to assist in comprehensive care to elderly persons with neurological disabilities.
9. Determine methods of delivering services to the elderly living in communities where such agencies do not exist.
10. Discuss possible methods of financing these service agencies.

Case

IV

Mr. Leonard Franklin: Trapped in the Cage of Age

INTRODUCTION

Mr. Leonard Franklin, age 74, was admitted to an episodic health care setting and later transferred to a tertiary care setting for skilled nursing care and general rehabilitation in preparation for transfer to the acute care hospital for a second major surgery. On admission to the skilled care facility, his primary physician and nurse identified the following list of initial problems:

1. Resected colon for cancer with perineal wound
2. Paralysis of right vocal cord
3. Transverse colostomy
4. Chronic cystitis with indwelling catheter
5. Loss, grief, and depression

The student should be able to identify at least twenty other interrelated problems that require resolution and evaluation. These

encompass components of biology, socioeconomics, psychology, psychotherapeutic modalities, and rehabilitation.

The questions deal only with one of the most frequently ignored problems of aging–sexuality. The aspiring nurse clinician should deal as thoughtfully with the remaining patient care problems.

THE CASE

Leonard Franklin had been well until two weeks prior to his admission to an acute care hospital. During those two weeks he had complained of general malaise but with no specific symptoms. He became semi-comatose and was brought to the emergency room by a friend with whom he occasionally played cards.

Mr. Franklin was uremic with staphylococcal septicemia. There was a large, fungating rectal mass with perineal breakdown. Immediate cystoscopy revealed hemorrhagic cystitis with bladder neck obstruction from clot formation and prostatic hypertrophy. An intravenous pylogram demonstrated bilateral hydronephrosis, ureter dilatation, and an enlarged bladder. EKG revealed atrial fibrillation with rapid ventricular response and right bundle branch block.

On admission Mr. Franklin was thin and dehydrated, weighing 120 lb (his height was 5 ft 9 in.). Initially, he was unable to give an accurate history of events and could not recall activities of the past months other than of feeling unwell and listless.

It was judged that Mr. Franklin's condition would not tolerate exploratory or corrective surgery at the time. Therefore intensive antibiotic therapy was begun, and he quickly responded to this. An indwelling catheter was inserted and irrigated three times daily with $\frac{1}{4}$% acetic acid; this measure rapidly mitigated the bladder hemorrhages.

Additional therapies included the following:

Digoxin	.125 mg p.o. q. A.M.
$FeSo_4$	325 mg p.o. t.i.d..
Folic acid	1 mg q. A.M.
Bismuth subcarbondate	3 gr t.i.d.
Benadryl	75 mg p.o. h.s.
Multivitamins	2 tablets q. A.M.
Ensure	1 can t.i.d.
General diet	

Mr. Franklin was not able to drink the large quantities of fluid required to correct the dehydration and urinary tract problems. Intravenous supplementation was initiated with the insertion of a catheter in the subclavian vein. This procedure caused a large hematoma to form at the catheter insertion site, the pressure from which caused respiratory stridor, necessitating intubation. The hematoma resolved, but residual damage was right vocal cord paralysis. An Otolarygologist estimated that Mr. Franklin would have only a 50% chance of complete return to full voice.

Within a week Mr. Franklin had recovered sufficiently to be considered a candidate for surgery. A biopsy of the rectal mass through protoscopy showed invasive adenocarcinoma. The lower bowel barium X-ray demonstrated diffuse diverticuli and a large rectal mass. Metastatic series showed no evidence of other organ involvement. A physician informed Mr. Franklin of his diagnosis and told him surgery was planned to remove the tumor. No mention was made of a colostomy. Mr. Franklin consented to the removal of the tumor. Mr. Franklin had an anterior and posterior resection of the tumor with formation of a transverse colostomy. Because of the lengthy surgery, the anesthesia, and underlying medical problems, resection of the prostate was postponed.

The postoperative course was uneventful. Mr. Franklin advanced to full diet without difficulty and ambulated with assistance within the first 24 hours. Foley catheter irrigations were continued. Irrigations of the perineal wound were begun every six hours with normal saline, followed by wound packing with fluffed wet gauze to prevent premature closure.

Postoperatively, Mr. Franklin gave no evidence of confusion, loss of memory, or lethargy, but he showed no interest in the colostomy and asked no questions relative to the surgery or diagnosis. The nursing staff felt Mr. Franklin could learn to irrigate his Foley catheter, the colostomy, and the perineal wound. After six days Mr. Franklin had not looked at his catheter or colostomy, insisting the nurse was there to take care of such matters.

In view of the expense of hospitalization in an acute care center, the physicians determined it was advantageous for Mr. Franklin to be transferred to a skilled care facility to await prostate surgery following perineal wound healing and general stabilization. Orders were written, and the transfer by ambulance to the new facility was effected within 24 hours.

The Geriatric Nurse Practitioner obtained the following information from Mr. Franklin on his admission to the skilled care facility.

The practitioner noted that Mr. Franklin is a thin, white male, appearing older than his stated age and in no acute distress. He speaks with obvious hoarseness and frequently whispers. The initial impression is of depression and apathy.

Mr. Franklin had been a taxi driver until he retired at age 65. At that time his hobby of "junk collecting" became his avocation. He opened a shop to sell his "junk," of which he said, "I don't make much money, but I like it." He owns his own home, beside the shop. He has never married and traveled little. He says he has many friends who visit his shop daily to exchange news. Sales from store items, a small pension and Social Security just about "make ends meet. It's a good thing I don't want much."

Familial History

Father died at age 80 from "old age." His mother died at age 50 from surgical complications. Mr. Franklin conveyed the impression that he regretted not having a wife and children and said, "I made a big mistake; it would be nice to have my own family. A wife to grow old with and some kids to care about . . . there might have been some grandchildren too."

His only living relatives are a younger brother, age 70, and a 68-year-old sister. The brother is well except for the loss of several fingers and toes due to frostbite years ago. This brother and his wife operate a hamburger shop, which they have owned for 40 years. The sister is married and lives in another state, rarely having contact with her brothers.

Mr. Franklin and his brother frequently visit and have always been on good terms, although he does not feel he could live with his brother.

Review of systems and physical examination were essentially unremarkable. Mr. Franklin wore loose fitting dentures and glasses for reading. A cataract had developed on the right lens. Vital signs were within normal limits.

Mr. Franklin could not recall any rectal pain but had noticed increasing constipation and difficulty defecating. He had also noted urinary changes: increasing nocturia, frequency during the day, and

difficulty starting the stream. He denied any blood or burning on urination.

Examination of his abdomen revealed a healed midline incision and a right transverse colostomy with bag attached. There was a 2-inch long and deep open perineal wound with sutures and moist packing in place. Granulation tissue had begun, and there was scant drainage.

The majority of the laboratory values were within acceptable limits; the exceptions were:

K+	3.8
Hgb	11.0
HCT	33.0
MCV	88.0

The original medication regime was continued in the new facility. No surgical report accompanied Mr. Franklin to indicate any metastasis found at that time. Mr. Franklin stated he was told "everything was very successful."

NURSING EVALUATION NOTE on admission: Mr. Franklin is very weak and will undoubtedly require physical therapy on a regular basis to regain his strength. In addition, to correct the low potassium and anemia, there will be a dietary consultation. The psychiatric nursing clinician will interview Mr. Franklin relative to his apparent depression. The feasibility of self-care teaching seems limited at this time.

Mr. Franklin was introduced to several patients sitting in the social room and was oriented to physical surroundings, ward policies, and routines. He was assigned to a large semiprivate room, and from his bed he could look out on a landscaped courtyard. His roommate was friendly, ambulatory, and in his early sixties.

On the second day, Mr. Franklin was evaluated by a physical therapist for an exercise program.

PHYSICAL THERAPY CONSULTATION NOTE: Mr. Franklin's perception and sensory motor systems are grossly intact. He responds slowly to instruction, and those responses are often inappropriate. He seems to have some difficulty with problem solving, appearing to wait for assistance or more direction.

Mr. Franklin maintains his balance but needs assistance standing and rising from a chair. He will require help in most activities of daily

living until he regains his strength. His activity tolerance is limited, and he has little endurance. Range of motion of all joints is within normal limits of his age.

A physical therapy exercise plan was developed to help Mr. Franklin gain optimal muscle strength and independence in care. He was to spend two hours each afternoon in therapy. By the end of the first week Mr. Franklin's usual daily schedule was:

6:30 A.M.	Perineal wound irrigation and repacking
7:30 A.M.	Colostomy irrigation
8:30 A.M.	Breakfast
9:00 A.M.	Morning care and vital signs
10:00 A.M.	Foley irrigation
10:15 A.M.	M.D. visit
10:30 A.M.	Various group activities
11:30 A.M.	Lunch in the dining room
12:15 P.M.	Perineal wound irrigation and repacking
12:45 P.M.	Physical therapy
2:45 P.M.	Group activity
3:45 P.M.	Rest period
5:00 P.M.	Dinner in the dining room
6:00 P.M.	Television news
7:00–8:00 P.M.	Visitors
8:00 P.M.	Preparation for sleep

Mr. Franklin refused to prepare for bed until midnight, as it was his custom at home to watch television all evening. "I used to read a lot, but my glasses don't help much with that cataract growing. I like to go out after dinner for a bit around town, but now that's all over too. Not much left for me, is there?"

The morning hospital routine was also a problem for Mr. Franklin, as he was not accustomed to rising at 6:30, preferring to sleep until 9:00. "I don't see why I have to have nurses bothering me so early when I don't get to sleep until after midnight. I'd rather watch the late movie than have these irrigations done. A man needs more than six hours sleep."

Soon after Mr. Franklin's admission, nursing staff realized that the expectations that Mr. Franklin would assume self-care might not be realized. He readily performed routine morning hygiene and often made his own bed without encouragement. However, he refused to irrigate his indwelling catheter and perineal wound and would not

look at the colostomy or participate in its care. Mr. Franklin's primary physician discussed with him reasons for caring for himself. Mr. Franklin was not convinced and said, "If I had to do this over again, I'd never have that operation. They didn't level with me about what it really meant, and I don't like the results at all. I don't see why I had to come to this place when I was already in a hospital. I was just getting used to it there." The physician had no answer for Mr. Franklin and expressed his frustration to the nurses.

The following is a nurse's progress note written one week after Mr. Franklin's admission: "Mr. Franklin is discouraged and depressed about the irrigations and colostomy care. He continues to refuse to learn the irrigation techniques, although he is well able to do so. I have told him repeatedly we are not avoiding him or his wounds by teaching him to care for himself, but that we are trying to make him independent and more in control of himself."

"Today Mr. Franklin again made sexual comments during the irrigations. 'How much could I pay you to kiss your body? . . . Would you be afraid to kiss mine?' He made frequent grabbing attempts and often touched me when I worked close to him."

Mr. Franklin's behavior was confirmed by other nurses and the physical therapist. A staff conference was held, but no solutions were forthcoming. Two days later Mr. Franklin exhibited variable behavior relative to his medications. At times he would take all the medicines and at other times none, stating, "Medicine is poison. If I don't like it, it's poison." This behavior confused and frustrated the nursing staff.

One morning, an elderly patient complained to the head nurse that Mr. Franklin had been making advances toward her in the dining room. He generally sat at her table and would fondle her leg, upsetting her. "He's always whispering little things to me. Why is he always so secretive? I wish he'd speak up." Mr. Franklin's speech problem was explained to the woman, and she was asked if possible not to reject him. The patient, however, arranged to sit at another table and avoided Mr. Franklin in the television room.

Following this episode, Mr. Franklin asked to have his meals served in his room, refusing to go to the dining room. It was explained to him that meals were served in bedrooms only to patients who were bedridden. Mr. Franklin was not satisfied and arranged with the dietitian to have his meals served in the television room. The

staff consented to this plan, realizing that Mr. Franklin would probably become bedridden to get his own way.

During the second week, Mr. Franklin attempted to irrigate the perineal wound and the colostomy on three occasions. Each time he became frustrated. "Doing these irrigations is too much work. It isn't worth the effort." He refused to irrigate the indwelling catheter, expressing disgust over constant hematuria.

The nurse's progress note reflected Mr. Franklin's attitude. "His manual dexterity is poor, and he gives up easily. During the procedure he asked for continual feedback and will not progress from step to step independently. He cried frequently and asked me to hold his hand."

Physically, Mr. Franklin had made satisfactory progress. He had gained eight pounds, the hematuria had decreased, the perineal wound was healing, and muscle strength had vastly improved. Emotionally it was felt, there might be deterioration or impending crisis.

In an attempt to raise Mr. Franklin's spirits, roommates were carefully chosen to provide someone with a sense of humor without serious illness or incapacitation. These attempts were in vain, as Mr. Franklin refused any overture of friendship. "Why should I make friends when I won't be here much longer?"

One Sunday morning, after refusing his irrigations, Mr. Franklin took his clothes off and wheeled himself around the unit in his roommate's wheelchair. As anticipated, there was much commotion among patients, staff and visitors preparing a religious service. Mr. Franklin was returned to his room, reprimanded, and redressed. He remained in his room until evening, refusing meals and visitors. Around 11 P.M. he came out and demanded food from the nurse.

Monday morning, a large printed note was left for the charge nurse: "Please have a conference on Mr. Franklin before we all go crazy."

STUDY GUIDE QUESTIONS

1. What attitudes toward the elderly, aging sexuality, and body image are operative within
   a. American society?
   b. Health care institutions?
   c. Yourself?

2. Identify popular myths and taboos concerning sexuality and the elderly.
3. What are the patient's rights to sexual expression in a long-term care facility?
4. Utilizing knowledge of normal aging physiology, aging of the reproductive system, and possible limitations imposed by chronicity,
   a. establish components of a sexual history pertinent to hospitalized elderly.
   b. develop a patient history form that incorporates those components.
5. Determine reasons for diminished sexual function and experience in the elderly.
6. Describe the effects of various categories of drugs on sexual functioning and sexuality.
7. Determine the impact of surgical alteration, intrusive procedures, physical deterioration, the disease process, and normal aging on Mr. Franklin's adjustment to his own aging.
8. Identify components of Mr. Franklin's lifestyle that have affected this adjustment.
9. Communication is essential to understanding sexuality. Discuss communication and interpersonal skills necessary for effectively dealing with sexual concerns of the elderly.
10. A nurse who is comfortable with her own sexuality and attitudes toward the elderly and their sexuality is essential for effectively providing such information to the institutionalized elderly. Develop a comprehensive teaching guide to assist the elderly patient to improve sexual expression and well-being.
11. The environment of long-term care institutions lacks warmth and normalcy. Determine ways in which the institutional milieu can be altered to enhance or encourage sexuality as part of total well-being.
12. Utilizing this case, discuss other major issues confronting the institutionalized elderly and health care staff.
13. Apply your problem-solving abilities to develop methods of dealing with those issues.

Case V

Mrs. Ida Conti: Dependent and Manipulative

INTRODUCTION

This community-oriented case is divided into two parts; the settings and level of care required. As you read Part 1, identify the significant events and the problems that occur and recur, and determine alternate interventions. In Part 2, two sample interactions are presented that lead to analysis of personal themes and techniques of interaction.

The questions raised at the end of each section lead to the acquisition of knowledge and development of skill in planning nursing intervention.

When collecting data, identifying problems and providing rationale for judgments made, it is suggested that consideration be given to the following:

Erikson's eight stages of life
Developmental tasks of later life

Physiology of the aging
Cardiovascular, respiratory, renal, digestive, and metabolic systems
Disengagement versus activity
Loss and grief
Guilt
Sensory deprivation
Drug interaction, compliance, and physiological responses
Interface of systems
Nursing management
Changes in pain perception and management
Alterations in sleep patterns
Family interaction

THE CASE: PART 1

The nurse discharge planner of the hospital identified Mrs. Ida Conti, age 76, as requiring home health supervision and assistance with the activities of daily living. Mrs. Conti had been hospitalized for a month with a diagnosis of pulmonary edema subsequent to left ventricular heart failure. The latter resulted from mitral valve disease. During the past three years she had been admitted annually for correction of acute congestive heart failure.

The treatment regimen during the current hospitalization was

Bedrest
O_2 at 4 ℓ/min, by nasal canula
Digoxin 0.25 mg, q. A.M.
Lasix 120 mg p.o., q.d.
Aldomet 250 mg, q.d.
Tylenol #3 q-4-h.p.r.n., for pain
Nitroglycerin tab. sublingual, p.r.n., for sternal pain

Fluid intake was restricted to 1500 cc p.o. and intravenously per day the first week of hospitalization, increased to 2000 cc per day the ensuing three weeks. Prescription diet was 1800 calorie, Na 2 gm per day. Except for the fluid restrictions of the first week, this regimen did not deviate from Mrs. Conti's prehospital home care.

Prior to hospitalization Mrs. Conti had been living alone, with some independence, for three months. A helpful neighbor had helped care for both Mr. and Mrs. Conti. But the neighbor had moved from the district, and Mr. Conti had been admitted to a long-term care facility following a myocardial infarction and "nervous breakdown."

The week of discharge, Mrs. Conti refused placement in a nursing home. Referrals were made for community health nursing visits, and a daily homemaker was engaged for an eight-hour day, five days a week, through a local Catholic charity.

Prior to hospital discharge, Ms. Sands, a community health nurse, met with Mrs. Conti to discuss mutual expectations and a realistic visiting schedule.

Mrs. Conti left the acute care hospital for home on September 8.

After Hospitalization

As arranged, Ms. Sands visited Mrs. Conti at home two days following discharge from the hospital. During this initial visit Ms. Sands assessed Mrs. Conti's social supports, physical status, home environment, and personal resources.

Social supports

The homemaker, a middle-aged woman, had spent the previous day in the house and appeared to have established rapport with Mrs. Conti. Also present was Mrs. Conti's younger brother, Tony, who came to be with his sister until she felt secure and comfortable staying alone at night. This arrangement was a temporary one, since Tony had family and job commitments some four hundred miles distant. In addition, Mrs. Conti's son, Alberto, spent as much time as possible on weekends with his mother. Alberto carried out tasks of grocery shopping, refilling medication prescriptions, general housekeeping and home repairs.

Physical status

General appearance: Mrs. Conti was a thin, pale, alert, elderly-appearing white woman of Italian decent. She was dressed in street clothes and seated at the kitchen table. There was some shortness of breath on speaking.

Mrs. Conti seemed delighted to see the nurse and, as was her custom, grasped Ms. Sands' hand and held it in both of hers throughout the interview phase of the physical assessment, the results of which follow:

	Findings	*Health History*
Height:	5 ft 3 in.	No change in 5 years
Weight:	112 lb	

	Findings	*Health History*
Vital Signs:	Blood pressure: 158/76 left arm sitting 168/84 right arm sitting Apical rate: 96 Respiration rate: 24 shallow Temperature: 98.2 (oral)	
Head:	Normal cephalic Cheek bones prominent Skin dry and pale Hair dry, white, thin distribution No sinus pain Circumoral pallor	No sinusitis No known allergies Few headaches
Neck:	No nodes or thyroid felt Trachea midline Neck veins not distended Throat not injected	"Arthritis" of cervical vertebrae, several years Few sore throats
Eyes:	Lenses somewhat cloudy Arcus senilis	Wears glasses for reading
Ears:	Drums intact Moderate cerumen	Hears normal conversation General decrease noted
Nose:	Turbinates pink	Few colds
Mouth:	Few teeth No prostheses No lesions Membranes pale and intact	
Lungs:	Clear (no rales) Breath sounds loudest at left base Fremitus loudest at left base	No cough or wheezing Dyspnea on walking or climbing three steps Three-pillow orthopnea Occasional pain at base of left rib cage Intermittent O_2 4 ℓ/min at night
Cardiac:	Irregular rate and rhythm S4 present PMI 11 cm from sternum at sixth intercostal space	Occasional sternal pain relieved with Nitroglycerin sublingual (TNG.SL)
Peripheral Vascular:	All pulses present and equal Absence of extremity hair Pigmented areas over anterior lower legs Feet cool	No history of calf cramping
Breasts:	Soft, small No masses or retraction	No surgeries
Gastro-intestinal:	Abdomen soft No masses, no scars Bowel sounds heard	No surgeries No diarrhea Occasional constipation

	Findings	*Health History*
		Took MOM Tbls. II once or twice a month Stool brown
Rectal:	Omitted	
Genitourinary:	Unremarkable	No burning, frequency, or foul odor
Gynecological:	Omitted	
Neurological:	No tremors Gait unsteady Essentially unremarkable for age	Intermittent short-term memory loss
Musculo-skeletal:	Scant muscle mass in flexors	General weakness

Mrs. Conti was assessed as being very apprehensive but an accurate and reliable historian.

Personal history

Mrs. Conti had been born in a large Midwestern city 76 years earlier (date of birth August 16, 1901) and lived her entire life in that city with no trips abroad or to tropical climates.

She completed an eighth-grade education at a Catholic girls' school. Until recently she had enjoyed reading and watching television. When asked why she no longer enjoyed these activities, Mrs. Conti said, "I'm too unhappy."

Until her husband's illness and her own deteriorating health, Mrs. Conti's sleeping pattern had been seven hours of uninterrupted sleep each night. She has never used tobacco in any form; her husband had smoked cigarettes. She rarely drank coffee, preferring tea or milk. Until three months ago she enjoyed a glass of wine with the midday and evening meals.

Since her marriage, at age 18, she had not worked outside her home. Before her marriage she had worked as a housekeeper for relatives.

Mrs. Conti had been married to the same man for 58 years. Mr. Conti was 78 years old, but his current health status was unknown. Since placement in a nursing home in June 1977, Mrs. Conti had not seen him because "he wouldn't know me anyway, and I'm not well enough to travel."

Alberto Conti, age 57, was the only child of this marriage. He was married with four adult children and six grandchildren. Alberto had a history of a "heart attack" five years earlier.

Economically, the Conti's had $5000 in a savings account. They owned no real property but had rented the house they lived in for 50 years. The current rental cost was $175 per month. Social Security Insurance was the only source of income. Medicare Plan B covered the cost of Mrs. Conti's current health care.

Home environment

The one-floor house was old and in poor repair. There were five rooms, including two small bedrooms. The bathroom was located off the kitchen, approximately thirty feet from the bedroom used by Mrs. Conti. There were two sets of seven out-of-door steps.

The large, comfortable furniture was in good condition. The surroundings were neat and clean. The temperature was excessively warm and the air dry.

Neighborhood

The neighborhood was in an old section of the city, inhabited by a mix of ethnic groups. There were no major shopping areas or large supermarkets within a three-mile radius. Three blocks from the Conti house were two small variety stores and a pharmacy. A large medical center was located one mile away.

The crime rate in the area had been rising sharply, with increasing assaults against the elderly.

Public transportation served the area well (there was a bus stop two blocks away), but it was not suitable for Mrs. Conti's use. She had to rely on taxi service, which was expensive, or Alberto for transportation.

Homemaker service

The homemaker from the Catholic charity prepared Mrs. Conti's meals, helped her bathe, and did the laundry and some light housekeeping.

Subjective findings

Mrs. Conti freely expressed concerns about difficulty in breathing, sleeplessness at night, dependency on oxygen, poor appetite, occasional sternal pain, and an increasing lack of independence in activities of daily living since this hospitalization.

Mrs. Conti remarked, "I am a sick woman. . . . I've gotten worse

these last six months. . . . They wanted me to have a valve replacement last year, but I wouldn't hear of it."

Health maintenance regimen

The following medications and administration schedule were followed:

At breakfast:	Aldomet	250 mg
	Digoxin	0.25 mg
	Lasix	40 mg
	Orinase	500 mg
At lunch and dinner:	Lasix	40 mg
	Aldomet	250 mg
	Orinase	500 mg

There was a bottle of Nitroglycerin 1 : 150 at her bedside.

Mrs. Conti showed adequate understanding of the purpose of each medication but was not interested in learning about their possible side effects. She had not been taught to take her pulse while in the hospital and did not know the significance of this monitoring technique, nor did she want to learn. Mrs. Conti took no responsibility for compliance with the treatment regimen in spite of a medication chart, provided by the hospital, that was readily visible on the dining room table. The homemaker reminded her to take the medications and also tested Mrs. Conti's urine for sugar and acetone each morning. Alberto assumed these responsibilities on weekends.

Mrs. Conti's prescription diet was the same as the hospital one. However, her poor appetite kept her well under the caloric allotment.

At the end of this home visit Ms. Sands contracted to be Mrs. Conti's primary nurse. Both Mrs. Conti and the homemaker were instructed to contact the nurse managed health agency if there were any questions or problems.

Subsequent Events

September 12: Mrs. Conti's homemaker telephoned the health agency to request an early visit by Ms. Sands. She reported that Mrs. Conti had developed breathing difficulty and was very apprehensive.

The home visit was made and Mrs. Conti was found to be in an anxious state with sweaty palms and short of breath with an Apical rate of 100 per minute. The main subjective complaint was left lateral chest pain, not relieved by TNG.

Within ten minutes Mrs. Conti was less anxious; her blood pressure was within normal range, and the heart rate dropped to 84 with no increased irregularities. The chest pain continued over the left lower lobe, where faint light rales were heard. There was no cough or sputum, no elevated temperature, and no increase in circumoral cyanosis.

The homemaker said that Mrs. Conti was following her prescribed medication and diet regimen but had slept badly the previous night, using O_2 continuously.

Mrs. Conti did not want the physician, Dr. Brown, notified because she felt better.

Tony voiced concern about his sister's condition and his own fatigue.

September 14: The homemaker contacted Ms. Sands and requested that a home visit be made that morning.

Ms. Sands responded and found Mrs. Conti in bed, very apprehensive, with generalized sweating, circumoral pallor, and shortness of breath. All vital signs except temperature were moderately elevated; faint rales were heard in the left lower lobe, and there was marked cyanosis of the buccal mucous membranes. Oxygen at 4 ℓ/min by nasal cannala was started.

Ms. Sands telephoned the physician, Dr. Brown, who ordered Lasix 40 mg I.M. stat. and an increase of Lasix p.o. to 240 mg daily. The intramuscular medication was administered, and the necessary adjustment was made on the medication chart kept on the dining room table. Both the homemaker and Mrs. Conti were reminded to expect the medication to increase frequency of urination.

September 15: Ms. Sands contacted Mrs. Conti, who reported frequent voidings of large amounts of urine the previous evening and night; there was decreased chest pain and improved breathing. She felt much better and had eaten breakfast.

September 16: Mrs. Conti appeared more vibrant and told Ms. Sands she had slept well without using any oxygen the previous night. Ms. Sands observed that cyanosis was absent, pallor was minimal, there was no significant shortness of breath, and the lung fields were clear.

September 19: Tony, Mrs. Conti's brother, phoned Ms. Sands and reported that his sister had "pain in her head" and "was not breathing well."

On her visit, Ms. Sands found Mrs. Conti lying on the living room couch in her night clothes. There was no evidence of cyanosis, chest pain, or rales. Mrs. Conti's general response was slow, and she answered questions with a weak voice. Her chief complaint was of neck and basal skull pain. After lengthy questioning, Mrs. Conti remembered Dr. Brown calling the pain "arthritis."

Since Tylenol was available in the house, it was recommended that Mrs. Conti take Tab. II q-4-h, p.r.n. Ms. Sands assured Mrs. Conti she would telephone later to learn the effect of the Tylenol.

On returning to her office Ms. Sands contacted Dr. Brown to discuss his treatment plan for Mrs. Conti. Dr. Brown stated that he was at a loss to offer anything more medically.

September 20: Ms. Sands' telephone call to Mrs. Conti found her to be in "good spirits," free of pain and with minimal shortness of breath.

September 23: Mrs. Conti's homemaker called to report Mrs. Conti had severe nausea and diarrhea. She had vomited breakfast and medications, had not slept the previous night, and had complained of sternal pain and increased difficulty in breathing.

Ms. Sands visited two hours later and found that Mrs. Conti had taken Nitroglycerin with relief of sternal pain. There was no cyanosis, and all vital signs were stable. She had frequent, watery brown stools; nausea was experienced only on eating solid foods.

Ms. Sands advised Mrs. Conti to take her afternoon medications with milk. Dr. Brown arranged to see Mrs. Conti at his office the following morning.

September 24: Ms. Sands telephoned Tony, Mrs. Conti's brother, to learn the results of the visit to Dr. Brown. Mrs. Conti had been found in stable condition, and no medication or dietary changes had been recommended.

Tony expressed concern about his sister's reaction to his leaving for home in two days time and the change of homemaker the ensuing Monday. He felt it was detrimental to be changing the aide with whom Mrs. Conti had such a good relationship. The agency policy, however, required that when an aide went on vacation, she was replaced and on return reassigned to another home. Ms. Sands' call to the homemaker's director was unsuccessful.

September 28: Ms. Sands called Mrs. Conti's new homemaker, who said the client appeared to be doing well. She was

accepting Tony's return home and the change in the homemaker. Alberto was spending the nights with his mother.

October 3: Ms. Sands' 9:00 A.M. telephone call revealed that Mrs. Conti had not slept well; she was experiencing sternal and left lateral chest pain and shortness of breath at rest and was in bed using oxygen. She had not eaten breakfast and had refused the morning medications. Ms. Sands told the homemaker to encourage Mrs. Conti to take her medications and that she would visit later. At 2:00 P.M. Ms. Sands found Mrs. Conti's condition as follows:

in bed, using oxygen
circumoral cyanosis when talking
stable vital signs
afebrile
alert but anxious and depressed
slight expiratory wheeze in left midaxillary area
no cough; no sputum
fine, crisp rales heard bilaterally in the lower lobes
occasional diarrhea, not being treated
no nausea
poor appetite, intake low

Ms. Sands talked with Alberto, who, on a leave of absence from his job, was staying with his mother. He appeared fatigued after four nights of interrupted sleep. He was anxious about his mother's physical status and frequently stated, "I know her heart is bad and that there's nothing more anyone can do for her." Part of his expressed concern centered on his father's recent, rapid deterioration in a nursing home. Alberto found the care of his aging parents increasingly expensive and emotionally draining and said he did not know how much longer he would be able "to take it." "I feel pulled in so many directions. I'm not a young man; I'm a grandfather, and I get tired. If only someone could relieve me for a few nights."

At noon Dr. Brown was called and promised to visit later that day.

THE CASE: PART 2

The specific considerations given below are to assist in analyzing Part 2 of Mrs. Conti's problems in depth. These considerations, the

case data, and the questions raised at the end provide a basis for developing realistic, holistic short- and long-range goals.

1. Medications
   - dosage range
   - physiological limitations
   - behavioral responses
   - management
2. Interpersonal relationships
   - nurse/patient
   - mother/son
   - ethnic considerations
3. Dynamics of interviewing
   - identification of personality themes
4. Rehabilitation
5. Long-term management
6. Community agencies
   - financial aspects
   - physical aspects
7. Federal assistance programs
   - benefits
   - eligibility
   - limitations (financial, temporal, institutional)

October 3: Dr. Brown visited Mrs. Conti and administered 0.25 mg I.M. of Digoxin and 40 mg I.M. of Lasix. He prescribed Isordil 5 mg q.i.d. Sublingual for the increased frequency and intensity of sternal pain.

October 5: Alberto contacted Dr. Brown to report his mother's lack of response to the drugs. She had developed increasing shortness of breath, peri auricular cyanosis, diarrhea with incontinence, and sternal and left midaxillary pain despite continuous oxygen use. Dr. Brown arranged for admission to an acute care hospital on a unit where she had previously been a patient.

October 6: Admitting medical orders were:

Lasix 280 mg p.o. t.i.d.

Dosage schedule:	9:00 A.M.:	80 mg
	2:00 A.M.:	80 mg
	7:00 P.M.:	120 mg

Hydrodiuril: 50 mg p.o. q. A.M.

Aldomet: 250 mg t.i.d.

Digoxin: 0.25 mg p.o. q. A.M.
Isordil: 5 mg Sublingual q. 2-h while awake
Kcl: 20 mg p.o. t.i.d.
$FeSO_4$: 30 mg p.o. t.i.d.
Kaopectate: 30 cc with each bowel movement
Multivitamins I p.o. t.i.d.
Orinase: 500 mg p.o. t.i.d.
Nitroglycerin: 1/150 Sublingual p.r.n. for chest pain
Diet: Na 4 gm, 1800 calories
Fluid restriction to 1600 cc
I.V. D_5W: 250 cc/24 hours
O_2 at 4 ℓ/min by nasal cannula

During the first two days Mrs. Conti experienced increasing diarrhea with incontinence of stool and urine, especially at night. Her sleep became more disturbed, with long periods of wakefulness and confusion, resulting in Mrs. Conti climbing over the bed side rails. Her appetite continued to be poor, indicating that the food was not to her liking.

Early in her hospitalization, Mrs. Conti was interviewed by a nurse in order to develop health goals and a care plan. The following is a representative sample of that interview.

Nurse: *What actually brought you to the hospital, Mrs. Conti?*
Patient: *My chest pain and diarrhea. But I know you girls will do the right thing.*
Nurse: *How did all this start?*
Patient: [Taking the nurses' hand] *You won't let me down, will you?*
Nurse: *No, Mrs. Conti. Do you think you could tell me what caused these problems?*
Patient: *Of course, dear. I've been taking all these medicines, and the nurse visiting and all, have been so helpful, I just know I'll be able to go home soon. You'll soon have me fixed up again so I can go home.*
Nurse: *I gather you've been ill before.*
Patient: *Oh yes! I have an old heart that just won't work well anymore. It needs a new valve.*
Nurse: *Are you going to have a new valve?*
Patient: *Oh no, I'll just take my medicine, and when I go home, my son Alberto will stay with me at night, just like he has been doing.*
Nurse: *What about your diarrhea and losing control of your urine?*

Patient: *Yes, and those are problems, but I'll get someone to come and stay with me. I had a lovely woman from the charities you know, and I'm sure they'll send someone again.*

Nurse: *Who could stay with you?*

Patient: *I don't know. All my friends have their own problems. I can't afford to pay anyone.*

Nurse: *What will you do if these still are problems next week?*

Patient: *I'm sure you girls will think of something. You're all such lovely people and so smart.*

Two days later the same nurse talked with Alberto.

Nurse: *How do you feel your mother is progressing?*

Son: *Well, she sure looks much better with her breathing and all. I'm just worried about her bowel and urine control. I can't take her home like that.*

Nurse: *What will you do?*

Son: *Well, my dad's in a nursing home, and that takes most of their money. Mother rents her house, and there isn't much left for her to live on after the bills are paid. She just makes ends meet.*

Nurse: *Is there anyone to stay with her?*

Son: *I won't ask anyone. It's my responsibility. The charities won't send anyone in; they said "we've used up our quota." I could manage if she hadn't lost control.*

Nurse: *What if she continues to sleep poorly at night? Doesn't that keep you awake?*

Son: *Yes it does. I've missed some days at work because I fall asleep on the job and I have to drive.*

Nurse: *I'm sure you see what a complicated problem this is.*

Son: *I know, but I won't put her in a nursing home, she wants her own home.*

Nurse: *What will you do?*

Son: *At this point, I don't know.*

STUDY GUIDE QUESTIONS

1. Determine the reasons for Mrs. Conti's isolation.
   a. Provide rationale for applying the Disengagement Theory and the Activity Theory to Mrs. Conti's situation.
   b. Develop appropriate strategies for her resocialization.
2. a. In view of the Italian matriarchal situation presented in the case, discuss Mrs. Conti's relationship with her son.

b. Determine the problems that exist for Alberto and offer solutions for their resolution.
c. Under what circumstances could Mrs. Conti retain a measure of independence? Predict the probable success of these solutions.

3. Pharmacotherapeutics are a source of many problems for the elderly. For Mrs. Conti's case, determine the pharmacokinetics, interactions (drug–drug; drug–food), utilization, dosages, and response to the pharmacotherapeutic regimen.

4. The role of the visiting nurse was unclear in this situation. To avoid such ambiguity, develop a contract of home care specific to Mrs. Conti. Delineate mutually achievable goals, appropriate time frames, and a system of client–provider evaluation.

Case VI

Mrs. Consuelo Martinez: A Case of Mismanagement

INTRODUCTION

The activities of seeking and maintaining health are dependent upon age, culture, economics, lifelong habits, and sex. For the elderly poor who live in the urban core, the availability or nonavailability of preventive illness clinics and multilingual educational programs are also important factors.

Most illness insurance coverage focuses on acute hospital care, *not* prevention or health maintenance. Sickness, a dependent state, is reinforced or rewarded. This creates a distortion in the value systems of independence and self-reliance.

Mrs. Martinez is an example of an elderly, poor woman who has been victimized by neglect—her own as well as that of social and health services. As a result, the quality of her life has been diminished.

Too frequently the theoretical premises for patient care are left in the classroom and are not translated to pragmatics of daily prac-

tice. The problems presented in Mrs. Martinez's case bring a dimension of reality to this chasmic situation.

Some of the salient considerations in this case are

- Aging in Puerto Rican culture
- Grandparenting and the ascribed role and status of the Hispanic grandmother
- Multigenerational families and kinship ties.
- Ethnomedicine
- Dietary requirements in wound healing, obesity, hypertension, and sedentary living for the elderly
- Rehabilitation
- The role of primary care nursing in continuity of care for the elderly
- Home environment hazards
- Rules and regulations for illness reimbursement

THE CASE

The Home Health Agency received an informal request from an orthopedic surgeon to visit an 80-year-old woman in her home. Mrs. Consuelo Martinez had been seen in his office five weeks after amputation below the right knee for routine followup and suture removal. The wound had not healed, and rehospitalization was recommended. Mrs. Martinez refused, but she did agree to assistance in wound care from a visiting nurse.

During the initial visit, the nurse learned that Consuelo Martinez had emigrated from Puerto Pico at the end of World War II. She and her husband, Angel, arrived in New England to live with their oldest son, Manuel, following his discharge from the Navy. Accompanying them were five other children ranging in ages from 16 to 28. Work was scarce, and the Martinezes, unable to speak English, found employment as migrant tobacco and onion pickers. In the winter they traveled south, cropping in Florida and Georgia. After three years, Angel Martinez secured a job as railroad yardman. Although he worked steadily and the children married and left home, finances were always limited. To supplement Angel's wages, Consuelo secured a job washing dishes in the cafeteria of a state college. She gradually learned to speak and read English and was promoted to the position of food handler. Soon there were grandchildren, and a large extended family grew.

When Angel was 63 years old, he was shot and killed by mem-

bers of a teenage gang while returning from a local grocery store. The boys were never identified. The Martinez family offered to take their mother into their homes, but Consuelo refused. Eventually, a compromise between her independence and family concern resulted in various grandchildren living with Mrs. Martinez on a rotating basis.

When she reached age 65, Mrs. Martinez was asked to retire. Her income was reduced to her state retirement pension. The house she owned had no mortgage, but money was still limited. Her income was supplemented by the children when they were able. As a state employee, Mrs. Martinez had not paid into Social Security nor was she eligible for Medicare. As a homeowner, she was ineligible for public assistance. Upon her retirement, the family assumed payments for health insurance, which covered only 80% of hospitalization.

Retirement did bring more leisure time for church activities, children, and grandchildren. She became more involved in the neighborhood and could be relied on to help others with baby-sitting, giving advice, cooking, or taking someone into her home.

Mrs. Martinez had always been a "strong, active woman," rarely ill. During her years as a cafeteria worker she had begun smoking cigarettes, "but never in front of the children or Angel." She had also begun experiencing leg cramps and complained of constantly "cold feet." Within the past ten years she had had stasis ulcers twice on her right inner ankle. "They would have healed faster with salve I learned to make when I was young in Puerto Rico," she said. "My grandmother had sores like mine, and they healed with the salve." With increasing compromised circulation to her right leg, pain forced Mrs. Martinez to seek help, initially from neighborhood women, ("some are good at healing folks") and finally from her family. The family took Mrs. Martinez, who could no longer bear weight on her right foot, to a hospital emergency room. From the emergency unit Mrs. Martinez was admitted to the hospital for surgical amputation of the right lower limb.

Five weeks later, the stump was still soft with no evidence of molding. An ace bandage was loosely wrapped in a circular manner and caked with brown, odorless drainage. The wound, approximately 14 cm $\times$ 9 cm, was covered with heavy, loose eschar. The skin around the eschar was dark and hard. There was a 30° contracture of the right knee and a 20° contracture of the hip. "I don't remember how to do the exercises the therapists did. No one told me I'd have to do them at home or I'd have paid more attention." Examination of the left leg showed cool, dark skin below the knee

with "woodlike" texture. Popliteal pulse was faint; posterior tibialis and dorsalis pedis pulses were absent. The nails were dark yellow, thick, and brittle. There were no lesions. Mrs. Martinez stated, "No one in the hospital looked at my left leg after the operation. The nurses and doctors never said anything was wrong, but I know it feels like the right one did a couple of years ago."

At 80 years of age, Consuelo Martinez was an alert and accurate historian. She smiled often, her round face with dark brown eyes framed in long, wavy, gray hair worn in a neat bun fastened with a comb. Despite many wrinkles, her skin and muscle tone were firm. She was heavy (160 lb) for her height of 5 ft 1 in. "They had me on a diet in the hospital, but I'd get so hungry I'd call someone to bring me a little something from home. That hospital food had no taste, and it's worse without salt. You can't expect me to be thin when I've been like this all my life."

The nurse reviewed dressing technique with Mrs. Martinez and learned that Mrs. Martinez did not wash her hands before beginning, opened the gauze packages onto the bed linen, and changed the dressing and rewrapped the stump every other day. "Every day was too much work, so I thought every other day would be enough." Mrs. Martinez's weight and the location of the wound added to the effort of stump care. "The nurses always changed it for me because they said I was too slow. They forget people have to do for themselves when they go home. They also told me to teach somebody at home to help me, but I don't want anyone to see how bad it looks."

Next, the nurse attempted to assess Mrs. Martinez's ability to walk with crutches; however, Mrs. Martinez was too weak to maintain her balance. "I've just been using a wheelchair I borrowed from a lady down the street. I don't think I'll be able to go downstairs until I get my new leg, since I'm too heavy to carry." The wheelchair was an ancient, high-backed, wooden one with no leg extensions and stationary arms, making transfer difficult.

Inspection of the second floor of Mrs. Martinez's home showed many hazards to ambulation: scatter rugs, poorly repaired floor boards in the hall, broken tiles on the bathroom floor, and no banister in the stairwell. The stairwell and hall lights did not work, and there were no windows to light the passages.

The house, an old, brick-and-wood, two-story structure, was in poor repair inside and out. There were few windows, and most curtains were drawn. The entire house smelled stale and musty with much clutter, dirty dishes, and dust. Mrs. Martinez occupied the

only bright room. Her bedroom was large, with three windows overlooking the street. From her bed she could observe her neighbors' houses. This room was also dusty and held remnants of yesterday's meals and an ashtray filled with cigarette butts. Mrs. Martinez's bed linen and nightclothes were clean. When asked whether or not she was supposed to smoke, Mrs. Martinez said, "The doctor told me to stop, but he never said why. I don't have much else to do up here, and I smoke more when I'm worried."

With the exception of her visit to the physician's office, Consuelo Martinez had not been downstairs and had been in sleepwear in bed. "When I'm well, I'll get dressed and start running my house again."

When Consuelo Martinez returned home, her granddaughter, Maria Theresa, and her 18-month-old son, Juan, moved in to help with household chores. Maria Theresa's husband was serving a two-year prison term for "fencing" stolen goods, and she did not like staying alone with the baby. Mrs. Martinez had refused offers to stay with any of her children. "I don't like being away from my own home. Besides, they all have such noisy houses, and I like to take naps."

Maria Theresa had been preparing all meals and was responsible for housekeeping duties. "My granddaughter don't do things like I do. She doesn't clean good, and the meals aren't so good either. I know she cooks with salt, but what can I do, she tries, and she has the baby to look after. The doctor told me I have high blood pressure and not to eat salt." On discharge from the hospital Mrs. Martinez had been given prescriptions for Aldactone 100 mg and Hydrodiuril 50 mg once daily, which she firmly stated she took as ordered.

The nurse discussed diet restrictions with Maria Theresa and received no cooperation with meal planning or housekeeping. "My grandmother doesn't like bland food. She always put lots of salt on everything she ate. And this house was dirty when I moved in; others in the family should help me if they want it cleaned up."

The nurse arranged to make daily visits during the initial week to wash the wound with Betadine solution.

Concerned over lack of communication between the hospital and home health agency, the visiting nurse sought reasons for not receiving a referral from the primary nurse for an elderly, handicapped woman.

Investigation of Mrs. Martinez's hospital record indicated gaps in care and service. The physical therapists had documented daily sessions of crutch walking, joint and muscle strengthening exercises, and stump wrapping. According to the physical therapy progress notes, Mrs. Martinez had negotiated the stairs only once with crutches and had been "extremely apprehensive." There had been no assessment of her home environment relative to areas for ambulation, stairs, or safety hazards; nor had any request from or by the physician for continued crutch training and exercises on an outpatient basis been recorded.

Further deficiencies existed in the progress notes of the primary nurse. Omitted from the nursing history were such data as smoking habits, support systems available, usual diet, bowel habits, and a home assessment. Dressing changes and wound status were documented in detail. Teaching of dressing technique, wound care, and limb exercises were not recorded. The nursing progress notes made no mention of any care or plan of teaching relative to secondary prevention for the left leg which was peripherally vascular deficient, although a statement by Mrs. Martinez was quoted: "I sometimes think its only a matter of time until my left leg goes, too."

On the fifth visit, Mrs. Martinez complained to the visiting nurse of pain in the stump. There was a foul odor with increased thick, brownish-yellow drainage. The eschar had loosened, revealing 3 cm of the stump of the tibia. Mrs. Martinez had forgotten to lock the wheelchair the previous night and had fallen, striking the stump on the floor. Since then her leg had throbbed continuously despite taking Tylenol extra-strength tablets every four hours.

The physician was called, but there were no hospital beds available that day. Four days later, Consuelo Martinez was readmitted to the hospital. After two weeks of whirlpool treatment, pain and wound status were unchanged. The eschar was then surgically debrided. The wound continued to be foul smelling and painful. One week later, an above-knee amputation was performed. The wound healed well and pain was minimal.

STUDY GUIDE QUESTIONS

1. Stereotyping can lead to nonindividualized, unsafe nursing practice.
   a. Determine what biases about aging and culture may have been present in this case.

b. How did those biases affect care of Mrs. Martinez?
c. Determine the relationship between bias and malpractice in this case.
d. Which professionals could be considered "at fault"?
e. In what way did those professionals practice in a negligent manner?
f. How could negligence have been avoided?

2. During hospitalization, a patient's support systems should be identified and included in planning for discharge.
   a. Utilizing knowledge of Hispanic culture, identify the support systems for Mrs. Martinez.
   b. Develop a realistic plan to include those support systems in discharge preparation.
   c. How could this preparation be initiated?

3. Standardized criteria for length of hospitalization have been developed by third-party reimbursers and are based on medical diagnoses.
   a. What problems does this pose for the hospitalized elderly?
   b. What criteria should determine the optimal discharge time for an elderly person?
   c. How should such criteria be established and by whom?

4. Accidents in the home are a major cause of morbidity in the elderly.
   a. Identify home safety hazards of specific concern to the elderly.
   b. How could these data be acquired for hospitalized persons?
   c. Of what significance was this knowledge to those caring for Mrs. Martinez?

5. The home care agency did not receive reimbursement for visits to Mrs. Martinez.
   a. What alternatives or solutions were feasible?
   b. Did the primary care nurse have a continued responsibility to Mrs. Martinez?
   c. What professionals could have provided services to Mrs. Martinez at home?

6. Ethnic food habits are a problem in designing a clinical nutrition regimen.
   a. Identify those foods preferred by the Hispanic population.
   b. From those preferred foods, list those that would be prohibited by her medical problems.
   c. Develop a balanced therapeutic diet based on cultural eating patterns.

Case VII

Ms. Adrienne Porter: The Taciturn Woman

INTRODUCTION

The case of Ms. Adrienne Porter is presented in two parts. Part 1 deals with her experiences of admission, intensive care, and surgery, and Part 2 with intermediate care leading to discharge from the hospital.

The rapidly changing nature of Ms. Porter's problems and overall acute situation necessitates problem solving and data analysis on a daily basis, a fact of the hospital milieu. Questions are raised following each day's data; they build on all that has previously occurred. As you progress through Ms. Porter's experience, identify long-term problems and those that were preventable. You will become aware of the lack of social data, which Ms. Porter refused to divulge.

The case is based on the medical model; no nursing history was taken. However, the medical data and laboratory findings suggest nursing interventions which, if identified and carried out,

would have hastened this woman's recovery. Failure by physicians and nurses to recognize and analyze significant data led to preventable complications.

Considerations

The following considerations are central to resolving the problems, making judgments, and providing rationale for Ms. Porter's nursing care:

- Home remedies and self-treatment
- Black Baptist culture in North America
- Sensory deprivation and overstimulation
- Social isolation and treatment modalities
- Eric Erikson's stages of growth
- Maslow's hierarchy of needs
- Attitudes toward health and illness prevention
- Fluid and electrolyte balance in the elderly
- Stress and nutrition
- Acceptance of the "sick role"
- Physiology of the aging:
  - Female reproductive system
  - Cardiovascular
  - Renal
  - Gastrointestinal
  - Metabolic and endocrine
- Stressors in the acute care environment
- Health maintenance education

THE CASE: PART 1

Ms. Adrienne Porter was brought to the emergency room by a friend on May 10 at 11:40 A.M., her chief complaints were hematemesis and frank rectal bleeding. The problem had begun four days previously with coffee ground emesis and tarry brown stools. Despite dizziness, fatigue, and shortness of breath, she had refused to seek medical help until "the red blood showed."

History of Present Illness

Ms. Porter was known to have had a duodenal ulcer of 25 years duration with frequent complaints of dyspepsia, distention, and epigastric

distress. Following the initial diagnosis, Ms. Porter had refused further contact with the physician, preferring to treat herself with various "home remedies." She had been consulting a dermatologist for the past three years for no readily discernible reason; she offered no explanation for these consultations.

Family and Social History

Ms. Porter was a taciturn, fiercely independent woman who volunteered no information she considered irrelevant. It was learned that she was 65 years old, divorced for many years, living alone, active in a Black Baptist Church, and highly antagonistic toward health professionals. She volunteered no family health history, and no one was available to provide additional information.

General Impression

Ms. Porter was a well-developed woman with brown, ashen skin and short gray-black hair. She appeared younger than her stated age of 65. Despite the acuteness of her condition, she was alert and mentally clear.

Physical Examination

Vital Signs:	Blood pressure 120/70 Apical pulse 96 Respiratory rate 24 Rectal temperature 100°F
Head:	Normocephalic; no scars or lesions.
Ears:	Moderate cerumen; drums pearly gray and intact
Eyes:	PEERLA. Peripheral vision intact. Eye grounds essentially unremarkable.
Neck:	No nodes. Thyroid not enlarged. Neck supple. Trachea midline.
Lungs:	Clear to percussion and auscultation. Respirations shallow. Breath sound equal throughout.
Cardiovascular:	Heart percussed outward from sternal border at fifth intercostal space to 2 cm beyond the midclavicular line; a grade III/VI holosystolic murmur heard at fourth intercostal space at left sternal border; ECG and auscultation revealed ectopic beats at rate of 5/min. Pedal pulses faint; 2+ pitting pedal edema present bilaterally. Nonradiating pain over right clavicle. A bottle of Aldomet was found in her purse.

Breasts:	Soft with no masses.
Abdomen:	Round, tense, and tender below the xyphoid. No bowel sounds heard. Liver, spleen, and masses not palpable.
Neuromuscular:	Pinprick sensation decreased in lower extremities. Strength 3+ and equal in all flexors. Gait staggering.
Genitalia:	Complete uterine prolapse with small ulcerated areas.
Rectal:	External hemorrhoids; no internal masses palpated; no stool present.
Laboratory Results:	Hematocrit 13% Hemoglobin 4.4 mm

Despite the seriousness of her situation, Ms. Porter appeared not to be in acute physical distress. She expressed anger toward her predicament, the inconvenience, and the staff. To allow for close observation, she was transferred to the medical intensive care unit.

Questions for May 10

1. Identify significant data for planning nursing care from the physical examination, emergency room observations, and laboratory results.
2. Determine the acute, potential, situational, and long-term problems operative at this time.
3. What hypotheses can be made relative to the probable causes of these problems?
4. What nursing observations will be necessary?
5. What nursing interventions are indicated?

May 11

Admitting Orders:	Medical intensive care Bedrest Clear liquids as tolerated Intravenous D_5 $\frac{1}{2}$ normal saline at 100 ml/hr Digotin 0.25 mg p.o. q.d. Record intake and output

Within the initial 24 hours Ms. Porter received 5 units of whole blood, which increased her hematocrit to 28%. Her vital signs remained stable; there were no obvious signs of bleeding, and she tolerated the clear liquid diet.

Laboratory Results:	Serum creatinine 1.8 mg BUN 32 mg/100 ml K 2.9 mEq Bicarbonate 32 mEq

May 12

Morning

Appeared stable. Abdomen remained tense with some tenderness. Bowel sounds were faint, and there was no evidence of bleeding. No family or health history was elicited from Ms. Porter, because she refused to answer any additional questions.

Evening

At 7 P.M. Ms. Porter vomited 500 ml of coffee ground material. Her arterial blood pressure dropped to 70/0. An immediate upper G.I. showed a deformed prepyloric area with a penetrating ulcer. She was prepared for surgery for the next morning (May 13).

Orders:
Type and cross-match 5 units fresh whole blood.
Insert nasogastric tube and irrigate with iced saline until returns clear.
Vital signs every 15 minutes.
Nasal oxygen with humidification at 4 ℓ/min.

Questions for May 11 and 12

1. Identify data relevant to redesigning the nursing care plan.
2. What data were not provided?
3. Determine actual and potential problems.
4. What nursing orders or interventions would be appropriate?
5. What surgical preparation would be necessitated and effective?

May 13

A laparotomy was performed; the gastric perforation was closed and the peritoneal cavity extensively lavaged. In view of the chronicity of the bleeding, the surgeon felt a vagotomy was not feasible procedure.

Secondary Findings:
Extensive free peritoneal air.
Diffuse cloudy fluid in the peritoneal cavity.
Purulent pelvic fluid required irrigation with 2 gm Keflin.

Postoperative Orders:
Nasal gastric tube with sump set for low, intermittent suction.
Irrigate tube with iced saline if frank bleeding occurs.
Intravenous D_5 in $\frac{1}{2}$ NS at 100 ml/hr.
Add 20 mEq KCl to each intravenous 1000 ml of intravenous fluid.

Keflin 2 gm intravenous in 100 ml of solution q 12 hrs.
Digoxin 0.25 mg IM q.d.
O_2 at 4 ℓ/min via nasal prongs with humidity.
NPO.
Demerol 50–100 mg I.M. q. 3–4 h p.r.n. for pain.
To sit in chair for $\frac{1}{2}$ hour b.i.d.

May 14–15

Nurse progress notes

Uncomplicated immediate postoperative course. No bleeding. Vital signs stable. Patient alert and angry. Pain moderate and controlled with Demerol. Skin color less ashen. Continuous O_2 at 4 ℓ/min.

Questions for May 13, 14, and 15

1. Identify significant data.
2. Determine the short-term problems.
3. Identify potential complications, relevant observations, and preventive measures.
4. What are the underlying principles for the iced saline nasogastric irrigations?
5. State the reasons for O_2 administration.

May 16

Nurse's note

Ms. Porter's respirations were 28–30 and shallow with fine bilateral basilar rales. She had a harsh, moist, and nonproductive cough. O_2 at 4 ℓ/min was continuous.

Vital signs: Blood pressure 136/76
Apical pulse 104
Temperature 100.4°F rectally

She appeared more irritable but neither confused nor restless.

Questions for May 16

1. Identify the significant data.
2. What problems are or may be developing?
3. Give appropriate rationale.
4. Identify nursing orders and interventions most effective at this time.

May 17

A right cardiac catheterization was carried out in the intensive care unit with continuous ECG monitoring. The procedure was tolerated well with no untoward effects.

Findings:

Right atrial pressure 4 mm Hg.
Right ventricular pressure 50.5 mm Hg.
Pulmonary artery pressure 51/16 mm Hg with a mean pressure of 26 mm Hg.
Mean pulmonary capillary wedge pressure 6 mm Hg.

A Swan-Ganz catheter was left in the right femoral vein to measure pulmonary pressures at intervals.

Questions for May 17

1. Why was a cardiac catheterization performed?
2. Identify potential problems resulting from cardiac catheterization and insertion of a Swan-Ganz catheter.
3. Identify the abnormal values and determine the significance of each.
4. What is the nurse's role in this situation?
5. Why did Ms. Porter require a Swan-Ganz catheter placement?
6. What specific care will Ms. Porter require relative to the Swan-Ganz?

May 18

Pulmonary consultation note

The problem is undoubtedly progressive azotemia with marked metabolic alkalosis. It appears that this patient may have developed aspiration pneumonitis with moderate hypoxemia and persistent alkalosis. The mild alveolar hypoventilation is probably a consequence of the alkalosis. Over the past few days the base excess has been in the range of 15–20 with the $APCO_2$ in the range of 50–60 with O_2 continuous at 4 ℓ/min.

Laboratory Findings: Serum Na^+ 150–160 mEq/ℓ
Serum K^+ 4.2 mEq/ℓ

Body Weight:
May 10 167$\frac{3}{4}$ lb
May 15 165 lb
May 18 161 lb

Urine and nasogastric secretions have exceeded intake by 8 liters since admission.

Questions for May 18

1. What factors contributed to the development of pulmonary problems?
2. How did alkalosis develop?
3. What acute physiological problem(s) are occurring?
4. What nursing interventions were appropriate?
5. What is nursing's role at this point?
6. Under what physiological circumstances does output exceed intake?
7. What are the consequences for this patient?

May 19

Laboratory Findings:	Urine chloride	31 mEq/ℓ
	Urine Na^+	42 mEq/ℓ
	Urine K^+	25 mEq/ℓ
	Serum creatinine	32 mg
Miscellaneous:	Intake:	3 liters/24 hours
	Urine:	4 liters/24 hours
	Nasogastric	2 liters/24 hours
Chest X-ray:	Diffuse left basilar rales; clear at the right base.	

No bowel sounds were audible.

Questions for May 19

1. On the basis of today's data, what physiological problems are developing or have developed?
2. What medical interventions can you anticipate?
3. What nursing orders and interventions are appropriate?
4. What additional data do you need?
5. Why does urinary output continue in excess of intake?

May 20

Ms. Porter's intravenous fluids were changed to D_5W at 200 cc/24 hours in excess of nasogastric and urine losses.

She continued for the next four days to produce large amounts of urine, and the gastric contents were intermittently bloody.

Total Intravenous intake average 7 liters per 24 hours
Urinary output average 4 liters per 24 hours
Nasogastric output average 2.5 liters per 24 hours
Oxygen utilization intermittent per patient request

She continued without bowel activity and developed a distended, tender, rigid abdomen. She refused all pain medication. Her tempera-

ture continued to rise, and the basilar rales remained. She developed a productive cough raising thick yellow sputum.

Nurse's notes (relative to behavior)

Ms. Porter is uncooperative and often hostile. She refused to get out of bed. She complains when any procedure is performed, asking to be left alone. She volunteers no information, does not engage in conversation, and never smiles. Her only visitors are two women from her church who visit every afternoon and an occasional visit from her dermatologist.

Physician's note

The uterine prolapse continues to pose difficulty for mobility in bed. There are now several dark areas, and the mucus membrane dries quickly and necessitates frequent damp towel changes. There is no associated pain or discharge.

Questions for May 20

1. What problems are continuing relative to the gastrointestinal system?
2. What problems would you expect to encounter in maintaining an adequate fluid electrolyte balance?
3. What factors are causing the elevated temperature?
4. What problems should be anticipated with the prolapsed uterus?
5. What new nursing orders or interventions are necessary at this point?

May 23

Gastric contents continued bloody, and an esophagogastroscopy was performed.

Findings:	An actively bleeding prepyloric gastric ulcer
	Fundal gastritis
	Reflux esophagitis

Surgery was scheduled for the following morning, but Ms. Porter refused to sign a consent form. She was weak and more lethargic but retained her independence. The visiting church women called Ms. Porter's dermatologist, who persuaded her to consent to the operation. The Swan-Ganz catheter was removed because of poor functioning.

Questions for May 23

1. What is nursing's role in the ethics of this situation?
2. What preparation is necessary for the forthcoming surgery?
3. What stressors place this patient at particular risk for surgery?

May 24

A subtotal (40%) gastrectomy with gastrojejunostomy and vagotomy was performed. A tube was inserted through a duodenostomy and attached to gravity drainage.

Surgeon's note

The prepyloric ulcer remained closed. This area was bleeding profusely, as the base of it was sitting on the gastroduodenal artery. The ulcerated area had eroded into and combined with the pancreas.

Postoperative orders

Intravenous Fluids:	Intralipids 500 cc q. 8 h. D_5 in normal saline 500 cc Freamine II 500 cc KCl 20 mEq	1000 ml to run over 24 hours through arterial line
	D_5 in $\frac{1}{2}$ normal saline KCl 20 mEq Berocia C 2 cc	to run at 100 m/hr
	Hyperalimentation via subclavian line. To contain 50% dextrose; Amino acids 8.5% per 500 cc Na lactate Ca^{++} gluconate.	
Medications:	Digoxin 0.125 mg IM q. A.M. Demerol 50–100 mg IM q. 3 h. p.r.n. for pain Keflin I gm q. 8 h. intravenously in 100 ml over 60 minutes Gentamicin 80 mg intravenously in 100 ml over 60 minutes q. 8 h.	
Miscellaneous:	Vital signs q. 2 h. when stable. O_2 at 4 ℓ/min with humidity p.r.n. Duodenostomy tube on gravity drainage. Nasogastric sump tube to low, intermittent suction. Irrigate with iced normal saline when drainage is bright red. Turn cough and deep breathe. NPO. To sit in chair $\frac{1}{2}$ hour b.i.d. IPPB with NS 2 cc q. 2 h. followed by routine chest therapy.	

Questions for May 24

1. What nursing observations are necessary following Ms. Porter's surgery?
2. What nursing orders and interventions would have been appropriate for Ms. Porter's postoperative care?
3. Why is Ms. Porter now receiving Freamine II and Intralipids intravenously?
4. Why is the nasogastric tube connected to low, intermittent suction and the duodenostomy tube to gravity drainage?
5. What is the purpose of sump drainage?

May 25

Physician's progress notes

Evening of surgery the patient looked better than she did preoperatively. Output good. This A.M.: Arterial blood gases in normal range. No bowel sounds. Abdomen slightly distended. Breath sounds decreased in both bases. Afebrile. Salt-poor albumin 150 cc given intravenously.

May 26

Temperature 100.6°F rectally
Intake: 2800 cc
Output: 2700 cc

Persistent abdominal pain only somewhat relieved by Demerol. She is alert and refusing oxygen. Fewer rales heard in the lung basis. Abdomen is softer and diffusely tender with profused bowel sounds. She has developed greenish-yellow vaginal drainage.

Body weight 161½ lb
Hematocrit 30%

May 27

Patient is alert and not cooperating with the nurses. Resists getting out of bed and refuses respiratory therapy.

No bowel sounds heard. Decreased breath sounds at the left basc. Nasogastric drainage is clear and guaiac negative. Her serum gentamicin sulfate level is 4.4 ug/cc.

Rectal temperature range: 100–101°F.

Laboratory results: Vaginal drainage culture: Heavy pseudomonas

Moderate proteus
Moderate staphylococcus
WBC 14,000
Thyroid-stimulating hormone 3.5 mu/ml (1.0–10)
Iron 28 mcg/ℓ
ECG: Sinus rhythm with occasional QSR observation and minor nonspecific ST depression with T-wave lowering. The axis and position normal.

Questions for May 25, 26, and 27

1. Why does the abdomen remain distended and absent of bowel sounds?
2. Why did Ms. Porter receive salt-poor albumin?
3. What is the significance of the vaginal drainage?
4. Why is her temperature elevated?
5. According to the laboratory data, what problems are continuing and what potentially new ones are developing?

May 28

Physician's progress notes

Nasogastric drainage became bright red this morning. Patient received 2 units packed cells, and nasogastric tube is continuously irrigated with iced normal saline.

Hemoglobin is 8.9 gm.

It is surgery's impression that the bleeding is from the gastrojejunostomy anastomosis.

Blood pressure remains around 120/84. Her apical pulse rate fluctuates from 94 to 124 beats per minute. Today she began passing small watery stools that are moderately guaiac positive.

May 29

Physician's note

The bleeding appears to have stopped, and she is alert. Her temperature continues to spike. Electrolytes are within normal range. Her BUN is 33, and her hematocrit is 31%.

Questions for May 28 and 29

1. What factors might have contributed to the new episode of bleeding?
2. What is the significance for Ms. Porter of the continual blood pressure of 120/84?
3. What caused the bleeding to stop?

May 30

Physician's progress notes

She appears more stable today. Her lungs are clear to auscultation; there is decreased pedal edema, abdominal pain, and rigidity. However, bowel sounds remain decreased. She has been able to sit in a chair twice a day for $\frac{1}{2}$ hour but tires easily. Blood pressure 150/92. Apical pulse rate 104 and slightly irregular. Stool continues watery but is now guaiac negative.

Laboratory results

Blood Findings:	Total protein 5.5 gm
	Albumin 2.5 gm
	Calcium 8.5 mg
	Phosphorus 3.5 mg
	Creatinine 1.6 mg
	Total bilirubin 1.5 mg
	Alkaline phosphatase 1.4 mg
	LDH 260
	SGOT 10
	Prothrombin time 100% of control

Chest X-ray report

Lungs relatively clear with improvement over previous film. Slight increased density in shrunken right middle lobe and left base. Pulmonary vascular engorgement and cardiac enlargement indicate congestive heart failure.

Questions for May 30

1. Identify any abnormal laboratory findings and/or other significant data.
2. Provide scientific explanations for the altered parameters.
3. In addition to the stress of surgery, what factors have contributed to Ms. Porter's fatigue?
4. What nursing interventions would have been effective?
5. How did congestive heart failure develop at this time?

May 31

Physician's progress notes

She is alert today with no further evidence of any bleeding. Out of bed three times yesterday with less fatigue. She continues to be

irritable and resistant to care. Her temperature ranged from 100°F to 101°F.

Laboratory results

Blood:

Sodium 138 mEq/ℓ
Potassium 4.3 mEq/ℓ
Chloride 104 mEq/ℓ
CO_2 24 mEq/ℓ
BUN 28 mg
Glucose fasting 109 mg
Hemoglobin 12.1 gm
Hematocrit 33%

Questions for May 31

1. What factors are now contributing to the elevated temperature?
2. What laboratory findings indicate further observation and/or intervention?
3. What observations and interventions would be within the role of nursing?

June 1

Physician's progress notes

There continues to be no bleeding. The abdomen is soft, and faint bowel sounds are present. The chest is clear to percussion, auscultation, and X-ray. Her temperature continues to be 101.4°F rectally. Her urine output is adequate. She now has no pedal edema.

Nasogastric secretions have diminished, and the tube is clamped for 2 hours and then reconnected to low suction for ½ hour. The duodenostomy drainage is yellow and foul. The sump is now connected to low, continuous suction.

Her weight today is 146 lb.

Questions for June 1

1. Account for the resolution of pedal edema.
2. State the rationale for a nasogastric tube clamping schedule.
3. What may be causing the foul duodenostomy drainage?
4. Why was the sump drainage tube connected to suction at this time?
5. What factors contributed to her weight of 146 lb?
6. What problems must be anticipated relative to continual hyperalimentation therapy?
7. What monitoring should have been instituted? Why?

June 2

Physician's progress note

No bleeding. Bowel sounds increased. Nasogastric tube removed. Duodenostomy tube plugged. Hyperalimentation intravenous continues at 100 cc/hr. Her temperature is 101°F rectally at 3 P.M. Hematocrit 36%. Blood pressure 160/94. Apical pulse 96. Respirations 22.

June 3

Physician's progress note

Her temperature is 99°F rectally. She is tolerating clear liquids and seems less irritable. She continues to resist conversation and all aspects of care but those she considers essential. Hematocrit 30 mm. Blood pressure 150/90. Apical pulse 100. Respirations 22.

June 4

Physician's progress note

Her temperature is stable at 99°F rectally. She continues to receive hyperalimentation therapy. She received 2 ml Imferon intravenously and magnesium sulfate 2 ml IM today.

She will be transferred to a two-bed room in the intermediate care unit this afternoon.

Questions for June 2, 3, and 4

1. Why does Ms. Porter continue to receive hyperalimentation therapy?
2. Is her blood pressure significantly high enough to warrant treatment?
3. What may have caused the drop in temperature?
4. To what would you attribute the sudden drop in hematocrit on June 3?
5. Was this an appropriate time to transfer Ms. Porter to intermediate care?
6. What factors may have affected this decision?

THE CASE: PART 2

June 5

The two-bed room in the intermediate unit was quiet with less machinery and personnel. Ms. Porter's bed, beside the window, afforded

a view. Her roommate, a 52-year old woman recovering from a myocardial infarction, was pleasant and gregarious. She tried unsuccessfully to engage in conversation. Ms. Porter preferred staring out the window.

Progress notes

Afebrile and tolerating fluids only in small amounts. Appetite poor, and patient complains of distention upon moderate fluid intake. Hyperalimentation therapy continues. "Patient looks the best she has since admission."

Laboratory results:	HCO_3:	16 mEq/ℓ
	WBC:	13,800
	HCT:	31%

June 6

Ms. Porter ambulated twice today and seemed stronger. Her intravenous was discontinued, and she began a soft diet. Communication with staff and patients continued at a minimum. She rarely issued any complaints or requests. Cardiac status stable.

Orders:	$NaHCO_3$	625 mg b.i.d. p.o.
	Maalox	20 cc q. h. p.o.
	Transferred to floor care.	

Questions for June 5 and 6

1. What factors would indicate an appropriate time for Ms. Porter's transfer from acute care?
2. What problems would you anticipate and attempt to correct relative to Ms. Porter's transfer following 27 days in an ICU?
3. What contributed to abdominal distention?
4. What measures could have been suggested/instituted to intervene in the communication difficulty?
5. What nursing interventions might be indicated from the laboratory data?
6. What nursing interventions and observations are necessary for safe hyperalimentation therapy?
7. Why were $NaHCO_3$ and Maalox ordered at this time?

On June 6, Ms. Porter was transferred to a general 30-bed medical/surgical unit. She was again in a two-bed room beside the window. Her new roommate was in her 80's and very lethargic. There was a television set on the wall, which Ms. Porter did not want turned on.

The staff did not attempt to relate to Ms. Porter, no nursing

history was done, and no care plan was developed to meet her specific needs.

June 6 and 7

Orders:	$NaHCO_3$ increased to 950 mg p.o. t.i.d. Feosol spansules 1 tab q.d.
Laboratory Results:	Serum HCO_3: 15 mEq/ℓ WBC: 12,000 Hemoglobin: 10 gm
Vital Signs:	Apical pulse 120. Premature ventricular contractions noted at 2–3 per minute. Blood pressure 100/60 when upright. Respirations 18–20.

Progress note

Ms. Porter continues to eat poorly but does take fluid well. Condition stable.

Questions for June 6 and 7

1. Why was the $NaHCO_3$ dosage increased?
2. What is the purpose of Feosol?
3. What is the significance of the laboratory results?
4. Why is the apical cardiac rate 120 per minute?
5. What is the significance of 2–3 premature ventricular contractions per minute?
6. What factors might cause the orthostatic hypotension?
7. What nursing measures would be appropriate in controlling this hypotension?
8. What methods could have been employed to elicit a nursing history?
9. How could an individualized nursing care plan have been developed?

June 8

Progress note

Ms. Porter is dizzy upon standing. Blood pressure range when upright is 96/60 to 50/40. She is not eating well, and her fluid intake has decreased. Will start her on $D_5\ \frac{1}{2}NS$ with HCO_3 at 75 cc/hr.

June 9 and 10

She is medically stable. There is no evidence of bleeding. Body weight 150 lb. Her fluid intake is 1500 cc p.o., and intravenous intake is 1820 cc for the past 24 hours. Her urine output is 2800 cc for this

period. Hemoglobin 9; hematocrit 32; creatinine 3.8. The duodenostomy tube is in place but not draining. She continues afebrile.

Questions for June 8, 9, and 10

1. Why is Ms. Porter dizzy when standing?
2. How could this be prevented or controlled?
3. Why was an intravenous of D_5 in $\frac{1}{2}$ normal saline ordered?
4. Why was $NaHCO_3$ added to the intravenous?
5. Evaluate her fluid balance.
6. What new nursing interventions may be indicated?
7. How could you evaluate urinary adequacy?

June 11

Upper gastrointestinal series reveals poor peristalsis with delayed emptying. There is no evidence of obstruction at the stoma or below.

June 12

Continues to have premature ventricular contractions 2–3 times per minute. Her blood pressure continues to drop to 100/60 when upright. She is able to ambulate with assistance and tolerates sitting in a chair. Weight 155 lb.

Orders

Increase intravenous glucose to 10%/bottle; decrease rate to 50 cc/hr.
Give one unit Intralipid intravenously b.i.d.
Meritene milkshake 10 oz t.i.d. p.o.
One unit packed cells intravenously.

June 13

Appetite improving slowly. Total intake: 2400 cc
Urine output: 1200 cc
Body weight 160 lb
Multiple soft, brown, formed stools; guaiac negative
Physician referral to dietitian for evaluation

Dietitian's note

Ms. Porter receives 800 calories intravenously. She refuses Meritene milkshakes, stating she "doesn't like the taste." She enjoys

snacks and tolerated 475 calories in excess of planned meals yesterday. Our department will begin a daily calorie count and a six-meal plan with snack supplements.

Questions for June 12 and 13

1. Account for the 5-lb weight gain on June 12.
2. Indicate reasons for the orders written on June 12.
3. What nursing measures would be dependent upon those orders?
4. Account for the second 5-lb gain on June 13.
5. What total caloric intake would be appropriate for Ms. Porter at this time?
6. Why was the dietitian consulted this time during the hospitalization?
7. When would a nutrition referral been most beneficial?

June 14

Duodenostomy tube removed. The site is clean, uninflamed, and not draining. There is 2+ pedal edema; weight is 160 lb.

BUN 29 mg.

Dietitians report a 2300 calorie daily intake: 880 cc intravenously and 1420 p.o.

June 16

Blood pressure more stable when upright, and she ambulates without assistance. Intravenous discontinued to see how well she tolerates exclusive oral intake. Pedal edema continues at 2+.

Questions for June 14, 15, and 16

1. Why is Ms. Porter's weight stable?
2. What factors are contributing to pedal edema?
3. Evaluate the intake of 1420 calories on June 15.
4. What is nursing's role in Ms. Porter's overall nutrition?
5. What factors might have stabilized her blood pressure?

June 17

The duodenostomy site is healing. Pedal edema continues.
Intake 1700 cc p.o.
Output 1400 cc
WBC 10,000

Gynecology note

Prolapsed uterus replaced and manipulated into place with doughnut pessary. Pap smear of cervix and vaginal walls done. Suggested Ms. Porter be examined by a gynecologist on a regular basis. She was not receptive to this idea.

June 18

Dietitian's note

Ms. Porter was given diet instructions for home maintenance. It was suggested she restrict obvious salt intake. Meritene has been added to puddings for her, which she usually refuses. I doubt that she will use Meritene at home to get the recommended extra 1200 calories.

Physician referred Ms. Porter to hospital social worker for evaluation of post-discharge needs.

Social worker's note

Ms. Porter was rather taciturn and volunteered little about her home situation and needs. She was vague about who would be able to help her with chores and the general activities of daily living, answering "friends will help me." I suggested a referral to the Visiting Nurse Association to assist her until she was independent. Ms. Porter did not want this service.

I will contact her friends for some information about this woman, as I have little to go on at present. The nursing staff does not react well to Ms. Porter and know very little about her. An antagonistic relationship exists among them.

Questions for June 17 and 18

1. Evaluate Ms. Porter's fluid balance.
2. Why did her WBC drop to 10,000?
3. What is the action of a pessary?
4. What implications does this have for followup?
5. What teaching is necessary relative to this apparatus for Ms. Porter?
6. What consequences could develop without gynecological followup?
7. Why might Ms. Porter be resistant to medical care?
8. What could have replaced the Meritene milkshakes?
9. Why was a social worker consulted?

June 19

Social worker's note

Met with Ms. Porter's two closest friends and found them most helpful. Ms. Porter has apparently always been an independent, taciturn person, refusing help from anyone. She tends not to share personal information except with very close friends. These women knew of no living relatives. They were very willing to provide all the help Ms. Porter would need and doubted that a visiting nurse would be accepted.

Questions for June 19

1. What could the nursing staff have done to correct the rift with Ms. Porter?
2. How could this situation have been prevented?
3. Was the social worker appropriate in her actions?
4. What knowledge would be necessary for Ms. Porter to maintain a health state and comply with the regimen?
5. What methods and timing of instruction would be most effective?
6. What predictions can be made about recurrent problems after discharge? What nursing followup is indicated?

June 20

Physician's note

Ms. Porter will be discharged home today. The gastrointestinal bleedings were resolved. There continues to be borderline renal insufficiency. Pap smear of cervix and vaginal walls negative. Her weight is stable at 160 lb, but there remains 2+ pedal edema. Occasional premature ventricular contractions continue.

Discharge Medications: Lasix 40 mg p.o. q. A.M.
Feosol 1 tab p.o. q. A.M.

Nurse's note

Diet and medication instruction given. Clinic appointments made for medical and gynecology followup and dates given to Ms. Porter. She had no questions and was relieved to be leaving.

STUDY GUIDE QUESTIONS

1. a. Patient stays in intensive care units can be stressful at best. This care setting often poses many problems for elderly pa-

tients. With these statements in mind, delineate those aspects of the intensive care unit that can be threatening to the well-being of the elderly person.

b. Meeting basic human needs when a person is unable to meet these for himself is a paramount nursing activity. In the intensive care setting, what should be done to prevent sensory deprivation? to prevent sensory overload? to provide for uninterrupted periods of sleep?

c. Orientation to time, place, space, and people are measures taken to promote reality, thereby preventing confusion in the elderly. Plan an improved orientation program to the intensive care unit for the aging and aged. As you design the plan, take into consideration how circadian rhythm is altered in the setting and other problems that are related to age-dependent physiological changes.

2. Mrs. Porter's age, race, and religion can have a direct bearing on her health values and practices. Determine the folkways or ethnomedicine factors that influence the health-seeking activities of elderly black females of strong Protestant religious persuasion.

3. What responsibilities do nurses have relative to preparing Mrs. Porter for discharge and following hospital discharge?

Case

VIII

Mr. Joseph Rumanski: Matters of Living and Dying

INTRODUCTION

This community-based case includes relevant information from Mr. Rumanski's hospitalization. Again, there are scant hospital nursing baseline data provided to assist the community nurse in evolving relevant care plans for implementation. Nor did adequate protocols for direct communication between the hospital and community agency exist.

The nursing resolutions of this case require the application of multidisciplinary knowledge in the analysis of the data as they pertain to the recurrent problems in maintenance care of the elderly. In this particular instance the central foci for consideration include:

ethnic background
developmental stage
self-perception
sexuality

financial problems concomitant upon retirement
health insurance programs
home and neighborhood assessment
mobility hazards in the home and community
the metastatic cancer process in the aging
radiation therapy in the aging
nutrition in terminal cancer
the aging cardiovascular system
development of a patient–nurse in-home contract
suicide in the elderly
care of the elderly dying at home
community support systems available for the family, the patient, and the nurse

As in previous cases, each day or event should be examined for pertinent data, goal modifications, appropriate nursing judgments, and interventions. No one caring for any patient has the luxury of designing a plan of care in retrospect.

THE CASE

On November 11 a visiting nurse agency received the following physician's referral for Joseph Rumanski, who had been discharged from a surgical unit of an acute care hospital the same day.

Because the referral information was minimal and time did not permit visiting Mr. Rumanski prior to hospital discharge, the community health nurse arranged with the hospital Medical Records Department to read the patient's record.

Background Data from Hospital Record (History of Present Illness)

On October 16 Joseph Rumanski, age 72, had been admitted to hospital following one week of anorexia and increasing jaundice. The previous year he had had a proximal esophagogastrectomy for gastric carcinoma. Over the past six months he had received chemotherapy with 5-fluorouracil and had lost twenty pounds.

Admitting Laboratory Data:	Total bilirubin	8
	SGOT	57
	LDH	159
	Alkaline phosphotase	265
	Prothrombin time	68%

REFERRAL FORM – POST HOSPITAL NURSING CARE

PATIENT'S NAME	DATE OF BIRTH	SEX	MARITAL STATUS
Rumanski, Joseph	2-16-07	M	M

ADDRESS – VISIT AT	APT./FLOOR	TELEPHONE
8218 84th St.	2nd	687-4357

RELATIVE ☐ FRIEND ☐	ADDRESS	TELEPHONE
Wife Sophie	Same	

HOSPITAL NO.	ROOM	BL. CR. NO.	ADMITTED	DISCHARGED	SOCIAL WORKER AND EXT.	OUT PATIENT NO.
	443			11-11		

PHYSICIAN	ADDRESS	TELEPHONE	CLINIC PHYSICIAN AND EXT.
J.P. Gray	284-3375		

	RESULTS
DATE CHEST X-RAY 10-16	Lungs clear
DATE CBC 11-3	Hgb 11.1, Hct 32.9, WBC 10.6
DATE BLOOD SUGAR 11-3	260
DATE URINALYSIS 10-27	1-3 WBC +1 sugar

FOLLOW UP: MEDICAL PLAN — DATE — TIME; CLINIC; OFFICE; RADIATION; CHEMOTHERAPY

AGENCY REFERRED TO:	ADDRESS	TELEPHONE
Visiting Nurse		

DIAGNOSIS — DATE OF SURGERY

PRIMARY: S/P Esophago-gastrectomy
Cholecystectomy with diffuse metastases

SECONDARY:

PT. & OR FAMILY INFORMED ☐ Yes ☐ No — ?

PROGNOSIS: Poor

Is patient home bound? Yes ☐ No ☐

MEDICATION	DOSAGE–FREQUENCY	MEDICATION	DOSAGE–FREQUENCY
1. Amoxicillin 500mg p.o. q6h		6.	
2. Quiniglute 1 tab q12h		7.	
3. Aldactazide 250mg p.o. q6h		8.	
4. Tylenol #3 1 tab p.o. q4h p.r.n.		9.	
5.		10.	

INJECTIONS — DOSE — FREQUENCY — MODE — TEACH FAMILY ☐ Yes ☐ No

DRESSINGS TO: T tube site ☒ Dry ☐ Moist
TREATMENT ☐ Clean ☐ Irrigate
SOLUTION
Rx
FREQUENCY p.r.n. ☒ Yes TEACH ☐ No

OSTOMIES ☐ Trach TEACH ☐ Yes ☐ No
SOLUTION AMT. FREQUENCY
☐ Colostomy
CHANGE BAG FREQUENCY
☐ Illeostomy

PHYSICAL THERAPY
☐ ROM ☐ Active ☐ Passive R L
☐ Stretching ☐ ☐
☐ Resistive ☐ ☐
☐ Weight Bearing – Amount
☐ Muscle Strengthening
☐ Transfer
☐ Brace ☐ Ambulate ☐ Stair Climbing

CATHETER TEACH ☐ Yes ☐ No ☐ Change ☐
SIZE # BALLOON C.C.
☐ Irrigate Frequency
SOLUTION Frequency of Change

DIET ☒ General CALORIES
☐ Lo Sodium
☐ ADA PUSH ORAL FLUIDS
☐ Other

SPEECH THERAPY ☐ Home ☐ Out Patient
MENTAL HEALTH ☐ Recommended
HOME HEALTH AIDE ☐
OCCUPATIONAL THERAPY ☐ Out Patient ☐ Home
RESPONSIBLE PERSON ☐ Family ☐ Other
EQUIPMENT SUPPLIED ☐ Yes ☐ No
☐ Chair ☐ Bed ☐ Commode ☐ Walker ☐ Other
SUPPLIED BY: DATE REQUESTED

Special Nursing Needs or Services (Home Health Aide, O_2, ETC.)

T tube clamped at present
Change T tube site dressing

Physician's Signature [signature] Date 11-11

This will certify that this patient is in need of the services outlined above.

COMMUNITY NURSING REFERRAL – REPORT FROM NURSING AND SUPPORTIVE SERVICES

NAME NUMBER: AGENCY:

ADDITIONAL REPORTS:
1. SOCIAL SERVICE
2. PHYSICAL THERAPY
3. OCCUPATIONAL THERAPY
4. SPEECH THERAPY
5. NUTRITION
6. DIABETIC CLINICIAN

USE OTHER SIDE IF NEEDED (TURN CARBON)

	INDEPENDENT	NEEDS ASSIST	UNABLE TO DO	CHECK LEVEL OF ABILITY
BED ACTIVITY	✓			Turns
	✓			Sits
PERSONAL CARE	✓			Face, Hair and Arms
	✓			Trunk-Perineum
	✓			Legs and Feet
				Bladder Progress
				Bowel Progress
DRESSING				Upper Ext.
		✓		Trunk
		✓		Lower Ext.
				Prosthetic Appliance
MOBILITY	✓			Transfer
		✓		Sitting
		✓		Standing
		✓		Tub
		✓		Toilet
		✓		Wheelchair
		✓		Walking
		✓		Stairs
FEEDING		✓		DENTURES ☐ YES ☐ NO SIGHT ☐ YES ☐ NO

MENTAL STATUS

☐ ALERT ☐ CONFUSED ☑ FORGETFUL

NURSING PROCEDURES TAUGHT

	Pt.	Family
DRESSING	☑	☐
INJECTIONS	☐	☐
CATH. CARE	☐	☐
DECUBITUS CARE	☐	☐
DIABETIC INSTR.	☐	☐
ORAL MEDS	☐	☐
VITAL SIGNS	☐	☐
OTHER	☐	☐
OTHER	☐	☐

RESPONSE TO INSTRUCTION

POOR ☐ FAIR ☑
EXCELLENT ☐ POTENTIAL ☐

NURSE'S REPORT

1) T______ P______ R______ B/P______

2) COMMENTS:

Patient resents wife's constant ongoing hovering. Occasionally very hostile towards wife's nagging about food. Patient sleeps much of the time.

Mr. Rumanski was shown how to do his own dressings but I think Mrs. Rumanski would do better. She was shown only once how to change the dressing and is very unsure of herself.

SIGNATURE OF NURSE *Jean Simms* UNIT EXTENSION DATE

Metastatic Workup:

Normal bone scan.
Chest X-ray normal.
Liver scan: increased uptake in the right middle lobe.
Spleen scan normal.
Liver biopsy: no evidence of metastatic disease.
Cholangiogram evidenced an extrinsic mass compressing the proximal common bile duct, thought to be an enlarged lymph node secondary to metastatic tumor.

At home Mr. Rumanski had taken Donnatol and Lomotil, which were continued in hospital.

Two days after admission, Mr. Rumanski went to surgery for celiotomy, cholecystectomy, and exploration of the common bile duct with T tube insertion. The surgical findings were metastatic adenocarcinoma consistent with gastroesophageal primary metastases causing porta hepatic obstruction.

Mr. Rumanski's postoperative course in the intensive care unit was unremarkable. He received intravenous therapy with Ancef 1 gm and Cleocin 300 mg, IPPB, and chest physical therapy for postoperative pulmonary congestion. (Mr. Rumanski had been a heavy smoker, and his cough had become productive of thick, greenish mucus.)

An ECG showed a sinus arrhythmia, and quinidine was started.

Questions

1. Determine the most effective form of quinidine for an elderly person requiring long-term therapy.
2. Provide rationale for the decision made.

October 20

Mr. Rumanski continued stable and afebrile. His wound was clean, and bowel sounds were heard. He was transferred to a two-bed room; the monitor and central venous pressure line were discontinued.

Nasogastric secretions were minimal, and the tube was clamped. Over the next five days, Mr. Rumanski progressed to six oral feedings daily. The intravenous infusions were discontinued, medications were given orally, and quinidine and Ancef were discontinued.

October 26

Mr. Rumanski developed an elevated temperature (104°F) orally with the complaint of midepigastric pain. Cholangitis was suspected. Blood and bile cultures showed enterococcus (gram-positive

cocci). Cleocin was increased to 600 mg q. 6-h., and gentamicin 80 mg intravenously q. 8 h. was started. ECG showed a return sinus arrythmia, for which Tuiniglute was ordered. Chest X-ray indicated clear lungs but enlargement of the central pulmonary vessels.

Mr. Rumanski continued febrile for the next four days. He received Tylenol and intravenous fluids with 2 cc Berocca C and was placed on a hypothermia blanket. On October 29, Ampicillin 2 gm q. 8 h. intravenously was started. Cleocin was discontinued.

November 1

Mr. Rumanski developed diarrhea and was started on Lactinex. Pedal edema 1+ was noted, and Aldactazide was begun. He continued febrile with midepigastric pain.

November 3

Mr. Rumanski began taking Vivonex but disliked it. He continued febrile with epigastric tenderness.

Laboratory Data on November 1:		
	Total bilirubin	93 mg
	Alkaline phosphotase	4.75 mg
	LDH	171 units
	SGOT	57 units
	CPK	33 units
	Na^+	129 mEq/ℓ
	K^+	4 mEq/ℓ
	Cl	88 mEq/ℓ
	PCO_2	24.8 mEq/ℓ
	BUN	22 mg
	Creatinine	1.4 mg
	Prothrombin time	85
	PTT	25 seconds

During the febrile period, nurses' notes recorded several hours of depression. He frequently asked, "Why do I have to live like this?" He expressed fear of dying, but there was no mention of anyone discussing death or his diagnosis with him. On two occasions he was "irritable and restless" and was given 25 mg of Thorazine.

The nurses' notes did not reflect investigation of the causative factors underlying the irritable state. Nor were any specifics of the irritable and restless behavior described.

The nursing history did not include the extent of Mr. Rumanski's knowledge of his illness; nor a family health history, an

interview of his wife (to discuss her problems or expectations) or a description of the home situation. There was no discussion of dying at home.

No social history was recorded.

Synopsis of Physical Examination by Attending Physician

Head:	Normocephalic with male pattern of balding. Hair scant and gray. No subcutaneous fat.
Skin:	Jaundiced, dry, and very loose.
Eyes:	Sclera dark yellow; arcus senilis present; PEERLA.
Ears:	Moderate cerumen; tympanic membranes intact.
Nose:	Unremarkable.
Lymph:	Nodes negative to palpation.
Lungs:	Clear to percussion and auscultation.
Cardiac:	$S_1 S_2$ normal. Grade III/VI systolic murmur over third left. Intercostal space with radiation to both carotid and axilla. Bruits heard bilaterally in femoral arteries. All pulses present.
Abdomen:	Liver palpated 6 cm below right costal margin. Edge sharp with nodules in the right lobe. Spleen and masses not palpable. Bowel sounds normal.
Rectal:	Tone poor. Prostate smooth and enlarged 2+. No masses felt. Stool yellow and guaiac negative.
Muscloskeletal:	Spine straight. Long bones unremarkable. Decreased flexion in left knee due to osteoarthritis. No other joint limitation or bone or joint pain. No costovertebral angle tenderness.
CNS:	Cranial nerves II through XII intact. Muscle status fair. Romberg test negative. Sensation equal and normal.

Questions

1. From the physical findings and laboratory data, determine the normal aging changes.
2. Identify the abnormal changes that will require monitoring at home.

November 13

The initial home visit was made by the community health nurse. Mrs. Rumanski was found to be quite agitated. Questioning revealed that the cause of Mrs. Rumanski's concern was centered on the fact

that Mr. Rumanski had not had a bowel movement in the past five days. She stated, "They should never send a sick man home that . . ." Mrs. Rumanski had given him Ex-Lax and two tablespoons of milk of magnesia the previous night and hot prune juice that morning with no results. Mrs. Rumanski then called the physician, who suggested she give her husband a Fleet's enema. However, Mr. Rumanski had a large, formed, light-colored stool before the enema could be given.

On assessment, the nurse found Mr. Rumanski's abdomen soft and nontender without bowel sounds. The abdominal skin was jaundiced and the turgor poor. He had no appetite, and no clear answer was obtained relative to fluid intake. Mr. and Mrs. Rumanski continuously contradicted each other and argued over seemingly minor details; this often brought Mrs. Rumanski to tears.

During the assessment of her husband, Mrs. Rumanski hovered in the bedroom doorway and constantly answered for her husband, which annoyed him. She was a formidable, 64-year-old woman, 5 ft 6 in. tall and weighing 250 lb, with a mound of bright red curls ("having my hair done is the only luxury I have"). She was anxious, wringing her hands frequently, repeating what the nurse said, and speaking in a loud voice that irritated her husband. She stated that both she and her husband were losing their hearing.

Mr. Rumanski's vital signs were stable (blood pressure 120/78, apical rate 80 and slightly irregular, respirations 24 with decreased rib excursion). There were no adventitious sounds despite long history of smoking and chronic morning cough. He was afebrile, and there was no drainage around the clamped T tube.

Obtaining a diet history was difficult because of the Rumanskis' constant bickering. Eventually it was learned that they preferred sausages, eggs, and bread or fried potatoes for breakfast. Lunch often consisted of meat, gravy, cheese, potatoes, hash, and cabbage in various combinations. Pie was a common dessert. Dinner was similar. Neither of the Rumanskis cared for green vegetables, and Mrs. Rumanski rarely bought fruit. They drank orange juice three times a week. Mr. Rumanski said he was not interested in changing his diet and had lost his appetite. Mrs. Rumanski was anxious to prepare foods that would benefit her husband and catered to any new craving. On one occasion, she had gone a great distance by bus to buy a special sausage he thought he'd like, only to have him refuse to eat it.

Mr. Rumanski's tolerance for activities of personal care showed him to be weak and easily discouraged but willing to try to build up

his strength. At present, he was able to shuffle to the bathroom, 15 feet from his bed, with assistance. Mrs. Rumanski said, "I'm so afraid to leave him alone, and yet I have so many errands to do."

Mr. Rumanski was able to shave and partially wash himself at the sink with support of his wife. He wanted to be able to watch television in the living room (there was no space for one near his bed). Most of his day was spent looking out the bedroom window or dozing. He had not yet eaten at the table, and it was suggested he try this to increase his appetite. He was too weak to negotiate any stairs and was carried to and from the car by his son.

After the assessment of Mr. Rumanski, the nurse sat in the kitchen to listen to Mrs. Rumanski discuss her problems and concerns for her husband. Mrs. Rumanski was found to have a history of hypertension and diabetes for 15 years. Daily medications included 20 units NPH, Aldomet t.i.d., and Dyazide each morning. She found it difficult to adhere to her diet, since she was "so nervous with Joseph home and so sick." She was also anxious about her ability to change his dressing. "The nurses in the hospital showed me how to do it, but they moved so quickly I couldn't be sure what they were doing. I didn't get a chance to try it myself." At this point, the nurse supervised Mrs. Rumanski's technique and reassured her she had remembered quite accurately.

Mr. Rumanski's medications were on the kitchen table, and the nurse checked them against the referral order. She then asked Mrs. Rumanski if she could recall why her husband was taking them. Mrs. Rumanski remembered the purpose of Amoxacillin and Aldactazide but not of Synalogs D.C., Donnatol, or Dalmane. "I didn't know Joseph would be taking medicine at home until the nurse gave me a bag of these pills just before we left. I know she told me what they were, but I guess my memory isn't as good as it was. Joseph only takes them when I remind him."

Questions

1. Determine those components of a home assessment of significance for this couple.
2. On the basis of the initial visit, what problems for both Rumanskis would you identify?
3. Assess the Rumanskis' dietary habits relative to their respective health problems.
4. What nutritional suggestions would be helpful for this elderly, terminally ill man?

5. What realistic changes can be expected?
6. Determine means to assist in increasing Mr. Rumanski's activity tolerance.
7. Identify the role food plays for Mrs. Rumanski and in her relationship with her husband.
8. Evaluate the adequacy of the hospital patient and family teaching program.
9. What modifications may be necessary for the elderly?
10. What problems in medication compliance might be anticipated?

The following brief description of Mr. Rumanski, his family, and his environment is based on the assessment made by the community health nurse on the first visit:

The Rumanski's had lived in their own home since their marriage forty years ago. The house was a two-story, two-family red brick building in poor repair with a large, fenced back yard bordering on the railroad tracks. Over the years, a trucking company and warehouses had replaced many of the houses. Only eight remained, all of them dilapidated. Two of the eight were vacant.

The Rumanskis' only son, Joseph, Jr., was divorced and lived on the first floor with his 15-year-old daughter. Joseph, Jr., worked as a security guard on the evening shift at a local factory. The granddaughter had left high school in the tenth grade and spent most of her time at home or at a neighbor's.

Originally, the residents of this street had been Polish, Czech, Lithuanian, and Hungarian blue-collar workers. Residents had been close, friendly, and proud of their neighborhood. However, beginning in the early 1960s, many residents had had to abandon their homes. Commercial businesses and a transient population moved in under rezoning provisions.

Joseph and Sophie Rumanski lived on the second floor, where they had moved when Joseph, Jr., returned home after leaving his wife. The second-story apartment had four small rooms and was crowded to bursting with the couple's lifelong possessions. The Rumanskis were large people, and a large, elderly dog added to the cramped conditions. Mr. Rumanski's bedroom was cluttered from floor to ceiling and wall to wall. There was space for only one person to stand beside the bed. There was nowhere to sit.

Mr. Rumanski had been a blacksmith in his native Iowa until he moved to a Midwestern city following service in World War II. He continued as a blacksmith and later worked at a local ironworks. He had married a woman from his home town; they had a

son and a married daughter and three grandchildren. The daughter lived four miles away but did not visit her father; she was quoted as saying, "I don't want to see him this way."

As a young man, Mr. Rumanski had weighed 250 lb and had been noted for his physical strength. He had completed the eighth grade and then had become a blacksmith's apprentice to supplement family income. He did not enjoy reading but did keep abreast of world news through television and the daily newspaper.

Mr. Rumanski was the sole survivor in a family of three sons and one daughter. His mother had died from burn complications at age 36. His father, a corn farmer, committed suicide by shotgun after being told he had cancer. His sister, a terminal tuberculosis victim at age 50, jumped to her death. Two paternal uncles had committed suicide when told they had cancer. Cause of death of the two brothers was not known.

Mr. Rumanski had always been a heavy smoker and continued to smoke two packages of unfiltered cigarettes per day. He had also been a heavy whiskey drinker as a young man but reduced his intake in later years to two cans of beer weekly and an occasional glass of wine with dinner. He now drank four to six large cups of strong black coffee each day (preferring coffee to water or other beverages).

November 21

Mr. Rumanski began a series of twenty daily radiation treatments to the right upper abdominal quadrant. Mrs. Rumanski had several questions to ask the community health nurse relative to the treatments: Did they cause pain? Would her husband's hair fall out? Would the skin be burned? Did he need special food? Another major concern was that they would not see the physician until the course of treatments were completed. Mrs. Rumanski interpreted this to be a result of indifference on the part of the physician and as a result called him frequently, only to have her questions answered evasively.

During this visit, the nurse found that Mr. Rumanski's jaundice had increased, but he seemed stronger, more alert, and less despondent. There was no drainage in the T tube area and no inflammation. He expressed no interest in his treatments. His only comment was, "I wish I knew what I have wrong with me." Mrs. Rumanski interrupted any further discussion of the subject.

November 29

Mr. Rumanski now spent afternoons in the living room watching television. He was experiencing epigastric pain when sitting and nausea associated with the pain. His liver was palpable 6 cm below the right costal margin and remained nontender. There was a moderate amount of clear, yellow, odorless drainage around the T tube, requiring three dressing changes daily.

These physical changes had increased Mrs. Rumanski's apprehension and taxed her coping abilities. The nurse learned that Mrs. Rumanski had altered her NPH Insulin dosage by a few units to accommodate for an increased carbohydrate intake. "I get so nervous I eat a couple of extra bites."

After this visit the nurse contacted the Rumanskis' physician to discuss his handling of the diagnosis. The physician felt he had discussed the prognosis and therapy adequately with both husband and wife. "They really aren't very intelligent, and I don't think Mr. Rumanski wanted to hear me." The physician felt Mr. Rumanski had two to three months to live despite radiation therapy. "It's all we have to offer him at this point."

Questions

1. From the data compiled at this time, identify problems for the nurse.
2. How would you handle Mrs. Rumanski's questions relative to radiation therapy?
3. What information would be helpful in this situation?
4. Which side effects of radiation might be expected to occur more frequently in the elderly?
5. Which side effects could be prevented? How?
6. Account for the changes in Mr. Rumanski's condition.
7. What is the significance of the yellow drainage?
8. Identify factors influencing the physician's attitude and response to this couple's problems.
9. As the nurse in this situation, what would have been your response to the physician?
10. What assistance would be beneficial to the nurse and to the Rumanskis at this time?

December 7

This visit began by focusing on Mrs. Rumanski. The nurse took her vital signs (blood pressure 180/100, apical pulse 80 and regular,

temperature 98.4°F) and asked Mrs. Rumanski to keep her own record). Mrs. Rumanski reported her urine had tested 4+ for sugar and negative for acetone yesterday and that she had given herself three extra units of NPH. "I should probably see a doctor one of these days. Mine died last year. I stopped taking my Diazyde a couple of weeks ago because I got a little dizzy. I thought my blood pressure was too low." Mrs. Rumanski also mentioned burning on urination and perineal itching. The nurse suggested Mrs. Rumanski discuss these problems with her husband's internist. Mrs. Rumanski agreed to call him that week.

The nurse and Mrs. Rumanski discussed dietary restrictions, consequences of adjusting medication dosages; the possible causes of her perineal discomfort and possible measures Mrs. Rumanski could try until she could contact the physician. During their talk, Mrs. Rumanski told the nurse she suspected her 15-year-old granddaughter of using drugs. "Last week she took one of my used insulin syringes before I had a chance to destroy it. My son can't control her at all. She hangs around with a tough bunch of kids since she quit school. There was a drug raid next door last summer. Things are so different now. Kids are so wild. I can't talk to my son about her; he thinks she's perfect. I wish Joseph was well. He was always the strong one."

Mr. Rumanski was in bed but seemed in better spirits. He continued the argument about his poor appetite and lack of interest in the food prepared. Mrs. Rumanski continued to travel long distances by bus to purchase special foods to try to satisfy her husband's food whims. After the food was prepared, Mr. Rumanski rarely ate it, saying, "She doesn't understand I lose interest in food after I ask for it." This exchange brought Mrs. Rumanski to tears.

The area around the T tube continued to drain moderate to large amounts of yellow, odorless fluid. Bowel sounds were present, and vital signs were stable. General skin turgor had improved, and 1+ pedal edema continued. His feet were cool and pale with no palpable pulses.

As the nurse was leaving, Mrs. Rumanski asked: "How long do you think Joseph has to live? I won't be able to take it when he dies; but he doesn't look like he'll get any better either. I asked the doctor not to tell Joseph he has cancer because he might kill himself if he knew."

Questions

1. Determine the stressors in Mrs. Rumanski's life.
2. What mechanisms is she using to cope with them?
3. Identify possible consequences of these mechanisms.
4. What nursing interventions would be realistic for Mrs. Rumanski?
5. Explain the occurrence of pedal edema.

December 14

Mr. Rumanski's general condition remained unchanged. He had no appetite and continued to argue with his wife about food. It was difficult to assess the adequacy of his fluid intake. His urine was dark amber, occasionally scant and brown. The T tube area was draining large amounts of yellow fluid around the tube, necessitating frequent dressing changes and a bath towel around his abdomen to protect the bedding.

Mr. Rumanski's pedal edema increased to 2+ in the right foot and 1+ in the left. The skin remained pale and cool. He was able to sit up for longer periods with less epigastric pain. His morale was good, and he expressed hope of feeling better now that his course of radiation therapy was nearing an end.

After the nurse had completed the dressing change and assessment, Mr. Rumanski engaged her in conversation, asking, "Do you think I have cancer?" The nurse responded by asking, "What would happen if you did have cancer?" Mr. Rumanski's reply was "I'd get a gun and kill myself. I've watched too many people suffer." At this point, Mrs. Rumanski began to sob and went to sit at the kitchen table. Mr. Rumanski told the nurse to "go calm her down."

The nurse joined Mrs. Rumanski in the kitchen. They discussed the previous week and Mrs. Rumanski's concerns. Mrs. Rumanski had contacted her husband's physician and received prescriptions for Pyridium tablets and Mycostatin vaginal suppositories. Her symptoms had disappeared within three days, so she had discontinued both medications. Her urine had been negative for sugar and acetone and she had not taken extra insulin, although she admitted cheating "a little" on her diet. Her blood pressure was 144/88, and she continued not to take Diazyde.

Questions

1. What factors have contributed to
   a. changes in urine color?

b. increased drainage around the T tube?
c. increased asymmetrical pedal edema?
d. decreased epigastric pain?
e. improved emotional outlook?

2. What additional data are necessary to assess these changes adequately?

December 28

Mrs. Rumanski commented that Christmas had been a very unhappy time. "The children didn't want to spend much time with their poor father, and the grandkids never even came to visit. I don't know if they'll ever see him again. Joseph was so disappointed. We're such an inconvenience to them all, I guess."

Mr. Rumanski had completed his radiation treatments. "I still don't feel any better, and I look terrible, all orange and skinny."

Copious amounts of yellow liquid continued to leak around the T tube. His vital signs remained stable. Pedal edema had increased to 3+ in the right foot and 2+ in the left. Mr. Rumanski's physician had seen him briefly that week and had not commented on the edema or fluid leakage.

Mrs. Rumanski expressed concern that they were no longer affiliated with a church and knew of no clergyman. "The only one I have to talk to is an old Mexican woman across the street and I can't always understand her. She's such a good soul, and sometimes she stays with Joseph so I can go shopping."

January 2

Mrs. Rumanski called to inform the nurse she thought her husband had suddenly become worse.

The nurse visited and found Mr. Rumanski in bed complaining of continuous, unrelieved, burning, midepigastric pain and frequent bouts of hiccups. The pain was triggered by hot fluids and rapid changes in body position. His skin, sclera, and urine were darker. His stools were yellow. His abdominal skin was flaccid and hung in folds. Blood pressure was 108/62; apical pulse rate was 78 and more irregular with an S_3 on auscultation. Respirations were 16 per minute, and his temperature was 100°F. Pedal edema was 4+ bilaterally. He was discouraged: "I hope I don't have to go to the hospital. They never make anyone better."

Questions

1. Keeping in mind aging physiology, assess the significance of:
   a. epigastric pain
   b. hiccups
   c. increasing color changes in urine, stool, and sclera
   d. decreased abdominal skin turgor
   e. decrease in blood pressure
   f. cardiac irregularity and occurrence of S_3
   g. increased pedal edema
2. Assess other pertinent data.
3. What is the nurse's responsibility in view of the above changes?

STUDY GUIDE QUESTIONS

1. Evaluate the effectiveness of the hospital referral for comprehensiveness for the terminally ill elderly.
   a. Assess the data presented for relevance and completeness.
   b. Recommend additions and alterations in information.
   c. Identify additional health care members whose contributions would have been helpful.
   d. Recommend alternative methods of communication between institution and community.
2. Identify the dynamics operative between the Rumanskis.
   a. What roles can be identified?
   b. What actual and potential problems in their relationship may be of relevance to the nurse?
   c. What interventions, if any, would be appropriate?
3. Determine components of an effective home assessment specific to the elderly.
4. Develop a realistic contract of home care for the Rumanskis reflecting
   a. time.
   b. long- and short-term goals.
   c. mutual agreement.
5. Acceptance of the wish to die at home is regaining professional support in the United States. This wish is accompanied by some difficulties.
   a. On the individual level:
      (1) Identify attitudes prevalent in caring for the terminally ill and for the elderly.

(2) Identify limitations and restrictions in delivering comprehensive care in this situation.
(3) What personal difficulties might the nurse encounter in delivering this care?

b. On the community level:
(1) What is the responsibility of the hospital-based health care team to this family?
(2) What support systems are essential for those involved in care of the terminally ill for nurses? for families? for patients?
(3) What is nursing's role in establishing such services for the community? Identify sources of funding.
(4) Legal implications: In the event of the patient's death at home, certain policies and procedures are operative.
(a) How does the family effectively prepare for the patients death at home?
(b) What is nursing's role in this preparation?
(c) Who is responsible for pronouncing the person dead?
(d) What policy is in effect if there has been no physician supervising the medical aspects of care?
(e) By what methods can the body be removed from the home?
(f) May the person be waked in the home? What restrictions are there?

6. Identify the mechanisms by which Mrs. Rumanski attempted to cope with caring for a terminally ill husband.

7. Determine the prevalence, incidence, and success of suicide in the white elderly male.

8. Within the limitations of case data, identify Mr. Rumanski's attitude toward his illness and toward his life.

Case

IX

Professor Anthony Llewlyn-Morgan: A Conflict of Wills

INTRODUCTION

Too frequently, health professionals make unilateral or bilateral decisions predicated on their own value systems or on assumptions rather than facts. In the first instance, physicians and nurses view themselves as the sole decision makers for others. This can be attributed to the status assigned them by their culture, middle class values, and limited life experiences. In the second instance, their knowledge about aging and the aged is often limited.

The situations in this case deal with social class in a supposedly classless society and invite retrospective as well as projective nursing actions and solutions.

THE CASE

Jean-Pierre Petit, M.D., a general practitioner on staff on the 100-bed community hospital, was worried about his friend and

patient Professor Llewlyn-Morgan. The physician expressed this concern to Maureen Hanley, a Visiting Nurse Association staff nurse who also served, on request, as the discharge planner for elderly patients in the community hospital.

Dr. Petit, seeing Ms. Hanley at the hospital, asked her to see Professor Llewlyn-Morgan. He concluded the brief interchange with "... see what you can do with the stubborn old goat. He needs supervised care on discharge and won't hear of it. A third-degree burn to the palm of his right hand with some second degree burns to both upper thighs and left hand—a nasty business. Let me know what you think by tomorrow, I'm off to surgery now."

Maureen Hanley smiled to herself and thought how typical the exchange was of Dr. Petit—he was concerned and volatile, wanted everything done yesterday, and provided little information. Where to begin? Talking with the staff nurses on the surgical care unit was not possible; they would be too busy, since this was elective major surgery day. One or two days each month, a visiting surgeon came from the university center, thirty miles away, to the community hospital. This practice reduced hospital costs and unnecessary family separations and introduced resident surgeons from the university hospital to a rural practice setting.

Two sources of information were readily available to Maureen: the hospital chart and the patient. The chart provided the following information:

Patient's Name:	Anthony Llewlyn-Morgan
Address:	Park Farm Mapeberry Rd. Old Greenwich, CT Telephone: 284-3963
Date of Birth:	October 12, 1884 (Wales, G.B.)
Insurance:	Blue Cross Master Medical and Blue Shield (independent policy holder) Medicare: not noted
Income:	Not noted
Social Security:	Not noted
Religion:	Not noted
Next of Kin:	Joan Morgan-Maxwell E. 65 St. and Third Ave. New York, NY Relationship: great-niece Telephone: (212) 924-4528 (212) 433-0076

Source of Information:	Patient (reliable, coherent)
Chief Complaint:	Burns to hands and thighs 7% "Rule of 9"; burned at home about 10:30 P.M. on July 18 and brought to hospital in an automobile by a neighbor; seen by Dr. Petit at 11:40 P.M. and admitted for treatment.
P.M.H.:	Not contributory
F.H.:	Not contributory
S.H.:	Height 5 ft 8 in.; weight 135 lb Rest not contributory
Systems Review:	**Eyes:** ⊖ except for: wears prescription bifocals. last eye examination six months ago (2/78). Cataract o.s. **Cardiovascular:** Aortic holosystolic murmur V/VI. Digoxin .125 mg × 5 per week. **Musculoskeletal:** Gait unsteady, uses cane.
Perceptual Skills:	Within normal limits

The therapeutic plan for Anthony Llewlyn-Morgan consisted of the following:

On admission: Tetanus toxoid booster 1.0 ml. subcutaneously and procaine penicillin G 300,000 u. I.M.; aspirin 0.6 gm p.o. q. 4 to 6 h. for pain. Intravenous therapy for the first 24 hours consisted of D_5 $\frac{1}{2}$ N.S. 500 cc. and D_5 in Lactated Ringer's Solution 1000 cc. The closed-method burn treatment was used with bilateral bandages to the hands at 10° flexion with interdigital padding.

July 19:	Intravenous infusion discontinued; Ensure 1500 cc. p.o. for next 48 hours. Additional pharmacotherapeutics were: Tetracycline 250 mg p.o. q.d. Vitamin C 500 mg t.i.d. Vitamin B complex Capsule I, t.i.d. p.c. Digoxin .125 mg × 5 per week. Passive range motion exercises all joints.
July 21:	Diet: high protein with roughage, 2000 calories, supplement with P.D.P. Liquid 30 cc t.i.d. No alteration or cancellation of any of the previously ordered pharmacotherapeutics. Bathroom ambulation with assistance and chair ad lib.
July 27:	Begin hydrotheraphy b.i.d. Vitamin C 500 mg b.i.d. D.C. vitamin B complex Capsule I, t.i.d. p.c. Vitamin B complex with C and iron Capsule I, q.d. Full ambulation with assistance

The progress notes gave every indication that Professor Llewlyn-Morgan was making a full recovery. The wound cultures were negative for pathogens, and healing by second intention was in evidence. There had been no elevated temperature, lung fields were clear, and urinary output was within normal limits. Manual dexterity was returning.

Maureen Hanley was puzzled. The information on the patient's chart was seemingly adequate for matters concerning illness care. There was nothing to suggest why posthospitalization supervised care might be needed. She determined to do her own interview; after all, a priori information was best.

Ms. Hanley found the professor in a private room, seated in a chaise longue and reading the *Wall Street Journal* with the use of a light magnifier view box placed over his knees. The sitting position for reading was attained with two oversized bolster pillows. She watched this 93-year-old man unobtrusively through the open doorway for a few minutes. He wore a full-length dressing gown of soft wool, long socks, and leather slippers. Both hands were bandaged, with only the last two digital joints exposed. He turned the page of the newspaper laboriously but ingeniously by using his fingers, elbows, chin, and mouth. The maneuver completed, the professor raised his head, saw Ms. Hanley, and said, "Do you plan to stand there all morning? I don't like being stared at; either come in or leave."

Ms. Hanley was startled by the order. She was not accustomed to patients or clients speaking to her in an authoritative manner; consequently, some of her composure was lost.

She lost further control of the situation when she explained the purpose of her visit, for Professor Llewlyn-Morgan retorted in a strong, firm voice, "I have no objection to talking with you; that will be a welcome relief from the daily tedium of hospital confinement. However, I have no doubt whatever that I shall be able to persuade you, and subsequently that idiot physician, that residential supervision is unwarranted." The bushy eyebrows on this craggy-faced man rose and the neatly trimmed full upper lip mustache twitched punctuating his statements. Despite a strong voice, penetrating steel-gray eyes, and well-barbered, thinning white hair, the skin of his face was almost translucent and wan. The eyes were exophthalmous, red rimmed, and watery.

THE HISTORY

The health history given by Anthony Llewlyn-Morgan during a period of two hours revealed the following:

He was lucid, rational, and accurate in relaying past and present events. Articulate in speech, he was inclined to rephrase questions to his advantage, conveying the impression that he would tell her what he wanted her to know and nothing else. Overall, he was a selective but good historian.

Identifying Data

Ms. Hanley was not familiar with the address listed; her district was in the southern sector of the community. She concluded that the client lived either in the west or the north. She found that Park Farm was north of town, set among rolling hills in a heavily wooded area, and consisted of five acres with a fourteen-room, three-story house. The market value of the property was in the range of $250,000 to $500,000.

Although a home telephone number was given on the hospital chart, the patient remarked, "There is no reason to give you the number; no one is there to receive the call. Martha, my homemaker-companion, has been gone for a month. There was a death in her family, and she has some matters to attend to in Southampton. That's in England, my dear."

The contact source listed in case of emergency was Joan Morgan-Maxwell, a great-niece who worked as a science editor in communications media. "She covers national and international events. One never knows what destination will be her assignment. Presently, she is in Moscow at a genetics conference. She plans to return home via India and Australia. I expect her at the farm sometime in late August.

"Joan is a lovely girl. When possible, she visits me for a long weekend each month. We spend those four days talking, walking, playing chess and backgammon. We have always spent a good deal of time together. She took her first steps at the farm, learned to ride horseback and sail. I taught her the games and activities. She was a very adept student. She took her baccalaureate at Radcliffe in science and journalism and went off to Stanford for graduate work in nuclear physics.

"When I die, the majority of my estate will go to Joan. Despite

her objective, scientific approach to things, she is a warm, sensitive, caring girl."

Place of Employment

Questions related to this area evoked a chuckle from Anthony Llewlyn-Morgan. "I suppose you think I retired some twenty-eight years ago; well, I didn't. As a matter of fact, I still go up to the university a couple of times a year to lecture on the history of constitutional law. I've been attached to the Faculty of Law at the university for well over fifty years and now have the dubious distinction of being an emeritus professor. The tragic part of it all is that one is not in contact with students on a weekly basis to see evidence of their intellectual growth. I miss that, but someone has to be put out to pasture, so to speak, to create a place for the younger chaps.

"One thing that disturbs me greatly is the lack of sense of history among the students and faculty these days.

"I work from my home, too; . . . have a rather extensive library, and what I don't have, I can have delivered by courier from the university law library.

"Oddly enough, I have a few private clients for estate closings and sales. As we oldsters die off, someone familiar with the property is needed. Death and family mobility have brought many changes in the district. But who am I to speak of mobility—I immigrated to the U.S.A. in 1919; . . . it's always been so for the adventurous young.

"There is consulting work, too, advising emergent so-called Third World countries on constitutional matters. Various representatives stop in to see me on their way home from Washington or New York.

"I have enough to do to keep me gainfully occupied. My income has declined, but prudent investments allow me to live comfortably and don't want for a great deal. As you get older, material acquisitions become less important.

". . . matter of fact, I never bothered about Social Security or Medicare, though I'm entitled to it. It's supplemental, and I don't need any supplemental income . . . it would move me into a higher income tax bracket."

Race, Nationality, and Religion

Caucasian, Welsh, Episcopalian (a lay reader and officer of the board).

Usual State of Health

"My usual state of health is very good, considering my age. Of course, things happen and body parts do wear down after 93 years."

Present Illness

Ms. Hanley had the basic information relative to the reason for Professor Llewlyn-Morgan's hospitalization and subsequent treatment. Not knowing the cause of the accident, she asked, "How did you get burned?"

The professor replied, "It was a clumsy accident. I was working in my study making notes from a law book that I brought from my basement repository. Hunting the book out must have tired me. I fell asleep smoking my pipe. The pipe dropped from my mouth onto the magnifer, and ashes from the bowl ignited the papers on my lap. I reacted by extinguishing the burning material with my hands.

"Martha was gone. I didn't feel a great deal of pain but thought some medical attention would be appropriate, so I called a neighbor for help.

"Mr. Roberts came to the house in ten to fifteen minutes time, made certain there were no smoldering embers remaining, and then brought me to the hospital. You see, I gave up driving an automobile twelve years ago."

Maureen Hanley was troubled. The answer was logical, and appropriate action had been taken. Accidents do happen. Did this warrant supervised retirement housing? She thought to herself, there must be more than one accident in this man's past medical history, or perhaps he is one of those confused elderly who has periods of lucidness.

Questions related to the professor's past medical history were pursued.

Previous Hospitalizations

Prostatectomy, 1952; three weeks hospitalization; no postoperative complications
Cataract surgery, o.d., 1968, five days hospitalization
Bacterial endocarditis, 1972, six weeks hospitalization

Professor Llewlyn-Morgan was very distressed during the discussion of his 1972 hospitalization. What seemed to annoy him most

was his scant recall of events during that time. He remembered going to the dentist for his semiannual examination and to have a filling changed in a lower left molar. Three or four days later, he did not feel very well. Joan was at the farm and wanted the professor to see a doctor, but he refused. This state of unawareness lasted about two weeks. He thought he had a "bout" of influenza, but his temperature was not elevated beyond 99°F. ". . . just out of sorts until I'm told I fainted. Martha couldn't rouse me so called an ambulance, and I was brought here. I vaguely remember having intravenous feedings and injections, people standing around talking in loud voices, and, at times, great pressure on my arms and legs. Obviously, I recovered.

"The only accident I ever had before this one was a soccer injury to my right foot when I was a lad at public school in England. In your terms, my dear, that would be a prep or private school. University preparatory education, at any rate. A few of the small bones were broken and, most likely, a tendon or two were damaged. It left me with a bit of a limp, so I started using a walking stick when I went up to the university and have used it ever since.

"Other than a month's bout with herpes zoster in March 1957 that was confined to the right side of my head and left me with a ptosis of the right eyelid, I have had no major illnesses as an adult.

"I had several childhood illnesses; we all did. The one I remember best was diphtheria. The doctor was called because I was choking on that gray membrane that develops in the back of the throat. Well, he removed it with a snare on the kitchen table by lamplight.

"My immunizations all are current. I travel a good deal."

Habits

"Well, that's really none of your affair. When you reach my age, then you can tell me what I may or may not do. I weary of the soap box you health people get on—can't take care of yourselves, so you tell others what they must do.

"Smoking—you know I smoke a pipe. I've had a pipe since I was twenty years of age. I drink, too, a couple of sherrys and a brandy and soda every day. What do you think of that, hah! Sherry before lunch and dinner every day, including prohibition, ever since I was eighteen years old. The only days I missed this treat was during hospitalizations. My brandy is taken after dinner; it's good for the digestion. The hospitals here are barbaric in their practices—won't let a man partake of the few remaining pleasures

in life. In the Old Country, they have a much more civilized approach to having a sherry or two in the hospital."

Genetic (Family) History

"People on both sides of the family came from Wales; too many generations to account for . . . the Morgans on my father's side got into coal in the early 1800s . . . with increased industrialization and colonization after the Napoleonic Wars . . . there was a great demand for coal for steam energy . . . we did quite well . . . comfortable, you might say . . . there were problems, too. Grandfather Morgan died in a mine explosion. . . . I was told the blast blew half the side of the mountain out, setting the slag heaps rolling right into the village.

"Not many years later, my grandmother Morgan died of consumption. I never knew them, of course. People didn't live to be very old in those days, and unless one married and had children early, the children seldom knew grandparents. Father, being the eldest son, took over the management of the coal mines after grandfather died. He had big plans for modernizing the operations. . . . He got some things done before he was shot in February 1912. That was the time when the coal unionists got out of hand. . . . David, my eldest brother, took over the mining operations when things settled down. That was an enormous undertaking for a young man. He was only thirty-two years old; neither John nor I could be bothered with that mess. . . . John was at the university, and I was clerking with a firm of barristers in London at the time. . . . John was killed just three years later at the Battle of Ypres in the spring of 1915 at the age of twenty-four; he was a calvary officer in the Great War.

"David didn't go to war; his position in the mines exempted him from service. I, because of my bad right foot and education, was an adjutant in charge of the colonial troops . . . I never did get to France.

"Yes, John was doing his degree in economics and commerce; he was to have gone with the Llewlyn Import and Export firm. He was a bright lad and would have done well in one of their overseas posts—got on well with people but could drive a hard bargain.

"My brothers and I had a great time when we got together—hiking, field games, sailing, and spelunking. Our sister, Amy, would sail or hike with us, but girl's clothes in those days were so cumbersome for sports. I will say this about her, she never complained.

"David was born in 1880 and died of a tired heart—a heart

attack—in 1965. He did a yeoman's job with the mines only to have them nationalized after World War II; what a pity, all that hard work. . . .

"Amy, born in 1890, came to the United States with her husband, Thomas Maxwell, in 1923. I haven't seen any of their three sons for quite some time; they all live in California. Amy is widowed and living in one of those retirement centers for the elderly in Arizona. She has a bit of arthritis in her hands and back now but seems to get on quite well; at least she was getting out a good deal when I visited her for a week this past April. We played golf together three or four times—just nine holes—it was a great holiday.

"I suppose you'd like to know something of the Llewlyn part of the family, too. Well, grandmother Llewlyn died before any of we Llewlyn-Morgan children were born. She died in childbed—fever.

"Actually, the only grandparent I did know was grandfather Llewlyn. He lived with us for a time until he died of old age, in 1891. I remember Amy was about a year old; mother was busy with her and getting things straight for the wake—grandfather was laid out in the living room, since the funeral was to be from our house. We boys took advantage of the situation and got into some mischief, for which we were soundly caned by father.

"Mother died in January 1919 from complications of the influenza that followed World War I.

"I didn't know the rest of the Llewlyn family. Three uncles were in overseas trade; two aunts married and immigrated—one to South Africa and one to Canada—and we were off to school in England a good part of our younger years.

"Barry (Barbara) Llewlyn-Morgan, my wife, died in December 1965 of inoperable metastatic cancer. She was a lovely person, a dear friend, a good sport and traveling companion. We didn't have children who lived—lost a boy and a girl at birth. As a consequence, Barry and I became very dear friends, closer than most married people. She really didn't deserve such a cruel death. The pain she suffered must have been ghastly. Those damn physicians wouldn't let me care for her at home—only managed to keep her unconscious with drugs the last weeks—poke, prod, poke, and prod, no decency or dignity in death for that beautiful person. I was furious, lost, and disgusted. To top it off they wouldn't let us say goodbye to each other. Just wanted permission to do an autopsy. I told them it was absolutely out of the question.

"Yes, Barry and I traveled to Europe and the Old Country

yearly after World War II—Nuremberg for six months during the trials; Berlin; the Hague; Paris, Vienna; Wales to visit David and his family; Cornwall to visit Barry's family; Jersey and Gurnsey Islands; Switzerland; Helsinki and Corfu . . . Corfu was Barry's favorite vacation spot. I haven't been back since the spring of 1956.

"We had a rose garden at the farm and couple of horses—rode every day when weather permitted. Golfed, sailed, and fished, too. We married after I finished reading for the bar at Temple Inn. Met in London—matter of fact, John introduced us. Barry was reading in economics, too, at the University of London, School of Economics. She was ahead of her time, a fiery lass. We married just before I went into the service and she to the Red Cross War Relief. I was quite lost without her—forty-two good years we had. She saw me through law school here and caring ever so deeply . . . I was fortunate indeed. Joan is much like Barry.

"After Barry died, I became absorbed in my work. Gave the rose garden over to the care of the gardener-handyman, the house to Martha and a semi weekly charwoman; all are still with me. Old Country people, you know, are loyal. Agnes was coming in daily to prepare meals and wash up during Martha's absence until my accident. Henry takes care of the house repairs and grounds on a daily basis."

Social History

"One can't talk of one's daily activities when you get to be my age; one day blends into another. That is why I keep a calendar of events—day book—have for years. Barry organized me into that habit.

"Usually, I take tea about 8:30 A.M. Then my toilet: wash, shave, and dress. 9:30 breakfast on a three-minute cooked egg, toast, marmalade, and tea. Monday, Wednesday, and Saturday, weather permitting, I ride my golf cart off to the links for nine holes at 11:00 A.M., a glass of sherry, a light lunch either at the club or at home (cheese, biscuits, fruit, and tea), read the paper and walk or ride the golf cart about the grounds, then to work on any pending legal matters. Usually have a cup of tea during this work period, a glass of sherry at 7:00 P.M. Dinner is at 7:30 P.M.—broiled fish or meat, cooked vegetables, a pudding or some other sweet, and tea. Back to the library for several hours of reading and work with a brandy and soda at 10:00 P.M. It helps relax me. I may go to a church

board meeting—again, it depends on the week. My average sleep time is four to five hours, but I stay in my room until 9:30 A.M.; the women don't like you underfoot too early.

"On Tuesdays and Thursdays I go to the University Club for the afternoon and evening, play bridge or chess and have dinner—usually a pie—steak 'n kidney or chicken. We old boys do a lot of socializing—some call it gossiping—recount old days. It's good fun. We get to know some of the new boys that way, too.

"Sunday is church and reading and listening to music. I may have difficulty seeing, but we Welsh don't lose our hearing easily, especially for music.

"If it's a weekend Joan comes, well, things are quite different. We go out or entertain our friends. Usually, there's a dinner party one evening during the time she's at the farm."

There was a pause; Maureen Hanley could think of nothing else to ask. Professor Llewlyn-Morgan's voice sounded tired. What was she to do next? Was this a problem of one-upmanship on the part of the professor? Did he tell her the truth? She was in a turmoil. Her position as part-time discharge planner for the elderly could be jeopardized by refuting Dr. Petit. What was to be done for and with Anthony Llewlyn-Morgan?

Case

Mrs. Yvonne Bolangier: A Self-Destructive Woman

INTRODUCTION

The nursing problems presented in this case require knowledge of physiology of aging, substance abuse, attitude toward medication regimen, and altered metabolism. Overriding patient depression curtails the nurse's efforts and challenges her skill in effecting health-seeking behaviors.

Prior to identifying the essential data for analysis and evaluation, it would be advantageous to understand the implications of the following considerations:

Considerations

- Coronary artery disease
  - Risk factors, early detection and prevention, chronicity
- COPD and related physiological compensations

Peripheral vascular disease in women
  Prevalence, incidence, causes, and treatment
Implications of cardiac surgery for aging physiology
Impaired liver function and medication therapy
Interaction of alcohol, medication, and aging liver and renal function
Prevalence, incidence, and social implications of alcoholism in elderly women
Cause of anemias in the elderly
Problems of anticoagulation therapy for the nonhospitalized elderly
Causes of pneumonia in the elderly
Noncompliance with medical regimen and medication therapy

THE CASE

Mrs. Yvonne Bolangier, age 70, was referred by the attending cardiologist to the visiting nurse agency one day prior to discharge from an acute care hospital.

A home visit was made on the basis of the following referral.

January 20

Mrs. Bolangier's husband Guy greeted the nurse at the door. He appeared more youthful than his 73 years—small, slim, and sprightly, with little gray hair. In contrast, his wife seemed older than her 70 years, white-haired, pale, thin, and anxious. She sat on the couch in a robe, covered with an afghan.

The Bolangiers were uncertain about the nurse's purpose in visiting and knew only that Mrs. Bolangier's physician had requested the service: "You're here to take my blood aren't you?" During the assessment, which took place in the living room, Mr. Bolangier found it difficult to remain seated, getting up frequently for small errands. He gave the impression of wanting to ask questions but did not do so.

Mrs. Bolangier volunteered little information about herself and answered questions in a clipped manner. She was not unfriendly but cautious and reserved. She had considered herself healthy until three years ago, when she experienced her "first heart attack." She was hospitalized and, while in the intensive care unit, suffered two additional "attacks."

REFERRAL FORM – POST HOSPITAL NURSING CARE

PATIENT'S NAME	DATE OF BIRTH	SEX	MARITAL STATUS
Bolangier, Yvonne	7-14-08	F	M

ADDRESS – VISIT AT	APT./FLOOR	TELEPHONE
410 Maple Lane		224-6236

RELATIVE [x] FRIEND [ ]	ADDRESS	TELEPHONE
Husb. Guy	Same	

HOSPITAL NO.	ROOM	BL. CR. NO.	ADMITTED	DISCHARGED	SOCIAL WORKER AND EXT.	OUT PATIENT NO.
	608		12-10	1-18		

PHYSICIAN	ADDRESS	TELEPHONE	CLINIC PHYSICIAN AND EXT.
Lawrence Phillips		626-7749	

DATE CHEST X-RAY	RESULTS
1-6	Lungs clear
DATE CBC 1-11	Within normal limits
DATE BLOOD SUGAR 12-13	Within normal limits
DATE URINALYSIS 12-13	Normal

FOLLOW UP: MEDICAL PLAN — DATE — TIME; CLINIC; OFFICE; RADIATION; CHEMOTHERAPY

AGENCY REFERRED TO:	ADDRESS	TELEPHONE
Home Health Service		

DIAGNOSIS — DATE OF SURGERY — PT. & OR FAMILY INFORMED [✓] Yes [ ] No — PROGNOSIS: Good

PRIMARY: Coronary artery bypass graft
Left ventricular aneurysmectomy

SECONDARY: Pacemaker insertion
COPD

Is patient home bound? Yes [ ] No [ ]

MEDICATION	DOSAGE–FREQUENCY
1. Digoxin 0.25mg p.o. qA.M.	
2. Dyazide 1 tab p.o. qA.M.	
3. Norpace 200mg p.o. q6h	
4. Coumadin 5mg p.o. qhs	
5. Tylenol #3 tabs 1-2 p.o. q3h p.r.n.	
6. K-Lyte 1 scoop p.o. qA.M.	
7.	
8.	
9.	
10.	

INJECTIONS — DOSE — FREQUENCY — MODE — TEACH FAMILY [ ] Yes [ ] No

DRESSINGS TO: [ ] Dry [ ] Moist
TREATMENT [ ] Clean [ ] Irrigate
SOLUTION
Rx
FREQUENCY [ ] Yes TEACH [ ] No

CATHETER TEACH [ ] Yes [ ] No [ ] Change [ ]
SIZE # — BALLOON C.C.
[ ] Irrigate — Frequency
SOLUTION — Frequency of Change

DIET [ ] General — CALORIES
[x] Lo Sodium
[ ] ADA
[ ] Other

OSTOMIES [ ] Trach — TEACH [ ] Yes [ ] No
[ ] Colostomy — SOLUTION — AMT. — FREQUENCY
[ ] Illeostomy — CHANGE BAG — FREQUENCY

PHYSICAL THERAPY [ ] ROM [ ] Active [ ] Passive — R — L
[ ] Stretching
[ ] Resistive
[ ] Weight Bearing – Amount
[x] Muscle Strengthening
[ ] Transfer
[ ] Brace [x] Ambulate [ ] Stair Climbing

SPEECH THERAPY [ ] Home [ ] Out Patient
MENTAL HEALTH [ ] Recommended
HOME HEALTH AIDE [ ]
OCCUPATIONAL THERAPY [ ] Out Patient [ ] Home
RESPONSIBLE PERSON [ ] Family [ ] Other
EQUIPMENT SUPPLIED [ ] Yes [ ] No
[ ] Chair [ ] Bed [ ] Commode [ ] Walker [ ] Other
SUPPLIED BY: — DATE REQUESTED

Special Nursing Needs or Services (Home Health Aide, O_2, ETC.)

Patient has had long post-op course complicated by cardiac arrhythmia, lung congestion, and congestive heart failure.

Monitor vital signs and neck veins and weigh patient.

Draw blood for prothrombin and potassium five days after discharge and then draw prothrombin weekly. Last pro-time was 37%

Physician's Signature L. Phillips — Date 1-18

This will certify that this patient is in need of the services outlined above.

COMMUNITY NURSING REFERRAL – REPORT FROM NURSING AND SUPPORTIVE SERVICES

	INDEPENDENT	NEEDS ASSIST.	UNABLE TO DO	CHECK LEVEL OF ABILITY
BED ACTIVITY	✓			Turns
	✓			Sits
PERSONAL CARE	✓			Face, Hair and Arms
	✓			Trunk-Perineum
		✓		Legs and Feet
	✓			Bladder Progress
	✓			Bowel Progress
DRESSING				Upper Ext.
				Trunk
				Lower Ext.
				Prosthetic Appliance
MOBILITY	✓			Transfer
	✓			Sitting
	✓			Standing
	✓			~~Tub~~ Shower
	✓			Toilet
				Wheelchair
	✓			Walking
		✓		Stairs
FEEDING				DENTURES ☐ YES ☐ NO SIGHT ☐ YES ☐ NO

MENTAL STATUS

☑ ALERT ☐ CONFUSED ☐ FORGETFUL

NURSING PROCEDURES TAUGHT

	Pt.	Family
DRESSING	☐	☐
INJECTIONS	☐	☐
CATH. CARE	☐	☐
DECUBITUS CARE	☐	☐
DIABETIC INSTR.	☐	☐
ORAL MEDS	☑	☐
VITAL SIGNS	☑	☐
OTHER	☐	☐
OTHER	☐	☐

RESPONSE TO INSTRUCTION

POOR ☐ FAIR ☑

EXCELLENT ☐ POTENTIAL ☐

ADDITIONAL REPORTS
1. SOCIAL SERVICE
2. PHYSICAL THERAPY
3. OCCUPATIONAL THERAPY
4. SPEECH THERAPY
5. NUTRITION
6. DIABETIC CLINICIAN

USE OTHER SIDE IF NEEDED (TURN CARBON)

She continues to have arrythmias. Holter monitor showed ventricular tachycardia and is being repeated.

She is very weak and tires easily. Her husband visited frequently but has medical problems as well, limiting his activity. The Bolangiers may need assistance with daily chores at home.

Mrs. Bolangier has been on a 2 Gm sodium diet with 2000 ml fluid restriction. She has lost 10 pounds since admission.

NURSE'S REPORT

1) T_____ P_____ R_____ B/P_____

2) COMMENTS:

Mrs. Bolangier has been a patient for two months. During her stay, she had two M.I.s and underwent surgery for coronary artery bypass, left ventricular aneurysm repair, and ~~a demand pacemaker.~~

There is no record of the rate of the pacer set in her chart. She has a history of COPD and received vigorous chest therapy to which she was generally resistant. She has been instructed on breathing exercises and should continue these at home.

After two months in the hospital, she went home with prescriptions for Lanoxin, Pronestyl, and nitroglycerin. Gradually she developed tightness in her left chest with nonradiating substernal pain on walking short distances. Eventually merely raising her arms above her head would elicit this pain. During those episodes she did not experience shortness of breath or nausea. The pain was alleviated by nitroglycerin and rest. Within the past year she had noticed the episodes increasing in frequency to four or five per week. She could not sleep without three pillows and occasionally experienced paroxysmal nocturnal dyspnea. At times she noted skipped beats but no palpitations. Three weeks prior to this hospitalization she developed swelling and coolness in both feet. "My fingers have always turned white and are freezing to touch, but I never noticed it in my feet until December; it scared me."

The evening of admission Mrs. Bolangier experienced crushing chest pain radiating to her jaw. Her husband called the ambulance, and she was admitted to the cardiac intensive care unit, where she remained one week. "I never thought much about my heart until I spent that week with a monitor hooked to my chest and watched the beats."

Mrs. Bolangier admitted to smoking one to two packages of cigarettes per day for over fifty years: "But I quit two months ago." She had had a "smoker's cough" for "years and years." "I don't even remember when I started getting short of breath; I guess it came on slowly." She denied alcohol abuse: "I like a cocktail occasionally and maybe a bit of wine on holidays." She had not decreased her coffee intake of five to six cups per day: "And I don't like that decaffeinated stuff either." When discussing diet, Mrs. Bolangier became evasive and avoided answering questions.

Physical assessment

Vital Signs:

Vital Signs:	Blood pressure 92/60 left arm; 104/68 right arm	
	Apical pulse	76 and irregular
	Radial pulse	72 and irregular
	Respirations	26 and shallow
	Temperature	98°F

General description

Mrs. Bolangier was an alert, thin, anxious, pale woman. Her hair was short, thin, and white. She appeared comfortable despite occasional hand wringing.

The following nursing assessment recorded only positive findings in the physical examination and review of systems:

	Objective Data *Physical Examination*	*Subjective Data* *Review of Systems*
Head:	Normocephalic. Prominent bony structure	
Ears:	Large amount of dark cerumen occluding left ear canal. Acuity decreased in left ear.	"I haven't been able to hear as well and sometimes it feels plugged. I use an ear wash occasionally."
Mouth:	Full dentures.	Has occasional sore spots under dentures. Otherwise no difficulty chewing.
Eyes:	PEERLA. Acuity not tested.	Eyes tire and become dry easily. "My glasses are for my nearsightedness. I've worn them since childhood."
Chest:	Decrease in subcutaneous and muscular tissue. Pacemaker mechanism on right anterior wall below clavicle. Well healed midsternal incision approximately 20 cm in length. Anterior/posterior ratio 1:1.	Area over pacemaker mechanism painful to touch. Postoperative pain along rib cage border and between scapulae.
Cardiac:	S_1 and S_2 auscultated. No splitting of S_2; no S_3 or S_4. Rhythm and rate irregular. PMI: 2 cm × 2 cm in the anterior axillary line at sixth ICS.	No cardiac symptoms since surgery.
Respiratory:	Diaphragmatic excursion 1.5 cm bilaterally. Breath sounds diminished bilaterally. Rhonchi heard over bronchi and clear with cough.	Cough productive of thick white sputum, especially upon arising.

Abdomen:	Not examined.	Chronic constipation; uses prune juice and milk of magnesia Generally soft diet Stools formed, light-colored.
Extremities:	Popliteal and pedal pulses absent. Fingers do not blanch; some clubbing. Toes blanch slightly Well-healed surgical incision, left upper thigh. Legs thin with little muscle mass. Nails brittle and thick.	Fingers cold and white. Surgical incision irritated by friction.
Neurological:	Bilateral hand and arm tremors. Gait unsteady but not staggering. Loss of vibratory sensation.	Nervousness. Occasional depression.
Current Medications:	Digoxin 0.25 mg p.o. q. A.M. Dyazide 1 tab p.o. q. 6° Coumadin 5 mg p. o. q. h.s. Tylenol #3, 1–2 tabs p.o. q. 3 h. p.r.n. K-Lyte I scoop p.o. q. A.M.	

Mrs. Bolangier had been relatively healthy, with hospitalizations for tonsilectomy as a child and surgery for right inguinal hernia, fractured wrist, and removal of rectal polyps as an adult.

Guy and Yvonne Bolangier lived in a single-family brick house on a tree-lined suburban street. The yard was well kept and the house neat inside and out. The Bolangiers had been married 52 years and had a divorced 50-year-old son in southern California. Mr. Bolangier expressed his disappointment: "He said he couldn't find himself here, but I think he can't take responsibility. He changes jobs so often, even with a good college education. We'd like to seem him settle down before it's too late." Their daughter was 42, married with three children, and lived nearby. She was attentive to her parents: "She's such a wonderful daughter."

The nurse reviewed with Mrs. Bolangier her knowledge of her disease, post surgical expectations, purposes and precautions relative to living with a pacemaker, and medication regimen. Mrs. Bolangier could not recall being taught about pacemakers and had not read the

brochure she received three days prior to discharge. She understood the respiratory exercises but had not done them: "I'm not up to it yet." She did not know how to take her radial pulse and felt the task too difficult to learn. Her husband volunteered to learn but after repeated attempts could not isolate either radial artery long enough for an accurate count. He indicated he would practice before the nurse's next visit.

When asked about his health problems, Mr. Bolangier said he was quite healthy and did not take any medication. "I used to have high blood pressure, but I took water pills for six months and now I'm fine." He refused to allow the nurse to check his pressure.

Arrangements were made for weekly visits for blood drawing and monitoring postoperative progress until Mrs. Bolangier was stable.

Questions

1. Identify problems the nurse encountered on this initial visit.
2. Which problems could have been prevented? Determine appropriate means.
3. Determine realistic short- and long-term goals for the Bolangiers based on this initial assessment.

Mrs. Bolangier's hospital record yielded the following information: On December 10 she was admitted to the emergency room with the symptoms previously described to the nurse. Additional findings noted by the admitting resident were a strong odor of alcohol and slurred speech. While in the emergency room, Mrs. Bolangier experienced a cardiac arrest but was successfully resuscitated and transferred to the medical intensive care unit. A second arrest occurred within five hours, again with successful resuscitation. During the next four days there were several episodes of ventricular tachycardia with right bundle branch block.

Physical examination by attending physician

The positive findings were as follows:

Respiratory:	Diffuse wheezing with bilateral lower lobe rales and rhonchi. Nonproductive cough.
Cardiac:	Nonradiating mitral systolic grade III/VI murmur. Physiological splitting of S_2. Bilateral femoral bruits.

Abdomen: Liver percusses at 14 cm in the left midclavicular line. Palpable 8 cm below right costal margin; slightly nodular and tender. No ascites or masses.

Rectal: External hemorrhoids.
Stool guaiac negative.

Neurological: Decreased vibratory sense in lower extremities.
Motor strength 3+.
Gait not tested.
Hand tremor.

Eyes: Vessels engorged.
Acuity 20/80 in the left and 20/100 in the right with corrective lenses.

Admission laboratory data:

Hemoglobin	16.9 gm
Hematocrit	50.4 mm
WBC	7400
LDH	193 units
CPK	36 units
SGOT	44 units
SGPT	80 units
Amylase	140 units
Serum alcohol	0.09%
Albumin	2.5 gm

Problems identified by the medical staff were

1. Coronary artery insufficiency with angina.
2. COPD.
3. Macrocytosis—folate anemia.
4. Alcohol abuse

There were no problems identified by nursing.

Surgical procedures (December 20)

1. Left ventricular aneurism repair.
2. Right coronary artery bypass graft using left autogenous saphenous vein.
3. Implementation of permanent epicardial electrode onto the anterior surface of the right ventricle.

Postoperative course was complicated by the preexisting compromised respiratory system, which became infected with *Candida albicans*. The left lower lobe was consolidated, and the right showed diffuse pleural effusion. Rigorous respiratory therapy was difficult because of nature of the surgery and lack of patient cooperation.

Mrs. Bolangier refused IPPB treatments and performed prescribed exercises as little as possible.

One week prior to discharge, X-rays showed the pacemaker wire tip in place, a tortuous aorta, parenchymal scarring of the left lung base, and distended pulmonary vasculature with pleural fluid.

At this time Mrs. Bolangier's hemoglobin was 11.1 grams and hematocrit was 33.7%. Her liver percussed at 10 cm with 4 cm palpable below the right costal margin with less tenderness. Macrocytosis was treated with diet.

During the final week, Mrs. Bolangier was given booklets about pacemakers, cardiac surgery, postoperative care, and respiratory exercises. Her medication regimen was discussed with her. There was no record of diet assessment, consultation, or instruction.

Questions

1. Incorporate information from the hospital record into your initial plan of care.
2. Identify conflicting data and establish methods of clarification.
3. On the basis of your knowledge of aging, health beliefs, and habits, determine problems with which the nurse can initially deal.

January 27

A routine home visit was made. Blood was drawn for CBC, potassium, and prothrombin time, which had been 30% the previous week.

The Bolangiers were less reserved and more willing to discuss their problems. Mr. Bolangier asked the nurse to take his blood pressure, as it had been 172/96 when checked two days previously at the fire department's screening program. An episode on New Year's Day, while his wife was still in the hospital, concerned him. He had been visiting his 93-year-old mother, hospitalized for rehabilitation for right-sided hemiparesis and aphasia from a stroke, when he experienced an episode of unconsciousness. He was resuscitated by the fire department rescue squad and taken to a local emergency room. After a series of tests, a prescription for a diuretic, and instructions to "take it easy," he was sent home. He had avoided telling his wife until two days ago because "I didn't want to worry her. I'm fine now and stopped my pills. I think my blood pressure is under control now." It was 148/88. The nurse reviewed his knowledge of the medication and of hypertension. She reinforced the need to continue taking the diuretic, take it easy, and have periodic blood pressure checks.

Mrs. Bolangier was understandably upset by the episode and her husband's attitude toward his hypertension. "I just wish he'd listen to the doctor. I'm afraid he'll have a stroke like his mother. Then where will we be?"

Mrs. Bolangier was still unable to take her pulse. However, her husband was accurate and had recorded three readings of the previous week: 72, 68, and 60. He was concerned that her pulse might be too slow.

Physical assessment

Vital Signs:	Blood pressure 88/56 left arm 110/60 right arm Temperature 98°F Apical rate 76 and irregular Radial rate 58 and less irregular Respirations 24 and shallow
Weight:	111 pounds.
Lungs:	Breath sounds greater on the left. Less wheezing. Decreased cough.
Chest:	Pain over pacemaker, between scapulae and along lower rib cage.
Cardiac:	Rate and rhythm irregular. No unusual sounds.
Extremities:	Cool, no changes.

Mrs. Bolangier was concerned about the discrepancy between her heart and pulse rates. She claimed she had taken her medications as directed and had adhered to the salt restriction. "I think I should have more energy by now. My husband has been doing all the work, even shoveling snow when he knows he shouldn't. I can't do anything with him, and I'm so afraid he'll pass out again. If he gets sick I won't be able to take care of him. I still get short of breath when I do any chores, just like before the surgery. How much longer will this go on?" She admitted not doing any respiratory exercises: "I don't see how I can do those exercises when I'm so tired."

Mrs. Bolangier continued to wear night clothing and had only worn street clothes for her daughter's last visit. "I didn't want her to think I wasn't recovering because she'd spend more time with me and she's too busy for that."

The Bolangiers' son was encouraging them to visit California

while his mother regained her strength and to consider moving there at a later time. Mrs. Bolangier's physician felt it would be many months before she would be able to travel. His caution was interpreted by the Bolangiers to mean she was not recovering satisfactorily. "I don't think he tells me everything I should know."

Although the Bolangiers did not want to move to California, they felt they needed a vacation from the severe winter weather. Mr. Bolangier said they should consider selling the house soon and move to an apartment. His wife became angry at this idea, stating she would soon be strong enough to help out. She did not want to leave "the neighborhood where we've lived so many years and know everybody. Apartments can be dangerous; no one knows or cares about anyone else."

Questions

1. What knowledge does Mrs. Bolangier need at this point relative to her medications? Of what side effects must she be aware? Outline preventive measures for her.
2. Explain Mr. Bolangier's "episode" at the nursing home.
   a. Determine possible causative factors.
   b. Evaluate the nurse's response.
   c. Evaluate the emergency care given him.
   d. What additional responsibilities does the health care professional have toward this elderly man?
   e. Beyond resuscitation and emergency room medical care, what is the nurse's responsibility?
   f. What is Mr. Bolangier's attitude toward the episode?

   Support your answers with scientific reasons.
3. Explain Mrs. Bolangier's attitude toward her restrictions and illness.
4. What reasons might explain her increasing pulse deficit? What is an appropriate nursing intervention? What information does Mrs. Bolangier need?
5. What explanation should the nurse give for pain over the pacemaker, between the scapulae and along the rib cage?
   a. Cite theories of altered healing attributed to normal aging.
   b. Identify additional factors in Mrs. Bolangier's lifestyle that may further complicate her progress.
   c. Develop realistic suggestions to aid her recovery.

February 3

This was the third home visit. Mrs. Bolangier continued pale and tired, but she was in street clothes, which improved her appearance. She was not sociable toward the nurse. However, conversation seemed

easier, partly due to a decreasing shortness of breath. The following dialogue occurred between Mrs. Bolangier and the nurse while Mr. Bolangier was making coffee.

Mrs. Bolangier: *I've been thinking of something that happened to me in the hospital. It's taken me a while to talk about it to anyone. I was wondering if you could explain what happened to me when I blacked out twice?*

Nurse: *Was this before your pacemaker was put in?*

Mrs. Bolangier: *Yes. I hadn't been in the hospital very long. I remember waking and seeing all those people around me; they looked concerned and I had the feeling something serious had happened to me.*

Nurse: *It sounds as though your heart wasn't functioning well for a while.*

Mrs. Bolangier: *Do you think it may have stopped? Like in television shows where they shock the body?*

Nurse: *It's very possible. How do you feel about it now?*

Mrs. Bolangier: *Actually, I'm quite amazed I'm here at all!*

At this point Mrs. Bolangier changed the subject. She wanted to know why she still had the same sore chest and back, why the pacemaker hurt, and why she was tired all the time. Her thoughts seemed to drift, and she did not wait for an answer. She appeared as anxious as usual.

Physical assessment

Vital Signs: Blood pressure
92/60 left arm
106/70 right arm

Apical rate	76 and irregular
Radial rate	64 and less irregular
Respirations	22 and shallow
Temperature	98.6° F oral
Weight	113 lb

Lungs: Breath sounds louder on the right side. Occasional cough productive of white, oily mucus. Fine rales heard over left middle lobe. No wheezing.

Heart: No S_3 or S_4 sounds. No change in irregular rhythm. No neck vein distension.

Extremities: Legs cool, pale with right peripheral 1+ nonpitting edema. Fingers ice cold.

The following data were obtained by telephone from the laboratory:

Hematocrit 33mm
Hemoglobin 11 gm.
Prothrombin time 26%
Potassium 5.1 mEq./ℓ.

When asked if she had any questions or concerns, Mrs. Bolangier said her constipation continued, making defecation painful. To remedy the situation she took 2 tablespoons of mineral oil immediately prior to lying down for the night. Although she felt this had decreased her rectal pain, she questioned a possible respiratory effect.

Mr. Bolangier asked the nurse to take his blood pressure; it was 176/104. He had not taken his medication for about three weeks. "Maybe I'd better start taking it again, although I don't feel any different." He had been shoveling snow several times that week and climbing the cellar stairs with laundry. "I know I was told to take it easy, but there's so much to do, and I'm not the type that can sit still anyway. I don't read much, and the TV programs get worse every year." The nurse reminded him that his mother had been symptom-free prior to her stroke.

Questions

1. Determine possible causes for Mrs. Bolangier's increased irritability.
2. What factors continue to contribute to her fatigue? Identify additional factors.
3. Assess the new laboratory data and develop realistic nursing interventions.
4. What problem resulted from Mrs. Bolangier's method of taking mineral oil?
    a. Of what significance is this for her?
    b. What alternatives to mineral oil could the nurse suggest?
    c. What safety measures should be utilized for the elderly taking mineral oil?
    d. What long-term potential problem could result?
5. Identify factors contributing to Mrs. Bolangier's peripheral edema. Determine interventions to aid in its resolution.
6. Determine the causes of compromised circulation in Mrs. Bolangier's fingers. Develop interventions to improve the circulation.

February 14

Mrs. Bolangier had taken the nurse's advice and seen her physician. She felt the physician had been vague in answering her questions and said she would "be fine." He had prescribed colace to replace mineral oil and suggested she "watch her diet for roughage." "He doesn't

seem very concerned about me or my pains. He said the pacemaker isn't working as well as it should but that I'm not to worry about it. How can I not worry about it when it's my heart that could stop again?"

Mrs. Bolangier was angry, and her words were slow and slurred. There was a strong odor of alcohol on her breath, and a half-empty glass sat on the coffee table. Her gait was unsteady, and there were several bruises on her legs.

"I'm tired of all this not being able to smoke, drink, help around the house, and go out. I'm just useless now. My husband's tired from all the work, and he won't take his medication every day. We had an offer for the house, and I guess we'll have to move." Shortness of breath and coughing stopped her tirade.

Mr. Bolangier did not want his blood pressure taken. "It's probably OK today. I take a pill if I think my pressure's up. I'll make an appointment to see my doctor soon."

Assessment of Mrs. Bolangier revealed no significant changes other than a probable high alcohol intake, a sprained right ankle (which had occurred the previous day after drinking), and multiple leg bruises. Mrs. Bolangier said she recalled bumping into furniture and tripping on the cellar stairs, wrenching her ankle. Mr. Bolangier had effectively wrapped the ankle in an elastic knit bandage.

Both Bolangiers were discouraged. Mrs. Bolangier had begun smoking again, with the result that her coughing increased, keeping her awake at night. She refused to discuss the return to alcohol and cigarettes with the nurse.

While Mrs. Bolangier was out of the room, her husband expressed his anxiety: "She was doing so well. For a long time she didn't drink at all, and now she's at it again. She drank for years, and I know its hard to give up a habit. It's because of her drinking we stopped going to church years ago, and after awhile the priest didn't come around to inquire how we were doing. She doesn't seem to think there's much to live for anymore."

STUDY GUIDE QUESTIONS

1. Evaluate the effectiveness of the hospital referral for comprehensiveness for the elderly.
   a. Assess the data presented for relevance and completeness.
   b. Recommend additions and alterations.

   c. Identify additional health care personnel whose contributions would have been helpful.
   d. Recommend alternative methods of communication between institution and community.

2. Identify the dynamics operative between the Bolangiers.
   a. What roles can be identified?
   b. What actual and potential problems in their relationship may be of relevance to the nurse?
   c. What interventions, if any, would be appropriate?

3. This illness has precipitated problems in lifestyle and housing for this couple.
   a. Identify those problems.
   b. What are the effects and problems of relocation for the elderly? For this particular couple?
   c. Determine alternative methods of maintaining their current housing and lifestyle.

4. Determine reasons for Mr. Bolangier's noncompliance with his medical regimen.
   a. What is nursing's role in this situation?
   b. What teaching and learning methods might be attempted? Give reasons to support your decision.

5. Stressors and life crises are usually dealt with by coping mechanisms, that may be as detrimental to the individual as the original stressors.
   a. Identify Mrs. Bolangier's coping behavior.
   b. Determine the effects of alcohol on aging physiology in general and on Mrs. Bolangier's physiology in particular.
   c. Determine the effects of smoking on aging physiology in general and on Mrs. Bolangier's physiology in particular.

6. Alcoholism (and abuse of other substances) may be on the increase among women in the United States.
   a. What are the incidence and prevalence of alcoholism in the elderly? In women?
   b. Compile a demographic profile to reflect.
      (1) The scope of the problem of alcoholism in the elderly.
      (2) Risk factors leading to potential alcoholism.

Case

Mr. Timothy O'Connor: A Case for an Advocate

INTRODUCTION

The problems presented in this case reinforce the contention that care for the aging person is multifaceted.

The roles of assessor, manager, modifier, collaborator, teacher, consultant and advocate are inherent in this specialized clinical practice area. The gerontological nurse clinician's attention is directed to those considerations delineated below and to additional ones that can be found on analytical study of Mr. O'Connor's case.

Considerations identified are:

Patient advocacy for the elderly
Role of the gerontology clinical nurse specialist
Chronicity
Alcoholism in the elderly
Peripheral vascular disease and the healing process
Attitudes of health care providers toward the elderly

Managing a population of elderly ill, including therapeutic modalities
Teaching self-care to the elderly
New health care skills for the elderly
Discharge planning to meet the needs of the elderly with problems of limited independence
Maintaining independence of the elderly after discharge

THE CASE

During the past two and a half years Mr. Timothy O'Connor, age 65, had been in four hospitals. In June 1975, while at work, he fell from a loading dock, incurring left-sided fractures of his arm, leg, pelvis, and ribs. After two months in traction in a general hospital, he spent an additional two months recuperating at the home of a married nephew. During this time Mr. O'Connor experienced approximately ten episodes of unconsciousness. He became obtunded, and his nephew brought him to the hospital again. He was diagnosed as having right subdural hematoma, which was treated successfully with burr holes.

The second hospitalization was complicated by gastrointestinal bleeding from esophageal varices and a recurrent gastric ulcer. The varices responded to Sengstaken–Blakemore intubation in three days. The gastric ulcer was treated with milk and Riopan through the nasogastric tube. After one week there was no further evidence of bleeding, and he was transferred to a nursing home, as his nephew did not feel he could adequately care for him at home.

Mr. O'Connor did not feel comfortable at the nursing home and discharged himself after three weeks. He felt he had recovered sufficiently to care for himself at home alone. At home Mr. O'Connor bumped his left ankle against a chair. The ankle bled, and within two days there was an open, draining area. Concomitantly he noted changes in his lower legs; the skin had become brownish purple. He became concerned and readmitted himself to the nursing home, where he was treated with soaks to the wound and bedrest. The ankle eventually healed, but an area 4.4 cm × 3 cm × 1 cm below the ankle sloughed. This ulceration was treated in a similar manner for several months with no improvement. He was subsequently transferred to a medical center (in November). During a month there he received systemic and local antibiotic therapy, soaks and periodic debridement, passive leg exercises, bedrest, and an adequate diet.

On December 10, Mr. O'Connor was transferred to a rehabilitation center for extended care. His foot decubitus had been reduced to 3.4 cm X 2.5 cm X 1 cm.

Previous Health History

Hospitalizations

1933: bullet wound three inches above right ear received while defending a neighborhood grocery store during robbery. Nonpenetrating; no residual damage.

1975: multiple fractures.

Illnesses

Mr. O'Connor had vague recall of any illnesses. He did remember episodes of "heavy drinking" resulting in loss of work time.

General health habits

Mr. O'Connor felt his general health had improved since his hospitalizations. He no longer drank alcohol but continued to smoke two packages of unfiltered cigarettes daily. In the rehabilitation extended care hospital, his sleep was approximately seven uninterrupted hours at night with an occasional afternoon nap. With inactivity his weight increased to 185 lb, at which point he adjusted his diet by omitting deserts and returned to his former weight of 175 lb.

The average hospital day included six hours of television, visits with other patients and nursing staff, and reading. One and a half hours were usually spent in physical therapy for whirlpool treatments and leg exercises. His nephew visited two or three times each week in the evening, and both seemed to enjoy time together. Mr. O'Connor's gait was unsteady, and he limped on his ritual walks around the unit.

Mr. O'Connor was often bored and became irritable. His roommates changed weekly, adding to his frustrations. He had no known allergies and denied use of medications other than an "occasional aspirin or antacid," for headache or "heartburn."

Genetic History

Father died age 35 and mother age 52 of heart disease. Sister and brother died in their forties, also of heart disease. Mr. O'Connor did not recall a family history of obesity, diabetes, arthritis, gout,

tuberculosis, or chonic respiratory problems. He knew no relatives outside his immediate family.

Family and Social Background

Timothy O'Connor did not know the year or place of his birth but thought it was "somewhere in Pennsylvania or Kentucky." Until he was about 20 years old he had no birth certificate; one was procured by a priest, enabling him to enter the Merchant Marine in World War II.

His recollections of childhood were vague. "We were always sick with colds and went hungry a lot." Mr. O'Connor, Sr., had been a coal miner, moving his family often before eventually settling in Illinois, where he had died, leaving a wife and three young children. Timothy had managed to graduate from high school while working to help support the family. In his spare time he had tried amateur boxing but found the competition stiff.

After World War II he had moved to New England, became a boiler engineer in a large factory, married, and had one son. Five years before his hospitalization his wife had died from chronic hepatitis following a blood transfusion. Timothy, Jr., a policeman, had not visited his father since the death of his mother despite living 10 miles away. Mr. O'Connor said he and his son "never got on that well; he always preferred his mother."

Mr. O'Connor was born Roman Catholic but had not practiced his religion for a number of years. "The church never did much for me and couldn't help my wife when she was dying."

Economic Status and Lifestyle

Mr. O'Connor described his financial situation as adequate to meet his decreased social needs. "I don't do much now with the wife gone. My insurance plan is good, especially with the help of workmen's compensation. I still get some of my regular pay as well. I'll be getting Medicare soon, too. I used to spend a lot of money on booze, and women are expensive too. Things are different now, being confined and all."

Prior to hospitalization, Mr. O'Connor ate his meals in restaurants. He preferred fried and starchy foods to vegetables and fruits and preceded his dinner with "two or three stiff whiskeys."

Evenings were often spent in a local tavern playing cards and drinking with friends, or he stayed home watching television and drinking beer. "I didn't like being alone very much."

Mr. O'Connor had continued to live in the house he and his wife had bought twenty years earlier. "It's too big for me now, and it's been sitting empty most of these past two years. A friend checks it for me once in a while. That house is all I own now, all I have left of my life, and I don't want to sell it."

Retirement was another issue of concern to Mr. O'Connor, who had hoped to work until age 70. "I've always enjoyed my job. This hanging around drives me crazy."

Physical Assessment

	Objective Data	*Subjective Data*
Integument:	Lower extremities dry, purplish brown and shiny Fingers red and smooth Spider angiomas on cheeks	Lower extremities itchy with occasional bruising
Head:	Normocephalic Hair dry, thin with normal male-pattern balding	Occasional headaches
Nails:	Clubbed, with slow blanching	Asymptomatic
Eyes:	Edema and redness of left lower lid; no drainage PEERLA Visual acuity 20/30 with corrective lenses Fundi unremarkable	Irritation, redness, and excessive tearing of left eye Has worn glasses for nearsightedness since age 42
Nose:	Left passage narrowed Turbinates red and dry	Broken while boxing forty years ago No sinus tenderness No difficulty inspiring
Ears:	Large amount of cerumen bilaterally Conversational tones heard Weber and Rinne tests unremarkable	Asymptomatic
Mouth:	Lips dry and pink Teeth in poor repair with several missing Gums reddened Tongue midline, uncoated	No sore throats and few colds Voice hoarse for several years

Neck:	Bruit heard over left carotid artery No nodes palpated Trachea midline Thyroid nonpalpable ROM of cervical spine full Crepitus on full ROM	No stiffness, swelling, or pain
Thorax and Lungs:	Anterior/posterior ratio 1:1 Symmetrical expansion Tactile fremitus and breath sounds decreased over left lower lobe; prolonged expiration with wheeze	Occasional morning cough (nonproductive) Shortness of breath on climbing more than five steps
Cardiovascular	Apical pulse 80 and regular PMI at fifth ICS, left midclavicular line No heaves, thrills, S_3 or S_4 Grade II/VI systolic, aortic murmur with carotid radiation No lower extremity pulses Righ femoral bruit Blood pressure 140/84	Shortness of breath on exertion Denies chest pain
Abdomen:	Liver percussed at 12 cm, right midclavicular line (6 cm below RCM); has decreased from 18 cm on admission Mild ascites Prominent venous pattern No tenderness or masses Bowel sounds present	Occasional constipation, relieved with Ex-Lax Frequent episodes of distention One episode of gastrointestinal bleeding (see "History of Present Illness")
Rectal:	Internal hemorrhoids Prostate soft with no significant enlargement Stool guaiac positive	Occasional mucus and blood-streaked stools Occasional bouts of cramping
Extremities:	No pulses palpated Ruborous integument Absence of hair Nails clubbed Spider angiomas present on lower extremities Left more involved than right Loss of pain and touch discrimination and vibratory sensation Left heel decubitus, which bleeds easily	Denies claudication Aching sensation appears after prolonged standing Occasional swelling and burning in both feet

Musculoskeletal:	Muscle strength 4+ except 3+ in left upper extremity Left handgrip weak (2+)	Aching on prolonged standing
Neurological:	Subtle hemiparesis Cranial nerves within normal limits	Left-sided weakness Loss of sensation in lower extremities

Reflexes:

	Right	*Left*
Biceps	+2	+2
Triceps	+2	+2
Radial	+2	+1
Patellar	+2	+4
Achilles	+2	omitted

Abdominal: present

Emotional:	Frequent episodes of irritability and depression since death of his wife. Less attentive to details.	
Genitourinary:	Normal male Uncircumcised	Nocturia X 2 No burning or difficulty initiating or stopping stream

Libido and Sexual Functioning

Activity and interest have steadily declined following wife's death. "What woman would look at an old wreck like me?"

Mr. O'Connor was admitted to a large, bright, semiprivate room in a new, modern extended care facility, where he was expected to remain until the decubitus healed. His roommate was 82 years of age with terminal cancer and had a large attentive family.

Physician's Orders

Aldomet 250 mg p.o. b.i.d.
Tylenol 1-2 tabs q. 3-4 hr for leg pain
Milk of magnesia 30 ml h.s. p.r.n.
Elevate legs when seated
May ambulate
Physical therapy evaluation
Whirlpool treatments to both legs daily
House diet

The following nursing assessment was recorded upon Mr. O'Connor's admission to extended care.

PATIENT DATA BASE
NURSING ASSESSMENT

DATE: Dec. 10 TIME: 2:00 a.m. / **p.m.** SEX: **Male** / Female AGE: 65

PHYSICIAN: Staff TIME NOTIFIED: a.m. / p.m. ADMITTED: Ambulant **Wheelchair** Cart

PRIMARY NURSE: S. Allen ACCOMPANIED BY: Nephew

ASSOCIATE NURSE: PRIOR PSL ADMISSION: yes **no**

REASON FOR THIS ADMISSION: Chronic left heel decubitus

MEDICATIONS (LIST): DISPOSITION OF MEDICATIONS:

1. 4. 7.

2. 5. 8.

3. 6. 9.

VITAL SIGNS:

BLOOD PRESSURE: 140/82 PULSE: 76 REG./IRREG. RESPIRATIONS:

TEMPERATURE: 98.2 HEIGHT: 5'6" WEIGHT: 165

ALLERGY: None

PROSTHETICS: None

EYEGLASSES/CONTACTS: **yes** / no ARTIFICIAL EYE: right / left **none** COLOR OF EYES: Brown

DENTURES: yes / **no** FULLPLATE: upper / lower PARTIAL PLATE: upper / lower

HEARING AIDE: yes / **no** – right / left HAIRPIECE (specify): COLOR OF HAIR: Gray

OTHER:

GENERAL PHYSICAL APPEARANCE:

Normally Nourished ✓ Obese ___ Thin ___

Chronically ILL ___ Emaciated ___ Acutely ILL ___

ELIMINATION HABITS:

BOWEL: Every 2 days

Frequency Color Brown

Diarrhea Constipation Occasionally

Laxative Used (what/when): Ex-Lax

BLADDER:

Frequency Nocturia Quantity

Color Yellow Odor Usual

Pain/Burning: yes / **no** (describe)

PRESENCE OF TUBES/APPLIANCES: yes / **no** (describe):

SKIN: Cyanotic ___ Dry ✓ Oily ___

FLUSHED: ___ JAUNDICED: ___ PALE: ___ TURGOR: ___

RASH (describe):

DECUBITI (describe): Left heel 3.4cm x 2.5cm x 1cm

NAILS: Yellow, brittle

FEMALE PATIENTS: Date of last Pelvic Exam.

DO YOU HAVE REGULAR MONTHLY PERIODS? yes / no

WHEN IS YOUR NEXT PERIOD DUE?

WILL YOU NEED: Pads ___ Tampon ___ Other ___

NUTRITION: (describe food preferences. Snacking patterns, diet, difficulty chewing, swallowing, condition of teeth, etc.)

REST AND SLEEP PATTERNS (describe regular patterns, insomnia, use of sleeping aides, number of hours slept etc.):

Naps in hospital. Sleeps 7 hours at night. No sleeping pills, prefers brandy.

ACTIVITY AND EXERCISE ROUTINES (describe ability to walk, daily activity, work habits):

Limited for the past 2 years by heel ulcer. Fairly active job for the past several years as a loading foreman and engineer in the boiler room. No interest in active sports.

RESPIRATORY FUNCTIONS (describe smoking habits, use of O_2 or medi-inhalers, shortness of breath):

Dyspnea Cyanosis Breath Sounds: (Clear) / Congested (Cough) (describe):

Heavy smoker/1-1½ packs of unfiltered cigarettes per day for 40 years. Denies cough except in the early morning on arising. Does complain of SOB on exertion of one flight of stairs. Also has noted some wheezing.

CARDIO-VASCULAR FUNCTIONS (describe any chest pain, duration, frequency, history of heart trouble):

Pacemaker: yes / (no) Blanching ____ Edema ✓ Location

SOB as noted above with some chest pain.

Extremities blue, cool, edematous without pulses. Nails clubbed.

NEURO-SENSORY LEVELS (describe pupil reflexes, movement of extremities, grasp reflexes):

Dizziness: yes / (no) Oriented to time, place, person: (yes) / no Unconscious: yes / (no)

Hearing difficulty/Visual difficulty (describe):

PSYCHO-SOCIAL PATTERNS:

Language(s) Spoken: English Occupation: Foreman & Boiler Engineer

Marital Status: Widowed Level of Education: High school

No. of Children: Oriented to Unit: (yes) / no Hospital Routine: (yes) / no

PROJECTED TEACHING NEEDS:

1.

2.

3.

OTHER PERTINENT DATA:

PSYCHIATRIC UNIT ADMISSION – ADMISSION CONSENT SIGNED: yes / (no)

SUICIDAL/HOMICIDAL GESTURE: yes / (no) (describe)

Interviewed By: S. Allen R.N. Date: 12-10

Primary Nurse: Date:

Questions

1. On the basis of the preceding data determine physical and emotional changes resulting from Mr. O'Connor's
   a. lifestyle.
   b. heredity.
   c. age.
   d. losses.
2. Develop interventions and effective schedule to facilitate
   a. elderly adjustment.
   b. optimal rest.
   c. healing process.
   d. individual interests.
   e. motivation/involvement, independence, and self-respect.
3. Identify environmental constraints inherent in most medical institutions.
4. Determine underlying factors contributing directly and indirectly to
   a. decubitus formation.
   b. subdural hematoma.
   c. gastrointestinal bleeding (acute and chronic).
   d. depression.
5. Develop restorative and preventive interventions.
6. Based on the case data and the foregoing questions, develop short- and long-term goals.

After one month in the new facility, a psychologist tested Mr. O'Connor's cognitive ability. His Intelligence Quotient was 128, and his areas of specific functioning were generally intact. Orientation, remote memory, receptive and expressive language, psychomotor skills, and social judgment were unimpaired. There were significant losses of attention span and recent memory, which did not interfere with daily routine functioning. Mr. O'Connor made errors of omission on tasks requiring sustained concentration. These changes were felt to be consistent with a history of prolonged alcoholism. The psychologist believed the depression over the loss of his wife contributed to his loss of memory and inattentiveness and recommended psychotherapy. Mr. O'Connor refused.

Mr. O'Connor's decubitus healed poorly despite adherence to the prescribed regimen. After six weeks the ulcer measured 3 cm × 2.2 cm × .5 cm with no further bleeding. The surrounding tissue had become dark and hard.

Mr. O'Connor had frequent outbursts of anger toward the staff, after which he apologized profusely. He refused to discuss the progress of the ulcer and no longer took an interest in the dressings and physical therapy. He continued to eat in the dining room and social-

ize with other patients. At this time Mr. O'Connor began discussing colorful aspects of his past life, often shocking his audience. He related episodes of heavy drinking, arrests, sexual activity, and plans following this hospitalization. "I'm going to make up for these past two years. I'll be back at work soon and have more money to spend on the things I like—women and booze."

Mr. O'Connor began taking lengthy afternoon naps, watched more television, and canceled many physical therapy sessions. "They weren't helping anyway. That ulcer isn't getting any smaller." He continued eating in the dining room but socialized less. He was no longer debating issues with the staff and often expressed anger without subsequent apology. His nephew began visiting less often, a further annoyance. "I know he doesn't want anything to do with an old grouch like me, but I can't help it, being cooped up like this all the time."

Questions

1. Determine the dynamics operative in this portion of Mr. O'Connor's hospitalization. Identify the role the setting has played in these dynamics.
2. Identify Mr. O'Connor's unmet needs.
3. Outline new goals for care of this man.
4. Determine methods of dealing with Mr. O'Connor's frustrations within the institutional setting (the extended care facility).
   a. Apply the results of the examination of cognitive ability to planning the interventions.
   b. Determine limitations of aging physiology and pathophysiological complications potentially affecting those interventions.
5. Identify factors affecting delayed wound healing.
   a. Determine appropriate interventions.
   b. Provide supportive data from knowledge of biological and psychosocial changes of aging.

Mr. O'Connor was asked to become a regular contributor to the hospital's weekly newsletter. He was excited at the offer and wrote voluminously. He interviewed patients and staff for issues and opinions. His essays appeared in each newsletter, and he received many compliments.

Another month passed, and Mr. O'Connor's elation declined. He returned to his withdrawn state. He continued to ignore the decubitus, which had healed very little. After three months the ulcer measured 2.6 cm × .5 cm. "That thing is never going to close over, and my legs are still so purple and cold. I'll never be able to wear my heavy shoes when I go back to work."

Mr. O'Connor limped around the ward, rarely using his crutch for support, subsequently complaining of frequent backaches. The physical therapists were discouraged because of his frequent cancellations and negative attitude. The nursing staff was frustrated and discouraged by his sarcastic abuse during dressing changes.

More and more Mr. O'Connor talked about going to his own home and returning to work. "I've decided not to sell the house. I called my friend last night and told him I'll be home on the weekend and to turn on the heat for me. I don't care if that thing is healed or not. I'll take care of it myself. I'm sure it'll get better if I'm outdoors in the fresh air. It isn't healthy being in a place like this where everyone is sick. Home will be quieter too; my roommates are always old, feeble, snoring men."

Mr. O'Connor intermittently showed guaiac positive stools throughout his hospitalization. A gastrointestinal series on admission revealed a healed peptic ulcer but chronic diverticulosis with mild ulceration. A repeat series was scheduled, but Mr. O'Connor refused the X-rays, stating that he was going home in a few days and would take care of himself.

True to his word, Mr. O'Connor discharged himself against medical advice and without preparation for self-care at home. He packed his belongings in paper bags, called a taxi, and limped to the front door.

STUDY GUIDE QUESTIONS

1. Discuss nursing's responsibility to Mr. O'Connor in this situation.
   a. Identify interventions that could have prevented
      (1) discharge against medical advice.
      (2) discharge without preparation.
   b. Determine the rights of patients in an intermediate care facility.
      (1) Who ensures these rights?
      (2) Are there any legal constraints in denying these rights?
      (3) Delineate the mechanisms currently operative in your community and/or institution to provide for patient rights. Assess their adequacy.
   c. Develop the role of nurse advocate for the elderly patient.
      (1) Identify constraints imposed on nurses in this role.
      (2) Determine methods of overcoming these constraints.
      (3) Identify bureaucratic and professional consequences of overcoming some of these constraints.

2. Mr. O'Connor is only one patient in a rehabilitation institution dealing with problems of the elderly ill. Many of his problems are representative of this population.
   a. Identify problems elderly patients commonly develop as a result of this situation.
   b. Determine attitudes toward the elderly that are inherent in this milieu and affect creative interventions.
   c. Develop methods of anticipating and preventing problems intensified by the setting.
   d. Develop a team approach to total care of the elderly.

3. Chronicity often implies change in lifestyle.
   a. Determine new health care behaviors or skills to assist the elderly person in adjusting to an altered lifestyle upon discharge.
   b. Develop methods of teaching these behaviors or skills to the elderly patient.
   c. Determine methods of reteaching or reinforcing these new skills or activities for long-term compliance at home.
   d. Identify community systems or agencies to assist in this long-term goal.
   e. Ascertain realistic financing of these services for the elderly.

Case

XII

Mr. Arthur James Grant III: A Case for Nurse Management

INTRODUCTION

Mr. Grant has dealt with the world on his own terms, deftly defying the established health system and the middle-class value system. As the title suggests, the nurse clinician is challenged to evolve imaginative long-range plans for health maintenance.

Unlike the previous cases, this one is not followed by a set of questions. Using the considerations identified, some of which are listed below, the student should identify questions and look for solutions based on the questions, what, why, where, when, how much, and by whom? All should require deductive and inductive thinking, synthesis, and peer evaluation.

Some of the considerations to be addressed are the following:

Problems of counterculture lifestyle.
Acceptance of an altered lifestyle in the elderly.

Maintenance of lifestyle.
Concomitant risks of aging physiology and lifestyle.
Effects of hypothermia (systemic and local).
Seizure disorders in the elderly.
Preventive measures.
Motivation for compliance with health care regimen.
Nurse–client health care contracts.
Long-term health maintenance goals.
Reimbursement policies.
Nurse-managed populations.
Role of the geriatric nurse clinician.

THE CASE

Arthur James Grant III was an 80-year-old New Englander. He was tall, slim, and straight. He had a mane of white hair, a full white beard, fair, ruddy skin, and bright blue, sparkling eyes. He was quick to smile, well-spoken, and a gentleman.

Five days earlier Mr. Grant had been brought unconscious to the emergency room by police who had responded to an anonymous call. He had been found covered with a thin, old blanket at a campsite beside railroad tracks. His temperature had been subnormal, but the presence of rales, shallow respiration, dehydration, and comatose state suggested pneumonia. He was immediately given antibiotics, fluids intravenously, and oxygen.

Within 24 hours Mr. Grant began producing such copious amounts of green sputum that nasotracheal suctioning was not sufficient. A tracheostomy was performed, allowing for vigorous removal of secretions. Forty-eight hours later he had regained consciousness and was able to cough.

It was winter, and Mr. Grant had not been warmly dressed. Several toes had been frostbitten and were gangrenous. There was no sensation in his feet, and pedal pulses were diminished on the right and absent on the left. The nails were long, yellow, and brittle. Those of the great toes curved across the other four, looking like four-inch ram's horns. He could not recall when they had last been trimmed.

During the initial five days, Mr. Grant experienced two grand mal seizures and was given Dilantin I.M. When the tracheostomy tube was removed and Mr. Grant was able to speak, he told the staff he had been diagnosed many years ago as having epilepsy. The seizures

had been controlled with Dilantin in the past, but he often sold the "pills" to buy food, claiming that each capsule could bring fifty cents to a dollar from someone who thought they were "uppers." After a time, the seizures would return and he would be brought to an emergency room and given more Dilantin.

On occasion he had sustained injuries from falls. These included concussion and fractures of the ribs, left ulna, and radius.

On the fifth day Mr. Grant was transferred from the intensive care unit to a general medical ward. The following is an excerpt from a nurse's interview with him:

"I must say, I've had quite a life. I've spent most of it traveling, and I'm not through yet; there's much more to see. I enjoy people, and in my eighty years I've known many people from professors to "bums," and I've liked them all.

"You probably won't believe me, but I was once a college professor of history. Ivy League education and all the rest. Now you might say I'm a student of life on the road. I never married, and to some I guess I never amounted to much. My family, they're all dead now, never understood why I gave up the security of a comfortable academic life. They all thought of me as a bum and not worth much; just an amusing character. I didn't want responsibility or routine, so a regular job or the efforts and demands of a career and family weren't for me.

"After I finished my Master's degree back in the 1920s, I taught in a small college for five years but couldn't tolerate the confinement of a job or the small town. So one day I sold everything and gave all my money to my father to invest, which he wisely did. I then took a train to Boston and have lived on the trains most of my life since then. Oh, once in a while I'd live with a woman for a few months, but it never lasted long. I tried settling long enough to write a book of my travels, but never finished it. It's the free lifestyle that I enjoy. I don't think I have any regrets. I may never have accomplished much, but then I don't know too many who have with all their hypocrisy and martyred attitudes. I've learned something new every day, and that's what's been important.

"As for my health, well, basically it has been pretty good. The seizures sometimes don't occur for months, and when they do I see a doctor. But doctors have a tendency to exaggerate your problems, and by the time they've examined, tested, and consulted you're much sicker than you were originally. Good food, fresh air, and

exercise will keep you healthy. I think I'm in pretty good shape for eighty.

"In the past fifty years, I've seen forty-nine states and Canada. But now I stick to the run from Boston to Maine in the good weather and in winter Boston to Florida. A few of us have traveled together for years, and it's a good life. We sleep in box cars while we're traveling and sometimes in empty rail cars if there is no one watching. I do admit it's harder getting on and off the trains now than when I was younger. I can't jump when they move, so I have to wait until we're at a station. Sure, I've been caught a few times, but a couple of nights in jail can be a blessing in damp weather. The joints do get stiff and sore. If the railroad men know you, or you're old, they are inclined to look the other way most of the time.

"People often wonder how we all manage financially. But as you can see, there isn't much overhead. The money that was invested years ago is still paying dividends, so I can live the way I want to. I pick up my checks at a Boston post office whenever I go through there. I'm not worried about money, as you can see. There's even enough to pay for a nursing home, but I'll never see the inside of one of those if I have my way.

"I'm glad my beard wasn't shaved off—it keeps my chin warm and I don't have much opportunity to shave anyway. We only bathe in the spring and fall, usually at a stream or lake. The Salvation Army is good about giving out clothes, and you can't carry extras anyway, in case you have to move fast. All I carry is in a backpack some college kid threw away. You can stuff a lot into it, and it makes a fine pillow.

"Usually our only worry is about getting sick. Most of us are old, and several have heart and lung problems. Some have bad coughs, and we've lost a few, especially in the winter. Sometimes we drink wine or whiskey to keep warm if we're caught North in bad weather, but on a couple of occasions a fellow hasn't wakened again.

"Sometimes if money is temporarily short, food becomes a problem. A home-cooked meal would be nice once in a while, but not worth the commitment. We share with one another when times get tough. Sometimes there are young fellows with us for a while, and we have some lively debates and good laughs. We're a loyal group. There's just no one to take care of some of our little medical problems, and I guess we wait until we're too sick before we get help. Medical care is too expensive for us."

Mr. Grant's lifestyle demanded alterations in routine nursing care. He refused to be bathed and insisted on wearing thermal underwear (the same pair continually). He did not want his toenails trimmed and stated that they just fit his shoes nicely. He preferred his hair long but consented to having both hair and beard trimmed. He refused to brush his few remaining teeth but did use a mouth rinse in the morning.

The medical staff and nursing staff formulated the following problem list:

Active	*Resolved*
Gangrenous toes	Pneumococcal pneumonia
Peripheral vascular disease	Tracheostomy
Seizure disorder	Hypothermia
Hypertension	Loss of hearing from packed cerumen
Dental caries	
Benign prostatic hypertrophy	
Underweight	

The following data from physical examination and review of systems include only those findings that indicate possible intervention.

Vital Sign Ranges:	Blood pressure 162/96–196/110 right arm 144/84–180/104 left arm (lying to standing) Apical rate 62–68 and regular Respiratory rate 16–20 and shallow Temperature 97.4–98.4°F
Height:	5 ft 10 in.
Weight:	130 lb
Head:	Occasional dizziness, tinnitus and occipital headaches. Several episodes of epistaxis. "Floaters" in the vitreous humor. Reading glasses that did not adequately correct vision; purchased 25 years ago.
Ears:	Minimal loss of conversational tones; improved following cerumen removal.
Mouth:	Ten remaining teeth with multiple caries.
Lungs:	Decreased breath sounds throughout. Diaphragmatic excursion 1 cm. Smokes one pack of cigarettes per day when available. Frequent productive morning cough. States he has bronchitis in cold, damp weather and occasionally wheezes.
Heart:	Grade II/VI systolic murmur. Pulses decreased in lower extremities; absent in left foot. Intermittent claudication in calves on exertion.

Gastrointestinal:	Occasional bouts of cramping and diarrhea. Alternate episodes of constipation, relieved with Ex-Lax.
Genitourinary:	Some difficulty initiating urinary stream. Nocturia X 3–4.
Neurological:	Seizures when not taking Dilantin. Begins with aura of darkened vision, tinnitus, and increased salivation. Seizure followed by long sleep and loss of short-term memory and generalized muscle aches.
Musculoskeletal:	Healed fractures of skull, ulna, radius, and ribs. Loss of muscle mass.

At the end of ten days the gangrene had not improved, and Mr. Grant was considered able to withstand the removal of the fifth toe bilaterally and partial removal of four other toes. Postoperative healing was slow but steady, with eventual closure of the wounds. Because of decreased circulation in his feet, the areas adjacent to the stumps on the left foot remained dark and friable. Ambulation was initially difficult and balance unsteady. After a week of physical therapy, Mr. Grant was independently mobile.

During the hospitalization Mr. Grant's seizure activity was controlled by Dilantin 100 mg daily and blood pressure stabilized around 148/90 on the left and 156/98 on the right with Hydrodiuril 50 mg daily. Other medications included multiple vitamins, potassium supplement, and Robitussin. For pneumonia, Ampicillin was given for three weeks.

An intravenous pyleogram showed normal aging kidneys. A voiding cystogram demonstrated increased bladder capacity with delayed emptying due to enlarged prostate. Mr. Grant refused palliative transurethral prostatectomy. The EEG tracings were within normal limits for his age.

At the end of a month Mr. Grant had gained 8 pounds and was anxious to be on his way. His feet had healed sufficiently to permit him to wear shoes and his nails had been trimmed. Without the long toenails, there was ample room for soft dressings to protect the amputation sites. He was given clothing left by other patients. Appointments were made for him at eye and dental clinics at the hospital and he was asked to remain in the city long enough for surgical followup. Mr. Grant agreed to keep these appointments but felt that within a month he would be on his way south to find his friends.

On the day of discharge, he was given a month's supply of Dilantin, Hydrodiuril, and potassium chloride. Arrangements were made for him to stay at a hotel for men close to the hospital.

Appendix A

GENERAL STUDY GUIDE QUESTIONS

The theory of education underlying these general study guide questions is that any successful learning process requires the students to develop a broad knowledge base before dealing with more specific knowledge.

To help the students maximize learning and develop attitudes and habits of logical thought, answers to those questions which have broad application should be developed in each instance before dealing with those questions that are peculiarly related to the clinical cases.

1. Identify those aging processes that will directly or potentially alter recovery or adaptation.
2. Based on normal aging within American society, determine appropriate developmental tasks.
   a. Identify factors complicating this development.
   b. Determine the individual's methods of accomplishing the task(s) or of avoiding or postponing the accomplishment.
3. Just as adequate kidney function is a physical asset to elderly persons taking medications, living in a high crime area is a sociological liability. Within the limits of the case data determine the additional physical, psychological, sociological, and environmental assets and liabilities.
4. Apply knowledge from theories and problems of aging, the introductory considerations, and previous questions to establish data bases for the identification of short- and long-term problems. For clarification, it may be useful to categorize the data as follows:

a. Anatomical
   Objective
   Subjective
b. Physiological
   Objective
   Subjective
c. Psychological
   Objective
   Subjective
d. Sociological
   Objective
   Subjective
e. Environmental
   (1) Home/community
      Objective
      Subjective
   (2) Institution
      Objective
      Subjective

5. Based on the data and foregoing questions, develop a list of problems in order of priority. These may also be stated as nursing diagnoses.
   a. Acute
   b. Intermittent/situational
   c. Long-term
   d. Potential

6. Determine those problems you might not address. Provide rationale for your decision.

7. Formulate health care goals or outcomes in behavioral terms:
   a. Short-term
   b. Long-term

8. Formulate health care interventions.
   a. Develop interventions for each problem identified, based on specific theories, the case data, and knowledge gained from case-specific questions. Capitalize on the patient's assets when formulating interventions.
   b. What difficulties must be anticipated in implementing the proposed interventions?
   c. Develop an evaluation tool for each intervention.
   d. Discuss the time and setting most effective for evaluation of each intervention.

   e. What restrictions would be anticipated in effecting the evaluation process?
   f. Project modifications for those interventions.
9. Nursing styles vary.
   a. Evaluate the nurse's role in each case, the interventions, and the interactions.
   b. What alternatives would you recommend? Why? When? And how?
10. Determine agencies and services available in your community with requisite skills applicable to each family's needs.
    a. Cost and reimbursement policy
    b. Eligibility
    c. Limitations of the agency
    d. Comprehensiveness of services
11. Develop additional questions for each case.

Appendix B

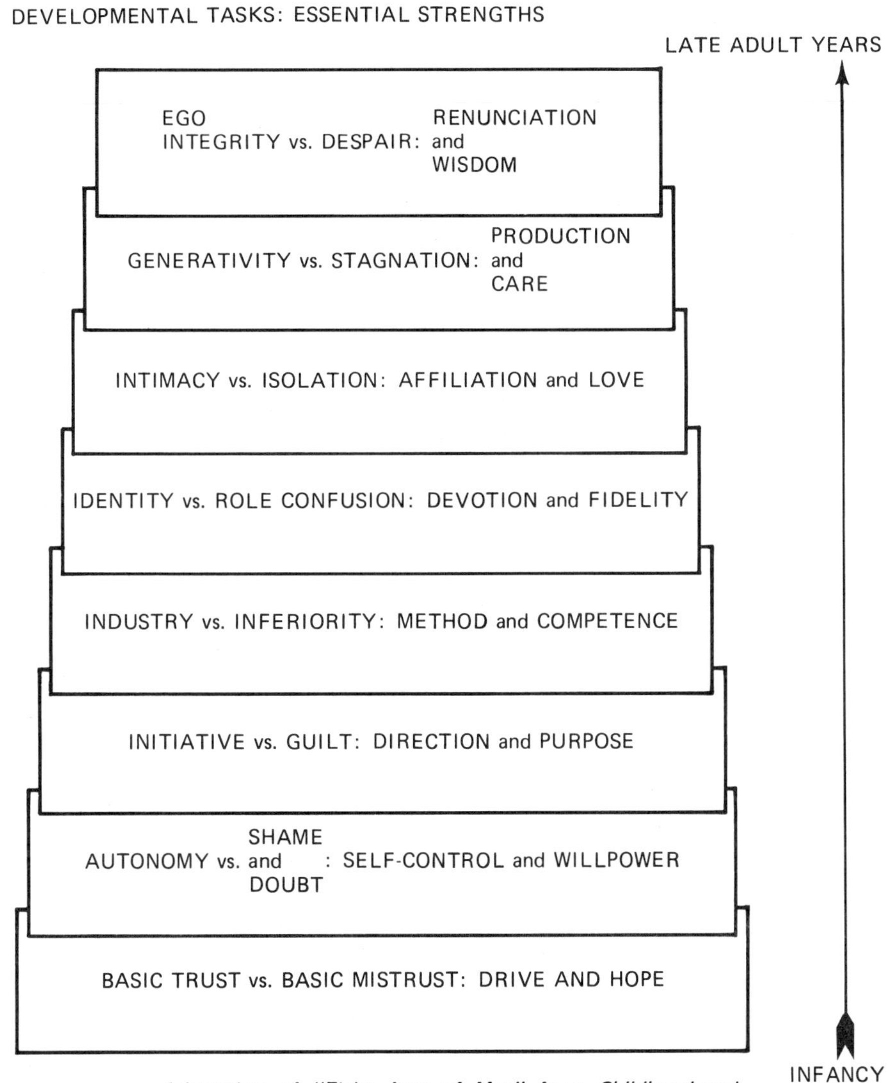

DEVELOPMENTAL TASKS: ESSENTIAL STRENGTHS
LATE ADULT YEARS
EGO INTEGRITY vs. DESPAIR: RENUNCIATION and WISDOM
GENERATIVITY vs. STAGNATION: PRODUCTION and CARE
INTIMACY vs. ISOLATION: AFFILIATION and LOVE
IDENTITY vs. ROLE CONFUSION: DEVOTION and FIDELITY
INDUSTRY vs. INFERIORITY: METHOD and COMPETENCE
INITIATIVE vs. GUILT: DIRECTION and PURPOSE
AUTONOMY vs. SHAME and DOUBT: SELF-CONTROL and WILLPOWER
BASIC TRUST vs. BASIC MISTRUST: DRIVE AND HOPE
INFANCY

Appendix C

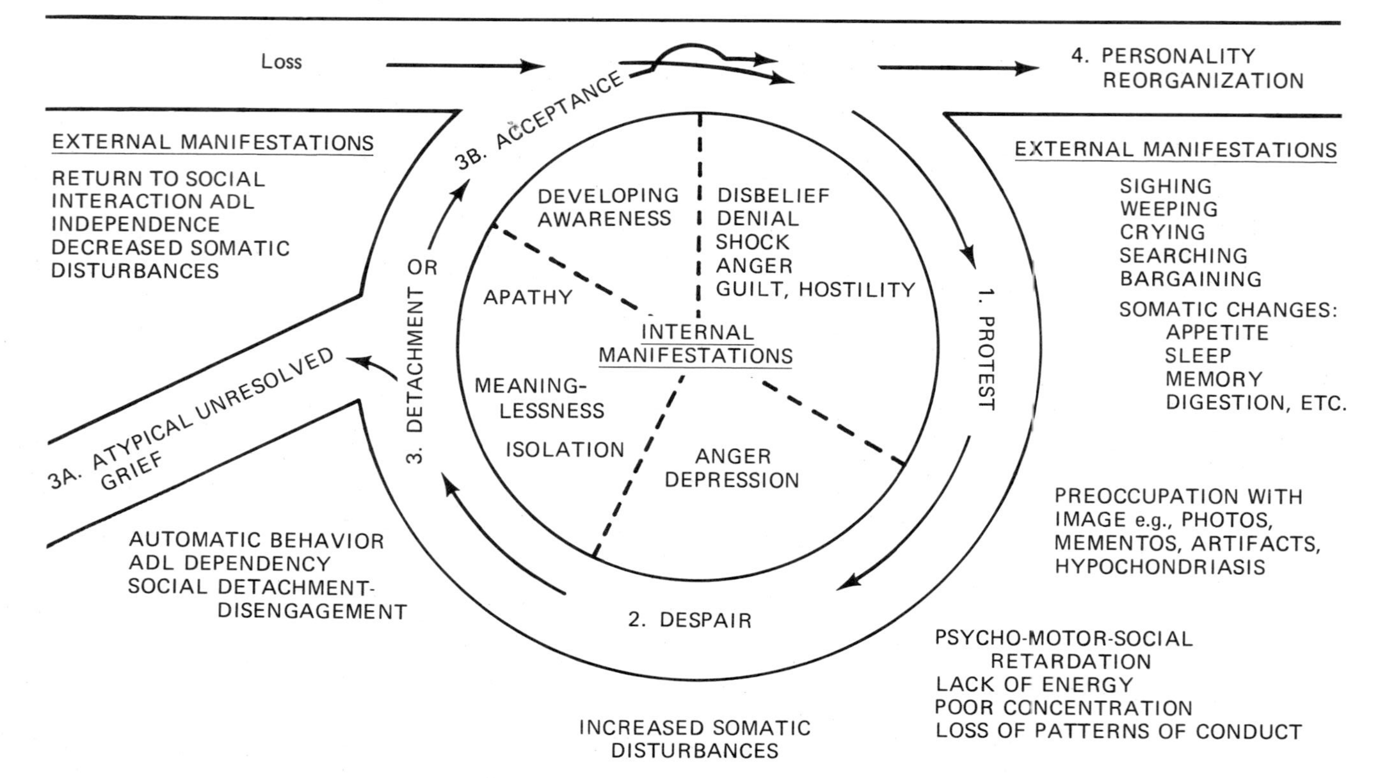

*APPLICABLE TO SEPARATION, GRIEF, GRIEVING, DYING, AND DEATH
Adapted from the theories of Bowlby, Engle, Kubler-Ross, and Lineman

Appendix D

THE CHRONOLOGY OF U.S. SOCIAL SECURITY*

1935: Social Security legislation enacted.

1939: (O.A.S.D.I.) Old Age, Survivors, Disability and Health Insurance Amendment: Benefits to be dispersed beginning in 1940 (originally 1942).

1950: Additional workers were included in the Social Security system (e.g., regularly employed farm and household employees, self-employed nonprofessional workers).

During the 1950s voluntary coverage was added for farm operators, most self-employed professionals, members of the armed forces, and workers for nonprofit organizations.

1950s: Husbands of retired women workers were included provided they were dependent on their wives for over 50% their income.

1955: Clergy could join on a voluntary basis.

1955: Mandatory participation of farm operators and self-employed professionals (except physicians and lawyers).

1957: Military personnel and lawyers were added to compulsory coverage; also firemen and police were eligible on a voluntary basis.

1957: Women could collect reduced benefits at age 62 (if retired, widowed, or wife of a retired worker).

1960: Coverage extended to U.S. citizens working for foreign governments or for international organizations.

1961: Men ruled eligible for Social Security at age 62 at a reduced rate (also included were female retired workers, dependent husbands, dependent widowers, and dependent parents).

*Prepared by Jane Perry, R.N., M.S.N., and Patricia C. Canty, R.N., M.S.N., as a course assignment while Masters students at Rush University, College of Nursing, Chicago, Ill.

1965: Widows and widowers became eligible at 60 instead of 62; mandatory participation of physicians.

1965: Medicare program enacted.

1965: Social Security benefits were adjusted upward (because of the wage-price spiral).

1973: Benefits to widows and dependent widowers were increased from 82% to 100% of the deceased worker's benefits.

1973: 1% bonus added to benefits for each year a worker works over age 65.

1975: Cost of living increase in benefits when consumer price index is 3% or greater.

1976: Widowers no longer had to be dependent for half their support to collect benefits.

1977: Maximum amount of taxable earnings increased to $16,500 per year at 5.85% taxation for employee and employer.

1977: Retiree may earn up to $3000 per year while on Social Security without reduction of benefits.

1978: Taxation rate increased to 6.05% with the base at $17,700 per year.

1978: A worker retiring at age 62 may collect 80% of benefits for life; the dependent spouse may collect 50% of the amount received by the worker.

1978: Retiree can earn up to $4000 per year without reduction of benefits; if under 65 and retired, can only earn $3240 without loss of benefits.

1979: Preexisting levels of benefits would be guaranteed to persons over 60 who marry or remarry (widows and widowers).

1979: Divorced wives qualify to apply for dependent spouse or survivors benefits if the marriage lasted ten years (previous requirement 29 years of marriage).

1979: Retiree under age 65 can earn up to $3480 without losing Social Security benefits.

Retirees 65–72 years of age can earn up to $4500; 72 or older, no income earning limit without losing Social Security benefits.

1979: Widows and widowers whose spouses worked past 65 years of age receive an average of $1000 extra over twelve months as delayed retirement credit.

1979: Taxation rate increased to 6.13% with the base at $22,900.

1979: Formula for calculating the base amount put on a par with the adjusted dollar value (one quarter worked = $260 base; 4 quarters = $1040).

1979: Social Security benefits to a dependent spouse who receives Civil Service pension has been reduced.

Future Changes

1980: Taxation rate 6.13% with the base increased to $25,900. (Amended 1977).

1981: Social Security tax rate paid by self-employed individuals would be increased $1\frac{1}{2}$ times the employee rate.

1981: Taxation rate increased to 6.65% with the base $29,700. (Amended 1977).

1982: Retirees who are 70 or older would be able to earn any amount without losing pension benefits.

1982: Workers would receive a benefit increase of 3% (currently 1%) for each year they continue to work past age 65.

1982: Taxation rate to be increased to 6.7%, the base amount to be determined.

1987: Workers and employers would each pay a tax of 7.15% on earnings up to $42,600, for a maximum payment of more than $3000 apiece.

Suggested References

The references that follow should not be viewed as exhaustive to the subject under study. They provide but a starting point for the synthesis of knowledge upon which to make judgments about nursing actions and provoke evaluative discourse.

Additional references can readily be found in national and international indexes, including *Index Medicus*; *International Index of Nursing*; Nathan W. Stock's review of "Current Publications in Gerontology and Geriatrics" *Journal of Gerontology*; *Technical Bibliographies on Aging, Series I and II* (Los Angeles: University of Southern California Press, Ethel Percy Andrus Gerontology Center, 1975–78); *Reader's Guide to Periodic Literature*, and *Cumulative Book Index*.

Nor should audiovisual materials be neglected. Three useful sources are: Mildred Allyn, *About Aging: A Catalog of Films* (Los Angeles: University of Southern California Press, The Ethel Percy Andrus Gerontology Center, 1977); *Media: Resources for Gerontology* (Ann Arbor, Mich.: Institute of Gerontology at the University of Michigan, 1977); and Lawrence Eidelberg, ed., *Health Sciences Video Directory 1978* (New York: Shelter Books, 1978).

Books and Monographs

Bell, Bill D., ed., *Contemporary Social Gerontology: Significant Development in the Field of Aging*. Springfield, Il.: Charles C. Thomas, Publisher, 1976.

Bellak, Leopold and Toksoz B. Karasu, eds., *Geriatric Psychiatry: A Handbook for Psychiatrists and Primary Care Physicians*. New York: Grune and Stratton, 1976.

Binstock, Robert H. and Ethel Shanas, *Handbook of Aging and the Social Sciences*. New York: Van Nostrand Reinhold Co., 1976.

Birren, James E. and K. Warner Schaie, *Handbook of the Psychology of Aging*. New York: Van Nostrand Reinhold Co., 1977.

Bonner, Charles D., *Homburger and Bonner's Medical Care and Rehabilitation of the Aged and Chronically Ill*, 3rd ed. Boston: Little, Brown & Co., 1974.

Brantl, Virginia M. and Sr. Marie R. Brown, eds., *Readings in Gerontology*. St. Louis: The C. V. Mosby Co., 1973.

Brearly, C. Paul, *Social Work, Aging and Society*. Boston: Routledge & Kegan Paul, 1975.

Brocklehurst, J. C. and T. Hanley, *Geriatric Medicine for Students*. Edinburgh and London: Churchill Livingston, Medical Division, Longman Group, 1976.

Brocklehurst, J. C., ed., *Textbook of Geriatric Medicine and Gerontology*, 2nd ed. Edinburgh and London: Churchill Livingston, Medical Division, Longman Group, 1978.

Brody, Elaine M., *Long-Term Care of Older People: A Practical Guide*. New York: Human Sciences Press, 1977.

Brown, Leo E. and E. O. Ellis, eds., *The Later Years*. Littleton, Mass.: Publishing Sciences Group, 1975.

Burnside, Irene M., ed., *Psychosocial Nursing Care of the Aged*. New York: McGraw-Hill Book Co., Blakiston Publications, 1973.

——, *Sexuality and Aging*. Los Angeles: University of Southern California, Ethel Percy Andrus Gerontology Center, 1975.

——, *Nursing and the Aged*. New York: McGraw-Hill Book Co., 1976.

——, *Working with the Elderly: Group Process and Techniques*. North Scituate, Mass.: Duxbury Press, 1978.

Burnside, Irene M., P. Ebersole, and H. E. Monea, eds., *Psychosocial Caring throughout the Life Span*. New York: McGraw-Hill Book Co., 1979.

Busse, Ewald W., and Eric Pfeiffer, eds., *Behavior Adaptation in Late Life*, 2nd ed. Boston: Little, Brown & Co., 1977.

Butler, Robert N., *Why Survive? Being Old in America*. New York: Harper & Row, Publishers, 1975.

Butler, Robert M. and Myrna I. Lewis, *Aging and Mental Health*, 2nd ed. St. Louis: The C. V. Mosby Company, 1977.

Cape, R. D. T., ed., *Symposia on Geriatric Medicine*, vol. 1. Birmingham, England: West Midland Institute of Geriatric Medicine and Gerontology, 1972.

——, *Symposia on Geriatric Medicine*, vol. 2, Birmingham, England: West Midland Institute of Geriatric Medicine and Gerontology, 1973.

——, *Symposia on Geriatric Medicine*, vol. 3, Birmingham, England: West Midland Institute of Geriatric Medicine and Gerontology, 1974.

Caughill, Rita E., ed., *The Dying Patient: A Supportive Approach*. Boston: Little, Brown & Co., 1976.

Colavita, Francis B., *Sensory Changes in the Elderly*. Springfield, Il.: Charles C Thomas, Publisher, 1978.

Davis, Richard H., ed., *Aging Prospects and Issues*, rev. Los Angeles: University of Southern California Press, Ethel Percy Andrus Gerontology Center, 1977.

Eisdorfer, Carl and W. E. Farr, eds., *Psychopharmacology and Aging*. New York: Plenum Publishing Corp., 1972.

Ethnicity and Health Care. New York: National League for Nursing (Pub. No. 14-1625), 1976.

Fields, W. S., *Neurological and Sensory Disorders in the Elderly*. New York: Stratton Intercontinental Medical Book Corp., 1975.

Finch, Caleb E. and Leonard Hayflick, *Handbook of the Biology of Aging*. New York: Van Nostrand Reinhold Co., 1977.

Goldman, Ralph and Morris Rockstein, eds., *The Physiology and Pathology of Human Aging*. New York: Academic Press, 1975.

Goldsmith, J., and S. Goldsmith, *Crime and the Elderly*. Lexington, Mass.: D. C. Heath & Co., 1976.

Gubrium, Jaber F., ed., *Late Life Communities and Environmental Policy*. Springfield, Il.: Charles C Thomas, Publisher, 1974.

——, *Time, Role and Self in Old Age*. New York: Human Sciences Press, 1976.

Harris, Raymond, *The Management of Geriatric Cardiovascular Disease*. Philadelphia: J. B. Lippincott Co., 1970.

Hershey, Daniel, *Life Span and Factors Affecting It: Aging Theories in Gerontology*. Springfield, Il.: Charles C Thomas, Publisher, 1974.

Herzog, Barbara R., ed., *Aging and Income: Programs and Prospects for the Elderly*. New York: Human Sciences Press, 1978.

Hymovich, D. and M. Barnard, *Family Health Care*. New York: McGraw-Hill Book Co., 1973.

Kalish, Richard A. and David K. Reynolds, *Death and Ethnicity: A Psychocultural Study*. Los Angeles: University of Southern California Press, Ethel Percy Andrus Gerontology Center, 1976.

Kayne, Ronald C., ed., *Drugs and the Elderly*, rev. Los Angeles: University of Southern California Press, Ethel Percy Andrus Gerontology Center, 1978.

Kerschner, Paul A., ed., *Advocacy and the Age: Issues, Experiences, Strategies*. Los Angeles: University of Southern California Press, Ethel Percy Andrus Gerontology Center, 1976.

Kubler-Ross, Elizabeth, *Death: The Final Stage of Growth*. Englewood Cliffs, N.J.: Prentice-Hall, 1975.

LaPatra, J. W., *Public Welfare Systems*. Springfield, Il.: Charles C Thomas, Publisher, 1975.

Legal Issues Affecting the Older Woman in America Today. Los Angeles: National Senior Citizens Law Center, 1975.

Medical Clinics of North America. Philadelphia: W. B. Saunders Co., 1976.

Nassau, Jean B., *Choosing a Nursing Home*. New York: Funk & Wagnalls, 1975.

Neugarten, Bernice L., ed., *Middle Age and Aging: A Reader in Social Psychology*. Chicago: University of Chicago Press, 1968.

Oyer, H. J. and E. J. Oyer, *Aging and Communication*. Baltimore, Md.: University Park Press, 1976.

Papers from the Economics of Aging: Toward 2001. (Ann Arbor, Mich.: Institute of Gerontology, The University of Michigan–Wayne State University, 1976).

Peterson, James A., *On Being Alone: Guide for Widowed Persons*. Washington, D.C.: Action for Independent Maturity, 1973.

Peterson, James A. and Barbara Payne, *Love in the Later Years: The Emotional, Physical, Sexual and Social Potential for the Elderly*. Wilton, Conn.: Association Press, 1975.

Political Consequences of Aging. Philadelphia: Annals of the American Academy of Political and Social Science, vol. 415, September 1974.

Portwood, Doris, *A Right to Suicide?* New York: Dodd, Mead & Co., 1978.

Reichel, William, ed., *Clinical Aspects of Aging*. Baltimore, Md.: Williams & Wilkins Co., 1978.

Rockstein, M. and M. Sussman, eds., *Nutrition, Longevity and Aging*. New York: Academic Press, 1976.

Rossman, Isadore, ed., *Clinical Geriatrics*. Philadelphia: J. B. Lippincott Co., 1971.

Schulz, J. H., *The Economics of Aging*. Belmont, Ca.: Wadsworth Publishing Co., 1976.

Senior Legal Rights Project, *Senior Legal Rights Manual: A Layman's Handbook*. Chicago: American Friends Service Committee, 1976.

Shanas, Ethel, Peter Townsend, and others, *Old People in Three Industrial Societies*. New York: Lieber-Atherton, 1968.

Shanas, Ethel and Marvin B. Sussman, eds., *Family, Bureaucracy and the Elderly*. Durham, N.C.: Duke University Press, 1977.

Silverstone, Barbara and Helen K. Hyman, *You and Your Aging Parent*. New York: Pantheon Books, 1976.

Social Security Handbook, 5th ed. Washington, D.C.: U.S. Department of Health, Education and Welfare, Social Security Administration, February 1974. (DHEW Publication no. (S.S.A. 73-10135.)

Solnick, Robert L., ed., *Sexuality and Aging*, rev. Los Angeles: University of Southern California Press, Ethel Percy Andrus Gerontology Center, 1978.

Spencer, M. G. and C. J. Dorr, eds., *Understanding Aging: A Multidisciplinary Approach*. New York: Appleton-Century-Crofts, A Publishing Division of Prentice-Hall, 1975.

Stevenson, JoAnn S., *Issues and Crises During Middlescence*. New York: Appleton-Century-Crofts, A Publishing Division of Prentice-Hall, 1977.

Stoddard, Sandol, *The Hospice Movement: A Better Way of Caring for the Dying*. Briarcliff Manor, N.Y.: Stein & Day Publishers, 1978.

Timiras, P. S., *Developmental Physiology and Aging*. New York: Macmillan, 1972.

Wey, Ruth B., *Nutrition and the Later Years*. Los Angeles: University of Southern California Press, Ethel Percy Andrus Gerontology Center, 1977.

Weiss, Jonathan A., ed., *Law of the Elderly*. New York: Practicing Law Institute, 1977.

Whitehead, J. M., *Psychiatric Disorders in Old Age: A Handbook for the Clinical Team*. New York: Springer Publishing Co., 1974.

Williams, Robert H., ed., *To Live and to Die: When, Why and How*. New York: Springer-Verlag, 1974.

Wilson, Sally H., *The Nursing Home Law Handbook*. Los Angeles: National Senior Citizens Law Center, 1975.

Woodruff, Diana S. and James Birren, eds., *Aging: Scientific Perspectives and Social Issues*. New York: Van Nostrand Reinhold Co., 1975.

Woodruff, Diana S., *Can You Live to be 100?* New York: Chatham Square Press, 1977.

Articles

Cardiovascular

Alford, W. D., Jr., "The Spectrum of Ventricular Aneurysms," *Heart Lung*, March–April 1973, 74–80.

Baker, W. H. and R. W. Barnes, "Revitalizing the Ischemic Limb," *Geriatrics*, December 1973, 56–60.

Burch, G. E., "Interesting Aspects of Geriatric Cardiology," *American Heart Journal* 89 (1975), 99–114.

——, "The Special Problems of Heart Disease in Old People," *Geriatrics*, February 1977, 51–54.

Burch, G. E. and N. P. DePasquale, "Geriatric Cardiology," *American Heart Journal 78* (1969), 700–708.

Bryant, R. B., "The Nursing Care and Management of Coronary Grafts," *Australian Nurses Journal*, November 1973, 24–26.

Courtes, T. S., "Pacemakers Today: All About Various Kinds, Nursing Implications and Counselling Problems," *Nursing '74*, February 1974, 23–29.

Dietzman, T. H. and others, "Pharmacologic and Mechanical Support for Managing Cardiogenic Shock," *Geriatrics*, December 1973, 69–79.

Ehtisham, M. and R. D. T. Cape, "Protocol for Diagnosing and Treating Anemia," *Geriatrics*, November 1977, 91–94 and 97–99.

Germain, C. P., "Helping Your Patient with an Implanted Pacemaker," *RN*, August 1974, 30–35.

Harris, Raymond, "Cardiopathy of Aging: Are the Changes Related to Congestive Heart Failure," *Geriatrics*, February 1977, 42–46.

Pool, P. E. and E. Braunwald, "Fundamental Mechanisms in Congestive Heart Failure," *American Journal of Cardiology*, 22 (1968), 7-15.

Pomerance, A., "Aging Changes in Human Heart Valves," *British Heart Journal*, 1967, 222.

——, "The Many Facets of Cardiac Pathology," *Geriatrics*, November 1973, 110-115.

Ritchie, M., "Heart Failure–The Geriatric Patient," *Nursing Clinics of North America*, December 1968, 663-674.

"Recognizing the 'Silent' Secondary Factor," *Geriatrics*, November 1973, 146, 147, and 150.

Stamler, J. and R. N. Epstein, "Coronary Heart Disease: Risk Factors as Guides to Preventive Action," *Preventive Medicine* 27 (1972), 48.

Syzek, B. J., "Cardiovascular Changes in Aging: Implications for Nursing," *Journal of Gerontological Nursing*, January-February 1976, 28-32.

Uesu, Chisher T., "The Problem of Dizziness and Syncope in Old Age: TIA vs Hypersensitive Carotid Sinus Reflex," *Journal of American Gerontological Society* 29 (March 1976), 126-135.

Verd, Z. and others, "Complications of Cardiac Pacemakers: Diagnosis and Management," *Geriatrics*, January 1975, 38-44.

Chronicity

Brickner, Philip W. and others, "Hospital Home Health Care Program Aids Isolated, Homebound Elderly," *Hospitals*, November 1976, 117-118, 120, 122.

——, "Outreach to Welfare Hotels, the Homebound, the Frail," *American Journal of Nursing*, May 1976, 762-764.

Felleson, J. A., "New Environment for Nursing Care: The Clinical Ecology Unit," *R.N.*, March 1977, 49-57.

Felstein, I., "After Care of Chronic Disease Following Hospital Discharge," *Midwife Health Visitor and Community Nurse*, August 1977, 257-260.

Halstead, L. S., "Team Care in Chronic Illness: A Critical Review of the Literature of the Past 25 Years," *Archives of Physical Medicine and Rehabilitation*, November 1976, 507-511.

Jaffe, E., "Letter of Seminar Students in 'Methods of Intervention with the Aging,'" *Death Education*, 1977, 325-337.

Jonsen, Albert R., "Dying Right in California," *Clinical Research* (Official Publication of the American Federation for Clinical Research), 26:2 (February 1978), 55-60.

MacVicar, M. G. and others, "A Framework for Family Assessment in Chronic Illness," *Nursing Forum*, 1976, 180-194.

Sabin, J. E., "Research Findings on Chronic Mental Illness: A Model for Continuing Care in the Health Maintenance Organization," *Comprehensive Psychiatry*, 17:1 (January-February 1978), 83-95.

Saunders, C., "A Therapeutic Community–St. Christopher's Hospice," in Bernard Schoenberg and others, eds., *Psychological Aspects of Terminal Care*. New York: Columbia University Press, 1972, 275-288.

Dental health and care

Block, Phillip, "Dental Health in Hospitalized Patients," *American Journal of Nursing*, July 1976, 1162-1164.

Borman, William, "Guidelines for Geriatric Dentistry," *Journal of the Indiana Dental Associates*, December 1972, 184-187.

Elfenbaum, B. A., "Who Are Our Elderly Patients, Parts I and II," *Dental Digest*, April 1971, 74-90.

Ettinger, R. L., "Dental Care of the Elderly," *Nursing Times* 71 (January 26, 1975), 1003-1006.

Franks, A., "The Mouth in Old Age," *Nursing Times*, October 4, 1973, 1292-1293.

Garverick, C. M. and others, "The Geriatric Patient," *Dental Clinics of North America*, July 1977, 637-645.

Kaplin, H., "The Oral Cavity in Geriatrics," *Geriatrics*, December 1971, 96-102.

Levin, Bernard, "Special Considerations for the Geriatric Complete Denture Patient," *Journal of the American Society for Geriatric Dentistry*, October 1970, 24-28.

Lotzkar, S., "Dental Care for the Aged," *Journal of Public Health Dentistry*, Summer 1977, 201-208.

Massler, Maury, "Oral Aspects of Aging," *Post Graduate Medicine*, January 1971, 179-183.

Murphy, W. M., "The Effects of Complete Dentures upon Taste Perception," *Journal of British Dentistry*, April 2, 1971, 94-98.

Palmer, J. D., "Dental Care for Elderly Patients," *Journal of British Dentistry*, July 19, 1977, 59-62.

Ramsey, W. O., "The Role of Nutrition in Conditioning Edentulous Patients," *Journal of Prosthetic Dentures*, February 1970, 40-48.

Ethnoculture

Clark, Margaret M., "Contributions of Cultural Anthropology to the Study of the Aged," in Laura Nader, and T. W. Maretzki, ed., *Cultural Illness and Health Essays in Human Adaptation*, Anthropology Studies #9 (Washington, D.C.: American Anthropology Association, 1973), 78-88.

Cohen, Elias and others, "Minority Aged in America," Occasional Paper No. 10. Ann Arbor, Mich.: Institute of Gerontology, University of Michigan-Wayne State University, 1971.

Delgado, Maria and G. E. Finley, "The Spanish Speaking Elderly: A Bibliography," *Gerontologist*, 18:4 (August 1978), 387-394.

Fabrega, H., "The Study of Disease in Relation to Culture," *Behavior Science*, 17 (1972), 183-203.

Jackson, Jacquelyne J., "Sex and Social Class Variations in Black Aged Parent-Adult Child Relationships," *Aging and Human Development* 2:2 (May 1971), 96-107.

Moriwaki, Sharon, "Ethnicity and Aging," in Irene M. Burnside, ed., *Nursing and the Aged* (New York: McGraw-Hill Book Co., 1976), 543-558.

Special Issue on Minority Aging, *Gerontologist*, Spring 1971.

Foods and nutrition

Berger, Ruth, "Nutritional Needs of the Aged," in Irene M. Barnside, ed., *Nursing and the Aged* (New York: McGraw-Hill Book Co. 1976), 113-122.

Bozian, M. W., "Nutrition for the Aged or Aged Nutrition?" *Nursing Clinics of North America*, March 1976, 169-177.

Carson, J. A. and others, "Taste Acuity and Food Attitudes of Selected Patients with Cancer," *Journal of the American Dietetic Association*, April 1977, 361-365.

Dwyer, L. S. and others, "Simplified Meal Planning for Hard-to-Teach Patients," *American Journal of Nursing*, April 1974, 664-665.

Exton-Smith, A. N., "Vitamins and the Elderly," in W. Ferguson Anderson and T. G. Judge, eds., *Geriatric Medicine* (London and New York: Academic Press, 1974), 247-264.

Hanson, R. Galen, "Considering Social Nutrition in Assessing Geriatric Nutrition," *Geriatrics*, March 1978, 49-51.

Harper, A. E., "Recommended Dietary Allowances for the Elderly," *Geriatrics*, May 1978, 73–75 and 79–80.

Hartahorn, Edward A., "Food and Drug Interactions," *Journal of the American Dietetic Association*, January 1977, 15–19.

Kritcheresky, D., "Are Dietary Components Risk Factors in Atherosclerosis?" *Geriatrics*, May 1978, 35–39.

MacDonald, J. S. and P. S. Schein, "Mechanisms and Management of Malnutrition Sites in Patients with Cancer," *Clinical Gastroenterology*, September 1976, 309–326.

Mann, George V., "Relationship of Age to Nutrient Requirements," *American Journal of Clinical Nutrition*, October 1973, 1150–1152.

Schlenker, E. D. and others, "Nutrition and Health of Older People," *American Journal of Clinical Nutrition*, October 1973, 1110–1119.

Shewood, Sylvia, "Sociology of Food and Eating: Implications for Action for the Elderly," *American Journal of Clinical Nutrition*, October 1973, 1108–1110.

Shifflett, P. A., "Folklore and Food Habits," *Journal of the American Dietetic Association*, 63:4 (April 1976), 347–350.

Steinberg, W. M. and P. P. Taskes, "A Practical Approach to Evaluating Maldigestion and Malabsorption," *Geriatrics*, July 1978, 73–78 and 82–85.

"Symposium on Nutrition," *Geriatrics*, May 1974.

Taylor, T. G., "Adding Protein, Subtracting Carbohydrate, Equals Better Nutrition," *Geriatrics*, November 1973, 154–156.

Thompson, F. F., "Dietary Problems in the Older Patient," *The Practitioner*, November 1975, 632–640.

Todhunter, E. N., "Life Style and Nutrient Intake in the Elderly," *Current Concepts of Nutrition*, January 1976, 119–127.

Todhurst, E. N. and W. J. Darby, "Guidelines for Maintaining Adequate Nutrition in Old Age," *Geriatrics*, June 1978, 49–51 and 54–56.

Troll, L. E., "Eating and Aging," *Journal of the American Dietetic Association*, November 1971, 456–459.

Weinberg, Jack, "Psychological Implication of the Nutritional Needs of the Elderly," *Journal of the American Dietetic Association*, April 1972, 293–296.

Wilson, T. C., "A Study of Vitamin C Levels in the Aged and Subsequent Mortality, *Gerontological Clinica* 14 (1972), 17–24.

Legal–economic

"Age Discrimination in Employment Act Amendments of 1978," *United States Law Week* May 9, 1978, 43.

Atchley, Robert C., "Adjustment to Loss of Job at Retirement," *International Journal of Aging and Human Development*, 1975, 17–27.

Ball, Robert M., "Federal Income Policy toward Elderly Neglects Chronically Ill," *Hospital Progress*, November 1976, 64–67 and 98.

Glamser, Francis and Gordon DeJong, "The Efficacy of Preretirement Preparation Programs for Industrial Workers," *Journal of Gerontology* 30:5 (September 1975), 595–600.

Goldsmith, J., "A Symposium on Crime and the Elderly," *Police Chief*, February 1976, 18–51 and 69.

Miller, Michael B., "Clinical Implications of Medicare upon an Extended Care Facility Population," *The Gerontologist*, 13:2 (Summer 1973), 171–172.

Randolph, D., "Sex Discrimination in the Family Benefits Section of the Social Security Act," *Clearinghouse Review* 8 (1974), 535–540.

Illness and clinical management

Bercaw, B. L., "When Loss of Consciousness is Not Caused by Epilepsy," *Geriatrics*, July 1976. 95–97.

Brody, Stanley J., "Evolving Health Delivery Systems and Older People," *American Journal of Public Health*, 64:3 (March 1974), 245–247.

Burnside, I. M., "Accountrements of Aging," *Nursing Clinics of North America*, June 1972, 291–301.

Cantor, Arthur, "How to Do Office-Based Screening for Ogranic Brain Disorders," *Geriatrics*, November 1978, 86–88 and 91.

Chopin, S. F., "Changes in Protein Metabolism with Age Affect Rehabilitation Potential," *Geriatrics*, May 1976, 52–57.

Davis, B., ". . . Until Death Ensues," *Nursing Clinics of North America*, June 1972, 303–309.

Donta, Saunt, "The Risk of Diarrhea and Colitis with Antibiotic Therapy," *Geriatrics*, March 1977, 103–106.

Duncan, T. G., "Diabetes: Diagnosis and Management in the Older Patient," *Geriatrics*, October 1976, 51.

Eton, Burce, "Gynecologic Surgery in Elderly Women," *Geratrics* 28:11 (November 1973), 119–123.

Faludi, Georgina, "Controlling Diabetes with Diet and Oral Hypoglycemic Agents," *Geriatrics*, October 1976, 67–70.

Fordyce, Wilbert E., "Evaluating and Managing Chronic Pain," *Geriatrics*, January 1978, 59–62.

Gerber, Irwin and others, "Anticipatory Grief and Aged Widows and Widowers," *Journal of Gerontology* 30:2 (March 1975), 225–229.

Greer, Melvin, "Uncommon Causes of Stroke, Part I: Diseases at the Vessel Wall," *Geriatrics*, December 1977, 28–32 and 39–41.

——, "Uncommon Causes of Stroke, Part 2: Changes in Blood Constituents and Hemodynamic Factors," *Geriatrics*, January 1978, 51–56.

Keim, Robert J., "Evaluating the Patient with Dysequilibrium," *Geriatrics*, January 1978, 87–92.

Kent, Saul, "The Aging Lung, Part I: Loss of Elasticity," *Geriatrics*, February 1978, 124, 126, 129, and 132.

——, "Decline of Pulmonary Function," *Geriatrics*, March 1978, 100, 104, 107, and 111.

Kohn, P., "Risks of Operation in Patients over 80," *Geriatrics*, November 1975, 100–105.

Libow, Lesli S., "Pseudo-Senility: Acute and Reversible Organic Brain Syndromes," *Journal of the American Geriatrics Society* 21 (1973), 112–120.

Melzack, Ronal and Paul Taenzer, "Concepts of Pain Perception and Therapy," *Geriatrics*, November 1977, 44–48.

Meng, H. C., "Parental Nutrition: Principles, Nutrient Requirements and Techniques," *Geriatrics*, September 1975, 97–102.

Nelson, R. S., "Gastrointestinal Carcinoma: Diagnosis, Staging and Follow-Up," *Geriatrics*, September 1976, 83–85.

Parsons, M. C. and others, "Post-operative Complications: Assessment and Intervention," *American Journal of Nursing*, February 1974, 240–244.

Pierson, D. J. and others, "Ventilatory Management of the Elderly," *Geriatrics*, November 1973, 86–95.

Ringrose, C. A. Douglas, "Geriatric Gynecologic Problems Increasing," *Geriatrics*, March 1978, 89–91.

Schuster, Marvin M., "Disorders of the Aging GI System," *Hospital Practice*, September 1976, 95–103.

Shuman, C. R. and O. E. Owen, "When and How to Use Insulin in the Elderly Diabetic," *Geriatrics*, October 1967, 75–79.

Sklar, M., "Functional Bowel Distress and Constipation in the Aged," *Geriatrics*, September 1972, 79–85.

Szauer, J. S. and C. Zukaukas, "The Problems of Abdominal Operations in the Elderly Patients," *Geriatrics*, September 1975, 57–59 and 63–64.

Thomas, K. P., "Diabetes Mellitus in Elderly Persons," *Nursing Clinics of North America*, March 1976, 157–168.

Webster, James and Richard Davison, "Aspiration Pneumonitis: A Serious Problem," *Geriatrics*, December 1977, 42–47.

Mental health, illness, and therapies

Barns, Eleanor and others, "Guidelines to Treatment Approaches," *The Gerontologist* 13:4 (Winter 1973), 513–527.

Brenner, C. and others, "The Concept and Phenomenology of Depression, with Special Reference to the Aged," *Journal of Geriatric Psychiatry* 7:1 (1974), 3–83.

Burnside, Irene M., "Multiple Losses in the Aged: Implications for Nursing Care," *The Gerontologist*, Summer 1973, 157–162.

——, "Caring for the Aged: Touching is Talking," *American Journal of Nursing*, December 1973, 2060–2063.

——, "Mental Health in the Aged," in Irene M. Burnside, ed., *Nursing and the Aged* (New York: McGraw-Hill Book Co., 1976), 136–147.

Busse, Ewald W., "Hypochondriasis in the Elderly: A Reaction to Social Stress," *Journal of American Geriatrics Society* 24:4, April 1976, 145–149.

Butler, Robert N., "Mental Health and Aging Life Cycle Perspectives," *Geriatrics*, November 1974, 59–60.

Cohen, Carl I., "Nocturnal Neurosis of the Elderly: Failure of Agencies to Cope with the Problem," *Journal of the American Geriatrics Society*, 24:2 February 1976, 86–88.

Conti, M., "The Loneliness of Old Age," *Nursing Outlook*, August 1970, 28–30.

Dénes, Z., "Old Age Emotions," *Journal of the American Geriatrics Society*, 24:10, October 1976, 465–467.

Ebersole, Priscilla E., "Reminiscing and Group Psychotherapy with the Aged," in Irene M. Burnside, ed., *Nursing and the Aged* (New York: McGraw-Hill Book Co., 1976), 214–230.

Ebersole, Priscilla P., "Crisis Intervention with the Aged," in Irene M. Burnside, ed., *Nursing and the Aged* (New York: McGraw-Hill Book Co., 1976), 270–282.

Gaitz, Charles M. and Judith Scott, "Mental Health of Mexican-Americans: Do Ethnic Factors Make a Difference?" *Geriatrics*, November 1974, 103–110.

Godber, Colin, "The Confused Elderly," *Nursing Times*, July 15, 1976, 7–8 and 10.

Haggerty, Judith, "Suicide in the Aging: Suicidal Behavior in a 70 Year-Old Man: A Case Report and Discussion," *Journal of Geriatric Psychiatry* 6:1, 1973, 43–69.

Hennessey, Mary J., "Music and Group Work with the Aged," in Irene M. Burnside, ed., *Nursing and the Aged* (New York: McGraw-Hill Book Co., 1976), 225–269.

Lee, R., "Self Images of the Elderly," *Nursing Clinics of North America*, March 1976, 119–124.

Lehnian, E., "Reality Orientation," *Nursing '74* (March 1974), 61–62.

Lewis, C. N., "Reminiscing and Self-Concept in Old Age," *Journal of Gerontology*, April 1971, 240–243.

——, "The Adaptive Value of Reminiscing in Old Age," *Journal of Geriatric Psychiatry* 6:1 (1973), 117–121.

Lewis, Myrna I. and Robert N. Butler, "Life Review Therapy: Putting Memories to Work in Individual and Group Psychotherapy," *Geriatrics* 29:11 (November 1974), 165-173.

Libow, Leslie, S., "Pseudo-Senility: Acute and Reversible Organic Brain Syndromes," *Journal of the American Geriatrics Society*, March 1973, 112-120.

Mayfield, D., "Managing Alcohol Problems in Geriatric Patients," *Nursing Care*, July 1974, 10-11.

Oberleder, M., "Emotional Breakdowns in Elderly People," *Hospital and Community Psychiatry*, July 1969, 21-26.

——, "Managing Problem Behaviors of Elderly Patients," *Hospital and Community Psychiatry*, May 1976, 325-330.

Opler, Marvin K., "Anthropological Aspects," in John T. Hawells ed. *Modern Perspectives in Psychiatry of Old Age*. (New York: Brunner/Mazel Publishers, 1975), 32-49.

Palmore, E. and V. Kivett, "Change in Life Satisfaction: A Longitudinal Study of Persons Aged 46-70," *Journal of Gerontology*, 32:3 (May 1977), 311-316.

Preston, T., "When Words Fail," *American Journal of Nursing*, December 1973, 2064-2065.

Rosin, A. J. and others, "The Influence of Emotional Reaction on the Course of Fatal Illness," *Geriatrics*, July 1976, 87-90.

Schulz, Richard and Gail Brenner, "Relocation of the Aged: A Review and Theoretical Analysis," *Journal of Gerontology*, May 1977, 323-333.

"Suicide in the Aging," *Journal of Geriatric Psychiatry* 6:1 (1973), 7-69.

Tuason, V. B., "Recognizing and Treating Depression," *Geriatrics*, December 1973, 99-102.

Taulbee, Lucille R., "Reality Orientation and the Aged," in Irene M. Burnside, ed., *Nursing and the Aged* (New York: McGraw-Hill Book Co., 1976), 245-254.

Turner, Thomas B., "Beer and Wine for Geriatric Patients," *Journal of the American Medical Association* 226:7 (Nov. 12, 1973), 779-780.

Volope, A. and R. Kastenbaum, "Beer and TLC," *American Journal of Nursing*, January 1967, 100-103.

Wahl, P. R., "Psychosocial Implications of Disorientation in the Elderly," *Nursing Clinics of North America*, March 1976, 145-155.

Miscellaneous

Alford, D. M., "The Affluent Elderly: Problems in Nursing," *Journal of Gerontological Nursing*, March-April 1978, 44-47.

Beverly, Virginia, "Lifelong Learning—A Concept Whose Time Has Come," *Geriatrics*, August 1976, 114-127.

Blazer, D., "Techniques for Communicating with Your Elderly Patient," *Geriatrics*, November 1978, 79-80 and 83-84.

Carlson, S., "Communication and Social Interaction in the Aged," *Nursing Clinics of North America*, June 1972, 269-279.

Gress, L., "Age vs. Agism," *Nursing '73*, 6-7.

Hayter, J., "Biologic Changes of Aging," *Nursing Forum*, 3:3 (1974), 289-308.

Jennings, M. and others, "Physiologic Functioning of the Elderly," *Nursing Clinics of North America*, June 1972, 237-252.

Kohnke, Mary F., "The Nurse's Responsibility to the Consumer," *American Journal of Nursing*, March 1978, 440-442.

Langer, Anselm, "Oral Signs of Aging and their Clinical Significance," *Geriatrics*, December 1976, 63-69.

Lemon, Bruce and others, "An Exposition of the Activity Theory of Aging: Activity Types and Life Satisfaction Among In-Movers to a Retirement Community," *Journal of Gerontology* 27 (October 1972), 511-523.

Lewis, Roger, "Anemia–A Common but Never a Normal Concomitant of Aging," *Geriatrics*, December 1976, 53–56 and 59–60.

McKenzie, H., "Help for the Single Woman with Elderly Dependents," *Nursing Times*, February 16, 1978, 292–293.

Parsons, Victor, "What Decreasing Renal Function Means to Aging Patients," *Geriatrics*, January 1977, 93–99.

Schwab, M., "Caring for the Aged," *American Journal of Nursing*, December 1973, 2049–2053.

Sherman, D., "Geriatrics: An Emerging Challenge to the Health Professions," *Journal of the American Geriatrics Society*, March 1971, 199–207.

Sonnefeld, J., "Dealing with the Aging Work Force," *Harvard Business Review*, 56:6 (November–December 1978), 81–92.

Tallmer, M., "A Current Issue in Social Gerontology," *Journal of Geriatric Psychiatry* 6:1 (1973), 99–108.

Nursing homes

Beverley, E. V., "Nursing Homes Matching the Facility to the Patients's Needs," *Geriatrics*, April 1975, 100–106 and 110.

——, "Helping Your Patient Choose and Adjust to a Nursing Home," *Geriatrics*, May 1976, 115, 118–120, and 125–126.

Edmond, S., "Baycrest Geriatric Centre: A Continuum of Care," *Canadian Nurse*, April 1977, 52–53.

Lawton, M. P., "Institutions and Alternatives for Older People," *Health and Social Work* 3:2 (May 1978), 108–134.

Libow, Leslie S. "Another Type of Iatragenic Problem," *Geriatrics*, March 1977, 92, 94, and 99.

Pablo, Renato Y., "Intra-Institutional Relocation: Its Impact on Long-term Care Patients," *The Gerontologist* 17:5 (1977), 426–435.

Poe, William D. and H. Laurence Rice, "Friendship Manor: A Community Geriatrics Model," *Journal of American Geriatric Society*, June 1976, 283–284.

Snyder, L. H., "Environmental Changes for Socialization," *Journal of Nursing Administration*, January 1978, 44–50.

Taseland, R. and J. Rasch, "Factors Contributing to Older Persons' Satisfaction with Their Community," *Gerontologist* 18:4, (August 1978), 395–402.

Williams, T. F. and others, "Appropriate Placement of the Chronically Ill and Aged," *Journal of the American Medical Association* 226:1 (December 10, 1973), 1332–1335.

Wooldrige, D. B., "The Geriatric Institution as a Therapeutic Modality," *Canadian Medical Association Journal*, July 1976, 27–29.

Pharmacological therapeutics and management

Blackwell, B., "Drug Therapy and Patient Compliance," *New England Journal of Medicine*, 289 (August 2, 1973), 249–252.

Brown, M. M. "Drug-Drug Interactions among Residents in Homes for the Elderly," *Nursing Research* 26:1 (1977), 47–52.

Cheraskin, E. and others, "Daily Vitamin C Consumption and Fatigability," *Journal of American Geriatric Society*, March 1976, 136–137.

Davidson, J. R., "Trial of Self-Medication in the Elderly," *Nursing Times*, March 14, 1974, 391–392.

Davidson, William, "Pitfalls to Avoid in Prescribing Drugs for the Elderly," *Geriatrics*, August 1975, 157-158.

Frohlich, E. D., "Use and Abuse of Diuretics," (editorial), *American Heart Journal*, January 1975, 1-3.

Gillum, R. and A. Barsky, "Diagnosis and Management of Patient Noncompliance." *Journal of the American Medical Association* 228:12 (June 17, 1974), 1563-1567.

Hanan, Z. I., "Geriatric Medications: How the Aged are Hurt by Drugs Meant to Help," *RN*, January 1978, 57-60.

Hollister, L. E., "Prescribing Drugs for the Elderly," *Geriatrics*, August 1977, 71-73.

Hulka, B. and others, "Communication, Compliance, and Concordance between Physicians and Patients with Prescribed Medications," *American Journal of Public Health*, September 1976, 847-853.

Isler, C., "Teaching the Elderly to Avoid Accidental Drug Abuse," *RN*, November 1977, 39-42.

Korcok, M., "Drugs and the Elderly," *Canadian Medical Association Journal*, May 20, 1978, 1320 and 1325-1326.

Libow, L. S. and B. Mehl, "Self Administration of Medications by Patients in Hospitals or Extended Care Facilities," *Journal of American Geriatric Society* 18 (1970), 81-85.

Lenhart, D. G., "The Use of Medications in the Elderly Population," *Nursing Clinics of North America*, March 1976, 135-143.

Lyle, W. M., "Drugs Prescribed for the Elderly," *American Journal of Optometry and Physiological Optics*, August 1977, 1029-1032.

Lyle, W. M. and D. A. Hayhoe, "A Literature Survey of the Potentially Adverse Effects of the Drugs Commonly Prescribed for the Elderly," *American Journal of Optometry and Physiological Optics*, June 1976, 768-778.

——, "Adverse Effects of the Drugs Most Frequently Administered to the Elderly—Part II," *American Journal of Optometry and Physiological Optics*, September 1976, 1132-1140.

MacLennan, W., "Dangerous Drugs," *Nursing Times*, July 15, 1976, 12.

Marston, M. V., "Compliance with Medical Regimens: A Review of the Literature," *Nursing Research* 19 (July -August 1970, 312-323.

Means, B. J. and P. P. Lamy, "Diagnostic Tests, Drugs and the Geriatric Patient," *Journal of the American Geriatric Society*, June 1974, 258-264.

Mollering, R. C., "Factors Influencing the Clinical Use of Antimicrobil Agents in Elderly Patients," *Geriatrics*, February 1978, 83-85 and 89-91.

Morrant, J. C. "Medicine and Mental Illness in Old Age," *Canadian Psychiatric Association Journal*, June 1975, 309-312.

Olson, J. and J. Johnson, "Drug Misuse among the Elderly," *Journal of Gerontological Nursing* 4:6 (November-December 1978), 11-14.

Plant, J., "Educating the Elderly in Self-Medication Use," *Hospitals*, April 16, 1977, 100-102.

Podell, R. N. and L. R. Gary, "Compliance: A Problem in Medical Management," *American Family Physician*, April 1976, 74-80.

Richey, D. P. and others, "Pharmokinetic Consequences of Aging," *Annual Review of Pharmacology Toxicology* 17 (1977), 49-65.

Rodman, J. J., "Adjusting Medications for the Needs of the Elderly," *RN*, May 1975, 65-67, 70, 72-74, 78, 80, 82, 84, 86, and 89.

Rogers, M. J., "Drug Abuse—Just What the Doctor Ordered," *Psychology Today*, September 1971, 16-24.

Rosenow, E. C., "Drugs That May Induce Pulmonary Disease," *Geriatrics*, January 1978, 64-68 and 73.

Schwartz, Doris and others, "Medication Errors Made by Elderly Chronically Ill Patients," *American Journal of Public Health*, December 1962, 2018–2029.

Shields, E. M., "Introduction to Drug Therapy for Older Adults," *Journal of Gerontological Nursing*, March–April 1975, 8–13.

Webb-Johnson, David C., "When Drug Therapy for Lung Disease Affects the Heart," *Geriatrics*, November 1976, 79–82 and 85–87.

Rehabilitation and long-term management

"Alcohol Benefit for the Geriatric Patient," *Journal of the American Medical Association* 227:4 (January 28, 1974), 439–440.

Barr, D. F., "Aural Rehabilitation of the Geriatric Patient," *Geriatrics*, June 1970, 111–113.

Canter, G. J., "Aphasia: Some Thoughts on the Problem of Word Finding," *Journal of Physical Medicine* 46 (1967), 1967.

Collis, Kathleen, "Aspects of Geriatric Care," *Nursing Times*, July 15, 1976, 14.

Coleman, L., "The Objectives and Final Goals of Physical Therapy," *Geriatrics*, May 1976, 91–95.

Cooper, M., "Voice Problems of the Geriatric Patient," *Geriatrics*, June 1970, 107–110.

Desautels, R. E., "Managing the Urinary Catheter," *Geriatrics*, September 1974, 67–70.

Geer, M., "Management of the Patient with Acute Stroke," *Geriatrics*, December 1973, 48–53.

Geshwind, Norman, "The Organization of Language and the Brain," *Science* 170 (1970), 940–944.

Greenberg, B., "Caring for the Aged: Reaction Time in the Elderly," *American Journal of Nursing*, December 1973, 2056–2058.

Grynbaum, Bruce B. and others, "Sensory Feedback Therapy for Stroke Patients," *Geriatrics*, June 1976, 43–47.

Hackler, E. S., "Expanding the Role of Nurses in Rehabilitation," *Geriatrics*, May 1976, 77–79.

Harrington, Robert, "Communication for the Aphasic Stroke Patient: Assessment and Therapy," *Journal of the American Geriatric Society*, June 1975, 254–257.

Hirschberg, G. G., "Ambulation and Self-Care Goals of Rehabilitation after Stroke," *Geriatrics*, May 1976, 61–65.

Lee, L. K. and J. L. Ambrus, "Collagenase Therapy for Decubitus Ulcers," *Geriatrics*, May 1975, 91–93 and 97–98.

Lye, M., "Defining and Treating Urinary Infections," *Geriatrics*, March 1978, 71–73 and 76–77.

Maney, J. Y., "A Behavioral Therapy Approach to Bladder Retraining," *Nursing Clinics of North America*, March 1976, 179–188.

Marks, Robert L. and George A. Bahr, "How to Manage Neurogenic Bladder after Stroke," *Geriatrics*, December 1977, 50–54.

McCann, B. Cairbre and Richard Culbertson, "Comparison of Two Systems for Stroke Rehabilitation in a General Hospital," *Journal of the American Geriatric Society* 24 (May 1976), 211–216.

Miller, M. B., "Iatrogenic and Nurisgenic Effects of Prolonged Immobilization of the Ill Aged," *Journal of the American Geriatrics Society*, August 1975, 360–369.

Ostfeld, A. M. and others "Epidemiology of Stroke in an Elderly Welfare Population," *American Journal of Public Health* 64:5 (May 1974), 450–458.

Pinel, C., "Disorders of Micturition in the Elderly," *Nursing Times*, December 18, 1975, 2019–2021.

Sheridan, Jane, "Restoring Speech and Language Skills," *Geriatrics*, May 1976, 83–86.

Steger, H. G., "Understanding the Psychologic Factors in Rehabilitation," *Geriatrics*, May 1976, 68–73.

Vetra, Helga and Derrick Whittaker, "Hydrotherapy and Topical Collagenase for Decubitus Ulcers," *Geriatrics*, August 1975, 53–58.

Wingerson, E'Lane, "The Value of Occupational Therapy in Rehabilitation." *Geriatrics*, May 1976, 99–101.

Sex and sexuality

Christensen, Cornelia and John Gagnon, "Sexual Behavior in a Group of Older Women," *Journal of Gerontology* 20:3 (July 1965), 351–356.

Christensen, Cornelia and A. B. Johnson, "Sexual Patterns in a Group of Older Never-Married Women," *Journal of Geriatric Psychiatry* 6:1 (1973), 80–98.

Comfort, A., "Sexuality in Old Age," *Journal of the American Geriatrics Society* 22 (1974), 440–442.

Finkle, Alex L. and Paul S. Finkle, "How Counseling May Solve Sexual Problems of Aging Men," *Geriatrics*, November 1977, 84–88.

Kaas, M. J., "Sexual Expression of the Elderly in Nursing Homes," *The Gerontologist* 18:4 (August 1978), 372–378.

Krizinofski, M. T., "Human Sexuality and Nursing Practice," *Nursing Clinics of North America* 8 (December 1973), 673–681.

Kroah, J., "How To Deal with Patients Who Act Out Sexually," *Nursing '73* 3 (December 1973), 38–39.

Mac Rae, I. and others, "Sexuality and Irreversible Health Limitations," *Nursing Clinics of North America*, September 1975, 587–597.

Masters, William and Virginia Johnson, "Human Sexual Response: The Aging Female and the Aging Male," in Bernice Neugarten, ed., *Middle Age and Aging* (Chicago: University of Chicago Press, 1968), 269–279.

——, "Sexual Inadequacy in the Aging Male" and "Sexual Inadequacy in the Aging Female," in *Human Sexual Inadequacy.* (Boston: Little, Brown, & Co., 1970), 316–335.

Pease, R., "Female Professional Students and Sexuality in the Aging Male," *The Gerontologist* 14 (April 1974), 153–157.

Verwoerdt, A. and others, "Sexual Behavior in Senescence, Part II: Patterns of Sexual Activity and Interest," *Geriatrics* 24:2 (February 1969), 137–154.

Sensory perception

Barnett, Kathryn, "A Survey of the Current Utilization of Touch by Health Team Personnel with Hospitalized Patients," *International Journal of Nursing Studies*, January 1970, 195–209.

Bolin, Rose H., "Sensory Deprivation: An Overview," *Nursing Forum* 13:3 (1974), 241–258.

Block, Irvine, "The Perception of Disoriential Figures," *Scientific American* 230:1 (January 1974), 78–86.

Burnside, Irene M., "The Special Senses and Sensory Deprivation," in Irene M. Burnside, ed., *Nursing and the Aged* (New York: McGraw-Hill Book Co., 1976), 380–395.

Cameron, C. F. and others, "When Sensory Deprivation Occurs," *Canadian Nurse* 68 (November 1972), 32–34.

Crombie, A. C., "Early Concept of the Senses and the Mind," *Scientific American* 10 (May 1964), 106–116.

Eisdorfer, Carl, "Developmental Level and Sensory Impairment in the Aged," *Journal of Projective Techniques* 24 (1965), 129–132.

Heron, Woodlim, "The Pathology of Boredom," *Scientific American* 196 (January 1957), 52–56.

Hess, E. H., "Attitude and Pupil Size," *Scientific American* 212 (April 1965), 46–54.

Hickey, T., "Simulating Age Related Sensory Impairments for Practitioner Education," *Gerontologist* (October 1975), 457–463.

Houston, A. and B. Royse, "Relationships between Deafness and Psychotic Illness," *Journal of Mental Diseases* (London) 100 (1954), 990–993.

Oster, Claude, "Sensory Deprivation in Geriatric Patients," *Journal of American Geriatrics Society*, 24:10 (October 1976), 461–464.

Prentice, W. C. H., "After Effects of Perception," *Scientific American* 206:1 (January 1962), 44–49.

Rock, Irvine and Charles S. Harris, "Vision and Touch," *Scientific American* 216:5 (May 1967), 96–104.

Siegel, R. K., "Hallucinations," *Scientific American* 237:10 (October 1978), 132–140.

Witkin, H. A., "The Perception of the Upright," *Scientific American* 200:2 (February 1959), 51–56.

Systems of health care

Abdellah, F. G., "H.E.W. Task Force Examines Ways to Upgrade and Expand Home Health Care Programs," *Geriatrics*, October 1976, 43 and 46.

Abdo, E. and others, "Elderly Women in Institutions versus Those in Public Housing: Comparison of Personal and Social Adjustments," *Journal of the American Geriatrics Society*, February 1973, 81–87.

Anderson, Odin W., "Reflections on the Sick Aged and the Helping Systems," *Journal of Gerontological Nursing* , March–April 1977, 14–20.

Cohn, G. M., "Defining Quality Care in Long Term Care Facilities," *Concern for Care of Aging*, April 1976, 23–26.

Garrison, John and Jo-Ann Howe, "Community Intervention with the Elderly: A Social Network Approach," *Journal of the American Geriatrics Society*, July 1976, 329–333.

Gartner, A. and F. Riessman, "Self-Help Models and Consumer Intensive Health Practice," *American Journal of Public Health*, August 1976, 783–786.

Harrison, C., "The Institutionally-Deprived Elderly," *Nursing Clinics of North America*, December 1968, 697–707.

Havinghurst, R. J., "Perspectives on Health Care for the Elderly," *Journal of Gerontological Nursing*, March–April 1977, 21–24.

"Know your Community Resources: Federal Council on Aging," *Journal of Gerontological Nursing*, November–December 1976, 47.

Kohn, J., "Hospices Movement Provides Humane Alternative for Terminally Ill Patients," *Modern Health Care*, September 1976, 26–28.

Miller, M. B., "A Physician Views Skilled Nursing Care," *Journal of Nursing Administration*, January–February 1973, 20–29.

Pomerantz, R., "The Nurse in an Expanded Role: A Proposed Solution to the Problems of Geriatric Health Care (editorial), *Journal of Chronic Diseases* 28 (1975), 561–563.

Rathbone-McCuan, E., "Geriatric Day Care: A Family Perspective," *The Gerontologist*, June 1976, 517–521.

Robertson, Duncan and others, "A Community-Based Continuing Care Program for the Elderly Disabled," *Journal of Gerontology*, May 1977, 334–339.

Rodstein, Manuel and others, "Initial Adjustment to a Long-Term Care Institution: Medical and Behavioral Aspects," *Journal of American Geriatric Society*, February 1976, 65–71.

Ross, D. N., "Geriatric Day Hospitals: Counting the Cost Compared with Other Methods of Support," *Age and Aging*, May 1976, 171–175.

Sammond, P. H. and S. Davis, "Hospital-Community Cooperation Brings Care to Senior Citizens," *Hospitals*, May 16, 1976, 117–120.

Saunders, C., "A Therapeutic Community: St. Christopher's Hospice," in Schoenberg, B. and others, eds., *Psychosocial Aspects of Terminal Care* (New York: Columbia University Press, 1972), 275–290.

Spagnolia, D. G., "Social Attitudes Affecting the Nursing Home Environment," *Nursing Homes*, July 1976, 5, 8, and 12.

Storz, R., "The Role of a Professional Nurse in a Health Maintenance Program," *Nursing Clinics of North America*, June 1972, 207–223.

Zerranzzano, A. R., "Seated Exercise . . . . Van Doren Nursing Home," *Nursing Homes*, June–July 1975, 18–19.